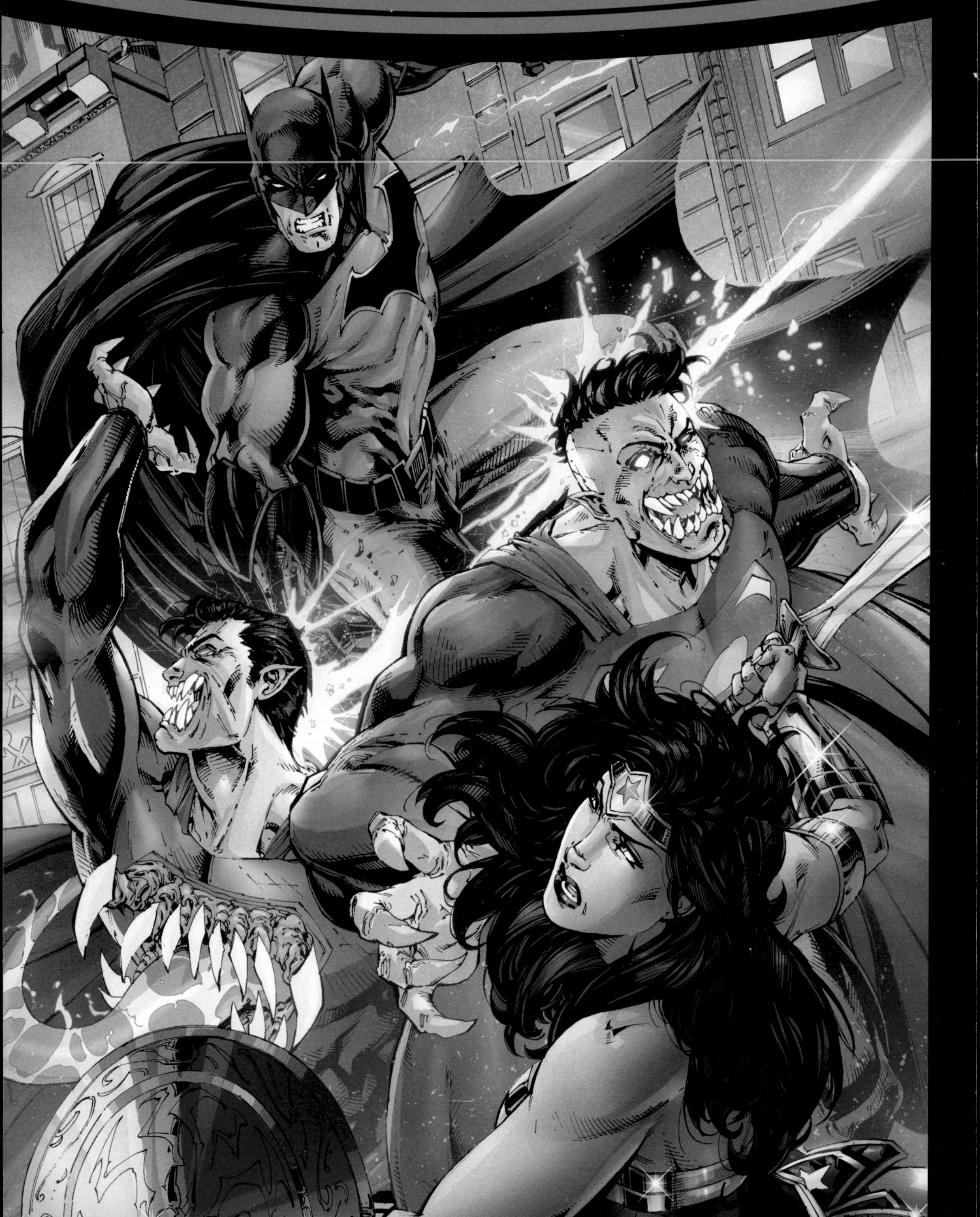

# TRINITY

## VOL.3 DARK DESTINY

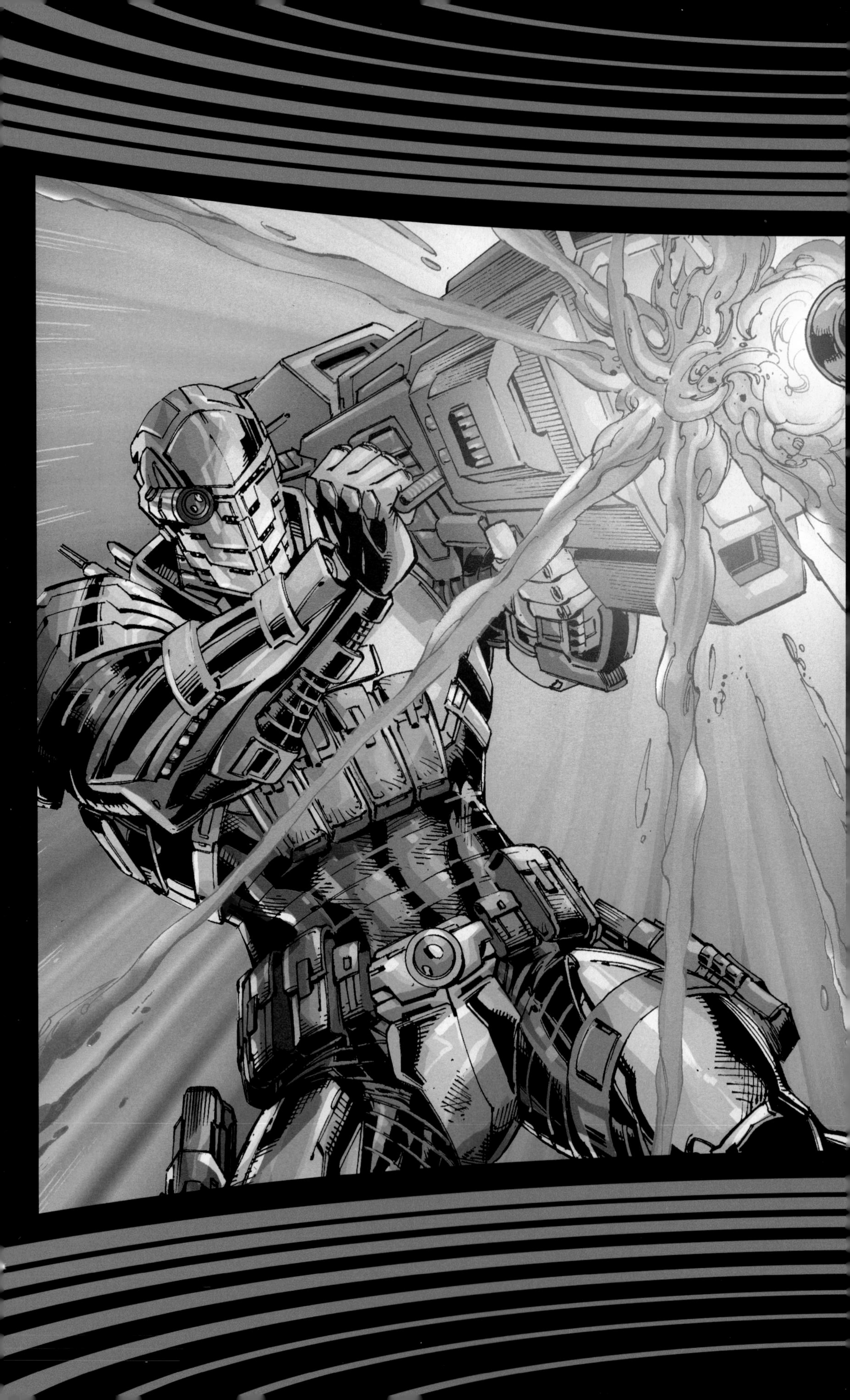

# TRINITY
## VOL.3 DARK DESTINY

**ROB WILLIAMS**
writer

**V KEN MARION** * **GUILLEM MARCH**
pencillers

**SANDU FLOREA** * **RAY McCARTHY** * **GUILLEM MARCH**
inkers

**DINEI RIBEIRO** * **TOMEU MOREY**
colorists

**CARLOS M. MANGUAL** * **JOSH REED**
**TOM NAPOLITANO** * **STEVE WANDS**
letterers

**CLAY MANN** and **TOMEU MOREY**
collection cover artists

**SUPERMAN** created by **JERRY SIEGEL** and **JOE SHUSTER**
By special arrangement with the Jerry Siegel family
**BATMAN** created by **BOB KANE** with **BILL FINGER**
**WONDER WOMAN** created by **WILLIAM MOULTON MARSTON**
**DEADSHOT** created by **LEW SAYRE SCHWARTZ**
**DEADMAN** created by **ARNOLD DRAKE**
**ZATANNA** created by **GARDNER FOX** and **MURPHY ANDERSON**
**JOHN CONSTANTINE** created by **ALAN MOORE, STEVE BISSETTE, JOHN TOTLEBEN** and **JAMIE DELANO** & **JOHN RIDGWAY**

**PAUL KAMINSKI EDDIE BERGANZA** Editors - Original Series ✳ **ANDREA SHEA** Assistant Editor - Original Series
**JEB WOODARD** Group Editor - Collected Editions ✳ **TYLER-MARIE EVANS** Editor - Collected Edition
**STEVE COOK** Design Director - Books ✳ **MEGEN BELLERSEN** Publication Design

**BOB HARRAS** Senior VP - Editor-in-Chief, DC Comics
**PAT McCALLUM** Executive Editor, DC Comics

**DIANE NELSON** President ✳ **DAN DiDIO** Publisher ✳ **JIM LEE** Publisher ✳ **GEOFF JOHNS** President & Chief Creative Officer
**AMIT DESAI** Executive VP - Business & Marketing Strategy, Direct to Consumer & Global Franchise Management
**SAM ADES** Senior VP & General Manager, Digital Services ✳ **BOBBIE CHASE** VP & Executive Editor, Young Reader & Talent Development
**MARK CHIARELLO** Senior VP - Art, Design & Collected Editions ✳ **JOHN CUNNINGHAM** Senior VP - Sales & Trade Marketing
**ANNE DePIES** Senior VP - Business Strategy, Finance & Administration ✳ **DON FALLETTI** VP - Manufacturing Operations
**LAWRENCE GANEM** VP - Editorial Administration & Talent Relations ✳ **ALISON GILL** Senior VP - Manufacturing & Operations
**HANK KANALZ** Senior VP - Editorial Strategy & Administration ✳ **JAY KOGAN** VP - Legal Affairs ✳ **JACK MAHAN** VP - Business Affairs
**NICK J. NAPOLITANO** VP - Manufacturing Administration ✳ **EDDIE SCANNELL** VP - Consumer Marketing
**COURTNEY SIMMONS** Senior VP - Publicity & Communications ✳ **JIM (SKI) SOKOLOWSKI** VP - Comic Book Specialty Sales & Trade Marketing
**NANCY SPEARS** VP - Mass, Book, Digital Sales & Trade Marketing ✳ **MICHELE R. WELLS** VP - Content Strategy

**TRINITY VOL. 3 DARK DESTINY**

Published by DC Comics. Compilation and all new material Copyright © 2018 DC Comics. All Rights Reserved.
Originally published in single magazine form in TRINITY ANNUAL 1, TRINITY 12-16. Copyright © 2017, 2018 DC Comics. All Rights Reserved.
All characters, their distinctive likenesses and related elements featured in this publication are trademarks of DC Comics.
The stories, characters and incidents featured in this publication are entirely fictional.
DC Comics does not read or accept unsolicited submissions of ideas, stories or artwork.

DC Comics, 2900 West Alameda Ave., Burbank, CA 91505
Printed by LSC Communications, Kendallville, IN, USA. 6/22/18. First Printing.
ISBN: 978-1-4012-8051-2

Library of Congress Cataloging-in-Publication Data is available.

**PEFC Certified**

Printed on paper from
sustainably managed
forests, controlled
sources

PEFC/29-31-337    www.pefc.org

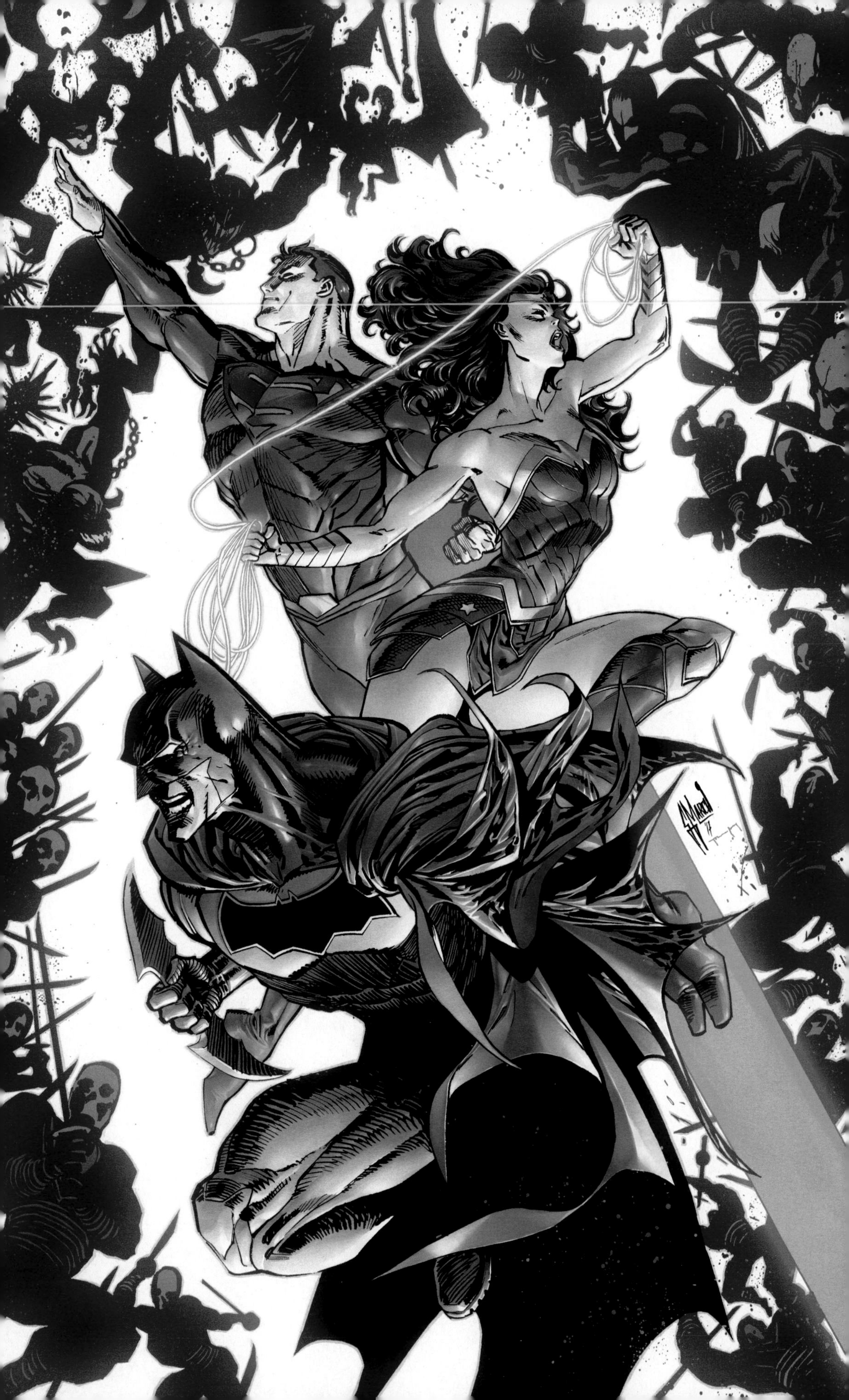

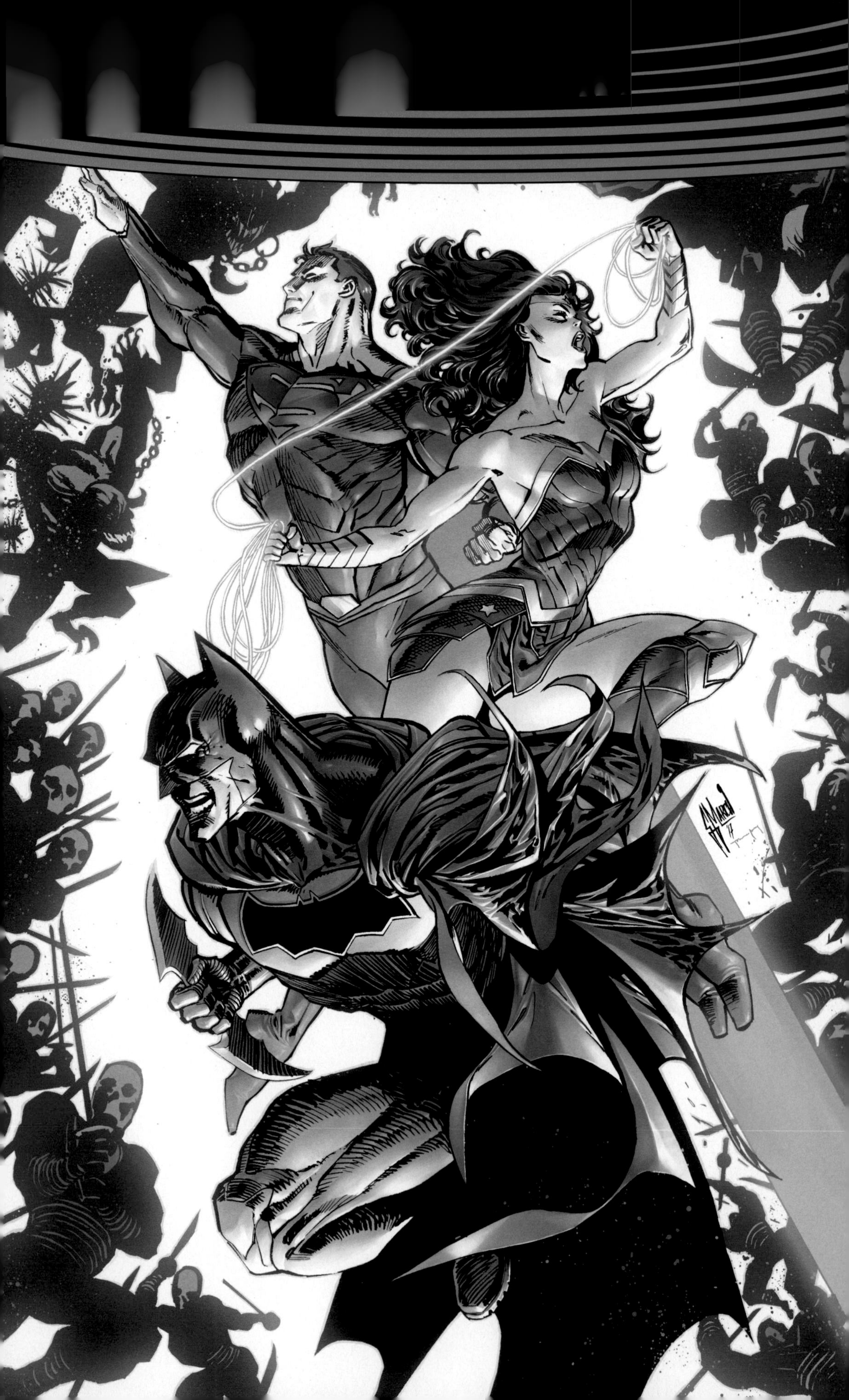

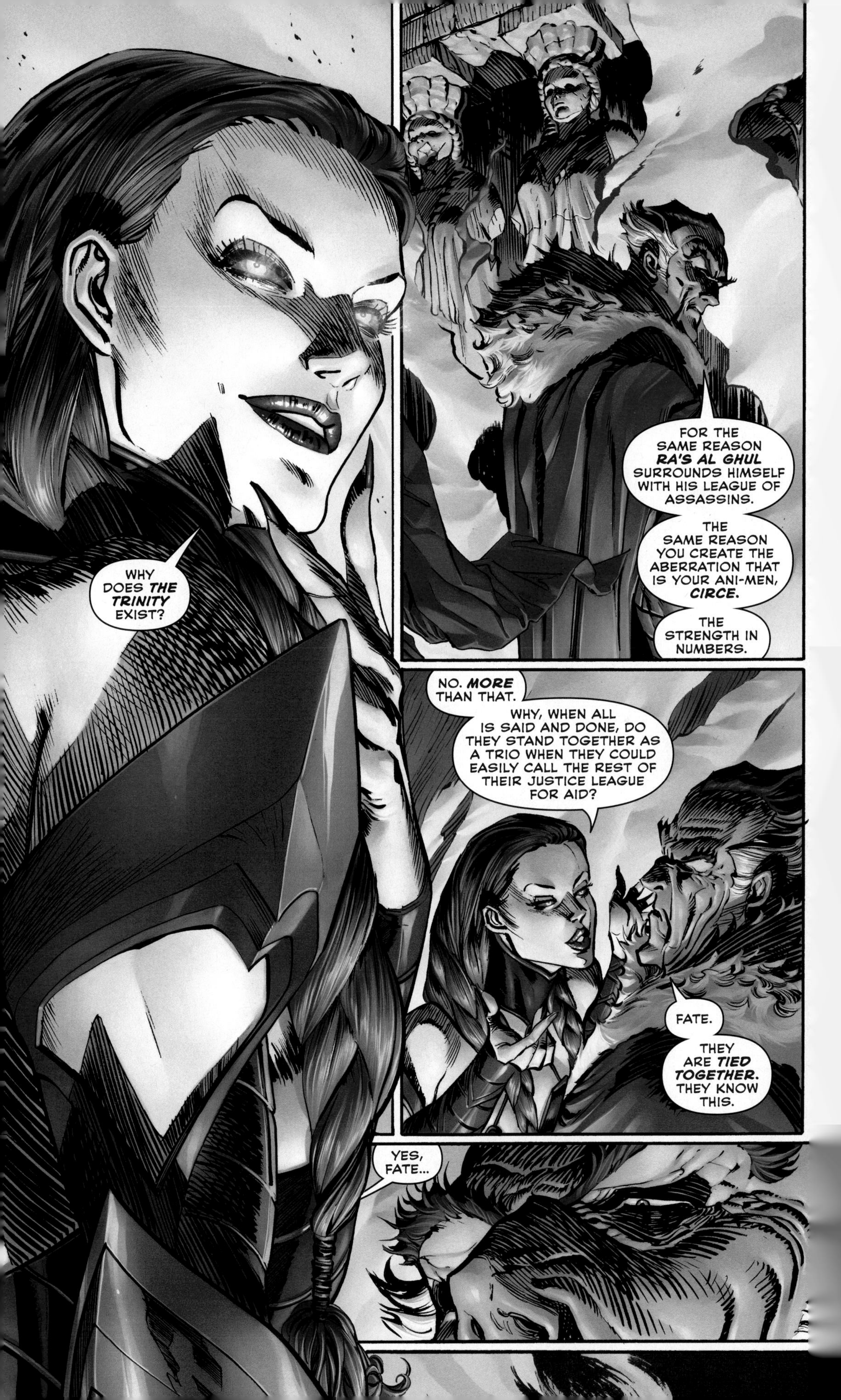
WHY DOES *THE TRINITY* EXIST?
FOR THE SAME REASON ***RA'S AL GHUL*** SURROUNDS HIMSELF WITH HIS LEAGUE OF ASSASSINS.
THE SAME REASON YOU CREATE THE ABERRATION THAT IS YOUR ANI-MEN, ***CIRCE.***
THE STRENGTH IN NUMBERS.
NO. ***MORE*** THAN THAT.
WHY, WHEN ALL IS SAID AND DONE, DO THEY STAND TOGETHER AS A TRIO WHEN THEY COULD EASILY CALL THE REST OF THEIR JUSTICE LEAGUE FOR AID?
FATE.
THEY ARE ***TIED TOGETHER.*** THEY KNOW THIS.
YES, FATE...

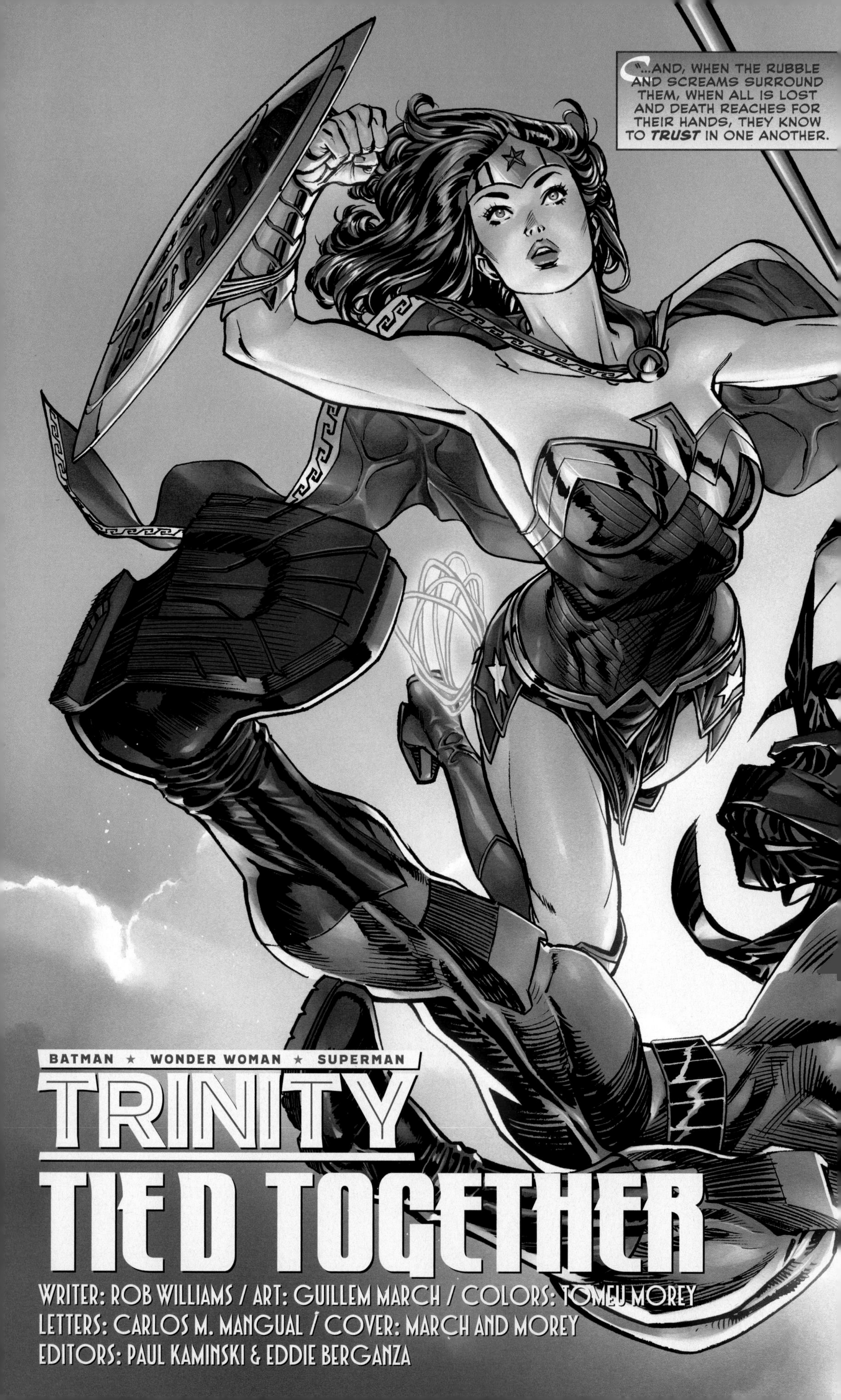
"...AND, WHEN THE RUBBLE AND SCREAMS SURROUND THEM, WHEN ALL IS LOST AND DEATH REACHES FOR THEIR HANDS, THEY KNOW TO *TRUST* IN ONE ANOTHER.
BATMAN ★ WONDER WOMAN ★ SUPERMAN
TRINITY
TIED TOGETHER
WRITER: ROB WILLIAMS / ART: GUILLEM MARCH / COLORS: TOMEU MOREY
LETTERS: CARLOS M. MANGUAL / COVER: MARCH AND MOREY
EDITORS: PAUL KAMINSKI & EDDIE BERGANZA

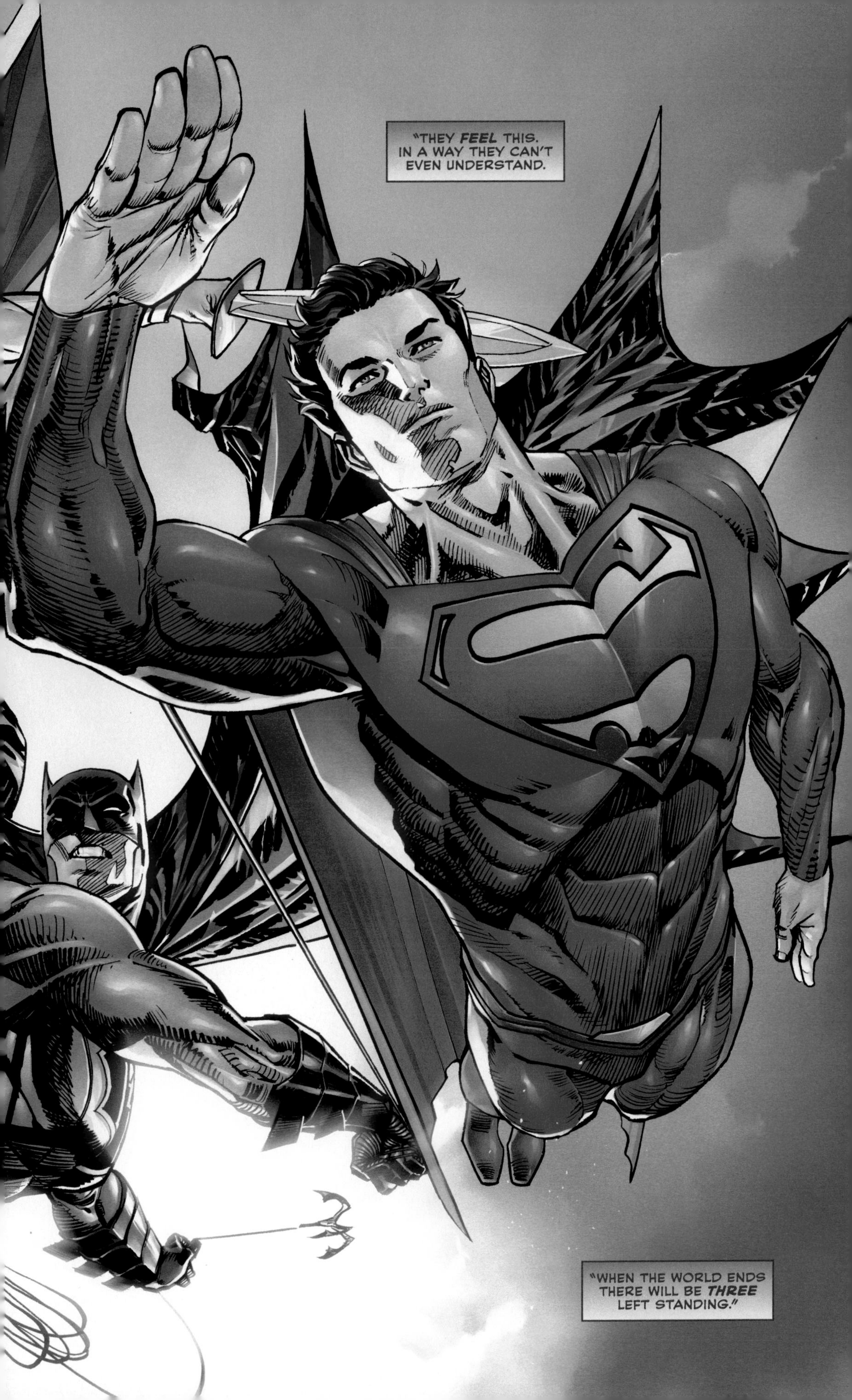
"THEY *FEEL* THIS. IN A WAY THEY CAN'T EVEN UNDERSTAND.
"WHEN THE WORLD ENDS THERE WILL BE *THREE* LEFT STANDING."

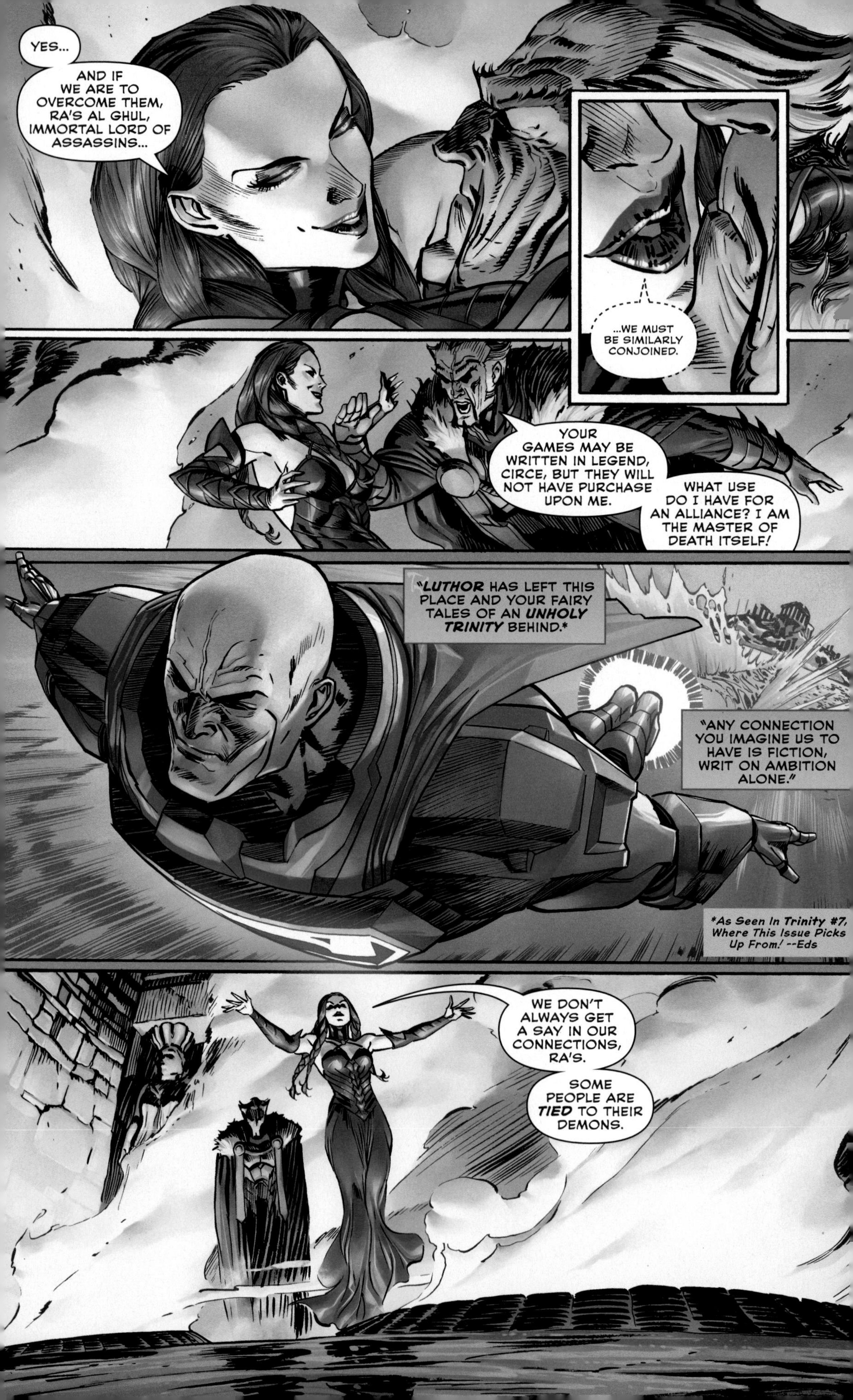
YES...
AND IF WE ARE TO OVERCOME THEM, RA'S AL GHUL, IMMORTAL LORD OF ASSASSINS...
...WE MUST BE SIMILARLY CONJOINED.
YOUR GAMES MAY BE WRITTEN IN LEGEND, CIRCE, BUT THEY WILL NOT HAVE PURCHASE UPON ME.
WHAT USE DO I HAVE FOR AN ALLIANCE? I AM THE MASTER OF DEATH ITSELF!
"LUTHOR HAS LEFT THIS PLACE AND YOUR FAIRY TALES OF AN UNHOLY TRINITY BEHIND.*
"ANY CONNECTION YOU IMAGINE US TO HAVE IS FICTION, WRIT ON AMBITION ALONE."
*As Seen In Trinity #7, Where This Issue Picks Up From! --Eds
WE DON'T ALWAYS GET A SAY IN OUR CONNECTIONS, RA'S.
SOME PEOPLE ARE TIED TO THEIR DEMONS.

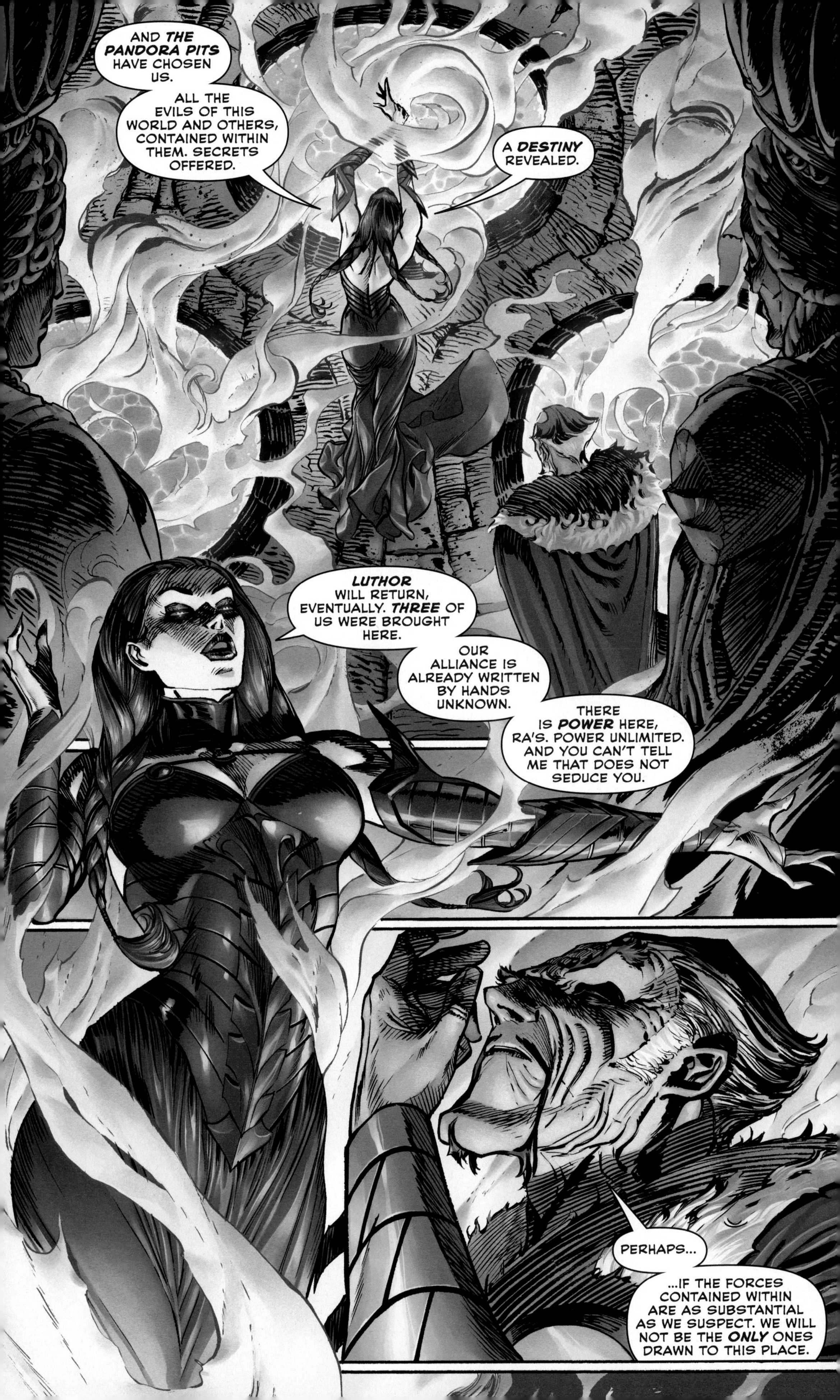
AND *THE PANDORA PITS* HAVE CHOSEN US.
ALL THE EVILS OF THIS WORLD AND OTHERS, CONTAINED WITHIN THEM. SECRETS OFFERED.
A *DESTINY* REVEALED.
*LUTHOR* WILL RETURN, EVENTUALLY. *THREE* OF US WERE BROUGHT HERE.
OUR ALLIANCE IS ALREADY WRITTEN BY HANDS UNKNOWN.
THERE IS *POWER* HERE, RA'S. POWER UNLIMITED. AND YOU CAN'T TELL ME THAT DOES NOT SEDUCE YOU.
PERHAPS...
...IF THE FORCES CONTAINED WITHIN ARE AS SUBSTANTIAL AS WE SUSPECT. WE WILL NOT BE THE *ONLY* ONES DRAWN TO THIS PLACE.

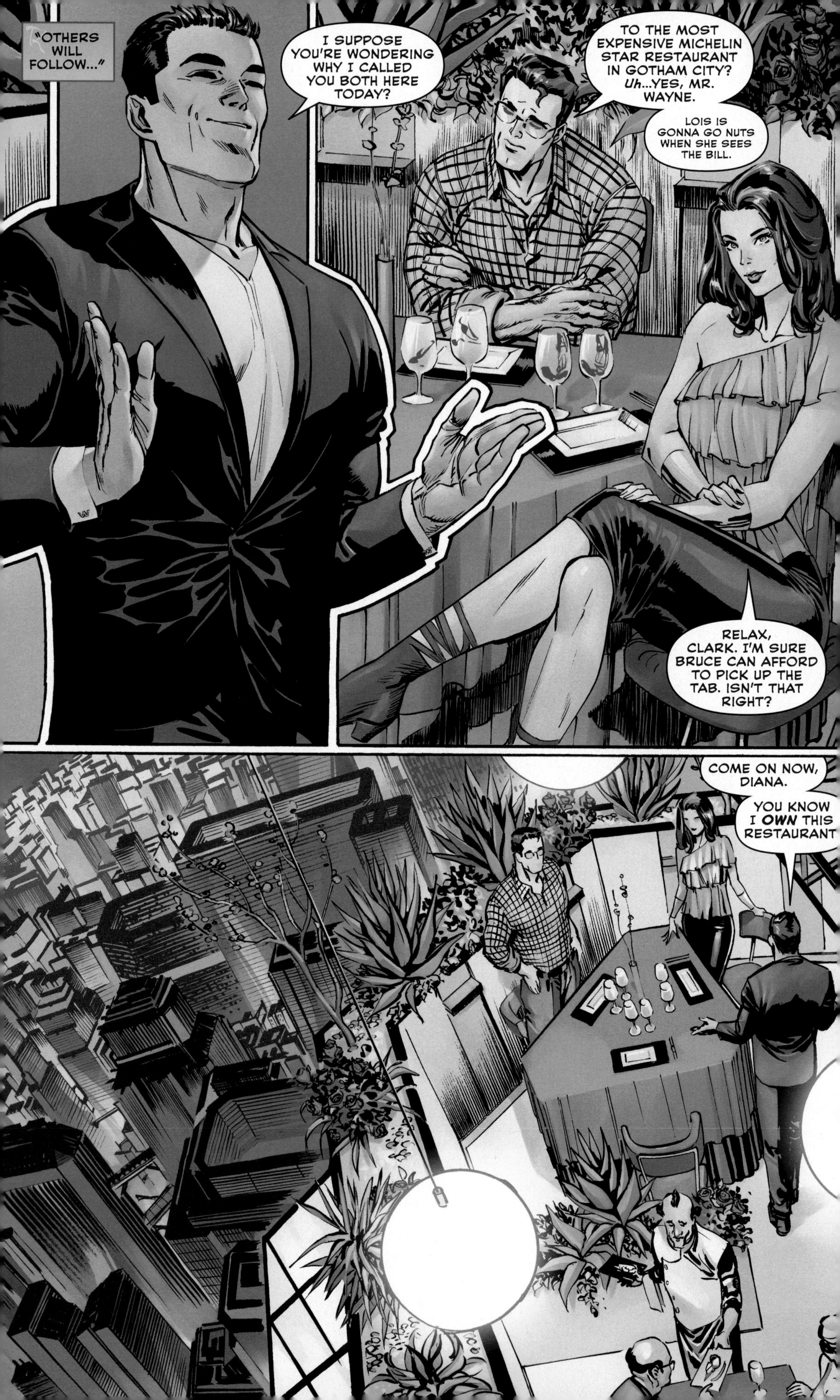

"OTHERS WILL FOLLOW..."
I SUPPOSE YOU'RE WONDERING WHY I CALLED YOU BOTH HERE TODAY?
TO THE MOST EXPENSIVE MICHELIN STAR RESTAURANT IN GOTHAM CITY? *Uh*...YES, MR. WAYNE.
LOIS IS GONNA GO NUTS WHEN SHE SEES THE BILL.
RELAX, CLARK. I'M SURE BRUCE CAN AFFORD TO PICK UP THE TAB. ISN'T THAT RIGHT?
COME ON NOW, DIANA.
YOU KNOW I ***OWN*** THIS RESTAURANT

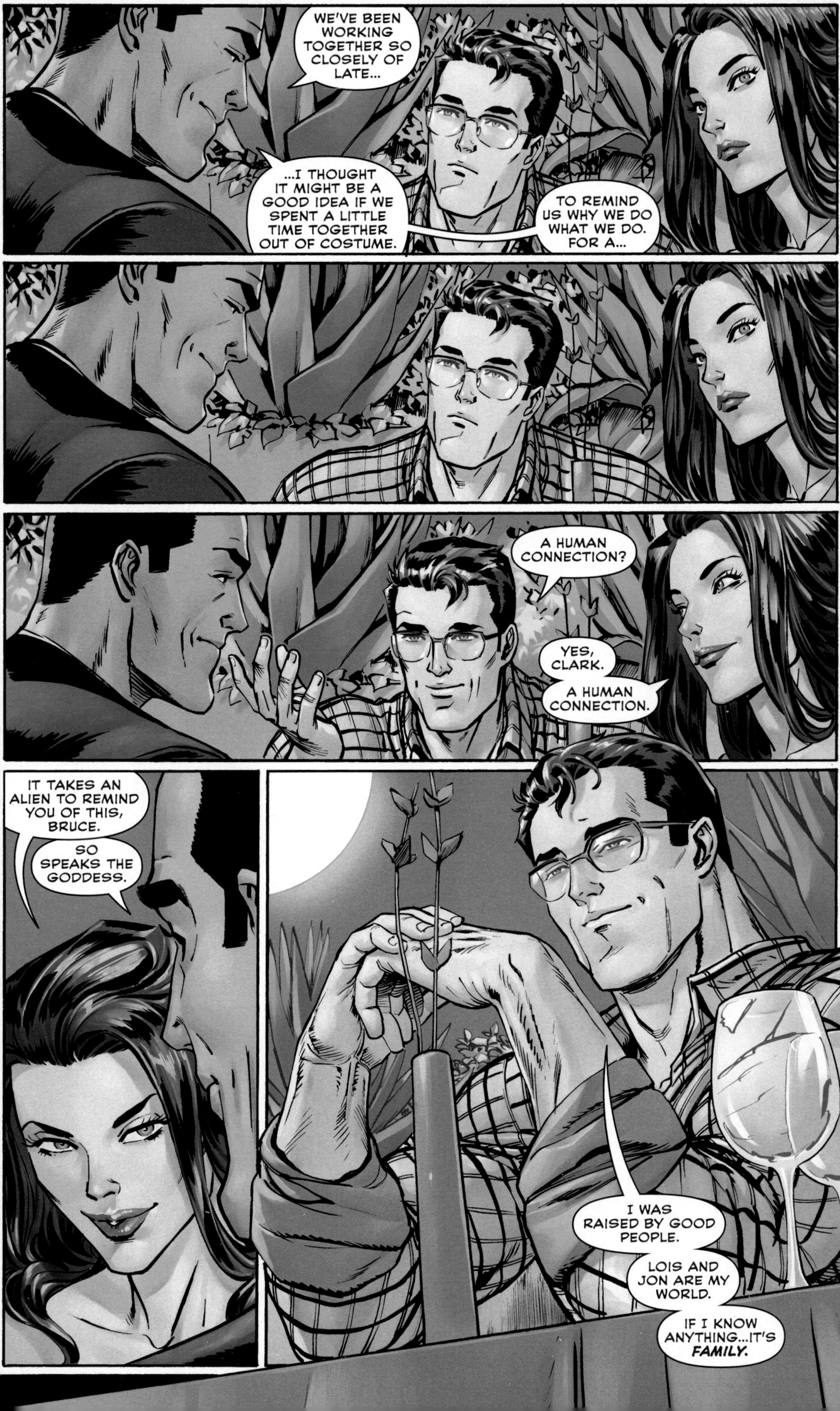
WE'VE BEEN WORKING TOGETHER SO CLOSELY OF LATE...
...I THOUGHT IT MIGHT BE A GOOD IDEA IF WE SPENT A LITTLE TIME TOGETHER OUT OF COSTUME.
TO REMIND US WHY WE DO WHAT WE DO. FOR A...
A HUMAN CONNECTION?
YES, CLARK.
A HUMAN CONNECTION.
IT TAKES AN ALIEN TO REMIND YOU OF THIS, BRUCE.
SO SPEAKS THE GODDESS.
I WAS RAISED BY GOOD PEOPLE.
LOIS AND JON ARE MY WORLD.
IF I KNOW ANYTHING...IT'S *FAMILY.*

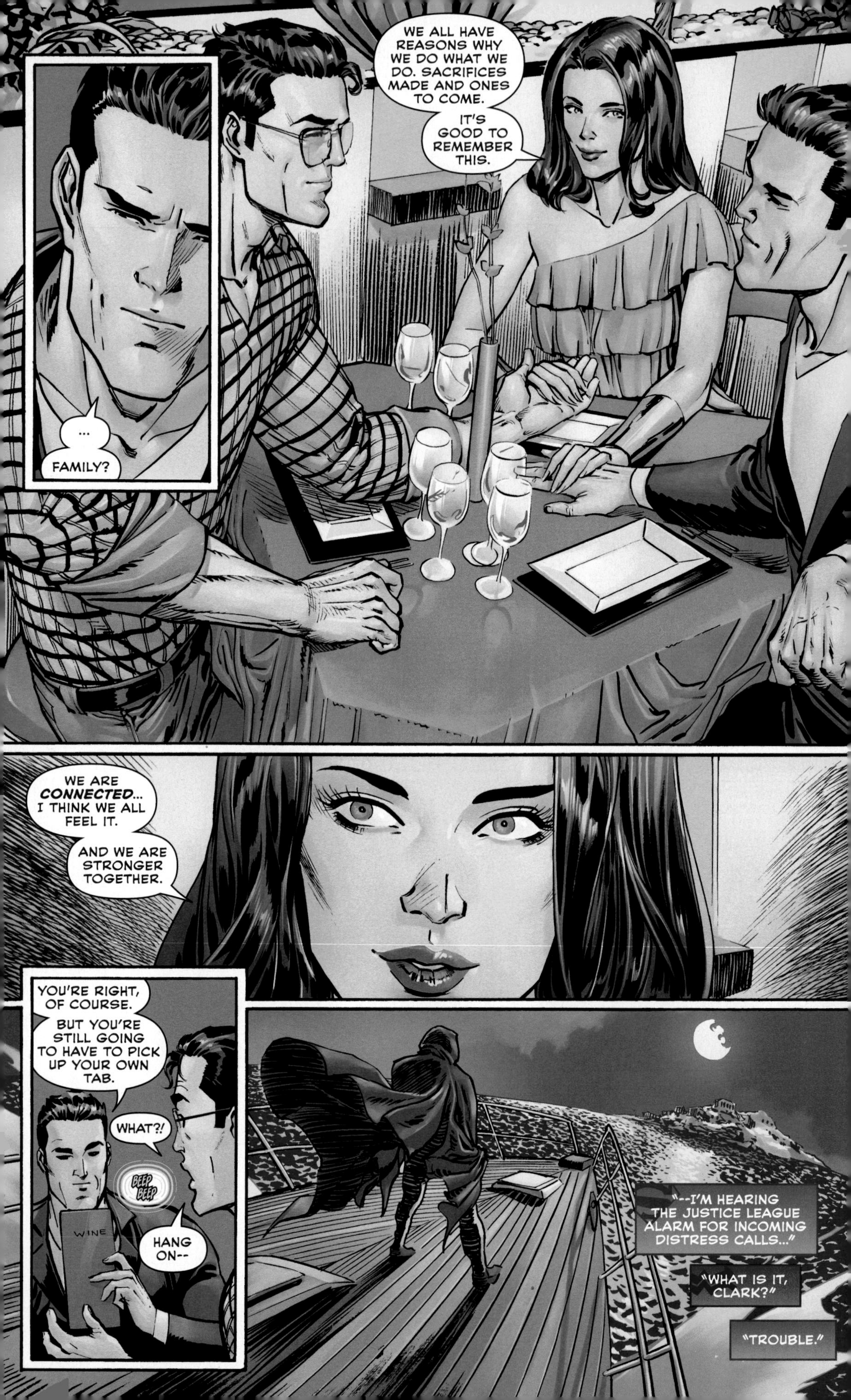

WE ALL HAVE REASONS WHY WE DO WHAT WE DO. SACRIFICES MADE AND ONES TO COME.
IT'S GOOD TO REMEMBER THIS.
... FAMILY?
WE ARE CONNECTED... I THINK WE ALL FEEL IT.
AND WE ARE STRONGER TOGETHER.
YOU'RE RIGHT, OF COURSE.
BUT YOU'RE STILL GOING TO HAVE TO PICK UP YOUR OWN TAB.
WHAT?!
BEEP BEEP
WINE
HANG ON--
"--I'M HEARING THE JUSTICE LEAGUE ALARM FOR INCOMING DISTRESS CALLS..."
"WHAT IS IT, CLARK?"
"TROUBLE."

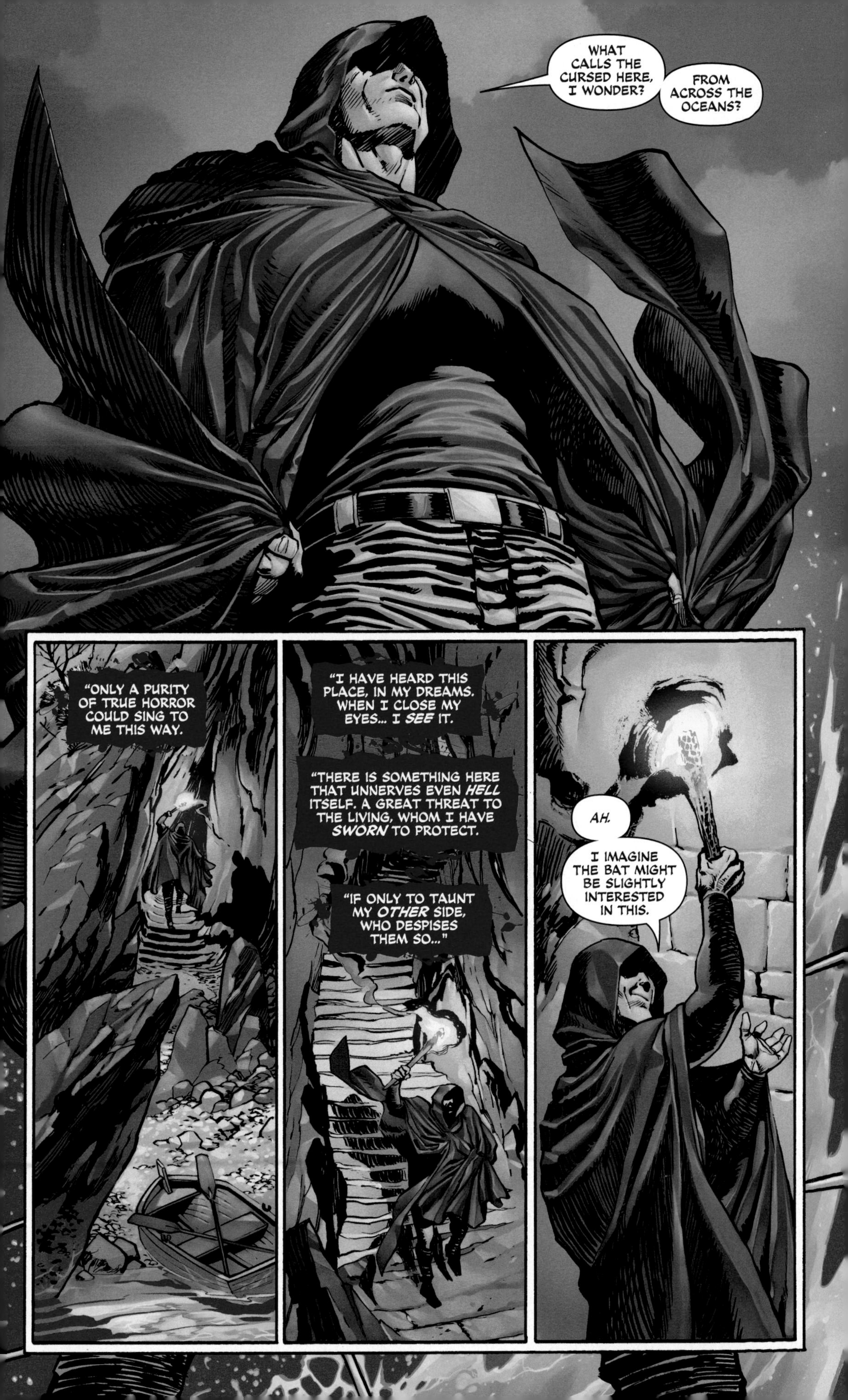
WHAT CALLS THE CURSED HERE, I WONDER?
FROM ACROSS THE OCEANS?
"ONLY A PURITY OF TRUE HORROR COULD SING TO ME THIS WAY.
"I HAVE HEARD THIS PLACE, IN MY DREAMS. WHEN I CLOSE MY EYES... I SEE IT.
"THERE IS SOMETHING HERE THAT UNNERVES EVEN HELL ITSELF. A GREAT THREAT TO THE LIVING, WHOM I HAVE SWORN TO PROTECT.
"IF ONLY TO TAUNT MY OTHER SIDE, WHO DESPISES THEM SO..."
AH.
I IMAGINE THE BAT MIGHT BE SLIGHTLY INTERESTED IN THIS.

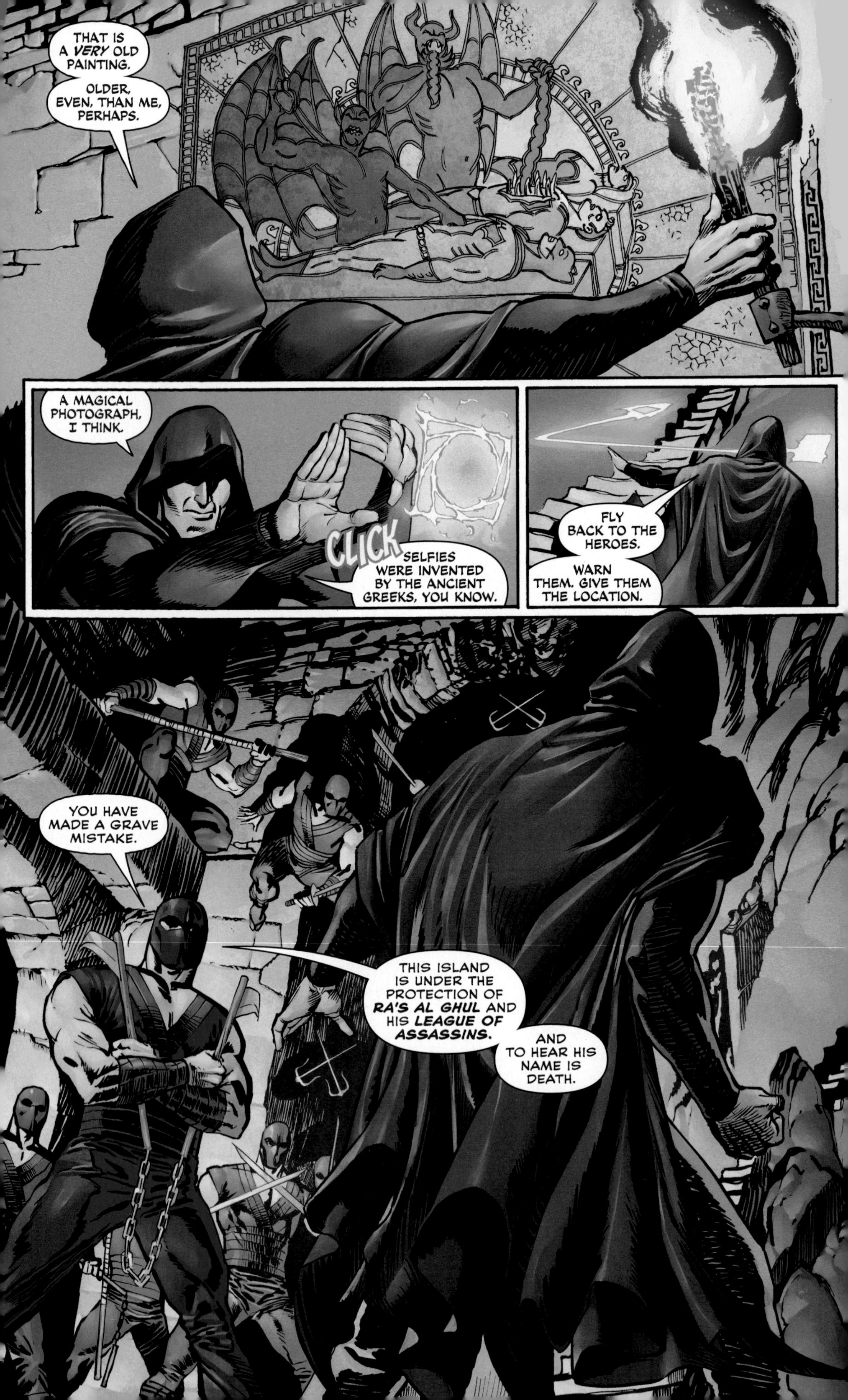
THAT IS A *VERY* OLD PAINTING.
OLDER, EVEN, THAN ME, PERHAPS.
A MAGICAL PHOTOGRAPH, I THINK.
CLICK
SELFIES WERE INVENTED BY THE ANCIENT GREEKS, YOU KNOW.
FLY BACK TO THE HEROES.
WARN THEM. GIVE THEM THE LOCATION.
YOU HAVE MADE A GRAVE MISTAKE.
THIS ISLAND IS UNDER THE PROTECTION OF ***RA'S AL GHUL*** AND HIS ***LEAGUE OF ASSASSINS.***
AND TO HEAR HIS NAME IS DEATH.

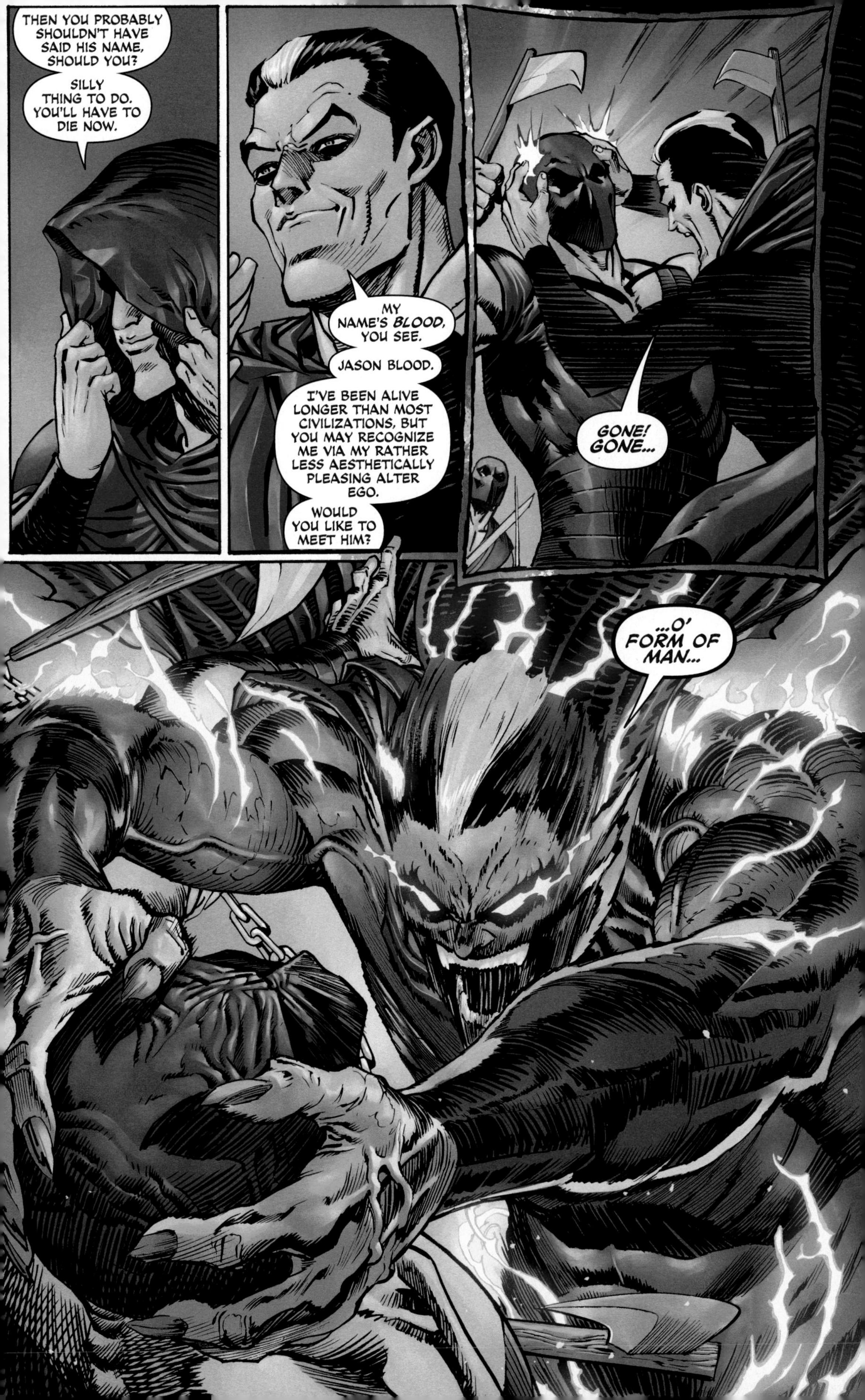
THEN YOU PROBABLY SHOULDN'T HAVE SAID HIS NAME, SHOULD YOU?
SILLY THING TO DO. YOU'LL HAVE TO DIE NOW.
MY NAME'S *BLOOD*, YOU SEE.
JASON BLOOD.
I'VE BEEN ALIVE LONGER THAN MOST CIVILIZATIONS, BUT YOU MAY RECOGNIZE ME VIA MY RATHER LESS AESTHETICALLY PLEASING ALTER EGO.
WOULD YOU LIKE TO MEET HIM?
GONE! GONE...
...O' FORM OF MAN...

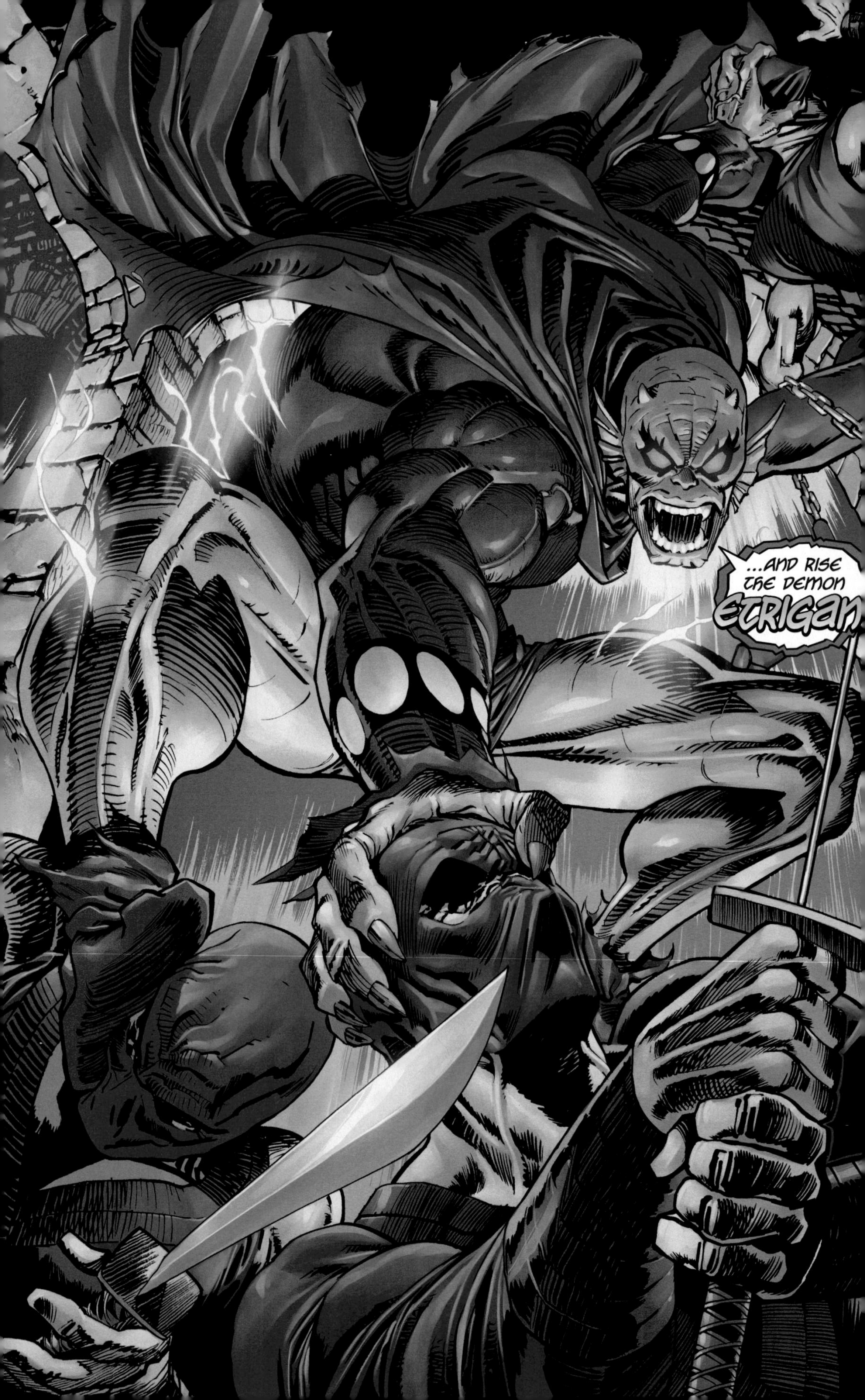
...AND RISE THE DEMON ETRIGAN

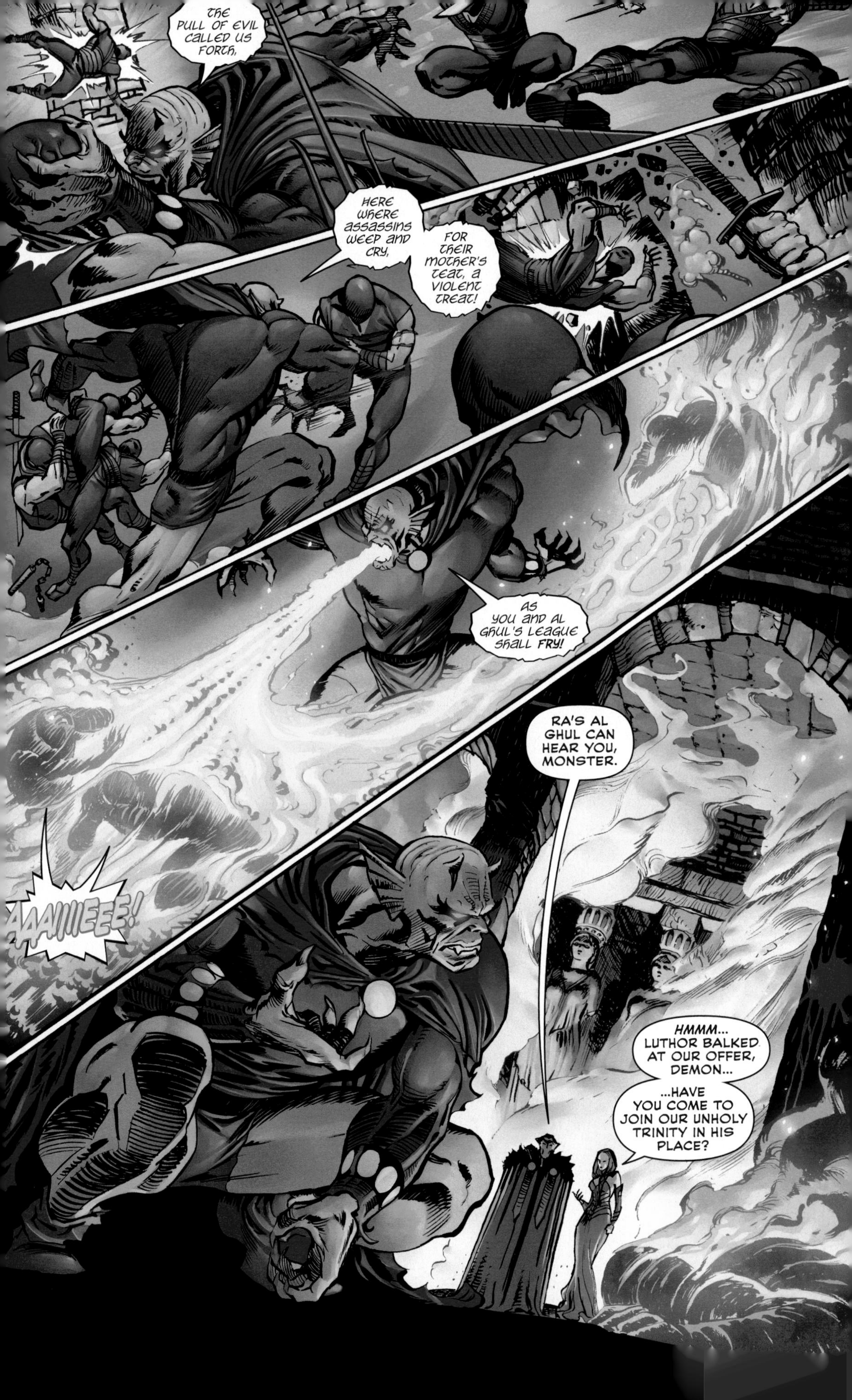
THE PULL OF EVIL CALLED US FORTH,
HERE WHERE ASSASSINS WEEP AND CRY,
FOR THEIR MOTHER'S TEAT, A VIOLENT TREAT!
AS YOU AND AL GHUL'S LEAGUE SHALL FRY!
AAAIIIIEEE!
RA'S AL GHUL CAN HEAR YOU, MONSTER.
HMMM... LUTHOR BALKED AT OUR OFFER, DEMON...
...HAVE YOU COME TO JOIN OUR UNHOLY TRINITY IN HIS PLACE?

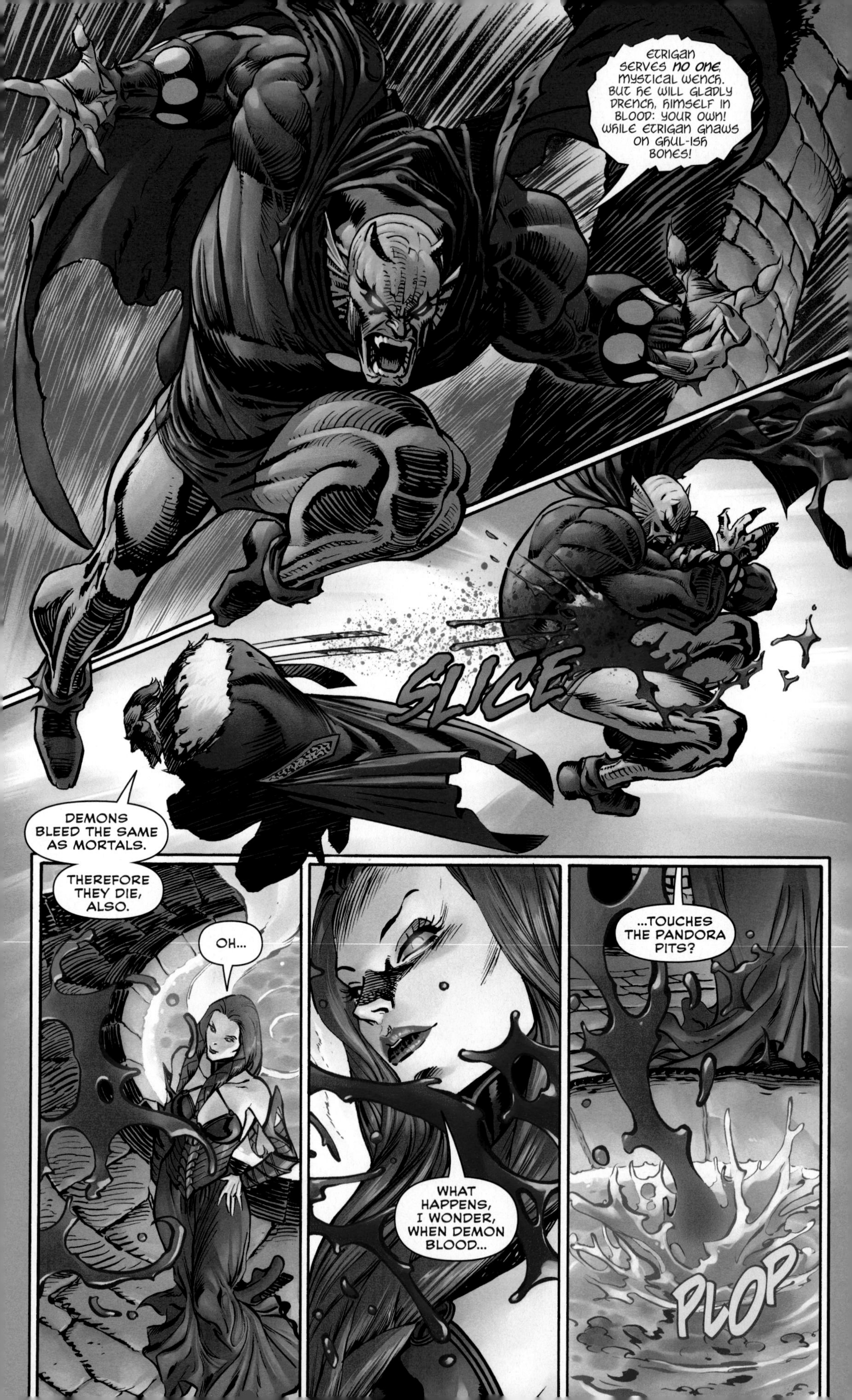
ETRIGAN SERVES NO ONE, MYSTICAL WENCH. BUT HE WILL GLADLY DRENCH, HIMSELF IN BLOOD: YOUR OWN! WHILE ETRIGAN GNAWS ON GHUL-ISH BONES!
SLICE
DEMONS BLEED THE SAME AS MORTALS.
THEREFORE THEY DIE, ALSO.
OH...
WHAT HAPPENS, I WONDER, WHEN DEMON BLOOD...
...TOUCHES THE PANDORA PITS?
PLOP

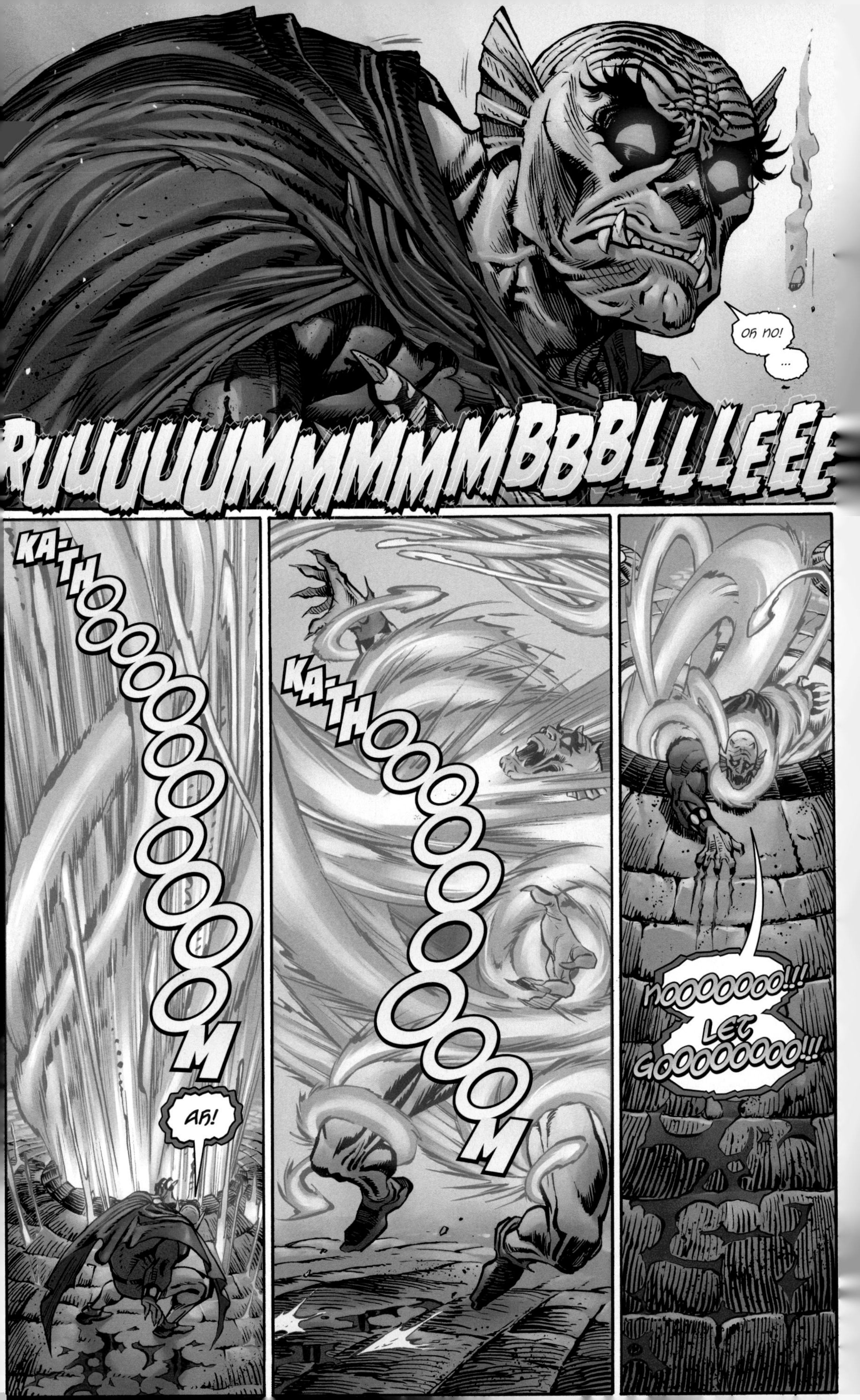
OH NO!
...
RUUUUUMMMMMMMBBBLLLLEEE
KA-THOOOOOOOOOOOOM
AH!
KA-THOOOOOOOOOOOOOM
NOOOOOOO!!!
LET GOOOOOOOO!!!

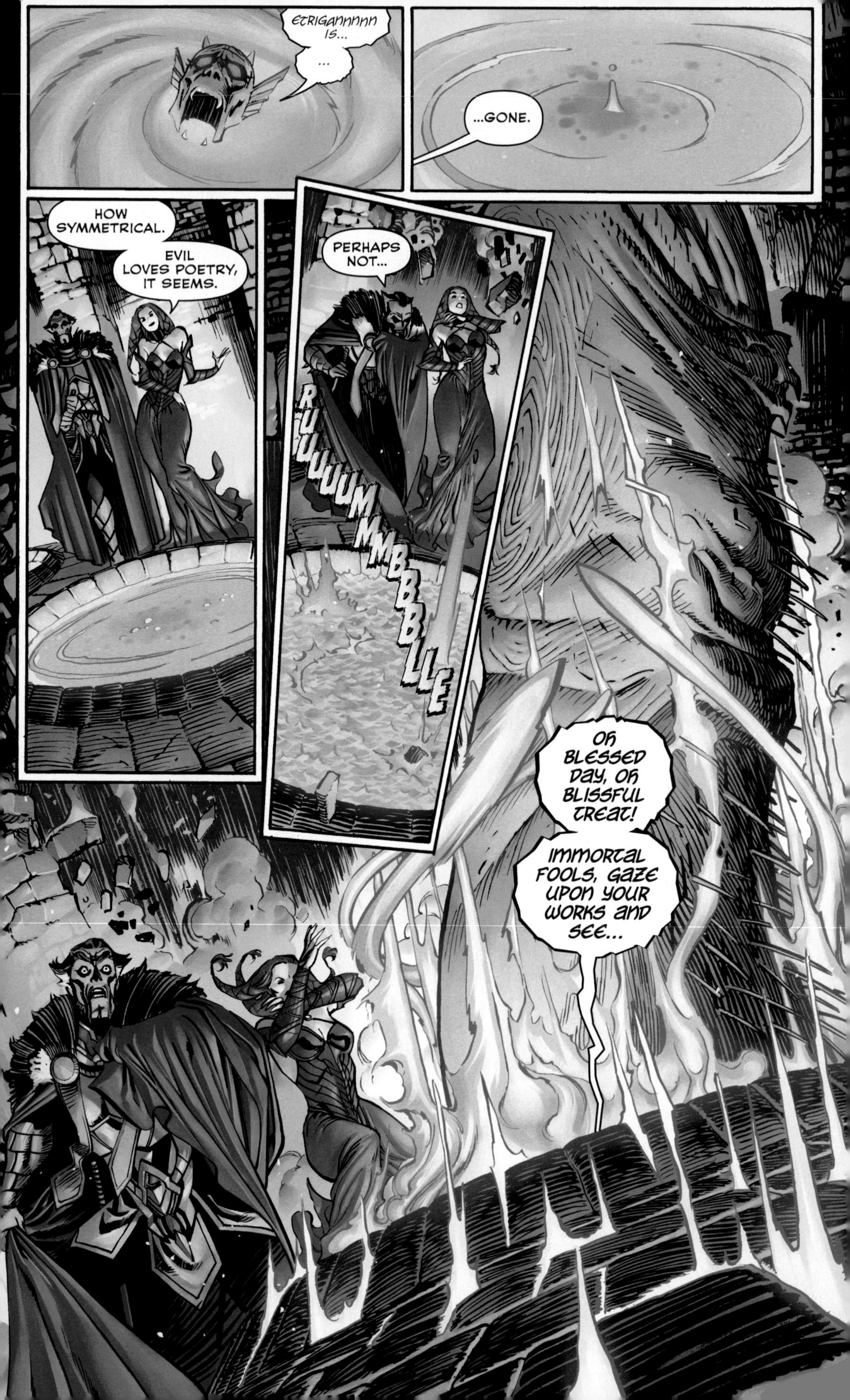

ETRIGANNNNN IS...
...
...GONE.
HOW SYMMETRICAL.
EVIL LOVES POETRY, IT SEEMS.
PERHAPS NOT...
RUUUUUMMMBBBLLE
OH BLESSED DAY, OH BLISSFUL TREAT!
IMMORTAL FOOLS, GAZE UPON YOUR WORKS AND SEE...

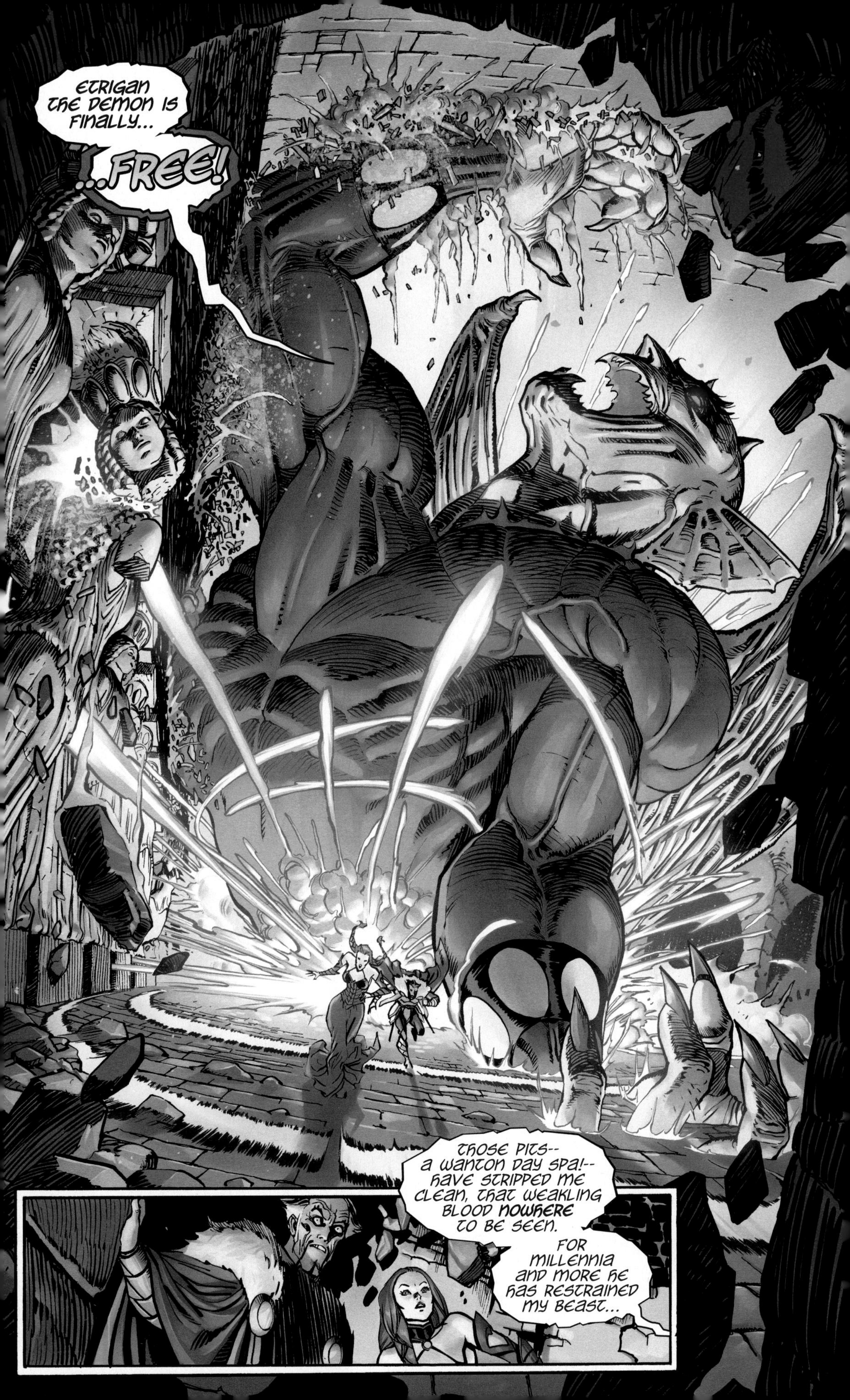
ETRIGAN THE DEMON IS FINALLY...
...FREE!
THOSE PITS-- A WANTON DAY SPA!-- HAVE STRIPPED ME CLEAN, THAT WEAKLING BLOOD **NOWHERE** TO BE SEEN.
FOR MILLENNIA AND MORE HE HAS RESTRAINED MY BEAST...

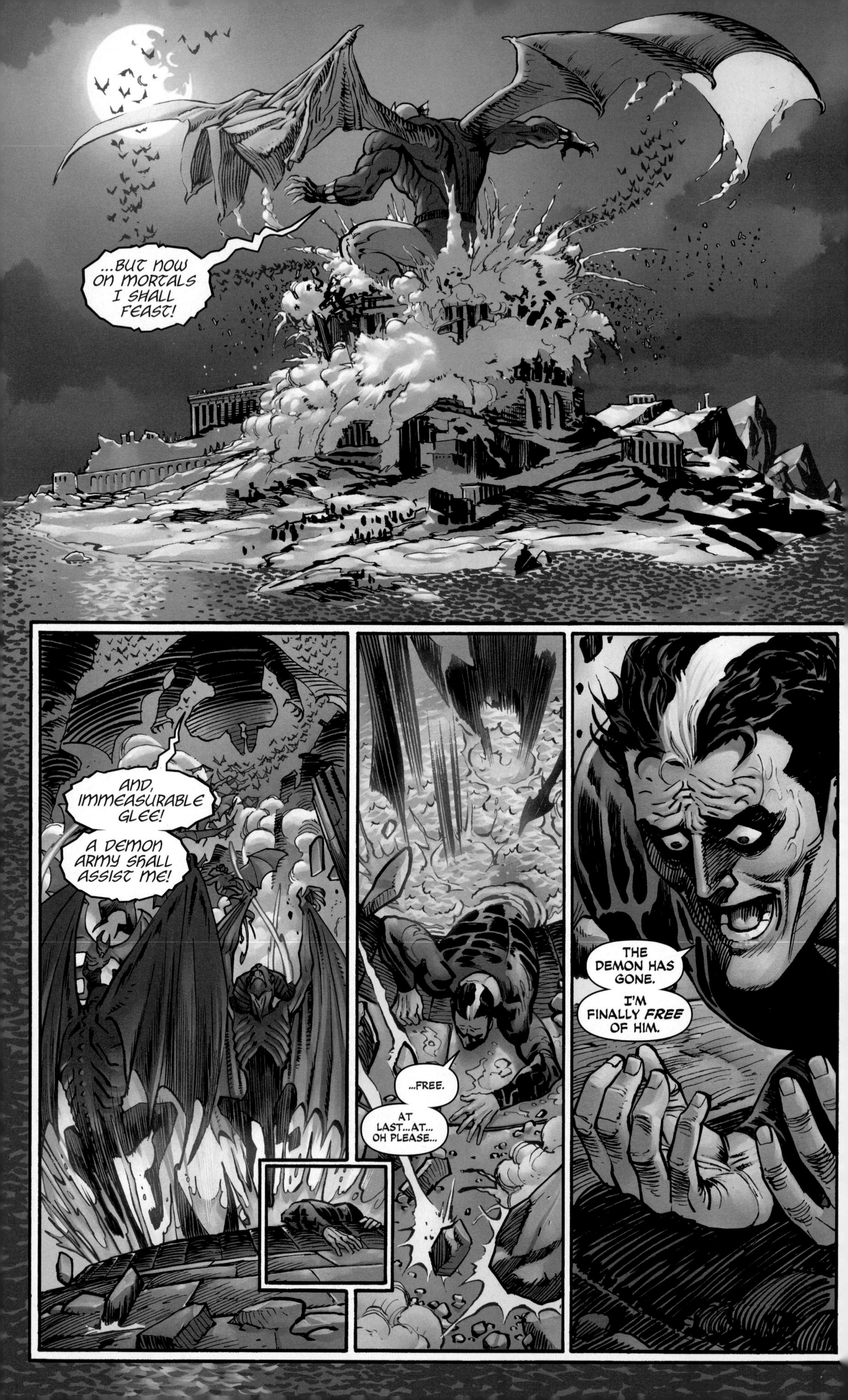
...BUT NOW ON MORTALS I SHALL FEAST!
AND, IMMEASURABLE GLEE!
A DEMON ARMY SHALL ASSIST ME!
...FREE.
AT LAST...AT... OH PLEASE...
THE DEMON HAS GONE.
I'M FINALLY *FREE* OF HIM.

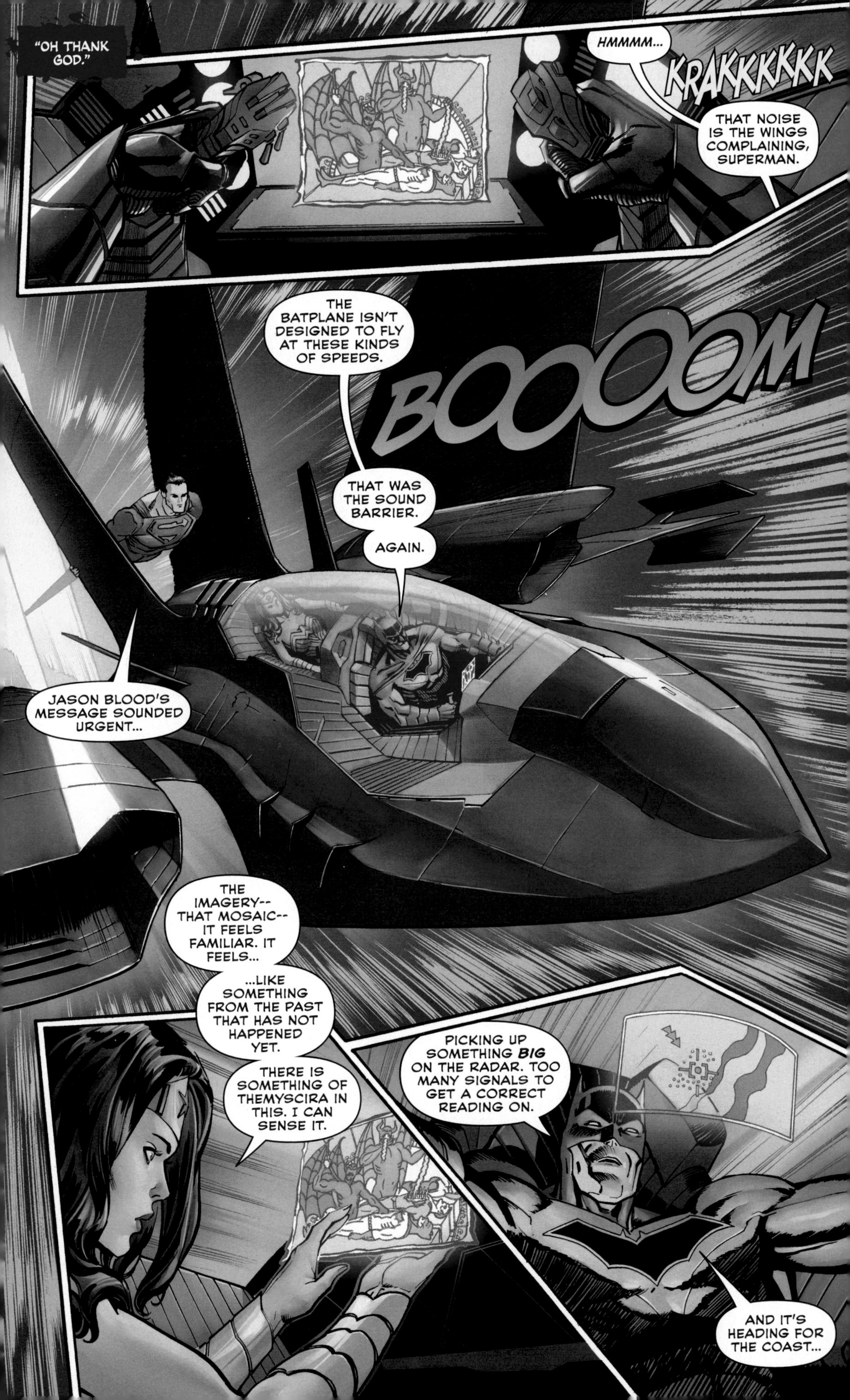
"OH THANK GOD."
HMMMM...
KRAKKKKKK
THAT NOISE IS THE WINGS COMPLAINING, SUPERMAN.
THE BATPLANE ISN'T DESIGNED TO FLY AT THESE KINDS OF SPEEDS.
BOOOOOM
THAT WAS THE SOUND BARRIER.
AGAIN.
JASON BLOOD'S MESSAGE SOUNDED URGENT...
THE IMAGERY-- THAT MOSAIC-- IT FEELS FAMILIAR. IT FEELS...
...LIKE SOMETHING FROM THE PAST THAT HAS NOT HAPPENED YET.
THERE IS SOMETHING OF THEMYSCIRA IN THIS. I CAN SENSE IT.
PICKING UP SOMETHING BIG ON THE RADAR. TOO MANY SIGNALS TO GET A CORRECT READING ON.
AND IT'S HEADING FOR THE COAST...

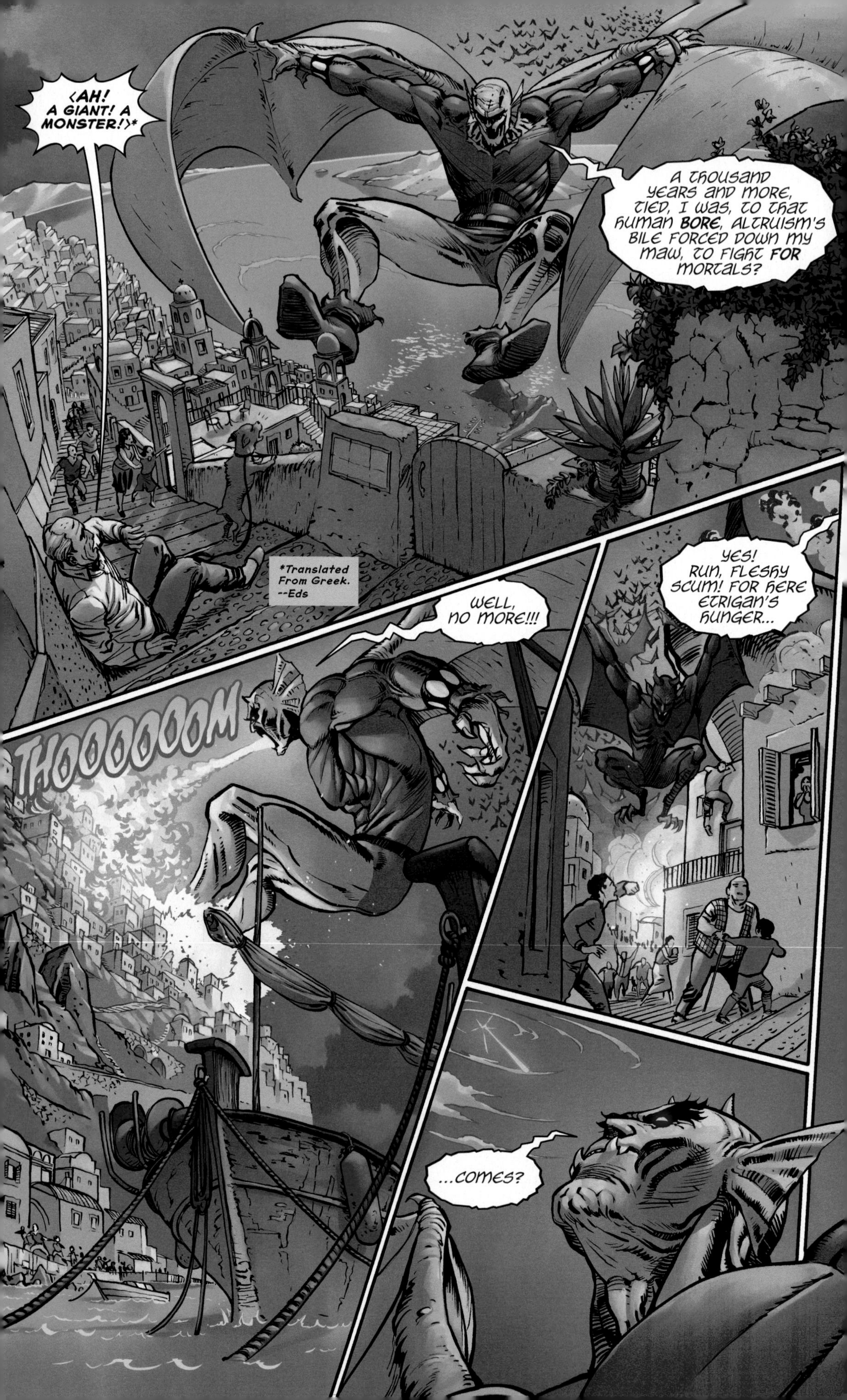
<AH! A GIANT! A MONSTER!>*
A THOUSAND YEARS AND MORE, TIED, I WAS, TO THAT HUMAN BORE, ALTRUISM'S BILE FORCED DOWN MY MAW, TO FIGHT FOR MORTALS?
*Translated From Greek. --Eds
WELL, NO MORE!!!
THOOOOOOM
YES! RUN, FLESHY SCUM! FOR HERE ETRIGAN'S HUNGER...
...COMES?

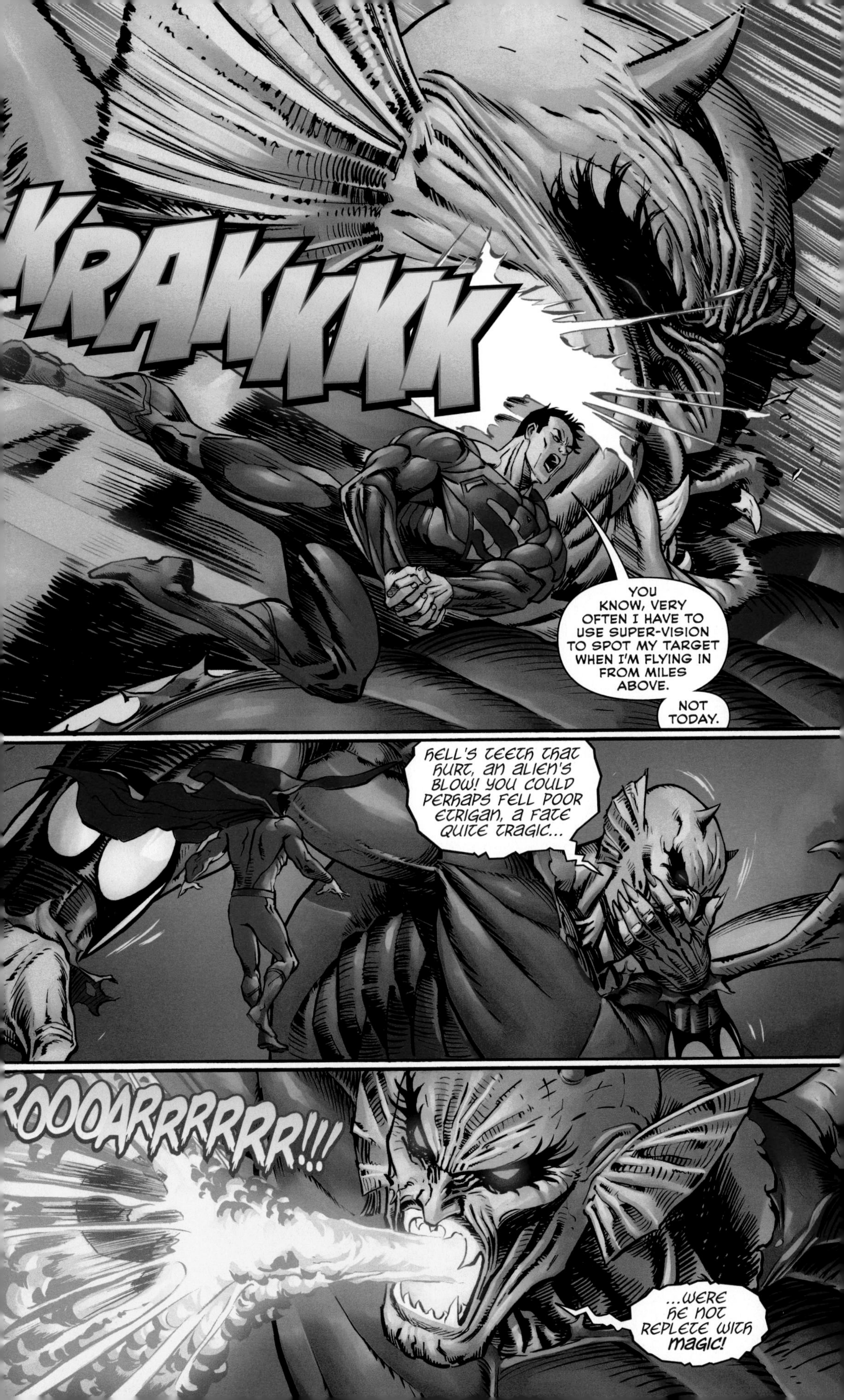
KRAKKKK
YOU KNOW, VERY OFTEN I HAVE TO USE SUPER-VISION TO SPOT MY TARGET WHEN I'M FLYING IN FROM MILES ABOVE.
NOT TODAY.
HELL'S TEETH THAT HURT, AN ALIEN'S BLOW! YOU COULD PERHAPS FELL POOR ETRIGAN, A FATE QUITE TRAGIC...
ROOOARRRRRR!!!
...WERE HE NOT REPLETE WITH MAGIC!

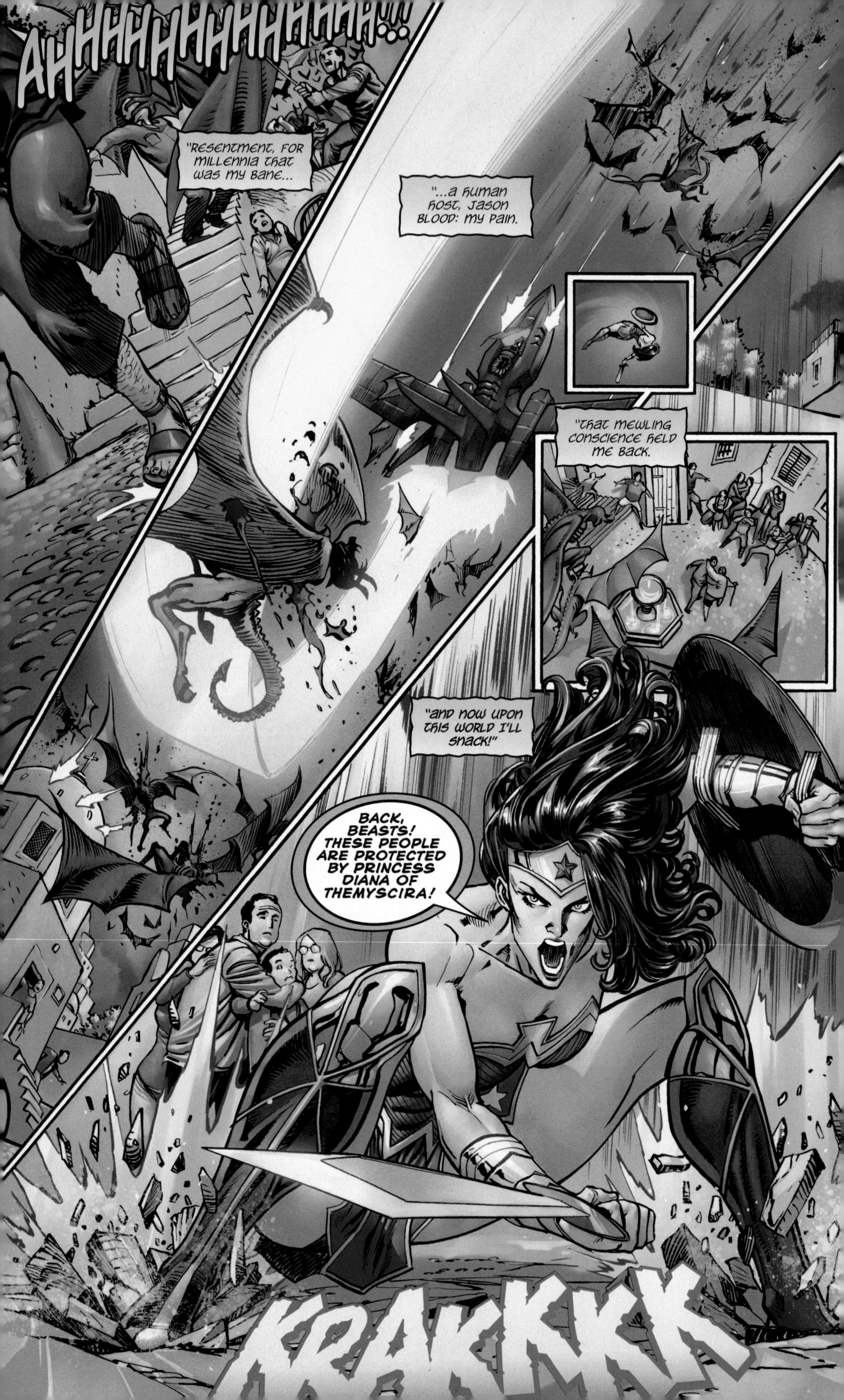
AHHHHHHHHHHHHH!!!
"RESENTMENT, FOR MILLENNIA THAT WAS MY BANE...
"...A HUMAN HOST, JASON BLOOD: MY PAIN.
"THAT MEWLING CONSCIENCE HELD ME BACK.
"AND NOW UPON THIS WORLD I'LL SNACK!"
BACK, BEASTS! THESE PEOPLE ARE PROTECTED BY PRINCESS DIANA OF THEMYSCIRA!
KRAKKK

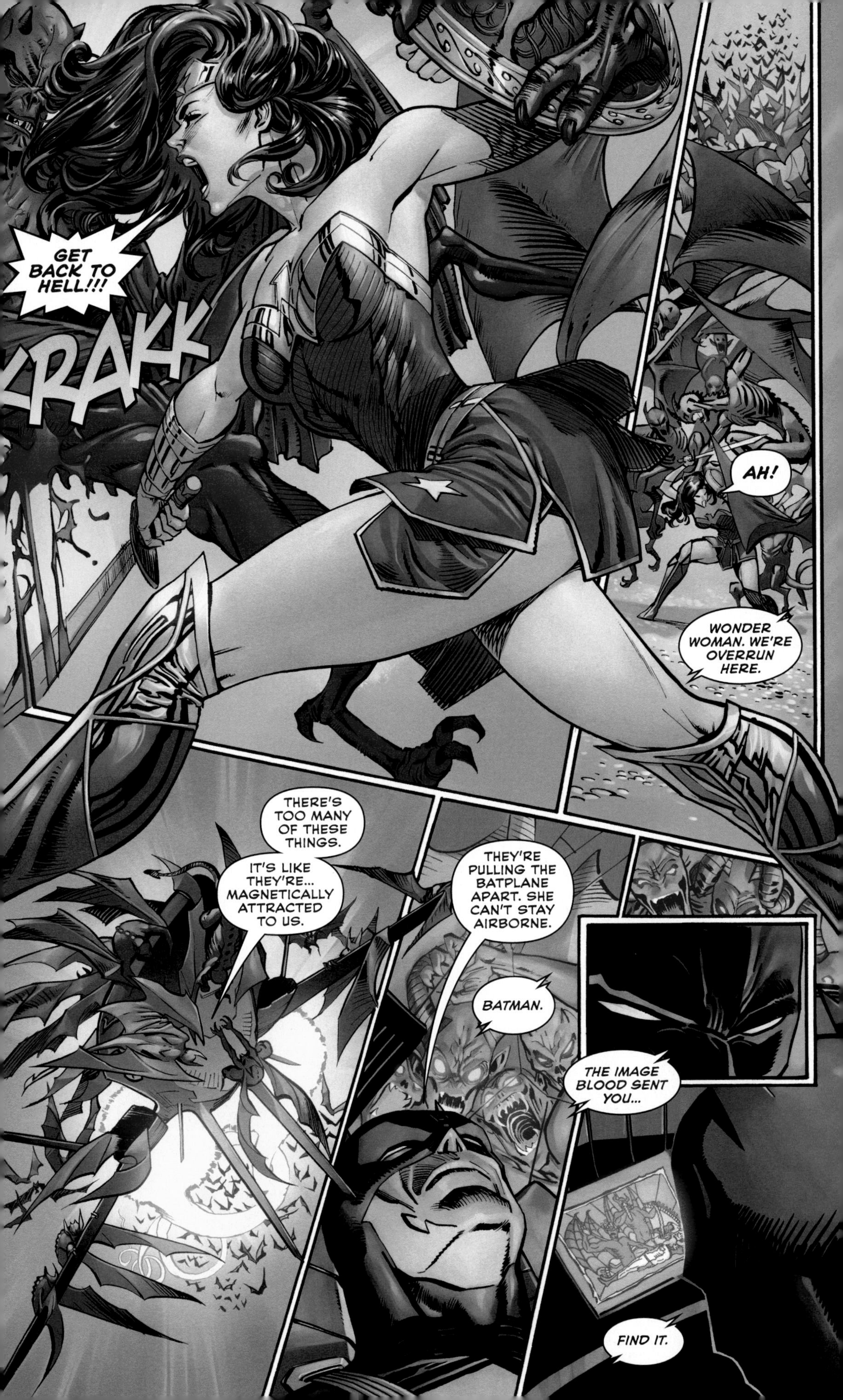
GET BACK TO HELL!!!
KRAKK
AH!
WONDER WOMAN. WE'RE OVERRUN HERE.
THERE'S TOO MANY OF THESE THINGS.
IT'S LIKE THEY'RE... MAGNETICALLY ATTRACTED TO US.
THEY'RE PULLING THE BATPLANE APART. SHE CAN'T STAY AIRBORNE.
BATMAN.
THE IMAGE BLOOD SENT YOU...
FIND IT.

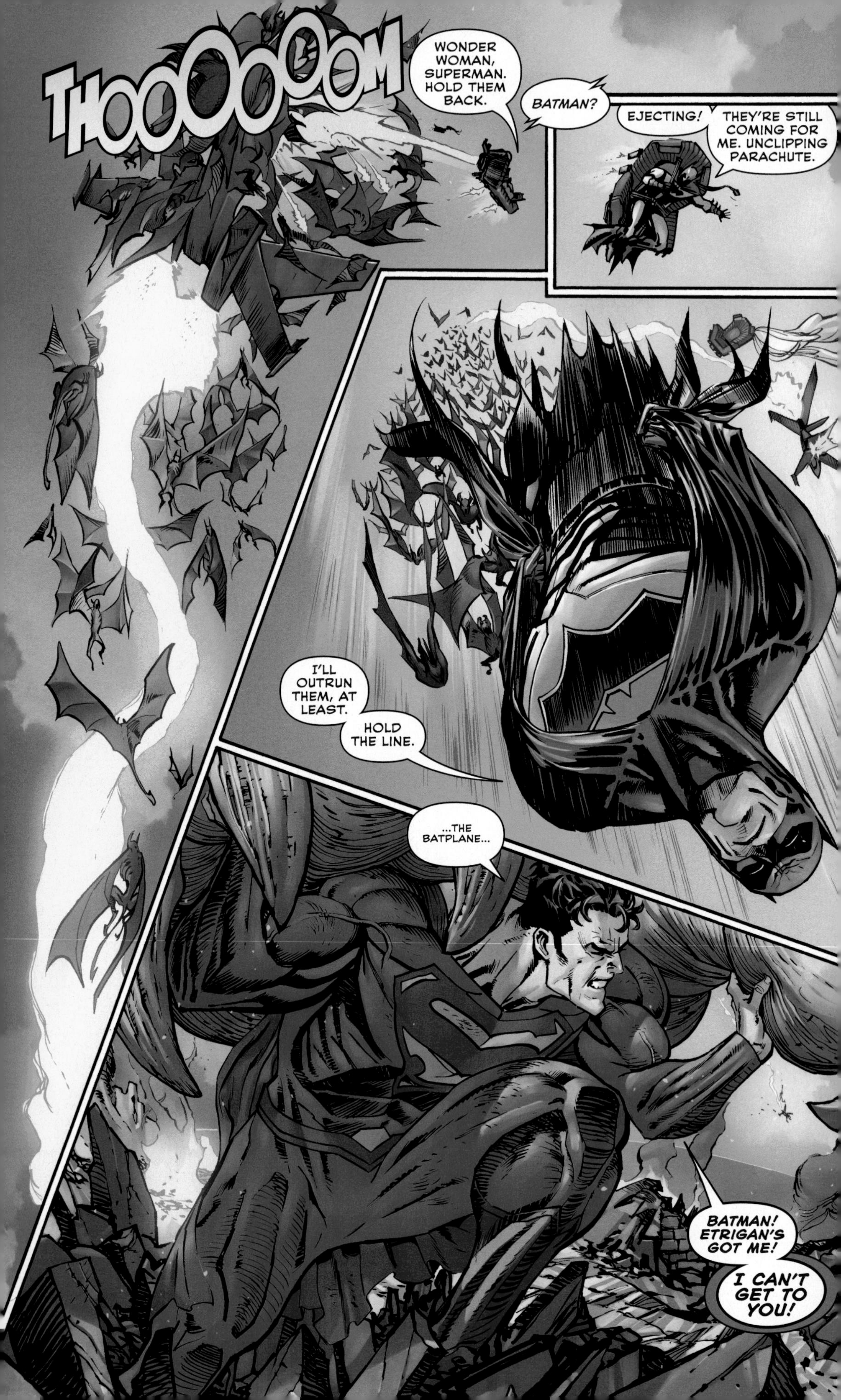
THOOOOOOOM
WONDER WOMAN, SUPERMAN. HOLD THEM BACK.
BATMAN?
EJECTING!
THEY'RE STILL COMING FOR ME. UNCLIPPING PARACHUTE.
I'LL OUTRUN THEM, AT LEAST.
HOLD THE LINE.
...THE BATPLANE...
BATMAN! ETRIGAN'S GOT ME!
I CAN'T GET TO YOU!

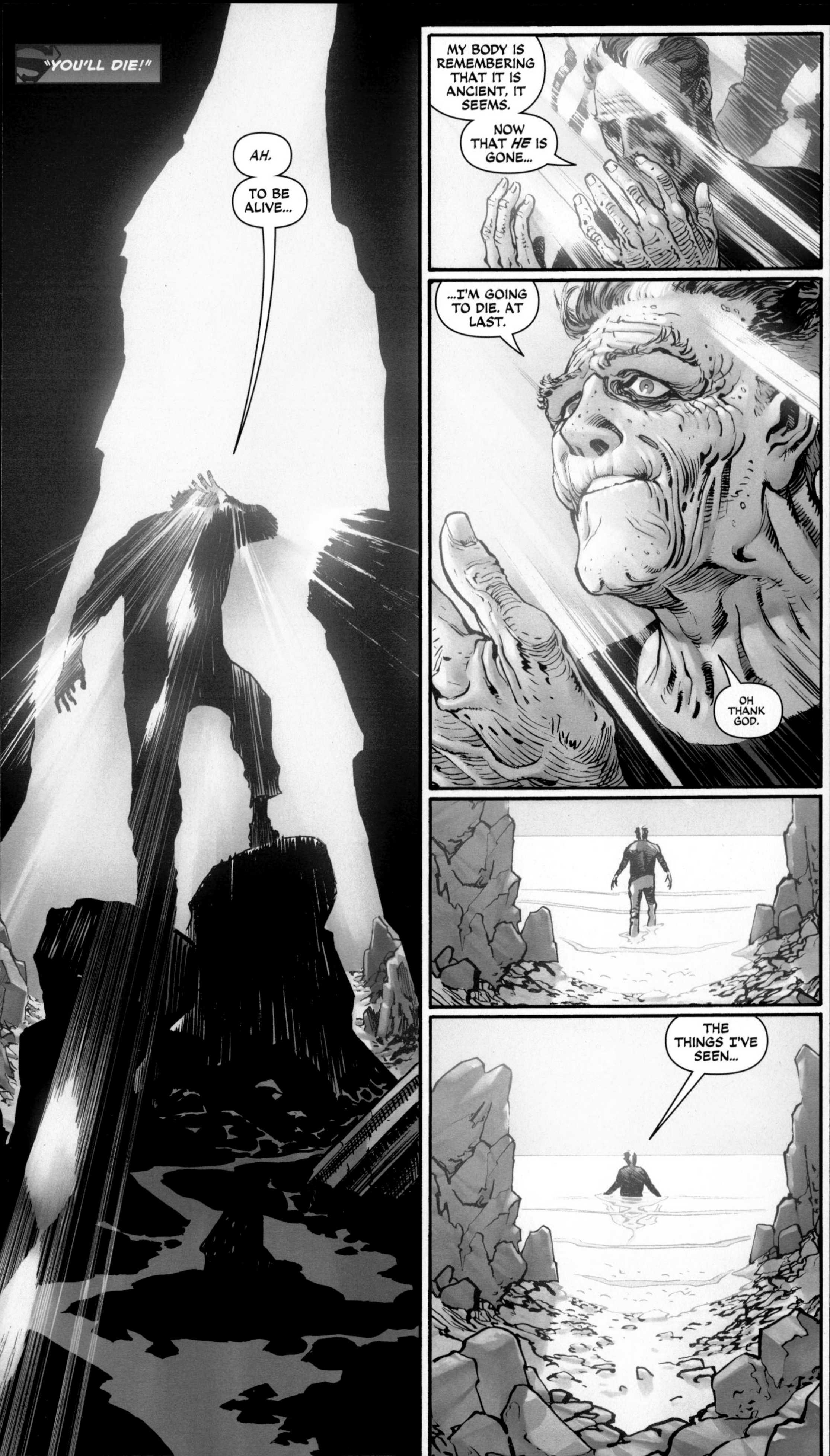

"YOU'LL DIE!"
AH.
TO BE ALIVE...
MY BODY IS REMEMBERING THAT IT IS ANCIENT, IT SEEMS.
NOW THAT *HE* IS GONE...
...I'M GOING TO DIE. AT LAST.
OH THANK GOD.
THE THINGS I'VE SEEN...

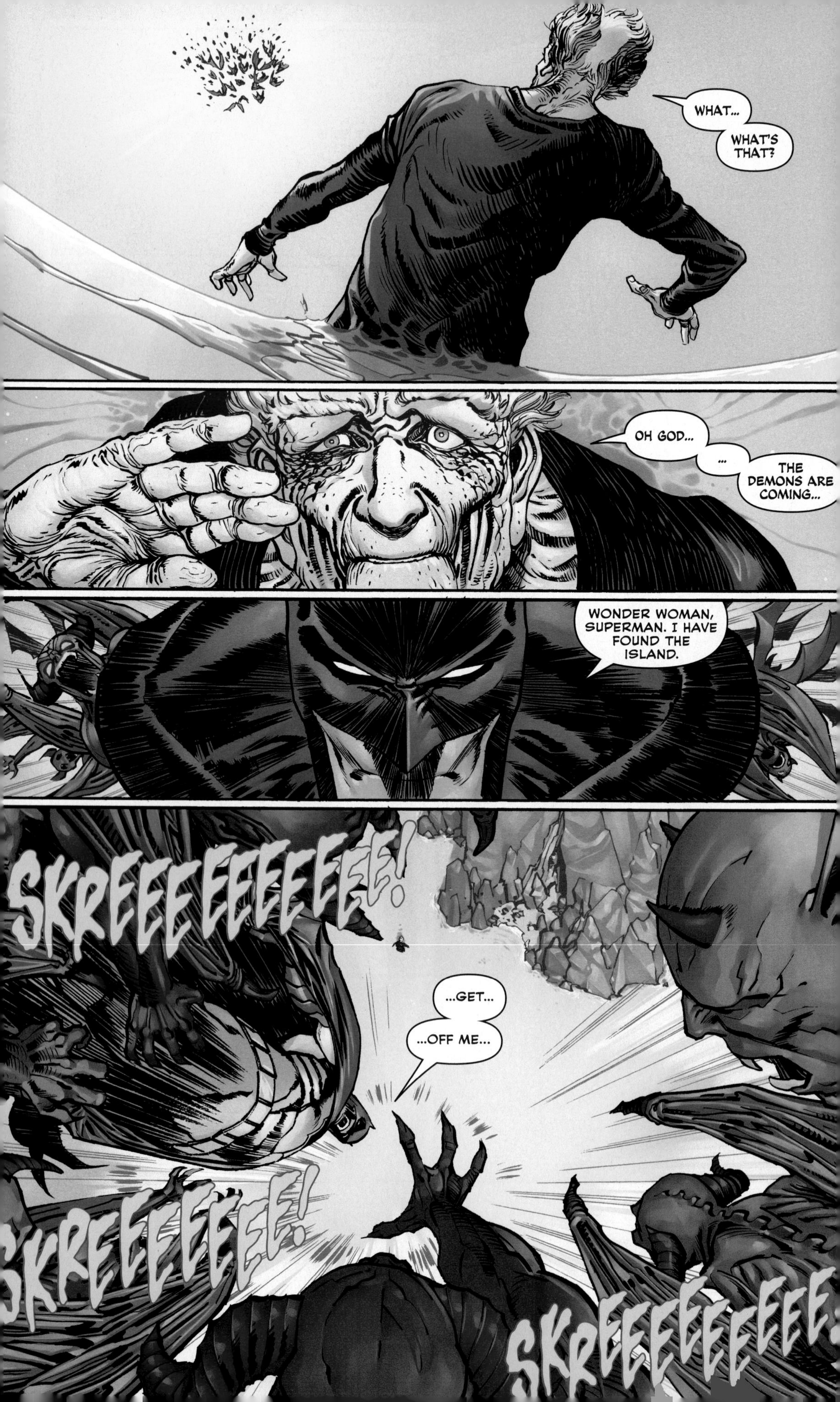
WHAT...
WHAT'S THAT?
OH GOD...
...
THE DEMONS ARE COMING...
WONDER WOMAN, SUPERMAN. I HAVE FOUND THE ISLAND.
SKREEEEEEEEEEE!
...GET...
...OFF ME...
SKREEEEEEE!
SKREEEEEEEEE

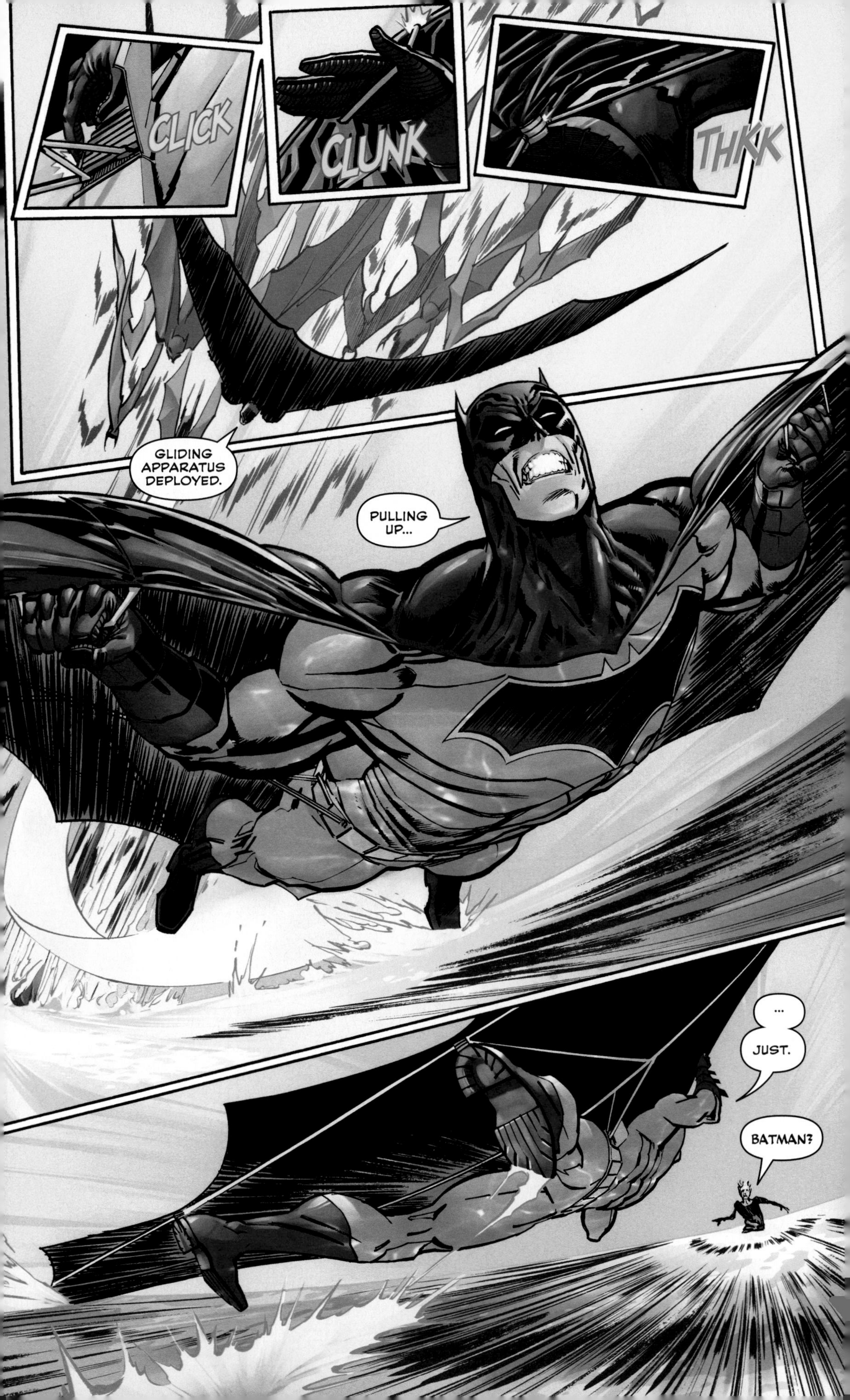
CLICK
CLUNK
THKK
GLIDING APPARATUS DEPLOYED.
PULLING UP...
...
JUST.
BATMAN?

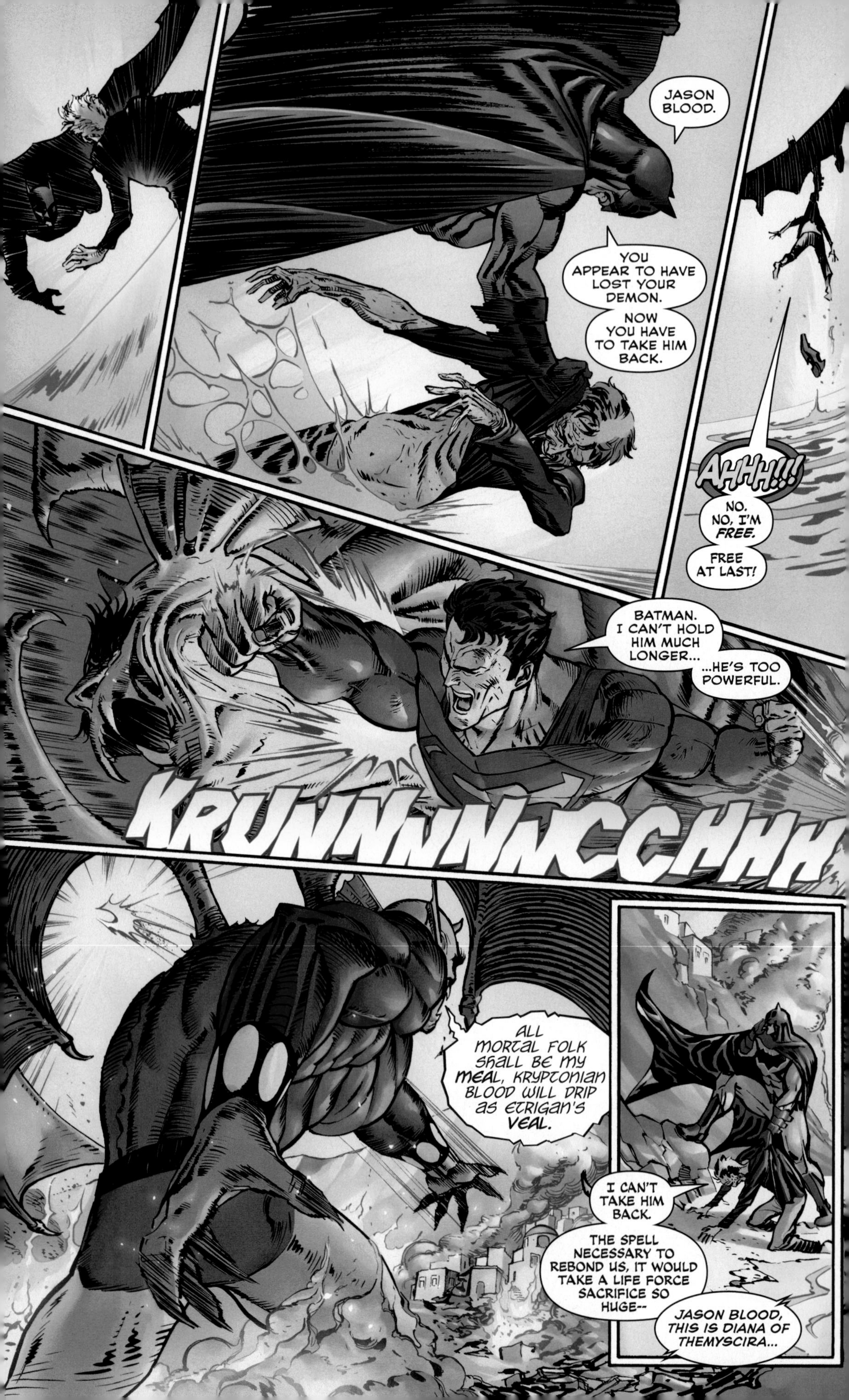
JASON BLOOD.
YOU APPEAR TO HAVE LOST YOUR DEMON.
NOW YOU HAVE TO TAKE HIM BACK.
AHHH!!!
NO. NO, I'M *FREE.*
FREE AT LAST!
BATMAN. I CAN'T HOLD HIM MUCH LONGER...
...HE'S TOO POWERFUL.
KRUNNNNNCCHHH
ALL MORTAL FOLK SHALL BE MY **MEAL**, KRYPTONIAN BLOOD WILL DRIP AS ETRIGAN'S **VEAL**.
I CAN'T TAKE HIM BACK.
THE SPELL NECESSARY TO REBOND US, IT WOULD TAKE A LIFE FORCE SACRIFICE SO HUGE--
*JASON BLOOD, THIS IS DIANA OF THEMYSCIRA...*

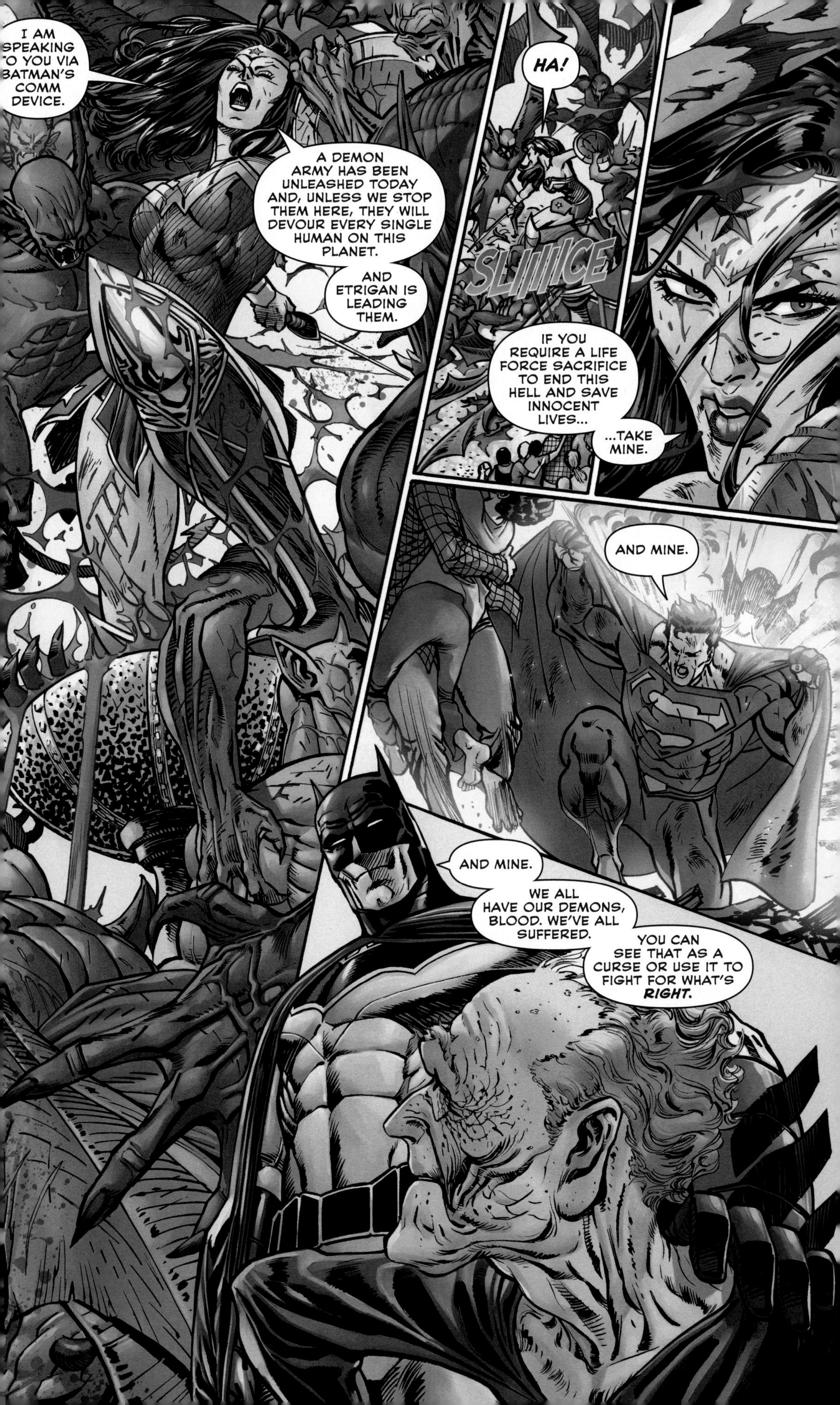
I AM SPEAKING TO YOU VIA BATMAN'S COMM DEVICE.
A DEMON ARMY HAS BEEN UNLEASHED TODAY AND, UNLESS WE STOP THEM HERE, THEY WILL DEVOUR EVERY SINGLE HUMAN ON THIS PLANET.
AND ETRIGAN IS LEADING THEM.
HA!
SLIIIICE
IF YOU REQUIRE A LIFE FORCE SACRIFICE TO END THIS HELL AND SAVE INNOCENT LIVES...
...TAKE MINE.
AND MINE.
AND MINE.
WE ALL HAVE OUR DEMONS, BLOOD. WE'VE ALL SUFFERED.
YOU CAN SEE THAT AS A CURSE OR USE IT TO FIGHT FOR WHAT'S ***RIGHT***.

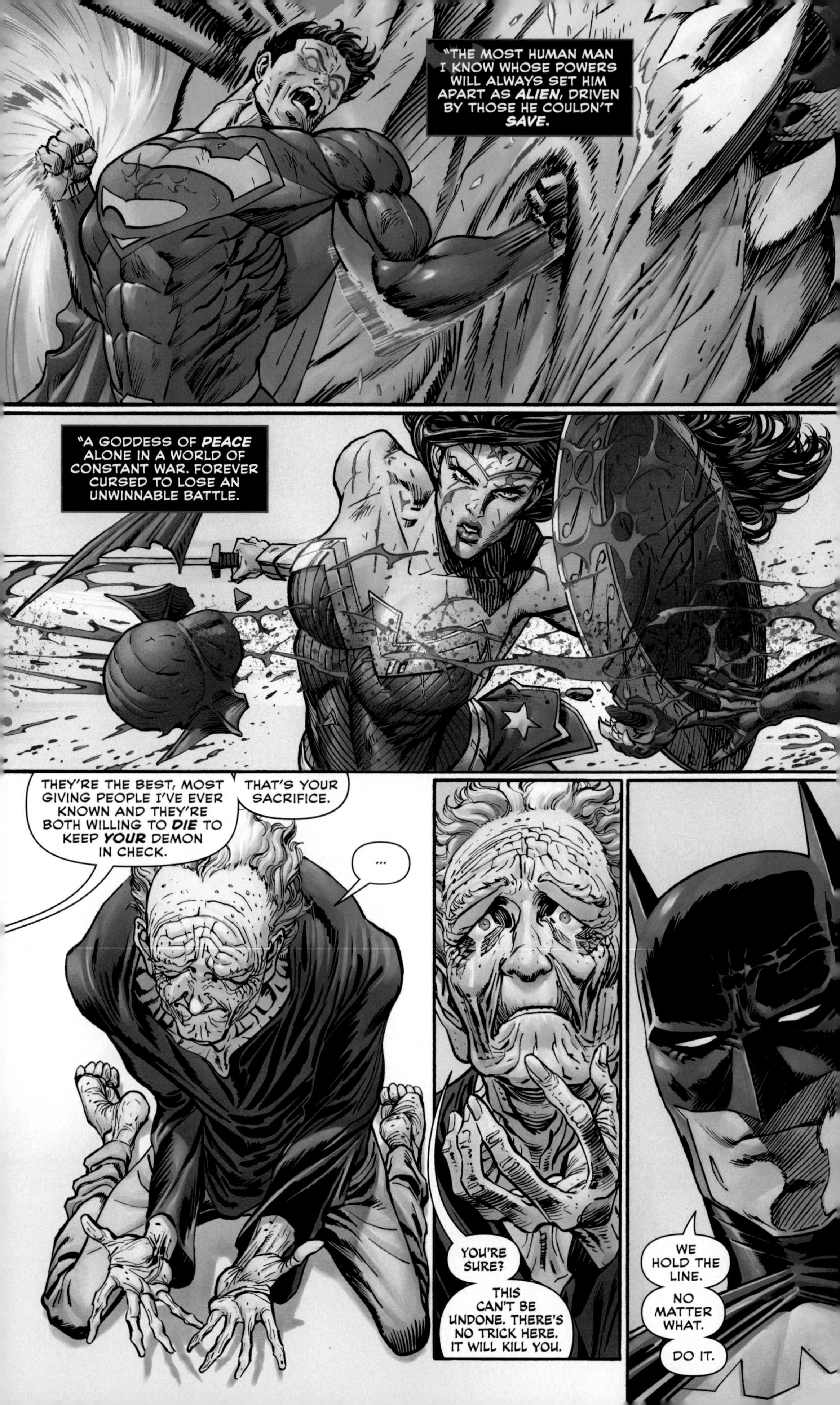
"THE MOST HUMAN MAN I KNOW WHOSE POWERS WILL ALWAYS SET HIM APART AS *ALIEN*, DRIVEN BY THOSE HE COULDN'T *SAVE*.
"A GODDESS OF *PEACE* ALONE IN A WORLD OF CONSTANT WAR. FOREVER CURSED TO LOSE AN UNWINNABLE BATTLE.
THEY'RE THE BEST, MOST GIVING PEOPLE I'VE EVER KNOWN AND THEY'RE BOTH WILLING TO *DIE* TO KEEP *YOUR* DEMON IN CHECK.
THAT'S YOUR SACRIFICE.
...
YOU'RE SURE?
THIS CAN'T BE UNDONE. THERE'S NO TRICK HERE. IT WILL KILL YOU.
WE HOLD THE LINE.
NO MATTER WHAT.
DO IT.

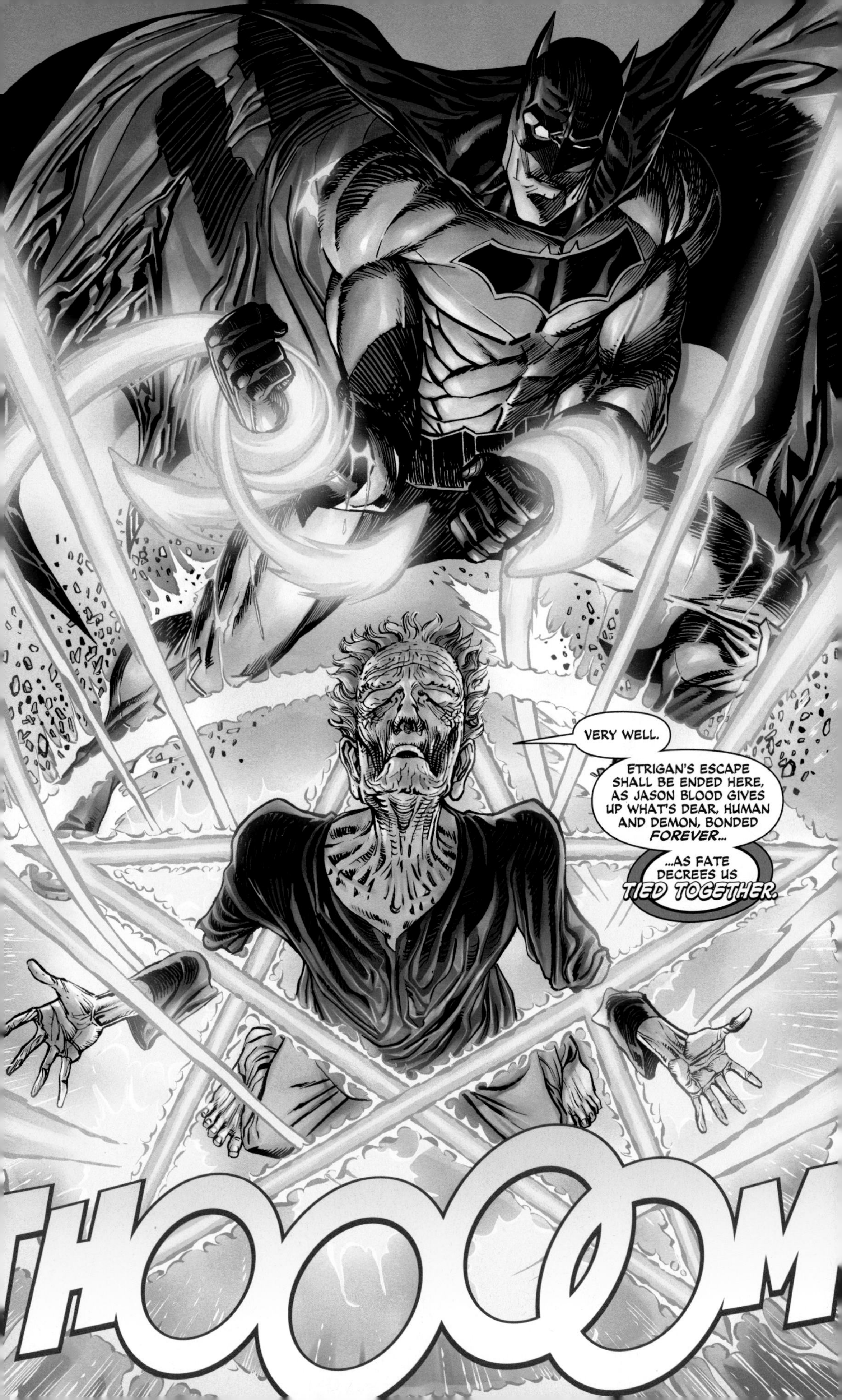
VERY WELL.
ETRIGAN'S ESCAPE SHALL BE ENDED HERE, AS JASON BLOOD GIVES UP WHAT'S DEAR, HUMAN AND DEMON, BONDED FOREVER...
...AS FATE DECREES US TIED TOGETHER.
THOOOOM

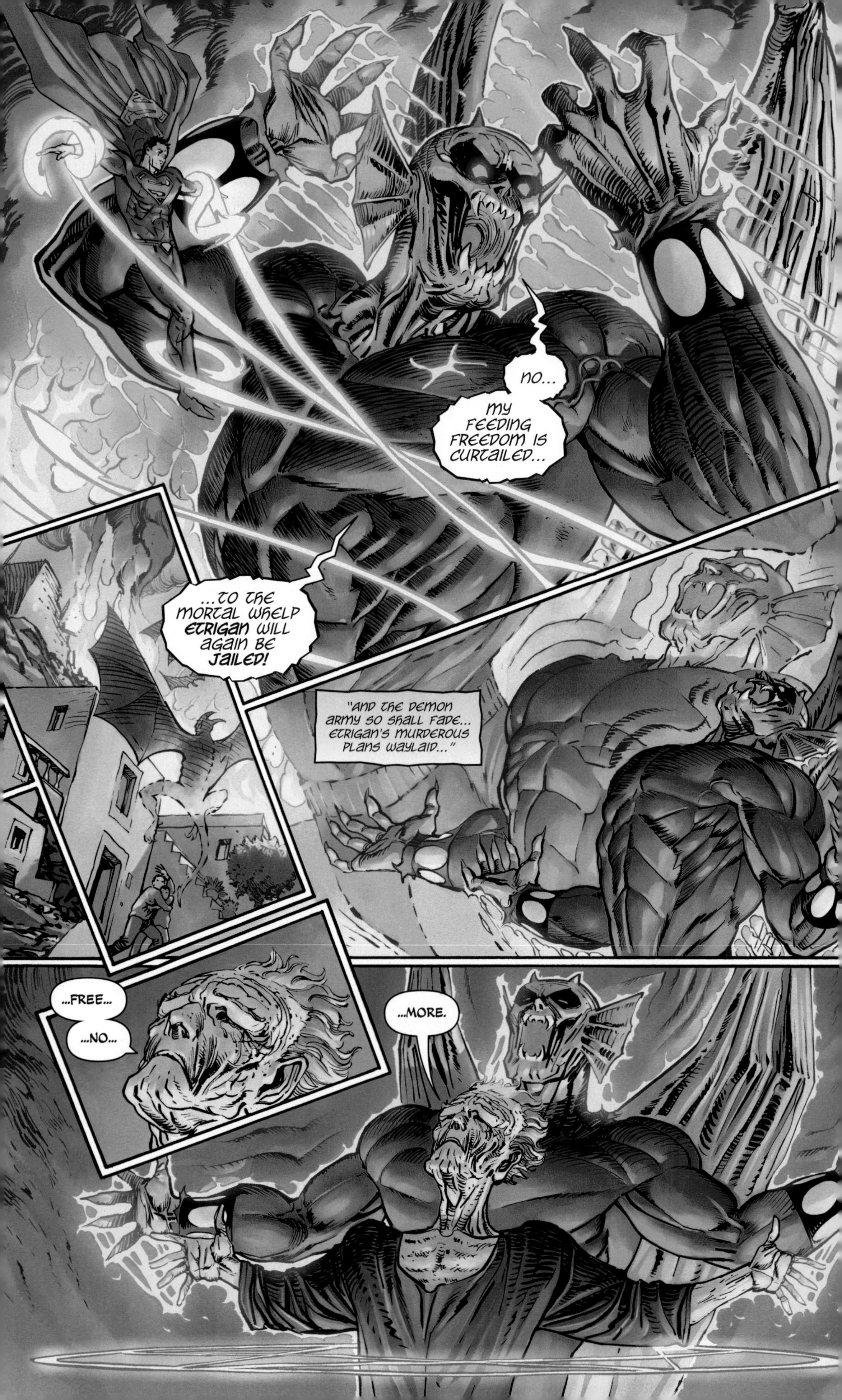

NO...
MY FEEDING FREEDOM IS CURTAILED...
...TO THE MORTAL WHELP ETRIGAN WILL AGAIN BE JAILED!
"AND THE DEMON ARMY SO SHALL FADE... ETRIGAN'S MURDEROUS PLANS WAYLAID..."
...FREE...
...NO...
...MORE.

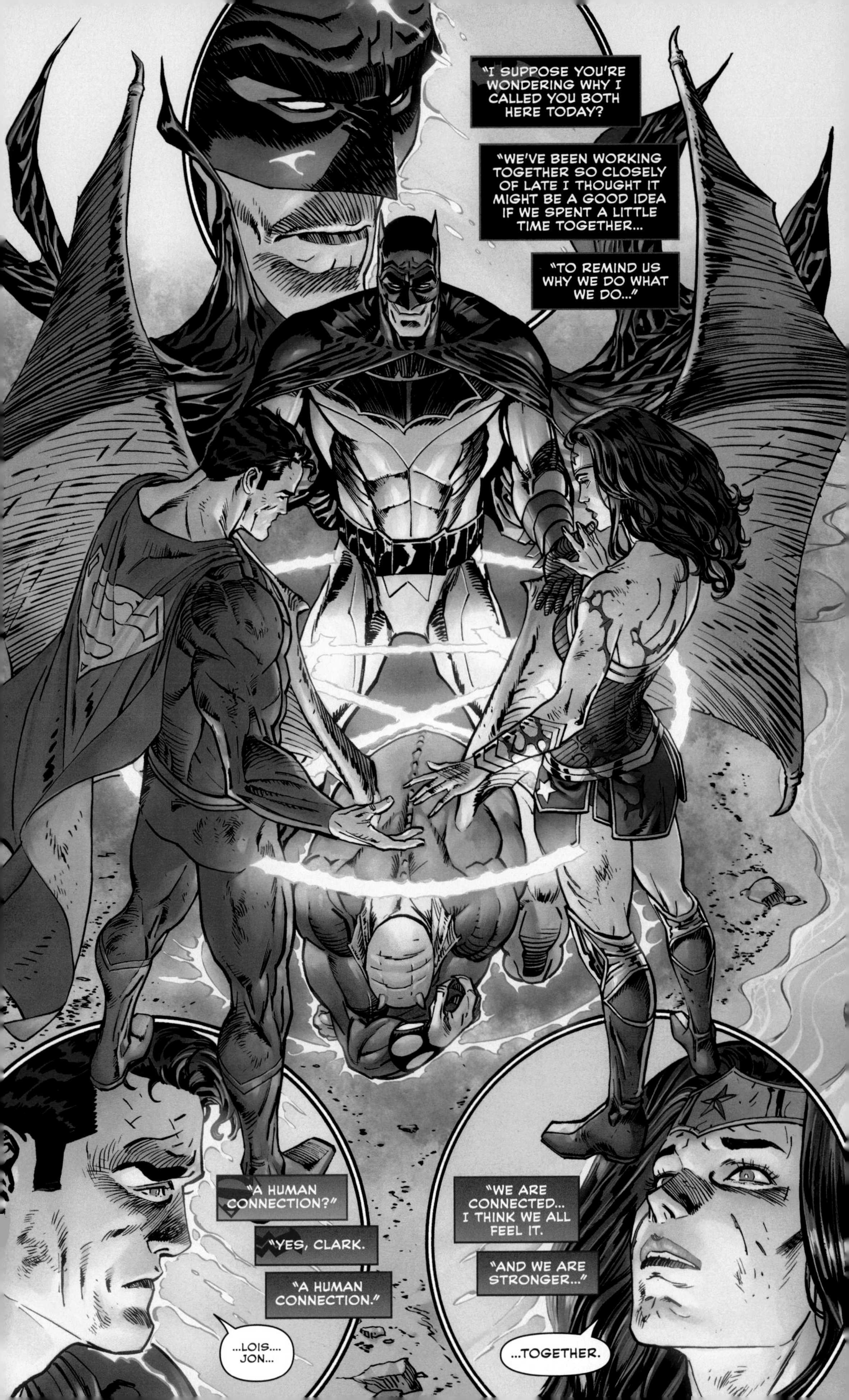
"I SUPPOSE YOU'RE WONDERING WHY I CALLED YOU BOTH HERE TODAY?
"WE'VE BEEN WORKING TOGETHER SO CLOSELY OF LATE I THOUGHT IT MIGHT BE A GOOD IDEA IF WE SPENT A LITTLE TIME TOGETHER...
"TO REMIND US WHY WE DO WHAT WE DO..."
"A HUMAN CONNECTION?"
"YES, CLARK.
"A HUMAN CONNECTION."
...LOIS.... JON...
"WE ARE CONNECTED... I THINK WE ALL FEEL IT.
"AND WE ARE STRONGER..."
...TOGETHER.

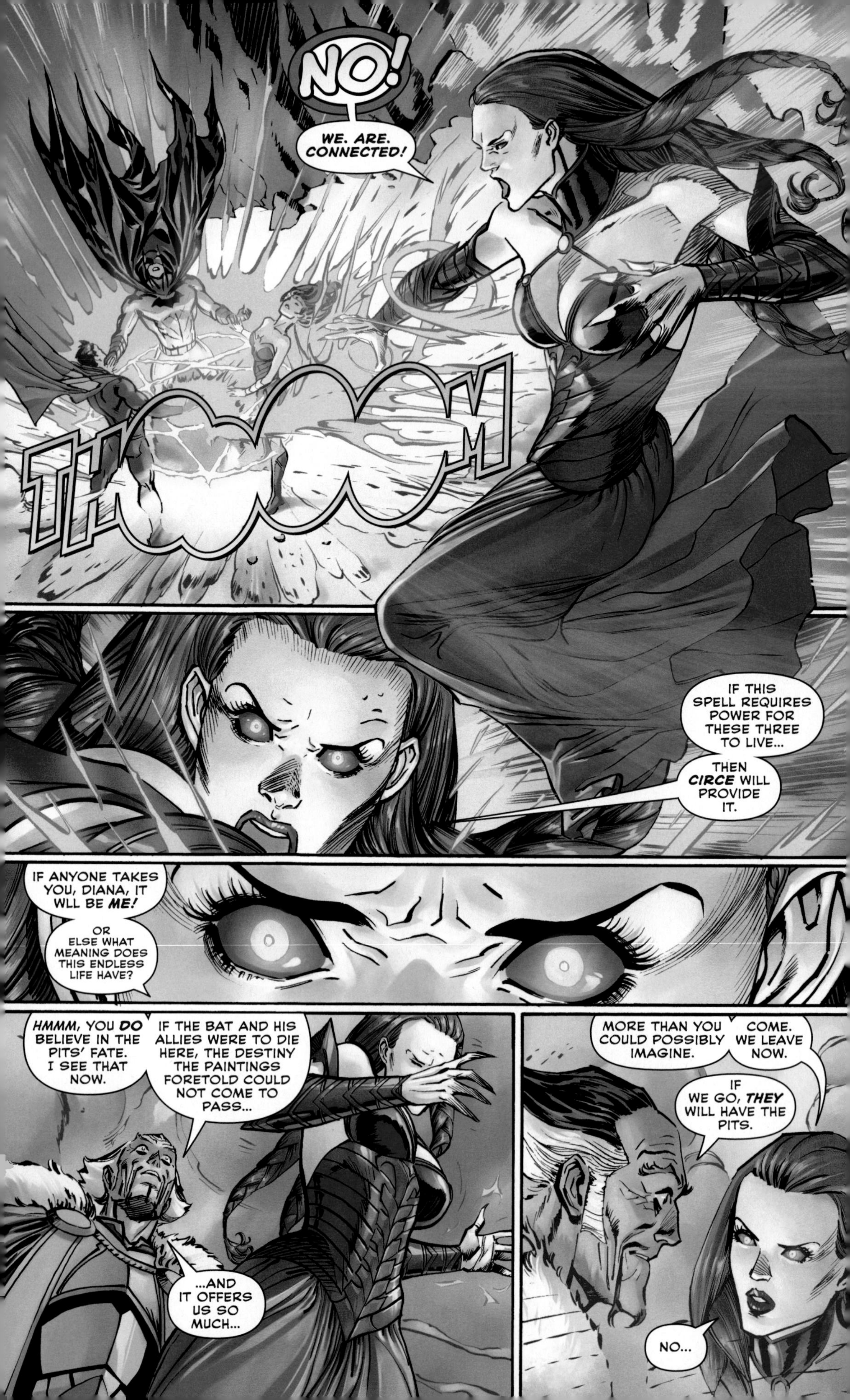
NO!
WE. ARE. CONNECTED!
THOOOOM
IF THIS SPELL REQUIRES POWER FOR THESE THREE TO LIVE...
THEN CIRCE WILL PROVIDE IT.
IF ANYONE TAKES YOU, DIANA, IT WLL BE ME!
OR ELSE WHAT MEANING DOES THIS ENDLESS LIFE HAVE?
HMMM, YOU DO BELIEVE IN THE PITS' FATE. I SEE THAT NOW.
IF THE BAT AND HIS ALLIES WERE TO DIE HERE, THE DESTINY THE PAINTINGS FORETOLD COULD NOT COME TO PASS...
...AND IT OFFERS US SO MUCH...
MORE THAN YOU COULD POSSIBLY IMAGINE.
COME. WE LEAVE NOW.
IF WE GO, THEY WILL HAVE THE PITS.
NO...

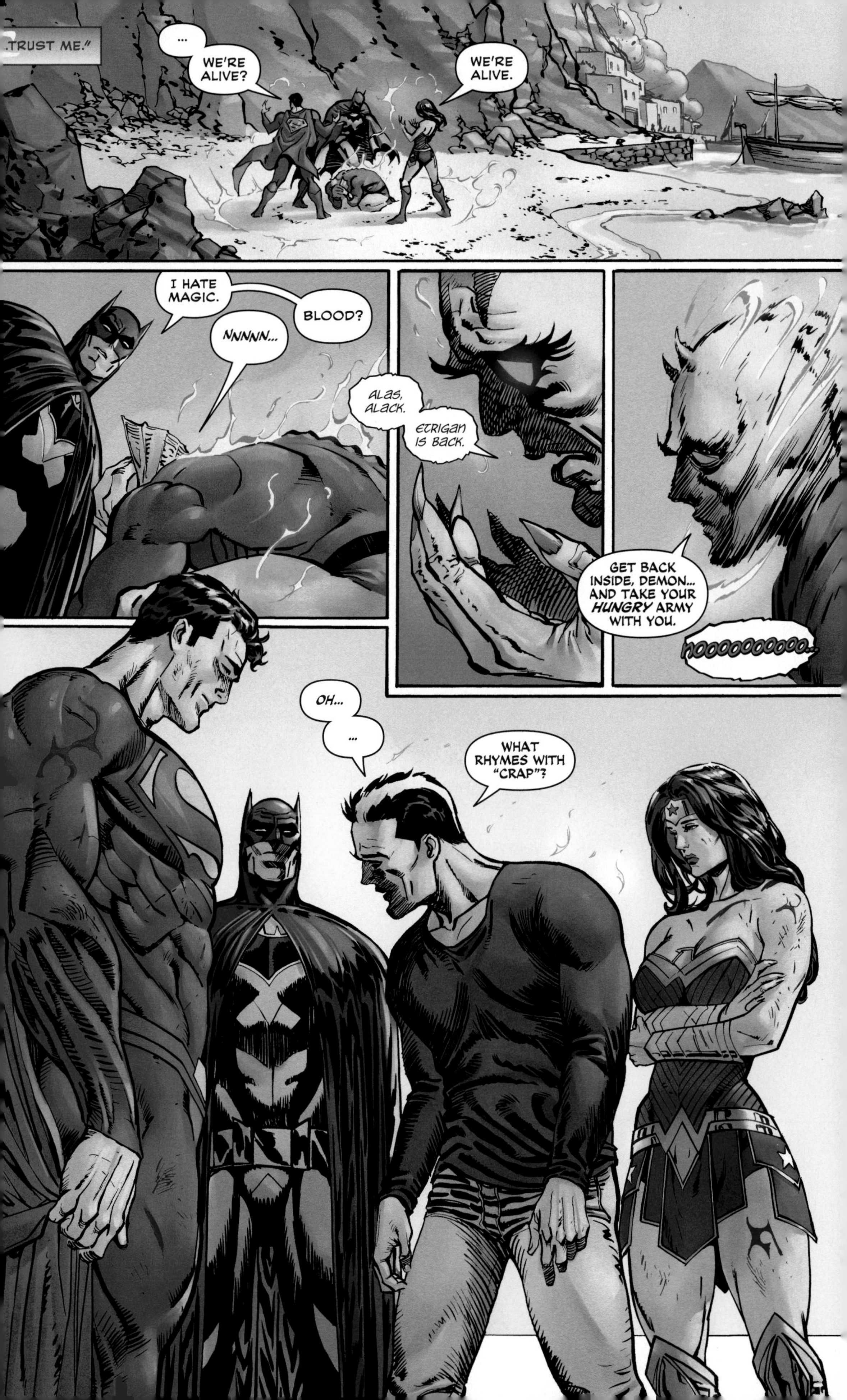

...TRUST ME."
...
WE'RE ALIVE?
WE'RE ALIVE.
I HATE MAGIC.
BLOOD?
NNNNN...
ALAS, ALACK.
ETRIGAN IS BACK.
GET BACK INSIDE, DEMON... AND TAKE YOUR HUNGRY ARMY WITH YOU.
NOOOOOOOOOO...
OH...
...
WHAT RHYMES WITH "CRAP"?

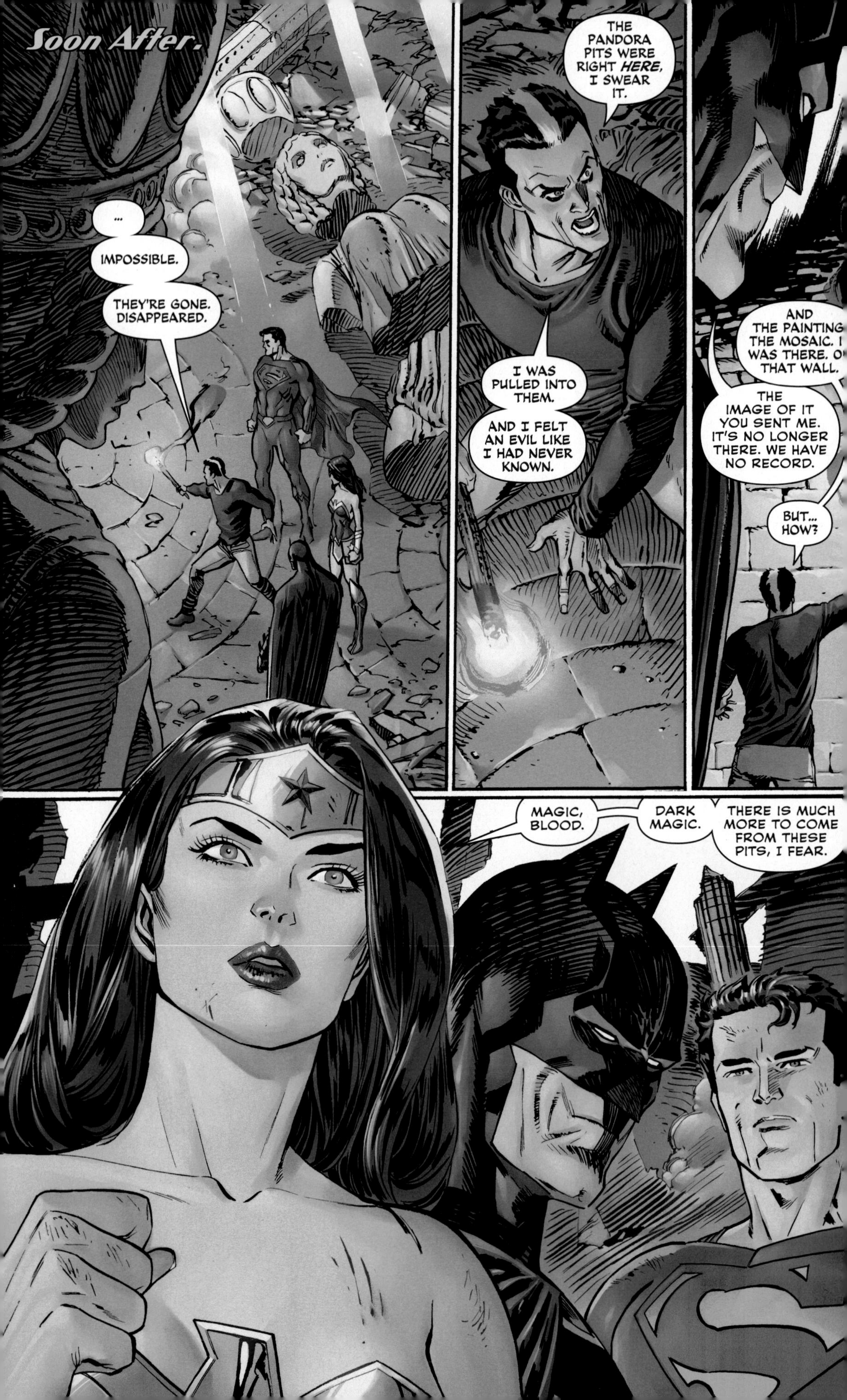
Soon After.
...
IMPOSSIBLE.
THEY'RE GONE. DISAPPEARED.
THE PANDORA PITS WERE RIGHT *HERE*, I SWEAR IT.
I WAS PULLED INTO THEM.
AND I FELT AN EVIL LIKE I HAD NEVER KNOWN.
AND THE PAINTING THE MOSAIC. I WAS THERE. O THAT WALL.
THE IMAGE OF IT YOU SENT ME. IT'S NO LONGER THERE. WE HAVE NO RECORD.
BUT... HOW?
MAGIC, BLOOD.
DARK MAGIC.
THERE IS MUCH MORE TO COME FROM THESE PITS, I FEAR.

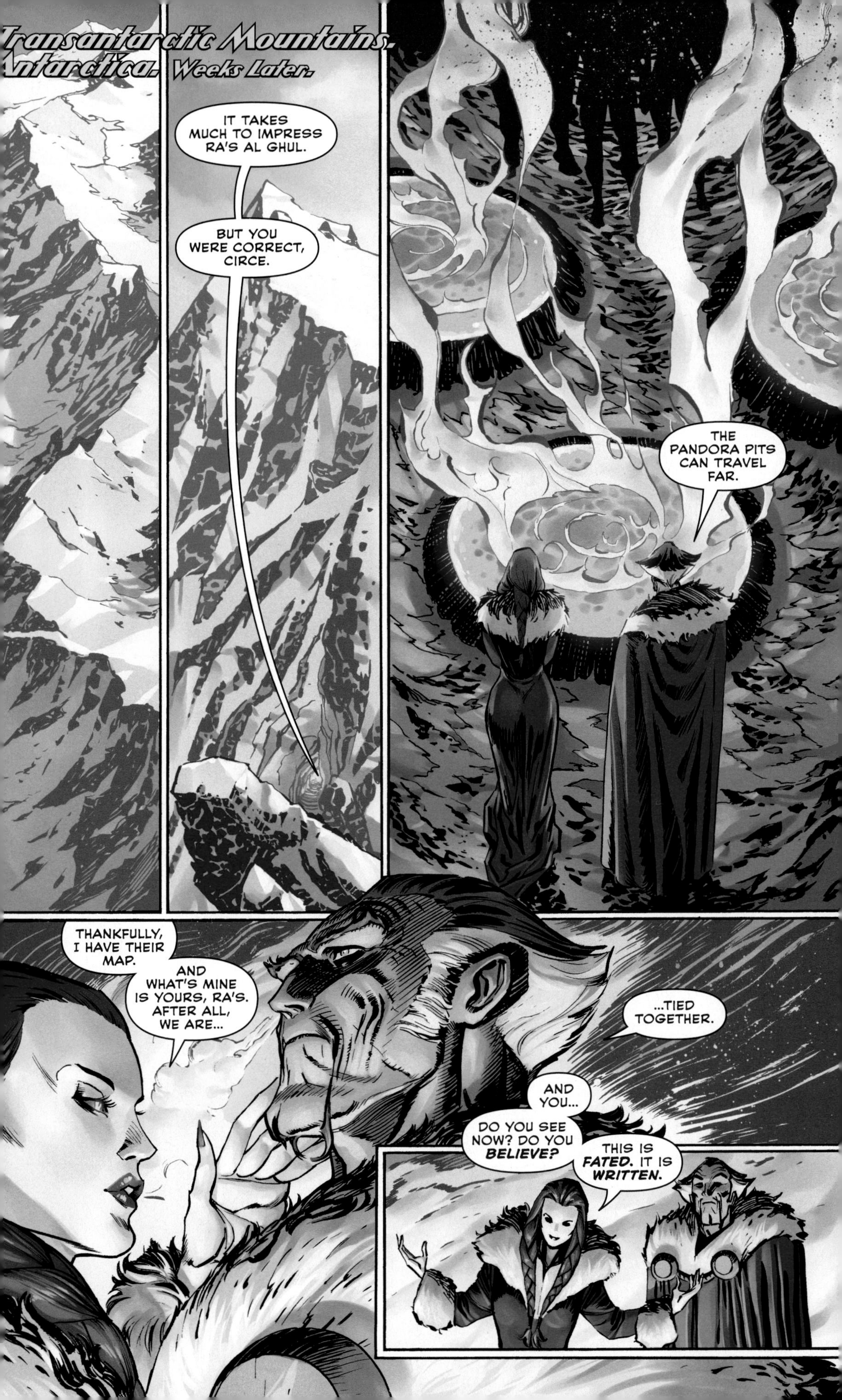
Transantarctic Mountains, Antarctica. Weeks Later.
IT TAKES MUCH TO IMPRESS RA'S AL GHUL.
BUT YOU WERE CORRECT, CIRCE.
THE PANDORA PITS CAN TRAVEL FAR.
THANKFULLY, I HAVE THEIR MAP.
AND WHAT'S MINE IS YOURS, RA'S. AFTER ALL, WE ARE...
...TIED TOGETHER.
AND YOU...
DO YOU SEE NOW? DO YOU **BELIEVE?**
THIS IS **FATED.** IT IS **WRITTEN.**

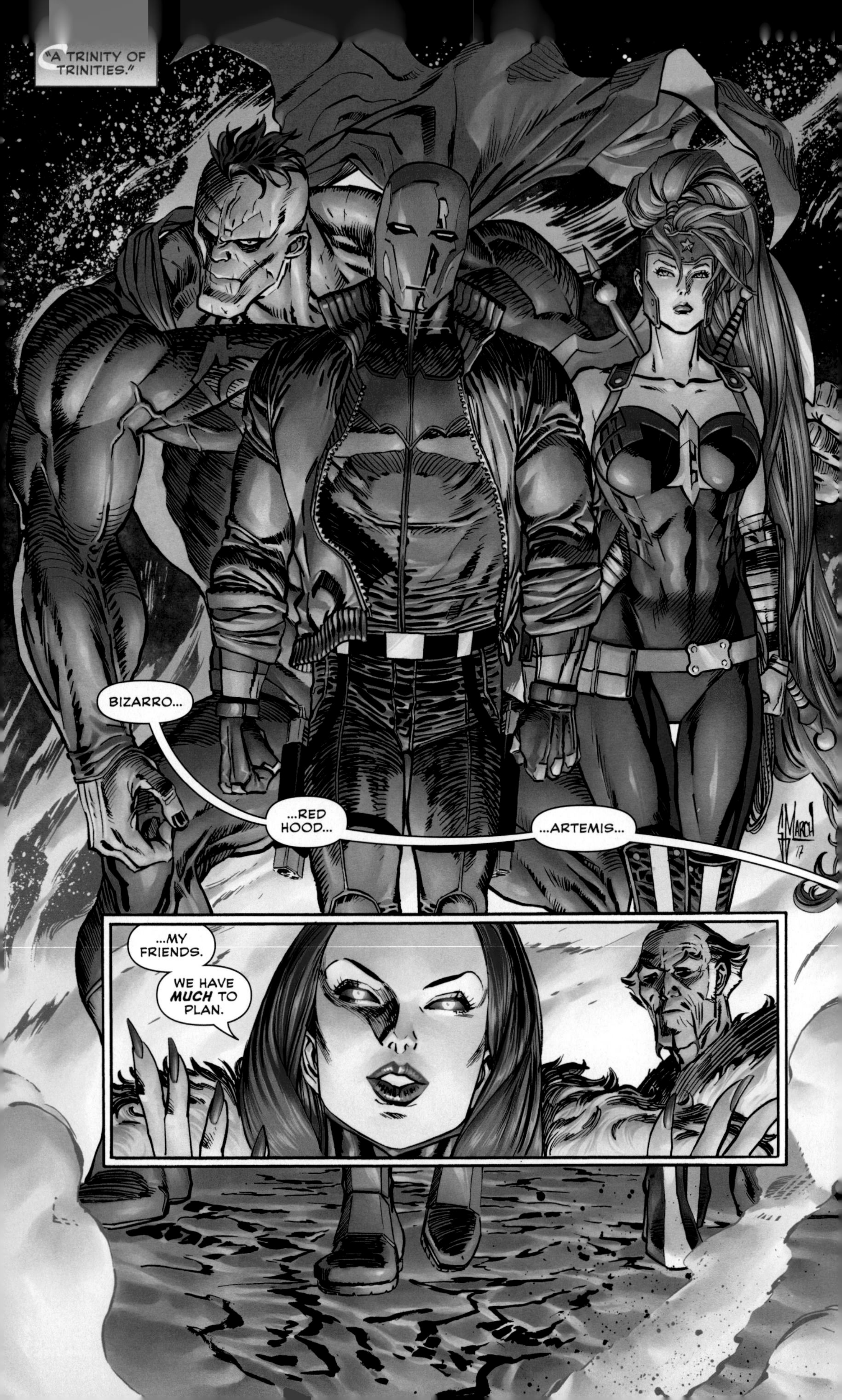
"A TRINITY OF TRINITIES."
BIZARRO...
...RED HOOD...
...ARTEMIS...
...MY FRIENDS.
WE HAVE MUCH TO PLAN.

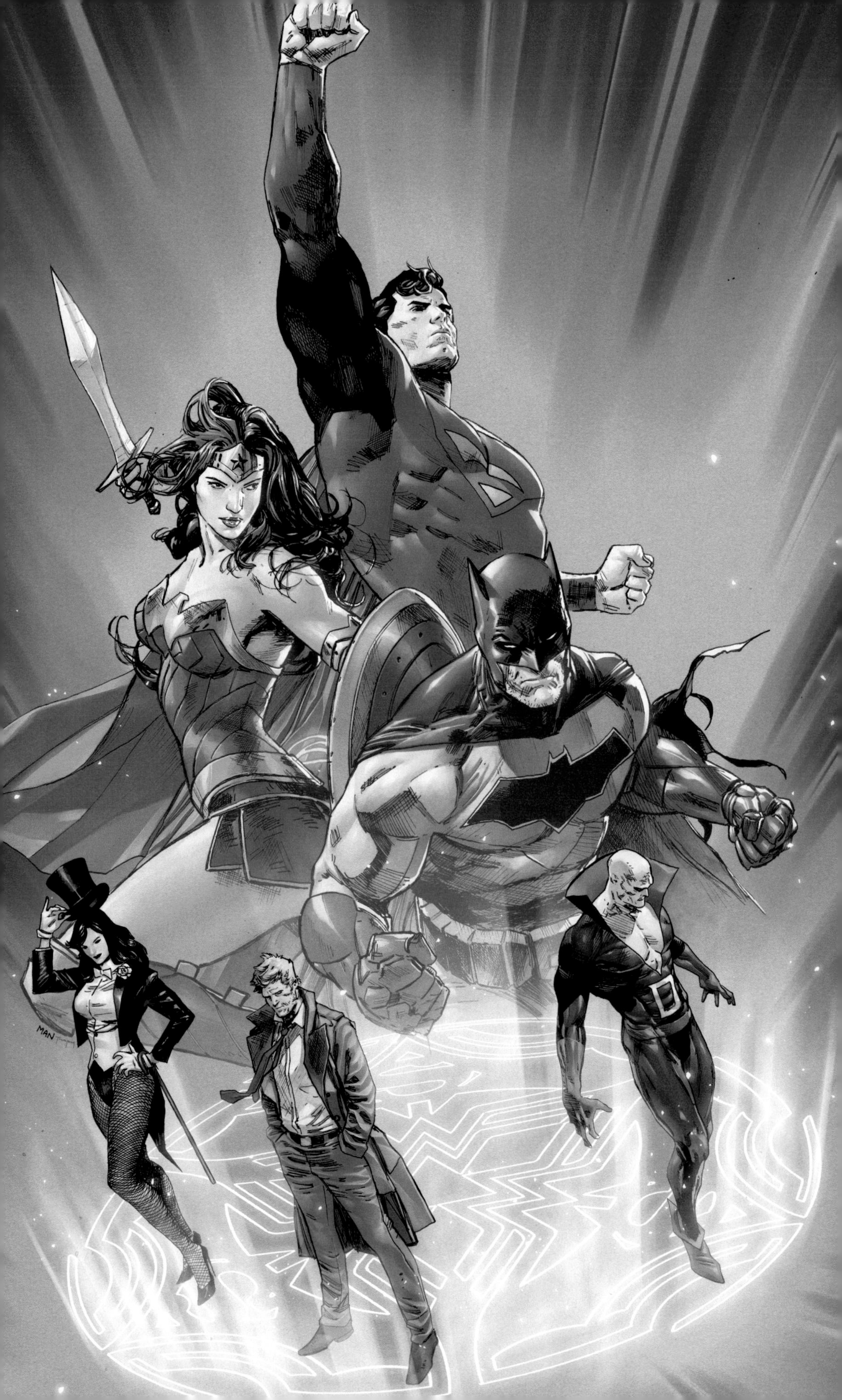
MAN

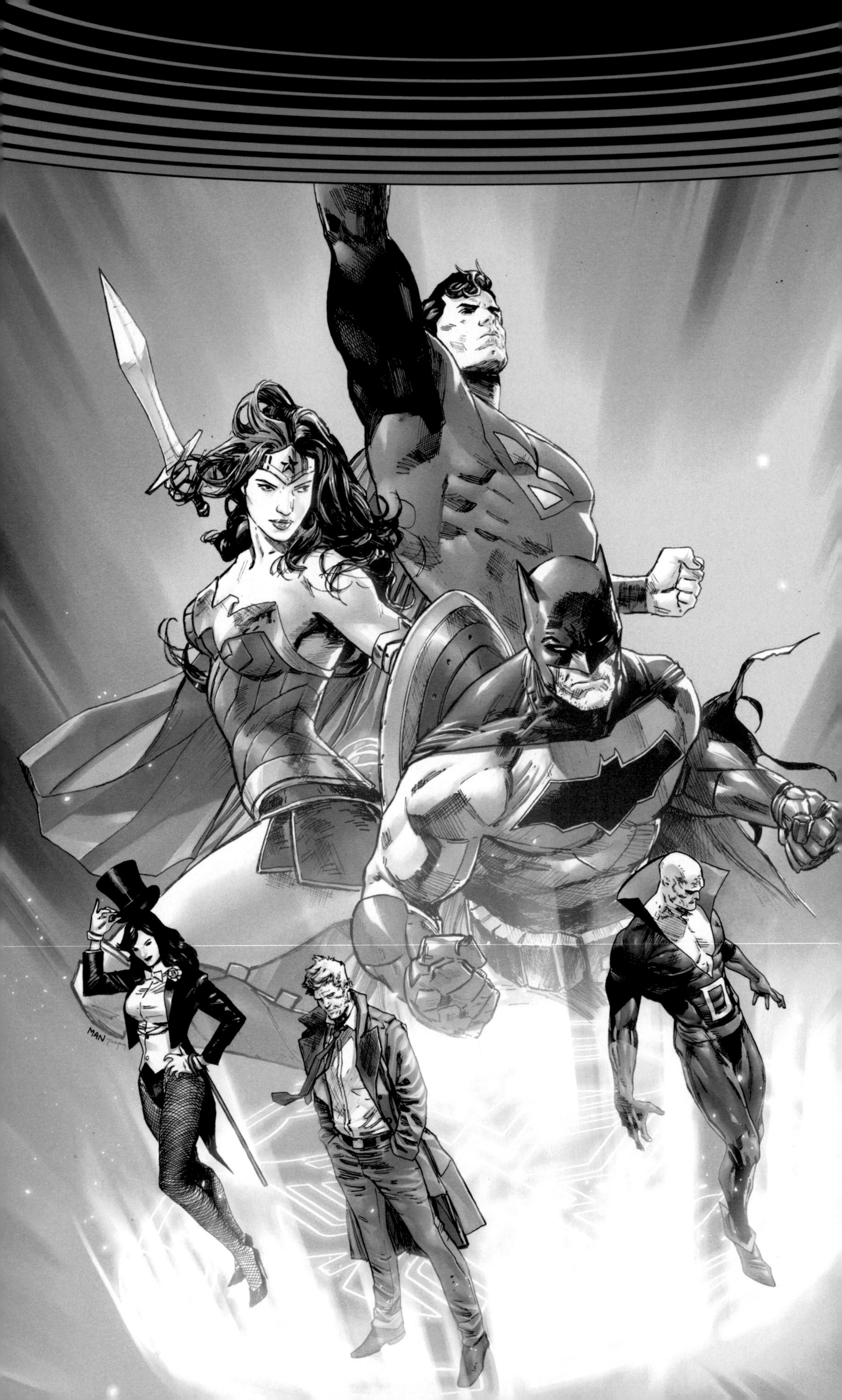
MAN

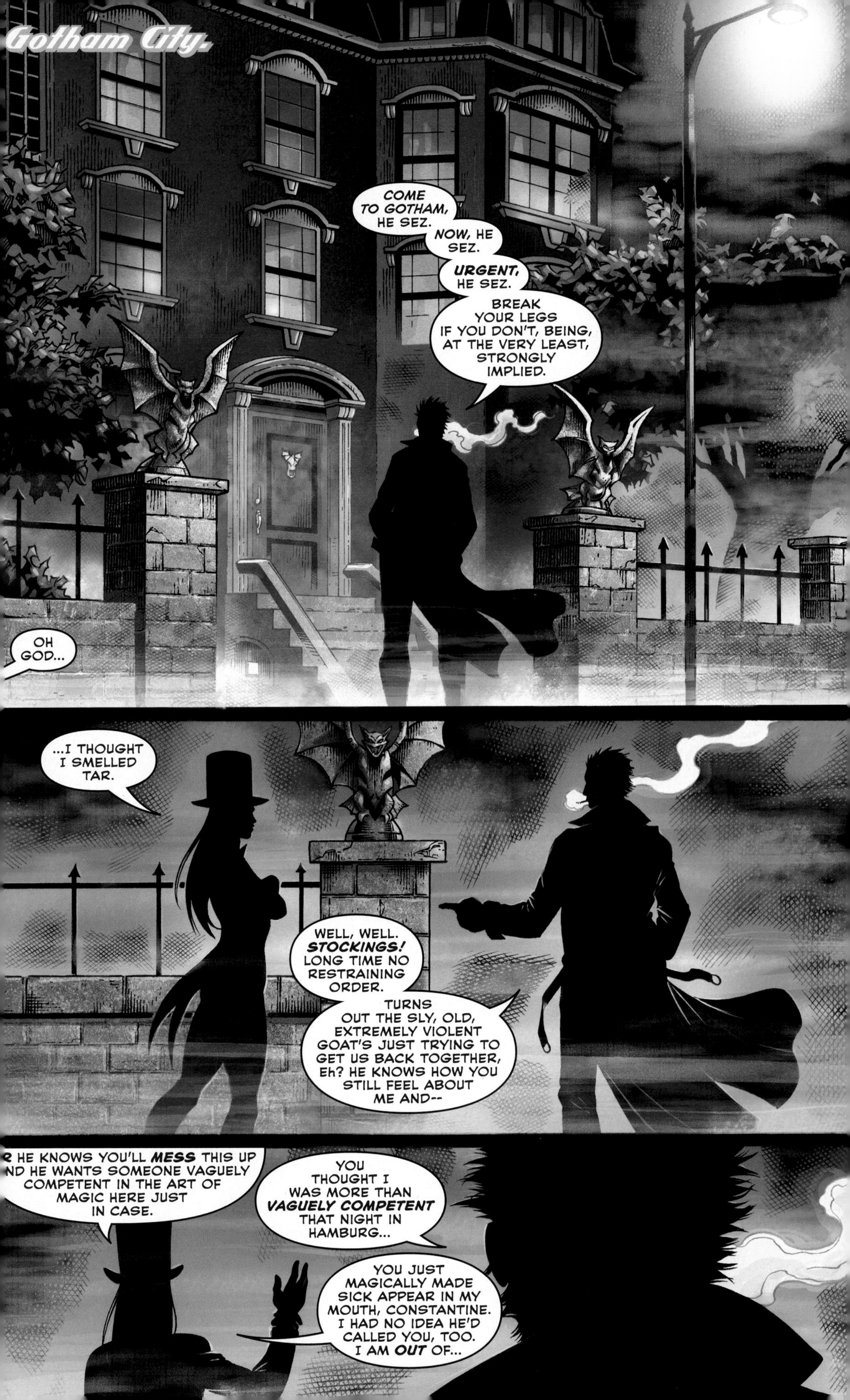
Gotham City.
COME TO GOTHAM, HE SEZ.
NOW, HE SEZ.
URGENT, HE SEZ.
BREAK YOUR LEGS IF YOU DON'T, BEING, AT THE VERY LEAST, STRONGLY IMPLIED.
OH GOD...
...I THOUGHT I SMELLED TAR.
WELL, WELL. STOCKINGS! LONG TIME NO RESTRAINING ORDER.
TURNS OUT THE SLY, OLD, EXTREMELY VIOLENT GOAT'S JUST TRYING TO GET US BACK TOGETHER, Eh? HE KNOWS HOW YOU STILL FEEL ABOUT ME AND--
HE KNOWS YOU'LL MESS THIS UP ND HE WANTS SOMEONE VAGUELY COMPETENT IN THE ART OF MAGIC HERE JUST IN CASE.
YOU THOUGHT I WAS MORE THAN VAGUELY COMPETENT THAT NIGHT IN HAMBURG...
YOU JUST MAGICALLY MADE SICK APPEAR IN MY MOUTH, CONSTANTINE. I HAD NO IDEA HE'D CALLED YOU, TOO. I AM OUT OF...

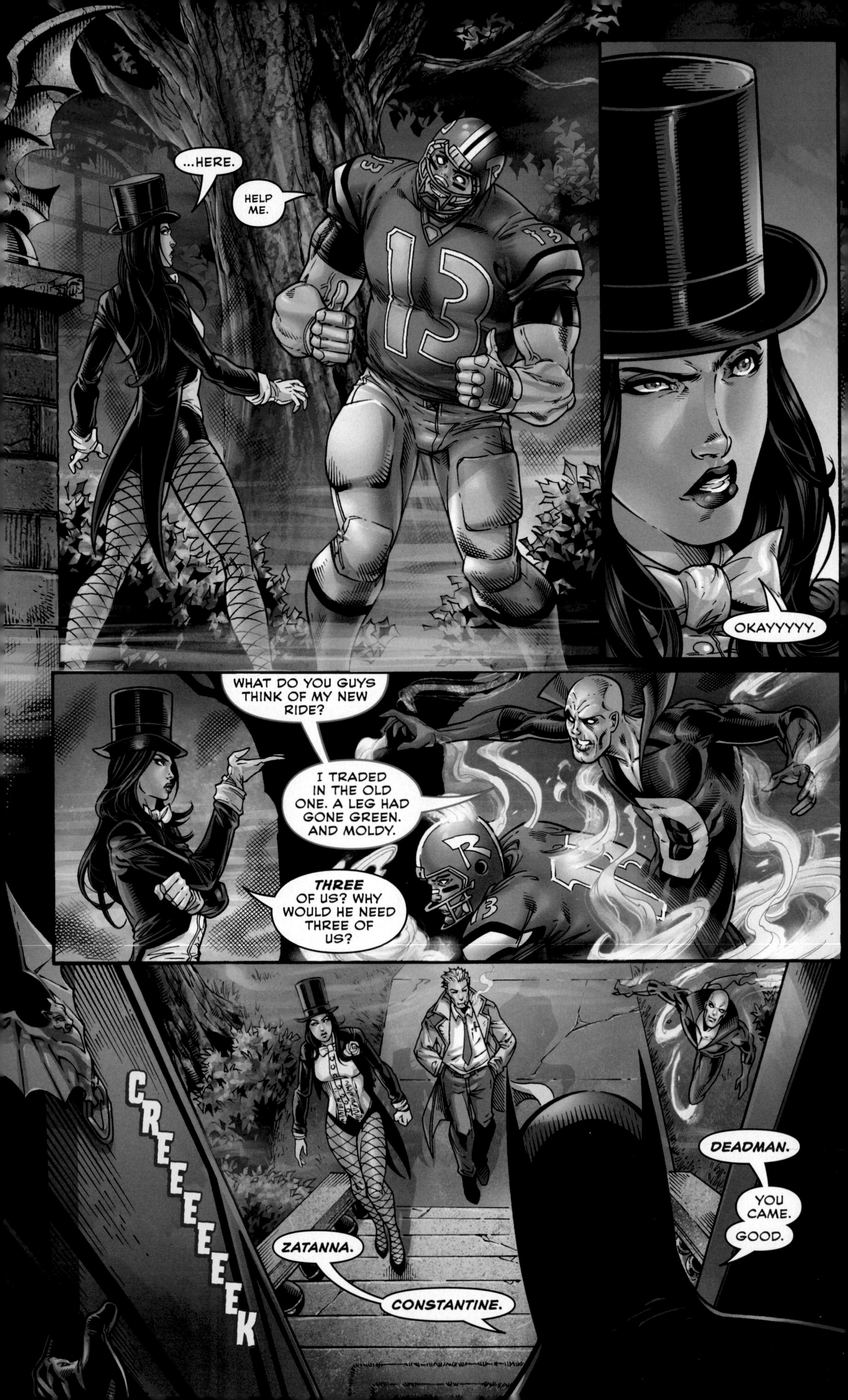
...HERE.
HELP ME.
OKAYYYYY.
WHAT DO YOU GUYS THINK OF MY NEW RIDE?
I TRADED IN THE OLD ONE. A LEG HAD GONE GREEN. AND MOLDY.
*THREE* OF US? WHY WOULD HE NEED THREE OF US?
CREEEEEEK
DEADMAN.
YOU CAME. GOOD.
ZATANNA.
CONSTANTINE.

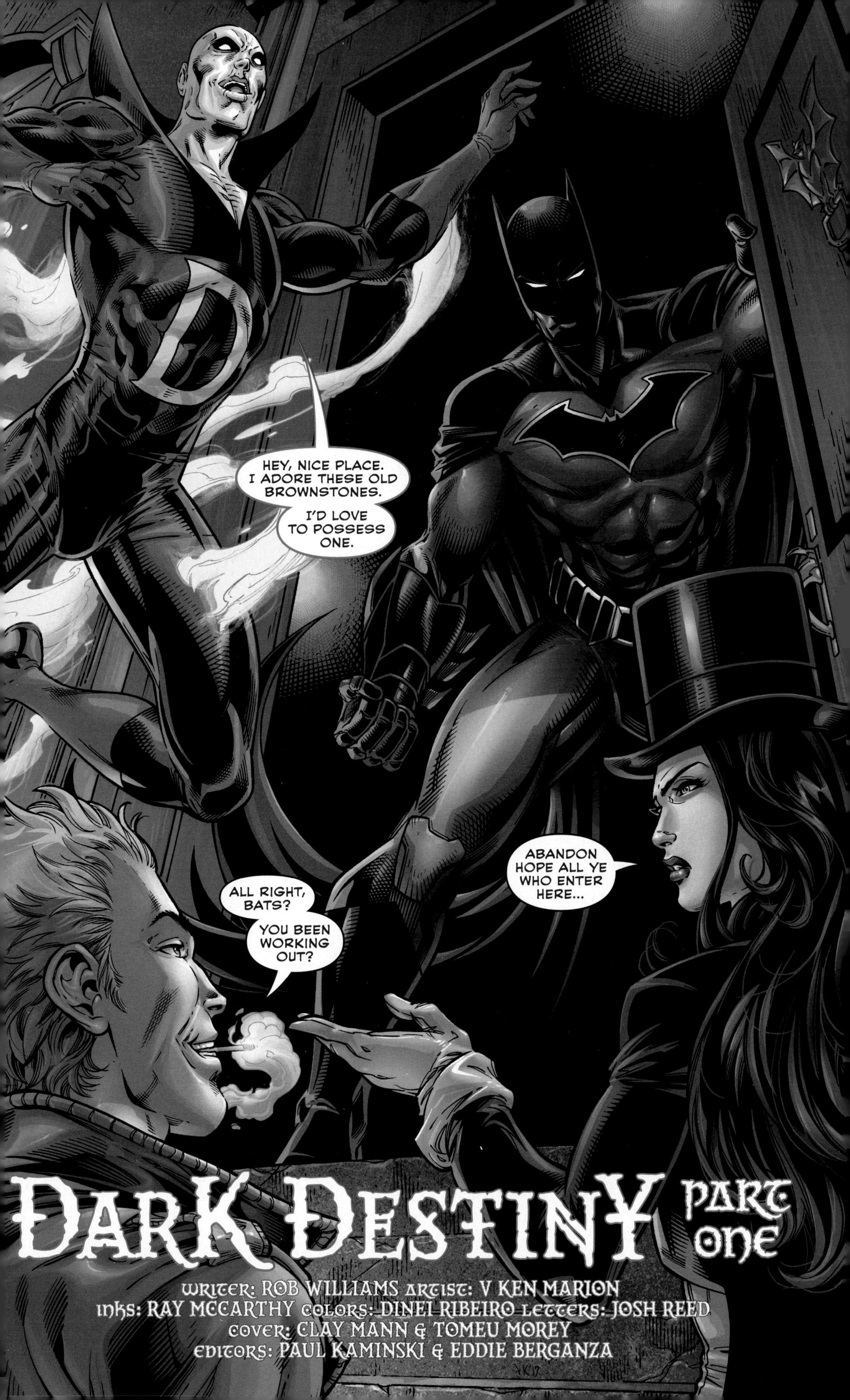
HEY, NICE PLACE. I ADORE THESE OLD BROWNSTONES.
I'D LOVE TO POSSESS ONE.
ABANDON HOPE ALL YE WHO ENTER HERE...
ALL RIGHT, BATS?
YOU BEEN WORKING OUT?
DARK DESTINY PART ONE
WRITER: ROB WILLIAMS ARTIST: V KEN MARION
INKS: RAY MCCARTHY COLORS: DINEI RIBEIRO LETTERS: JOSH REED
COVER: CLAY MANN & TOMEU MOREY
EDITORS: PAUL KAMINSKI & EDDIE BERGANZA

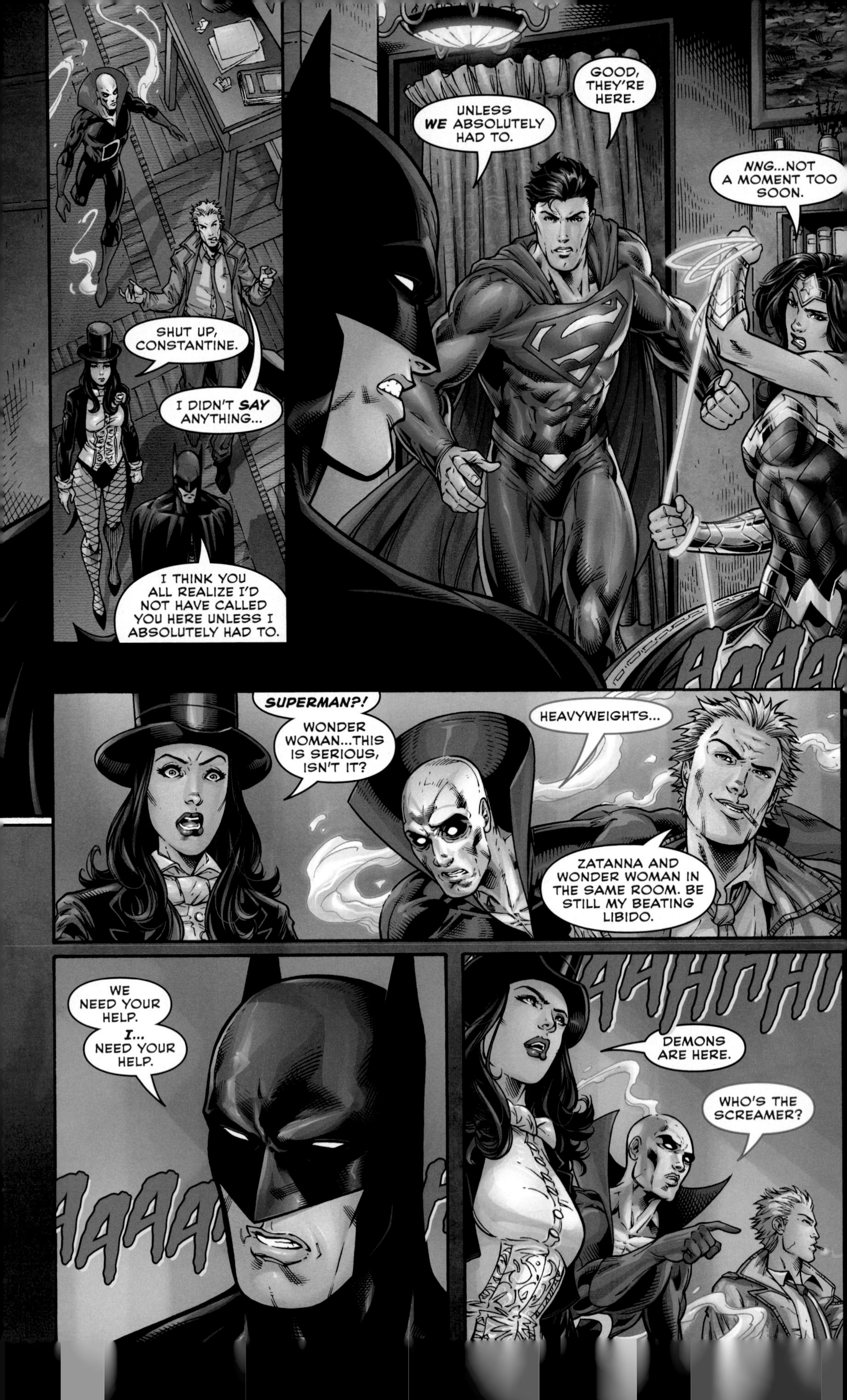
SHUT UP, CONSTANTINE.
I DIDN'T SAY ANYTHING...
I THINK YOU ALL REALIZE I'D NOT HAVE CALLED YOU HERE UNLESS I ABSOLUTELY HAD TO.
UNLESS WE ABSOLUTELY HAD TO.
GOOD, THEY'RE HERE.
NNG...NOT A MOMENT TOO SOON.
SUPERMAN?!
WONDER WOMAN...THIS IS SERIOUS, ISN'T IT?
HEAVYWEIGHTS...
ZATANNA AND WONDER WOMAN IN THE SAME ROOM. BE STILL MY BEATING LIBIDO.
WE NEED YOUR HELP. I... NEED YOUR HELP.
DEMONS ARE HERE.
WHO'S THE SCREAMER?

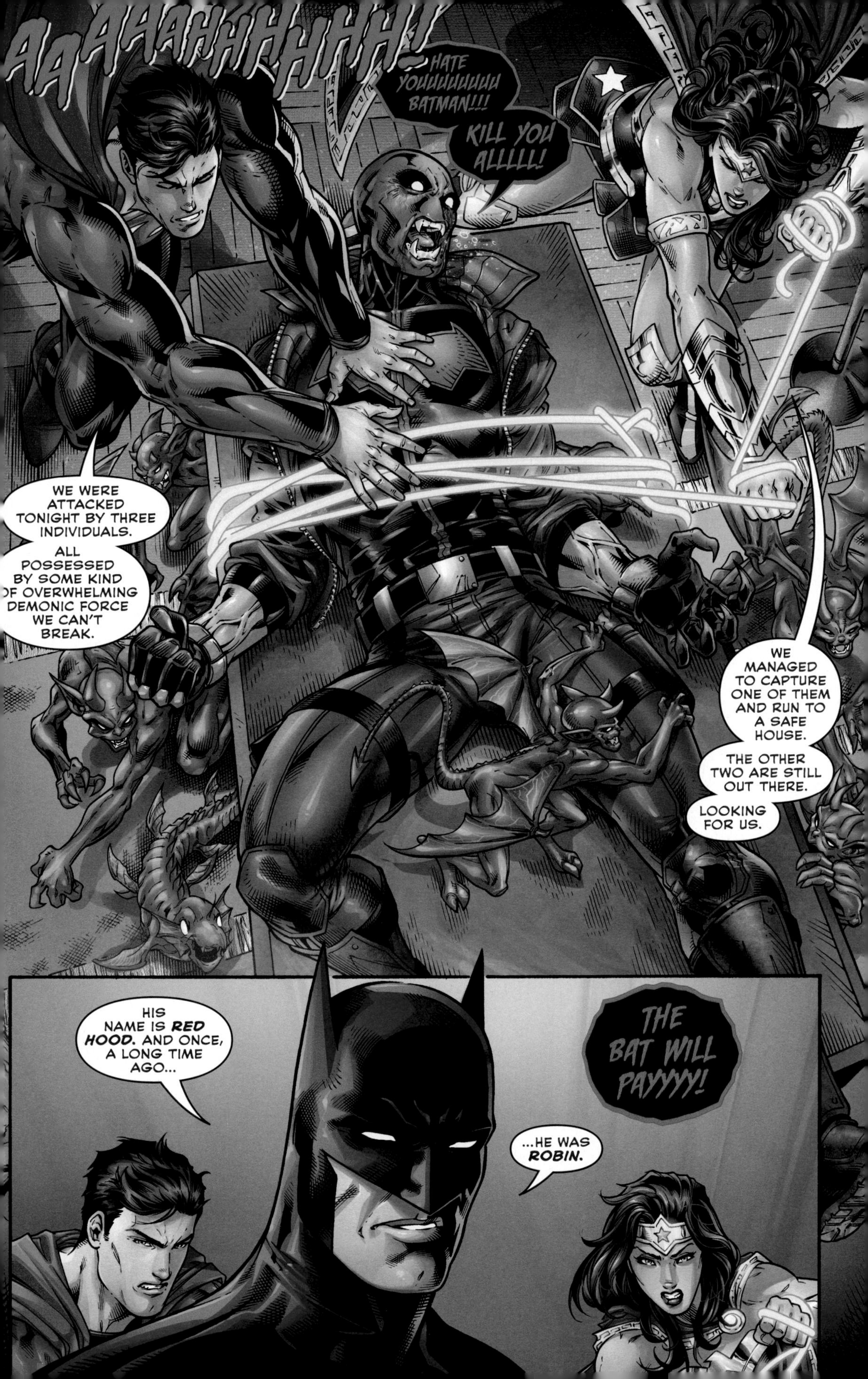
AAAAAHHHHHH!
HATE YOUUUUUUUU BATMAN!!!
KILL YOU ALLLLL!
WE WERE ATTACKED TONIGHT BY THREE INDIVIDUALS.
ALL POSSESSED BY SOME KIND OF OVERWHELMING DEMONIC FORCE WE CAN'T BREAK.
WE MANAGED TO CAPTURE ONE OF THEM AND RUN TO A SAFE HOUSE.
THE OTHER TWO ARE STILL OUT THERE.
LOOKING FOR US.
HIS NAME IS **RED HOOD.** AND ONCE, A LONG TIME AGO...
THE BAT WILL PAYYYY!
...HE WAS **ROBIN.**

THE BAT WILLL BUURN AND HIS INNARDS SHALL BOIL IN THE CARNAL BLOOD POT OF MY REVENGE.

THIS IS THE BAT-FAMILY VERSION OF "MUSICAL DIFFERENCES," I'M GUESSING.

HE'S POSSESSED. AND NOT BY ANY OF THE USUAL SUSPECTS. YOU NEED US TO FREE HIM.

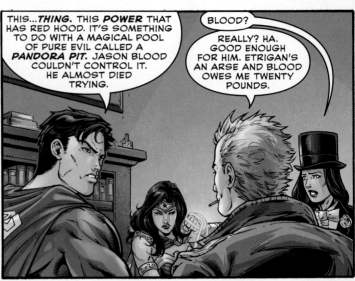

THIS...THING. THIS POWER THAT HAS RED HOOD. IT'S SOMETHING TO DO WITH A MAGICAL POOL OF PURE EVIL CALLED A PANDORA PIT. JASON BLOOD COULDN'T CONTROL IT. HE ALMOST DIED TRYING.

BLOOD?

REALLY? HA. GOOD ENOUGH FOR HIM. ETRIGAN'S AN ARSE AND BLOOD OWES ME TWENTY POUNDS.

WHAT IF I POSSESS HIM?

I GO IN. KICK OUT WHOEVER'S IN THERE?

THEN YOU TWO BIND IT.

AND YOU THREE KNOCK THE CRAP OUT OF IT.

OH, THAT WE CAN DO.

PLEASE DON'T TALK TO EACH OTHER, YOU TWO. IT'S... DISTRACTING.

CAN IT, CONSTANTINE.

YOU WILLLL FAILLLLL. HEHHEHHEH...

SAVE HIM, BRAND.

BE CAREFUL.

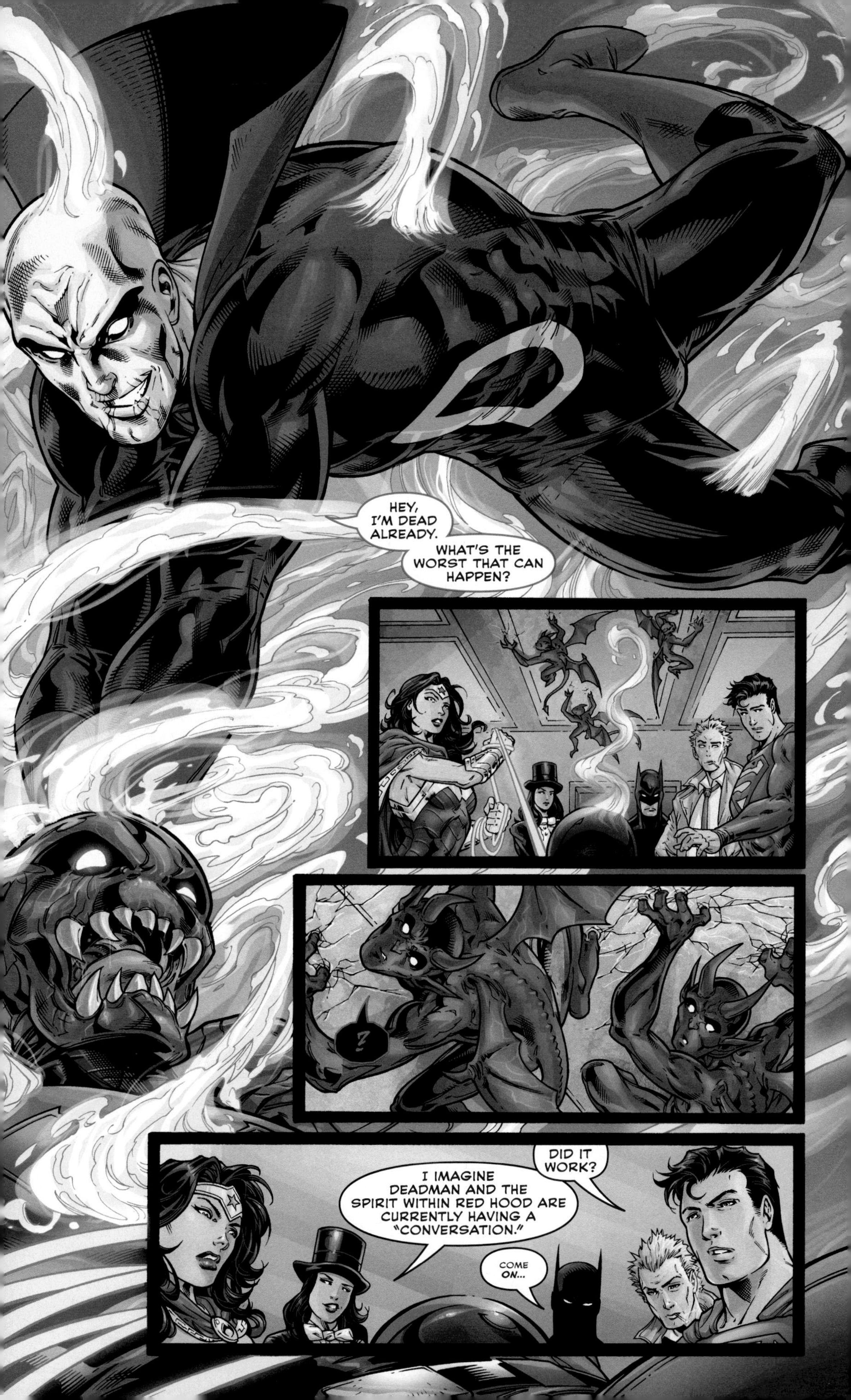
HEY, I'M DEAD ALREADY.
WHAT'S THE WORST THAT CAN HAPPEN?
?
DID IT WORK?
I IMAGINE DEADMAN AND THE SPIRIT WITHIN RED HOOD ARE CURRENTLY HAVING A "CONVERSATION."
COME ON...

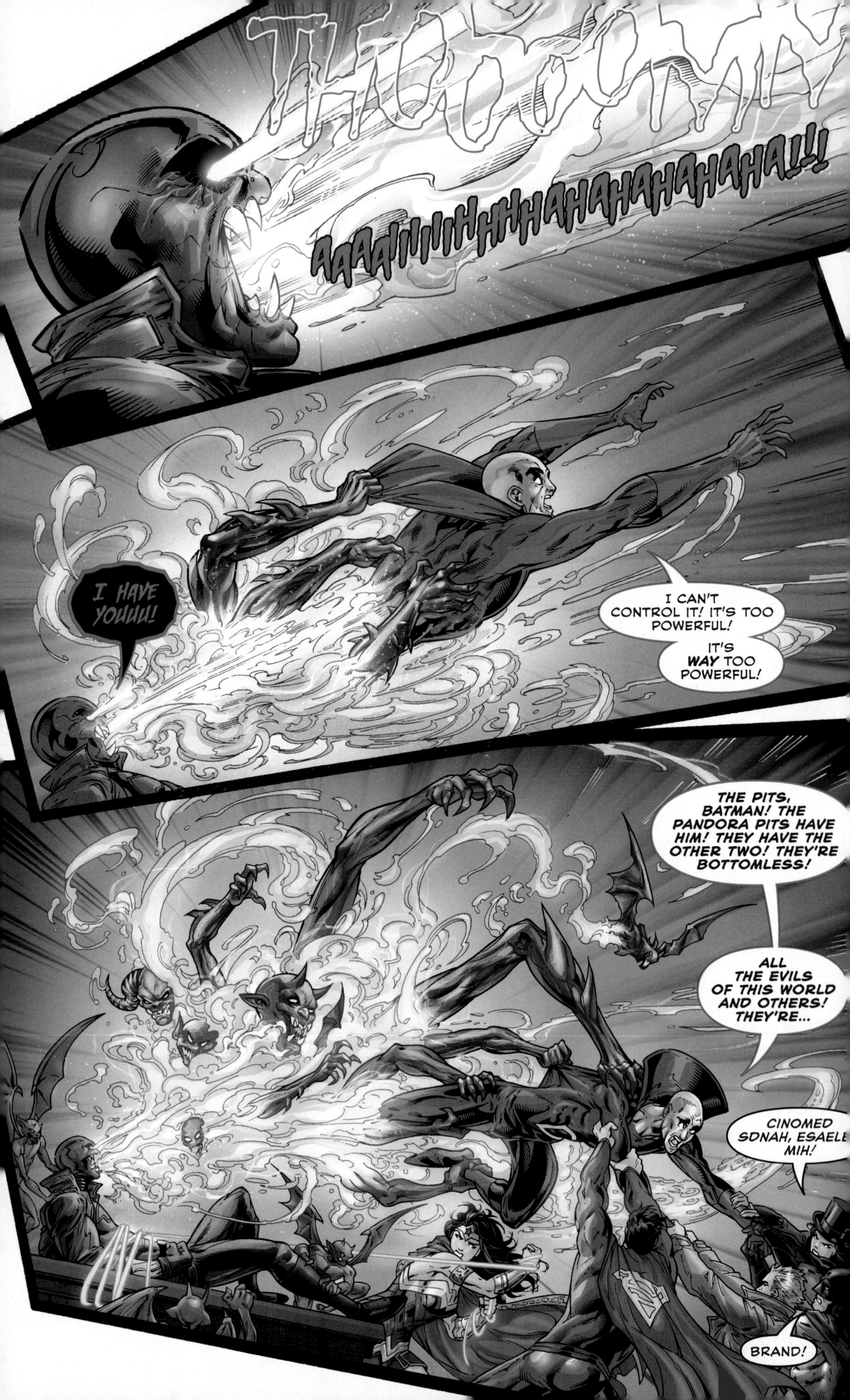

THOOOOOMM
AAAAIIIIIHHHHAHAHAHAHAHAHAHA!!!
I HAVE YOUUU!
I CAN'T CONTROL IT! IT'S TOO POWERFUL!
IT'S **WAY** TOO POWERFUL!
THE PITS, BATMAN! THE PANDORA PITS HAVE HIM! THEY HAVE THE OTHER TWO! THEY'RE BOTTOMLESS!
ALL THE EVILS OF THIS WORLD AND OTHERS! THEY'RE...
CINOMED SDNAH, ESAELE MIH!
BRAND!

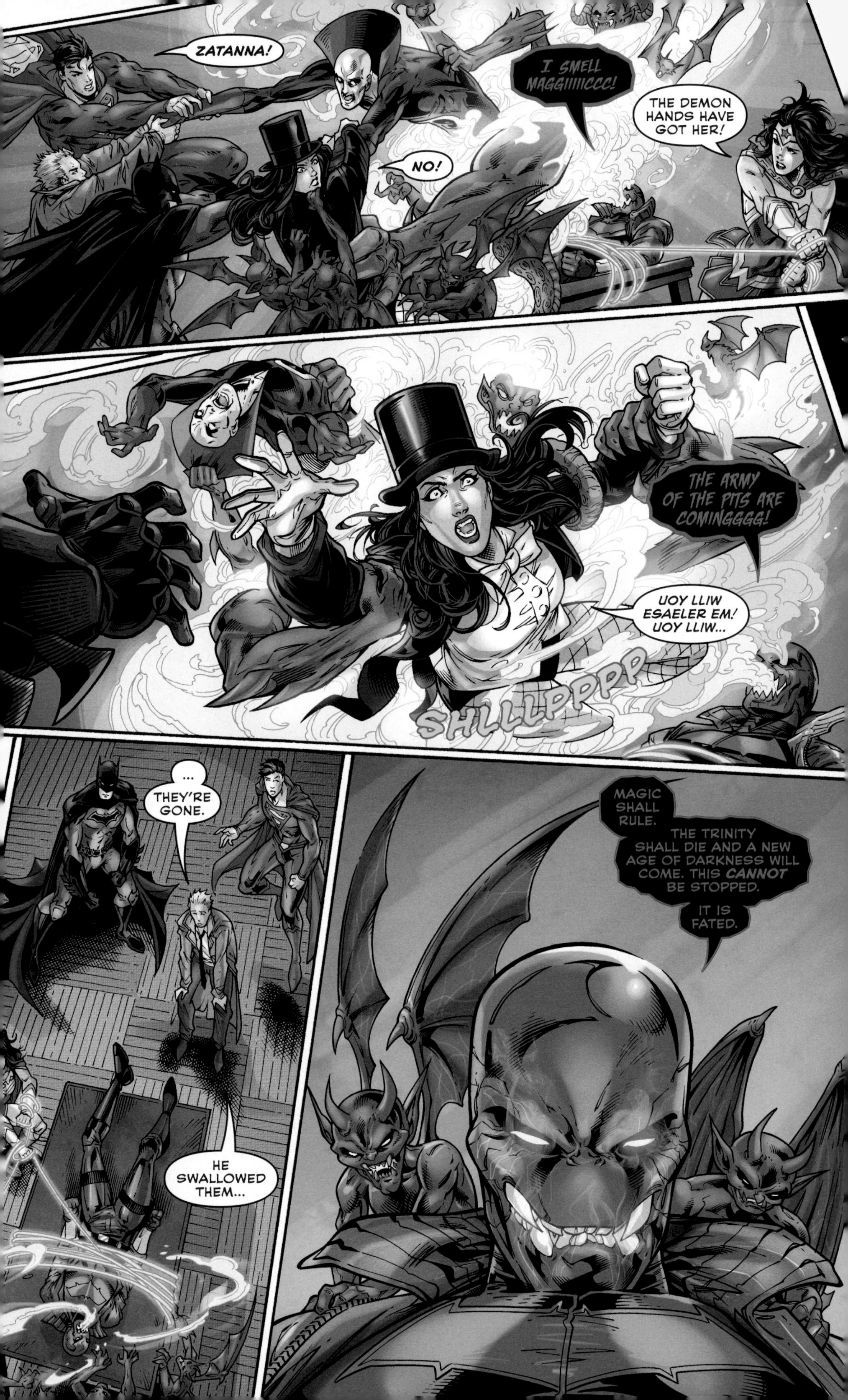
ZATANNA!
I SMELL MAGGIIIIICCC!
THE DEMON HANDS HAVE GOT HER!
NO!
THE ARMY OF THE PITS ARE COMINGGGG!
UOY LLIW ESAELER EM! UOY LLIW...
SHLLLPPPP
... THEY'RE GONE.
HE SWALLOWED THEM...
MAGIC SHALL RULE.
THE TRINITY SHALL DIE AND A NEW AGE OF DARKNESS WILL COME. THIS CANNOT BE STOPPED.
IT IS FATED.

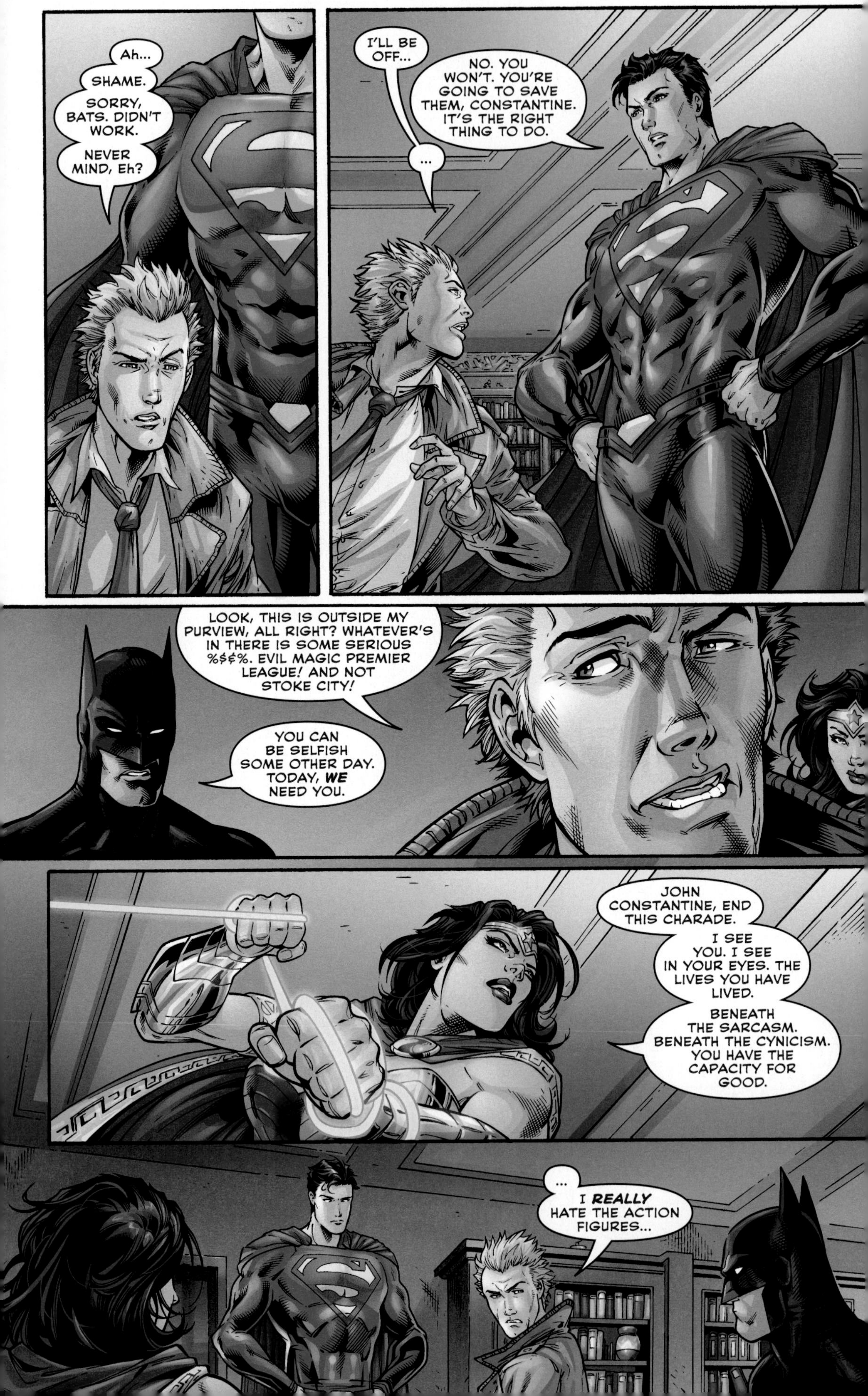
Ah...
SHAME.
SORRY, BATS. DIDN'T WORK.
NEVER MIND, Eh?
I'LL BE OFF...
NO. YOU WON'T. YOU'RE GOING TO SAVE THEM, CONSTANTINE. IT'S THE RIGHT THING TO DO.
...
LOOK, THIS IS OUTSIDE MY PURVIEW, ALL RIGHT? WHATEVER'S IN THERE IS SOME SERIOUS %$¢%. EVIL MAGIC PREMIER LEAGUE! AND NOT STOKE CITY!
YOU CAN BE SELFISH SOME OTHER DAY. TODAY, WE NEED YOU.
JOHN CONSTANTINE, END THIS CHARADE.
I SEE YOU. I SEE IN YOUR EYES. THE LIVES YOU HAVE LIVED.
BENEATH THE SARCASM. BENEATH THE CYNICISM. YOU HAVE THE CAPACITY FOR GOOD.
...
I REALLY HATE THE ACTION FIGURES...

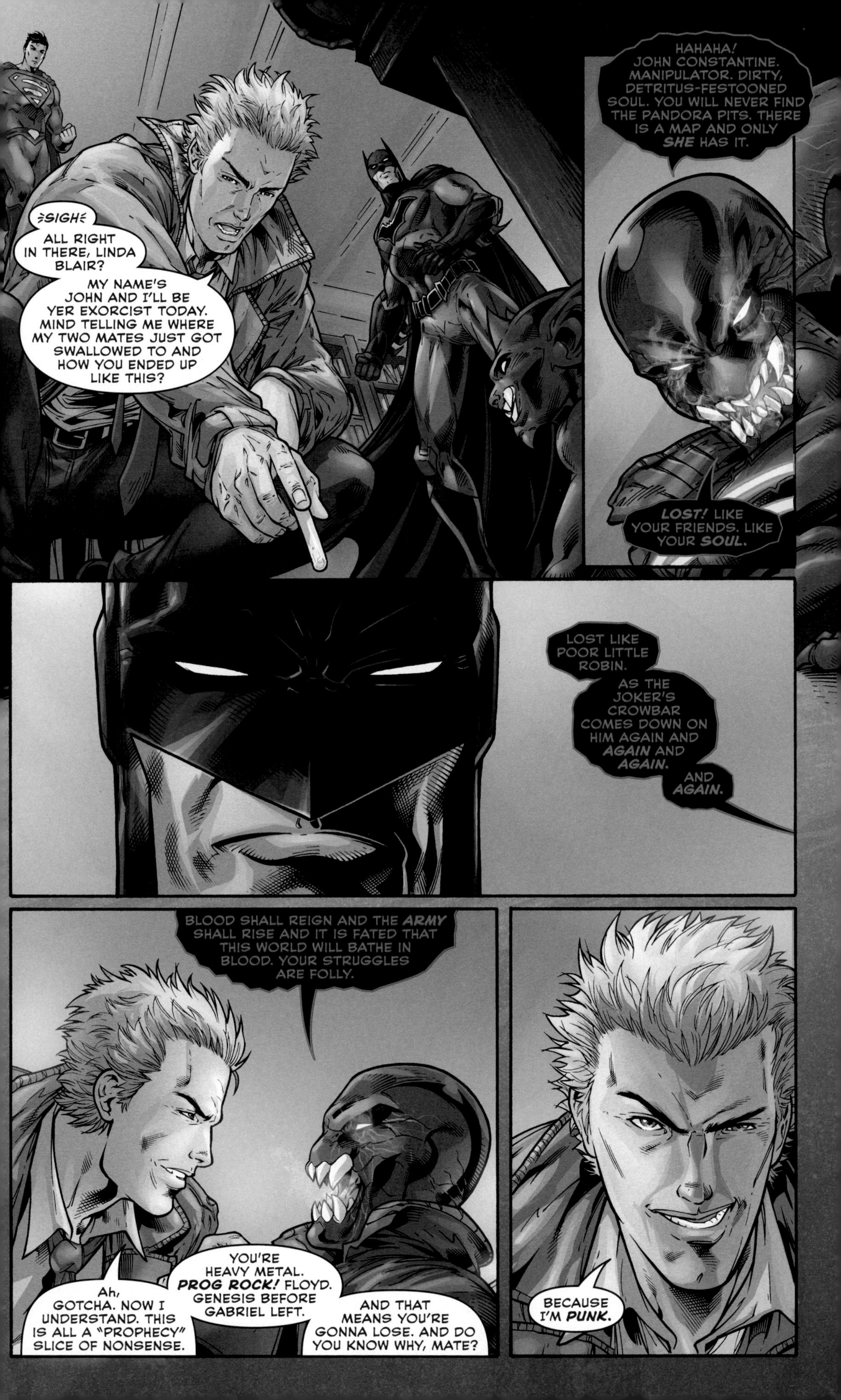

SIGH
ALL RIGHT IN THERE, LINDA BLAIR?
MY NAME'S JOHN AND I'LL BE YER EXORCIST TODAY. MIND TELLING ME WHERE MY TWO MATES JUST GOT SWALLOWED TO AND HOW YOU ENDED UP LIKE THIS?
HAHAHA! JOHN CONSTANTINE. MANIPULATOR. DIRTY, DETRITUS-FESTOONED SOUL. YOU WILL NEVER FIND THE PANDORA PITS. THERE IS A MAP AND ONLY SHE HAS IT.
LOST! LIKE YOUR FRIENDS. LIKE YOUR SOUL.
LOST LIKE POOR LITTLE ROBIN.
AS THE JOKER'S CROWBAR COMES DOWN ON HIM AGAIN AND AGAIN AND AGAIN.
AND AGAIN.
BLOOD SHALL REIGN AND THE ARMY SHALL RISE AND IT IS FATED THAT THIS WORLD WILL BATHE IN BLOOD. YOUR STRUGGLES ARE FOLLY.
Ah, GOTCHA. NOW I UNDERSTAND. THIS IS ALL A "PROPHECY" SLICE OF NONSENSE.
YOU'RE HEAVY METAL. PROG ROCK! FLOYD. GENESIS BEFORE GABRIEL LEFT.
AND THAT MEANS YOU'RE GONNA LOSE. AND DO YOU KNOW WHY, MATE?
BECAUSE I'M PUNK.

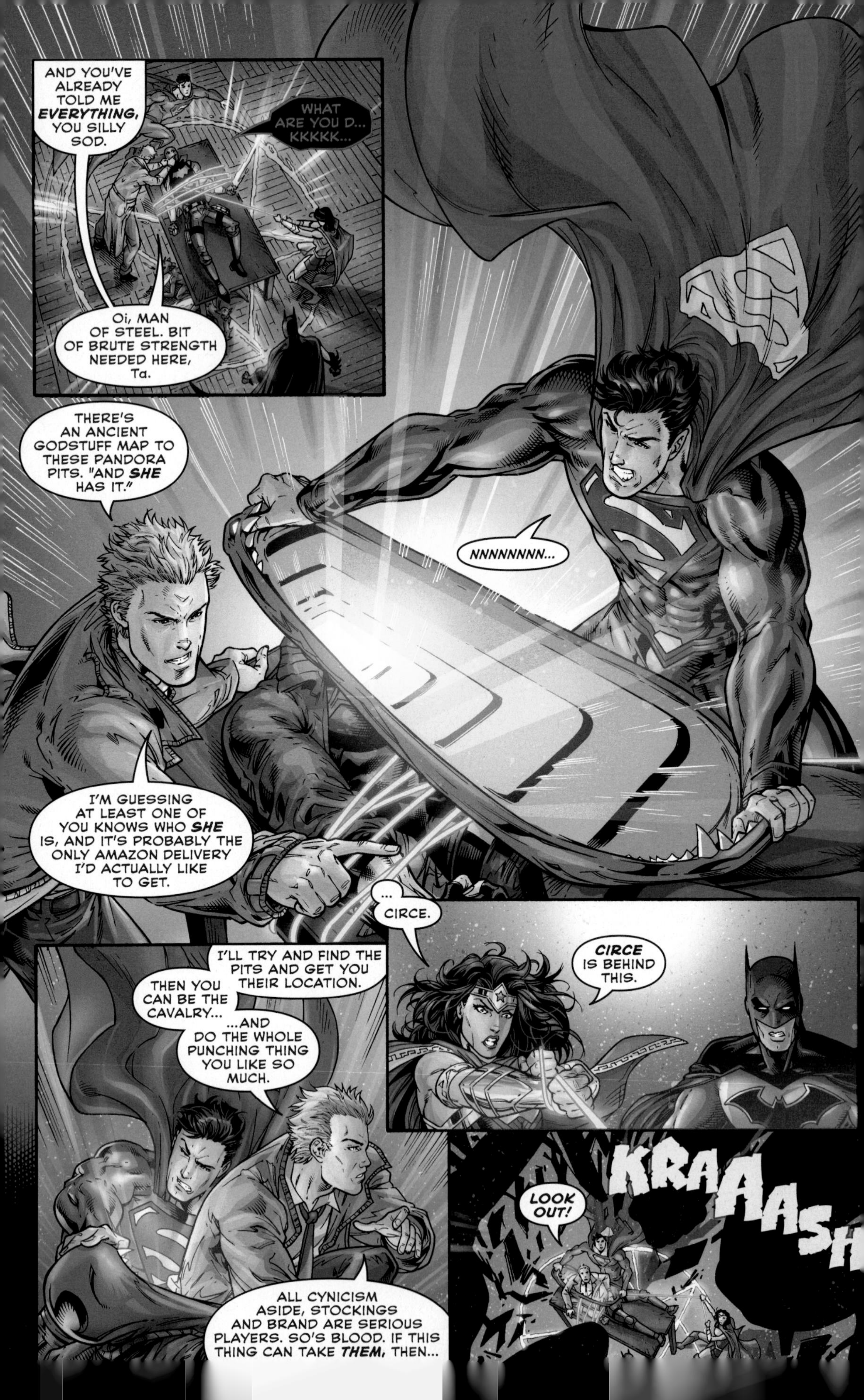
AND YOU'VE ALREADY TOLD ME EVERYTHING, YOU SILLY SOD.
WHAT ARE YOU D... KKKKK...
Oi, MAN OF STEEL. BIT OF BRUTE STRENGTH NEEDED HERE, Ta.
THERE'S AN ANCIENT GODSTUFF MAP TO THESE PANDORA PITS. "AND SHE HAS IT."
NNNNNNNN...
I'M GUESSING AT LEAST ONE OF YOU KNOWS WHO SHE IS, AND IT'S PROBABLY THE ONLY AMAZON DELIVERY I'D ACTUALLY LIKE TO GET.
... CIRCE.
CIRCE IS BEHIND THIS.
I'LL TRY AND FIND THE PITS AND GET YOU THEIR LOCATION.
THEN YOU CAN BE THE CAVALRY...
...AND DO THE WHOLE PUNCHING THING YOU LIKE SO MUCH.
ALL CYNICISM ASIDE, STOCKINGS AND BRAND ARE SERIOUS PLAYERS. SO'S BLOOD. IF THIS THING CAN TAKE THEM, THEN...
KRAAAASH
LOOK OUT!

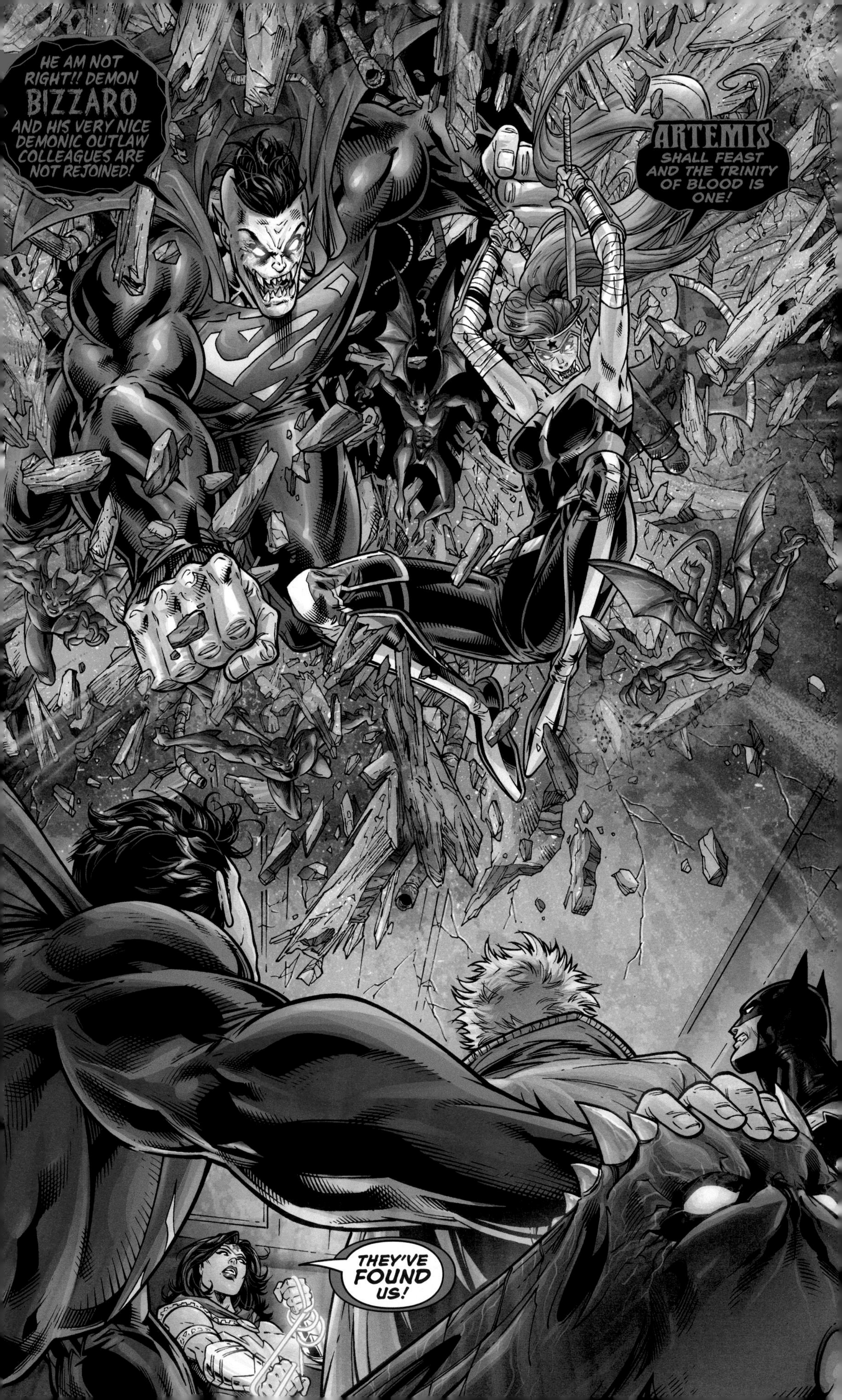
HE AM NOT RIGHT!! DEMON BIZZARO AND HIS VERY NICE DEMONIC OUTLAW COLLEAGUES ARE NOT REJOINED!
ARTEMIS SHALL FEAST AND THE TRINITY OF BLOOD IS ONE!
THEY'VE FOUND US!

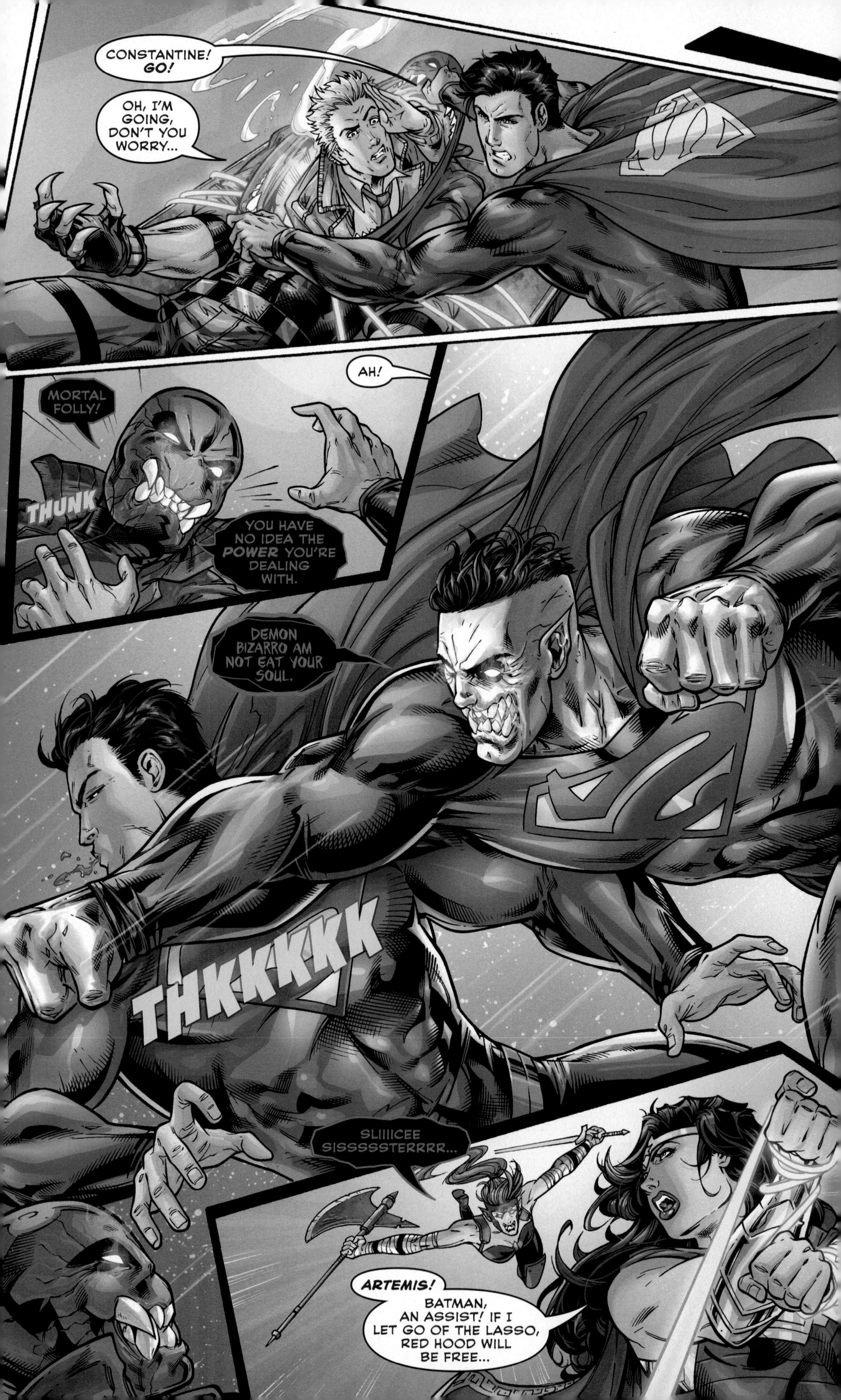
CONSTANTINE! GO!
OH, I'M GOING, DON'T YOU WORRY...
MORTAL FOLLY!
THUNK
YOU HAVE NO IDEA THE POWER YOU'RE DEALING WITH.
AH!
DEMON BIZARRO AM NOT EAT YOUR SOUL.
THKKKKK
SLIIIICEE SISSSSSTERRRR...
ARTEMIS!
BATMAN, AN ASSIST! IF I LET GO OF THE LASSO, RED HOOD WILL BE FREE...

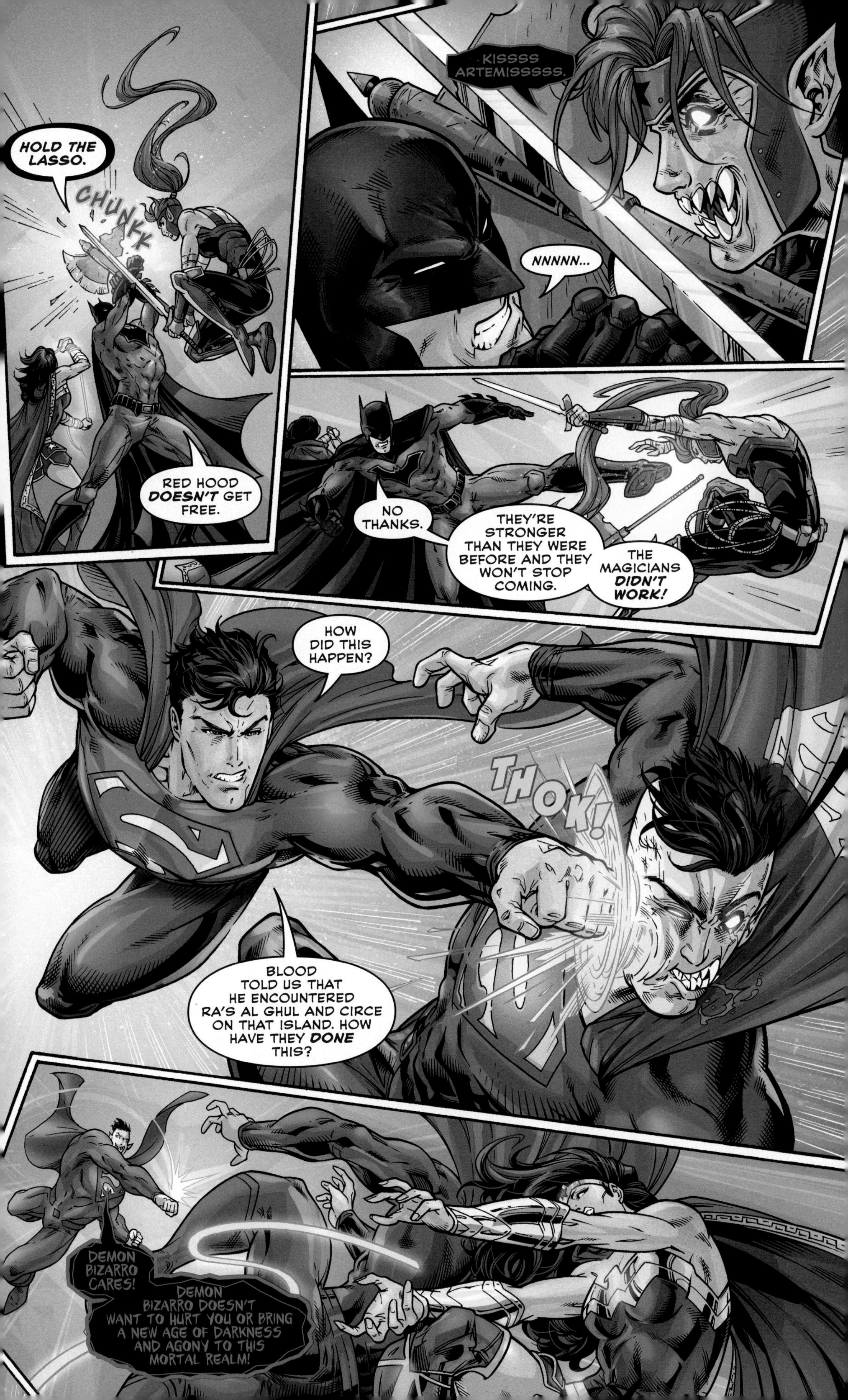
HOLD THE LASSO.
CHUNKK
KISSSS ARTEMISSSSS.
NNNNN...
RED HOOD DOESN'T GET FREE.
NO THANKS.
THEY'RE STRONGER THAN THEY WERE BEFORE AND THEY WON'T STOP COMING.
THE MAGICIANS DIDN'T WORK!
HOW DID THIS HAPPEN?
THOK!
BLOOD TOLD US THAT HE ENCOUNTERED RA'S AL GHUL AND CIRCE ON THAT ISLAND. HOW HAVE THEY DONE THIS?
DEMON BIZARRO CARES!
DEMON BIZARRO DOESN'T WANT TO HURT YOU OR BRING A NEW AGE OF DARKNESS AND AGONY TO THIS MORTAL REALM!

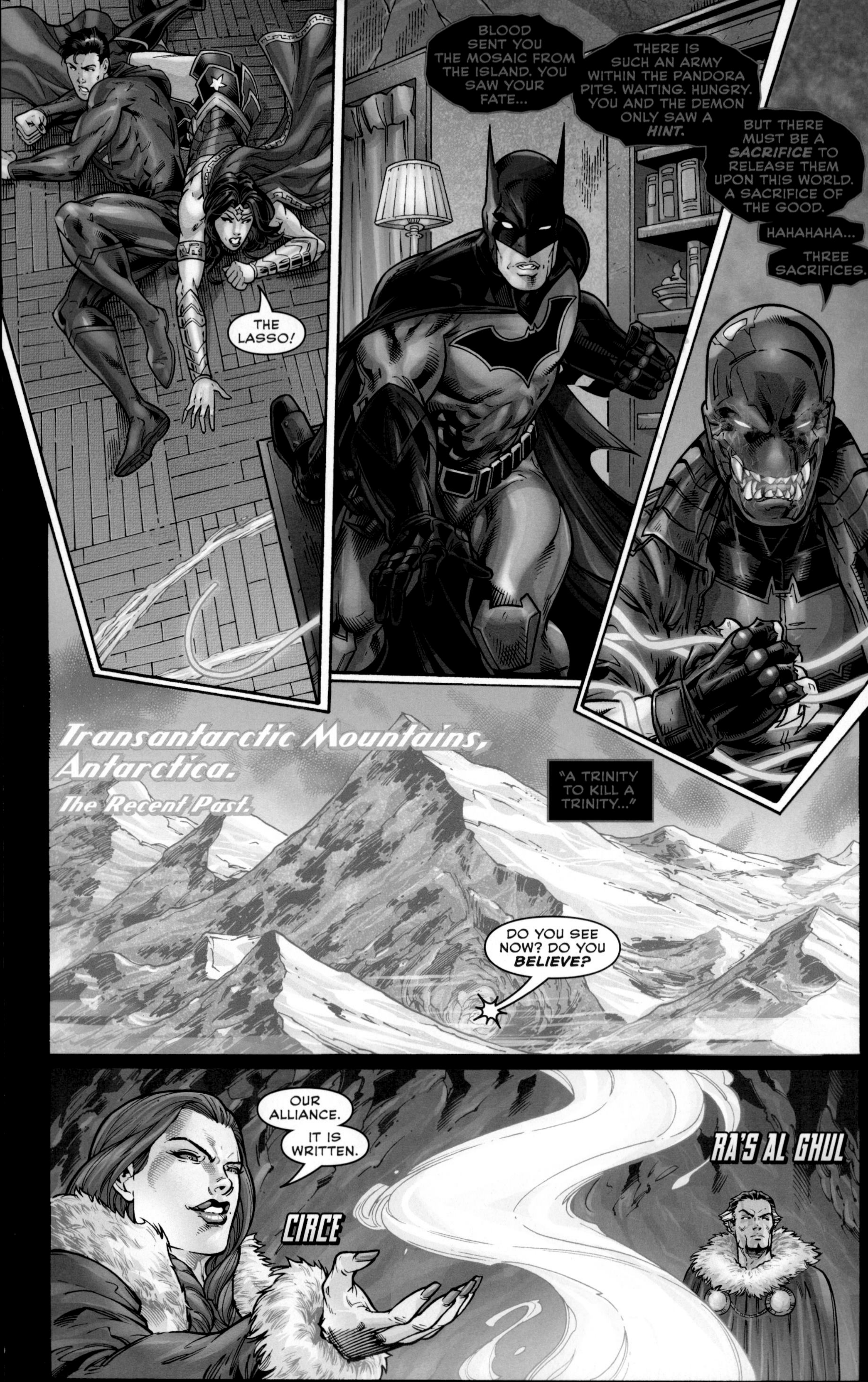
THE LASSO!
BLOOD SENT YOU THE MOSAIC FROM THE ISLAND. YOU SAW YOUR FATE...
THERE IS SUCH AN ARMY WITHIN THE PANDORA PITS. WAITING. HUNGRY. YOU AND THE DEMON ONLY SAW A HINT.
BUT THERE MUST BE A SACRIFICE TO RELEASE THEM UPON THIS WORLD. A SACRIFICE OF THE GOOD.
HAHAHAHA...
THREE SACRIFICES.
Transantarctic Mountains, Antarctica.
The Recent Past.
"A TRINITY TO KILL A TRINITY..."
DO YOU SEE NOW? DO YOU BELIEVE?
OUR ALLIANCE.
IT IS WRITTEN.
RA'S AL GHUL
CIRCE

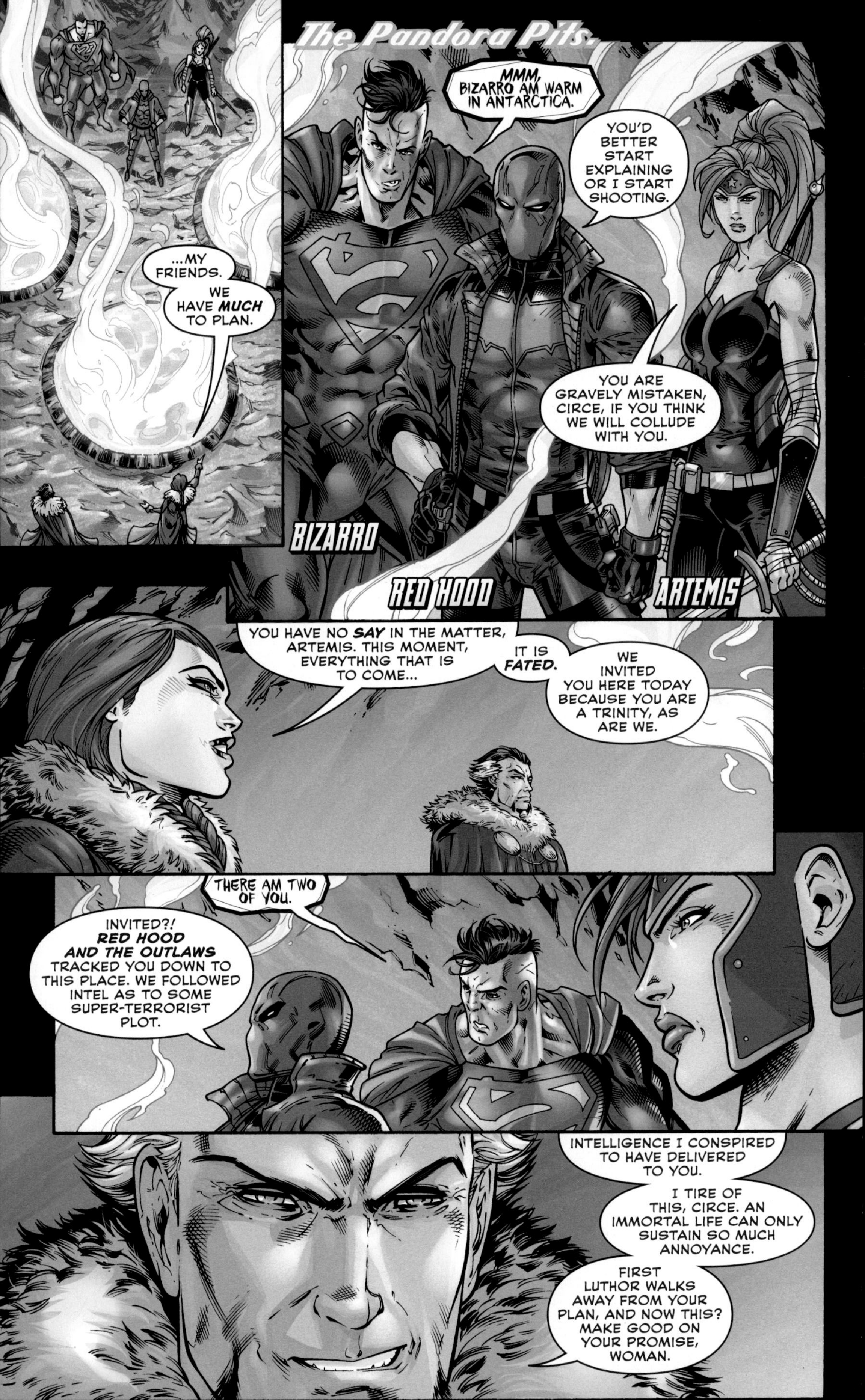

...MY FRIENDS.
WE HAVE MUCH TO PLAN.
The Pandora Pits.
MMM, BIZARRO AM WARM IN ANTARCTICA.
YOU'D BETTER START EXPLAINING OR I START SHOOTING.
YOU ARE GRAVELY MISTAKEN, CIRCE, IF YOU THINK WE WILL COLLUDE WITH YOU.
BIZARRO
RED HOOD
ARTEMIS
YOU HAVE NO SAY IN THE MATTER, ARTEMIS. THIS MOMENT, EVERYTHING THAT IS TO COME...
IT IS FATED.
WE INVITED YOU HERE TODAY BECAUSE YOU ARE A TRINITY, AS ARE WE.
THERE AM TWO OF YOU.
INVITED?! RED HOOD AND THE OUTLAWS TRACKED YOU DOWN TO THIS PLACE. WE FOLLOWED INTEL AS TO SOME SUPER-TERRORIST PLOT.
INTELLIGENCE I CONSPIRED TO HAVE DELIVERED TO YOU.
I TIRE OF THIS, CIRCE. AN IMMORTAL LIFE CAN ONLY SUSTAIN SO MUCH ANNOYANCE.
FIRST LUTHOR WALKS AWAY FROM YOUR PLAN, AND NOW THIS? MAKE GOOD ON YOUR PROMISE, WOMAN.

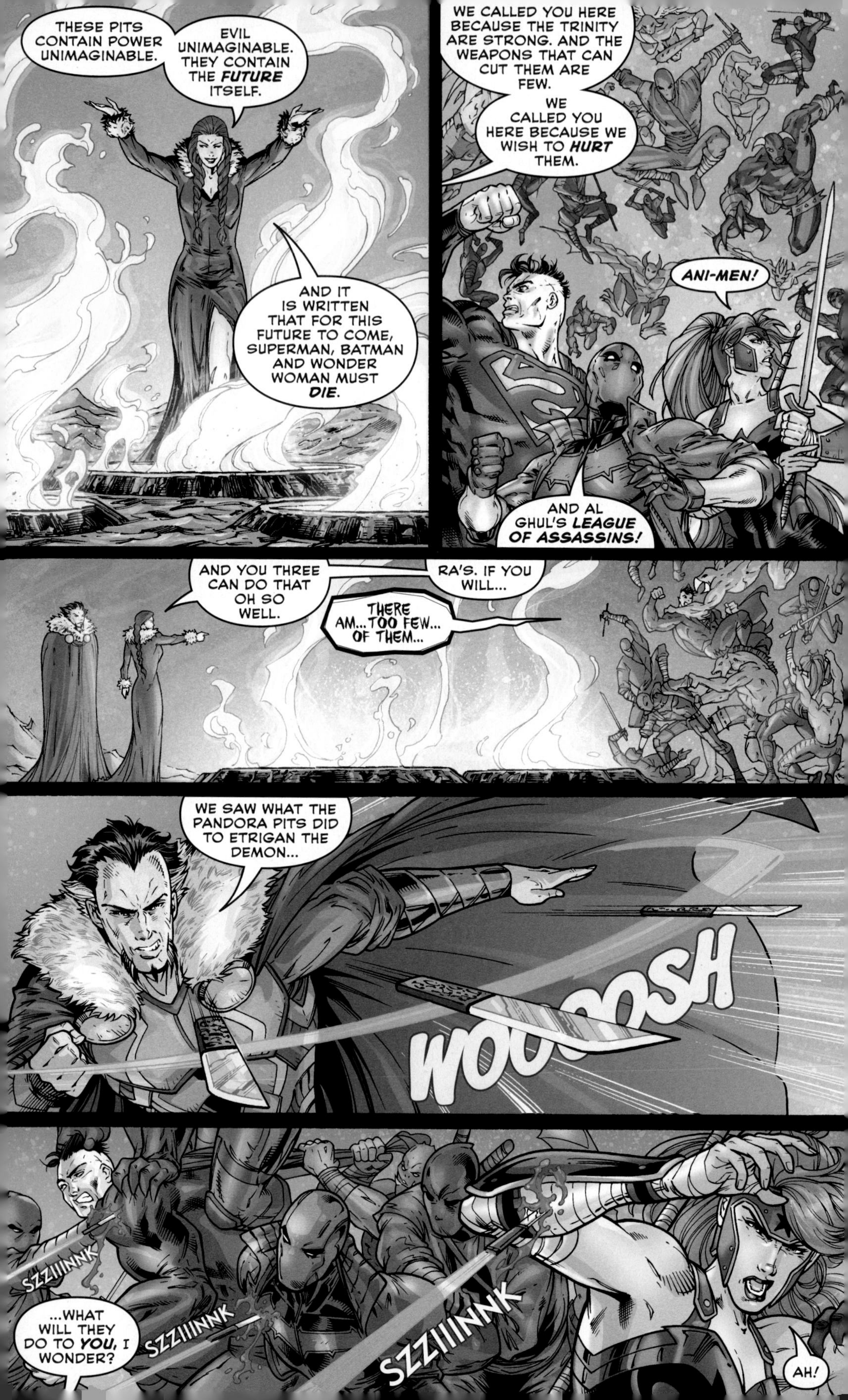
THESE PITS CONTAIN POWER UNIMAGINABLE.
EVIL UNIMAGINABLE. THEY CONTAIN THE FUTURE ITSELF.
AND IT IS WRITTEN THAT FOR THIS FUTURE TO COME, SUPERMAN, BATMAN AND WONDER WOMAN MUST DIE.
WE CALLED YOU HERE BECAUSE THE TRINITY ARE STRONG. AND THE WEAPONS THAT CAN CUT THEM ARE FEW.
WE CALLED YOU HERE BECAUSE WE WISH TO HURT THEM.
ANI-MEN!
AND AL GHUL'S LEAGUE OF ASSASSINS!
AND YOU THREE CAN DO THAT OH SO WELL.
RA'S. IF YOU WILL...
THERE AM...TOO FEW... OF THEM...
WE SAW WHAT THE PANDORA PITS DID TO ETRIGAN THE DEMON...
WOOOOSH
SZZIIINNK
...WHAT WILL THEY DO TO YOU, I WONDER?
SZZIIINNK
SZZIIINNK
AH!

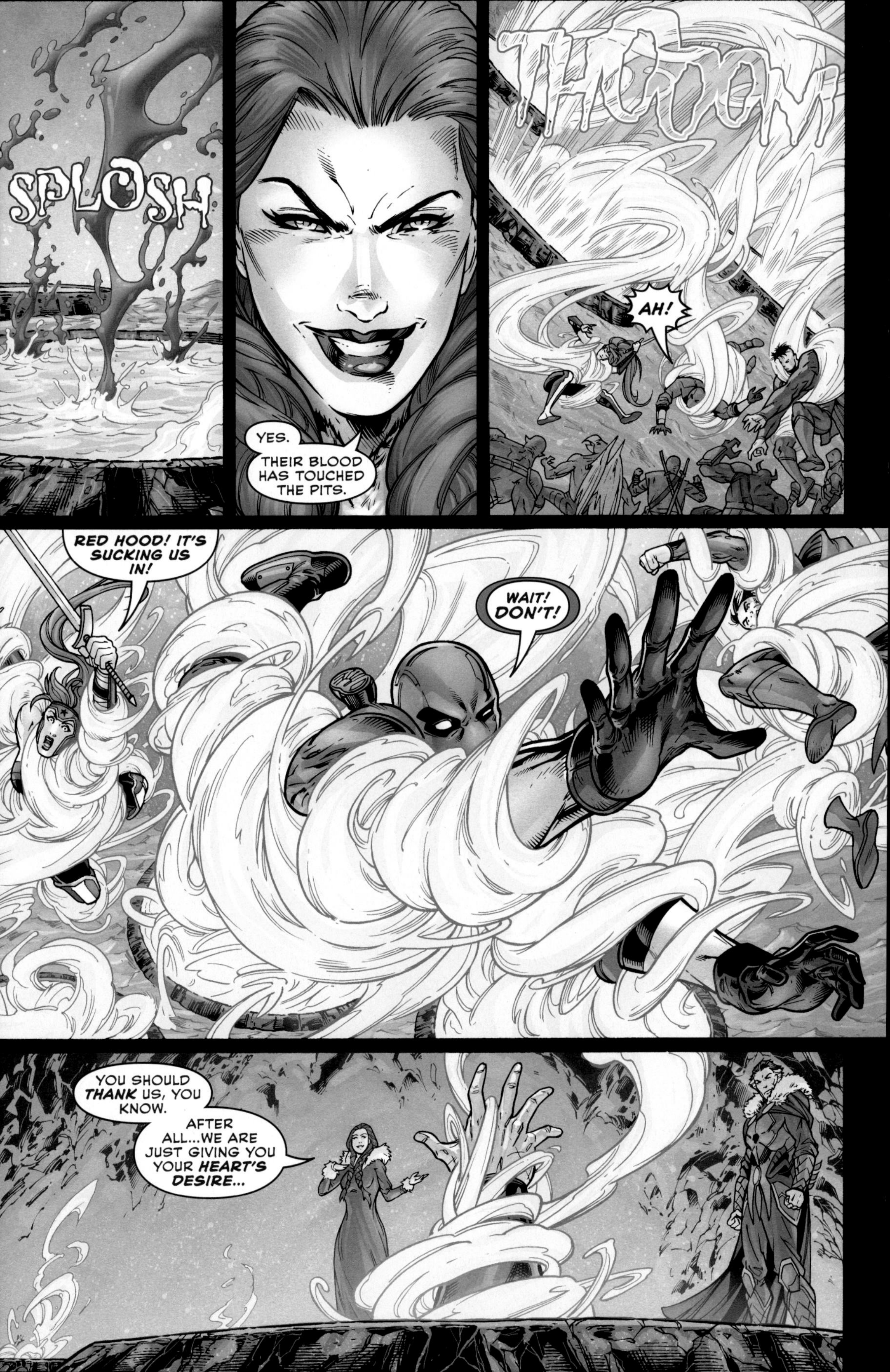
SPLOSH
YES.
THEIR BLOOD HAS TOUCHED THE PITS.
THOOOM
AH!
RED HOOD! IT'S SUCKING US IN!
WAIT! DON'T!
YOU SHOULD THANK US, YOU KNOW.
AFTER ALL...WE ARE JUST GIVING YOU YOUR HEART'S DESIRE...

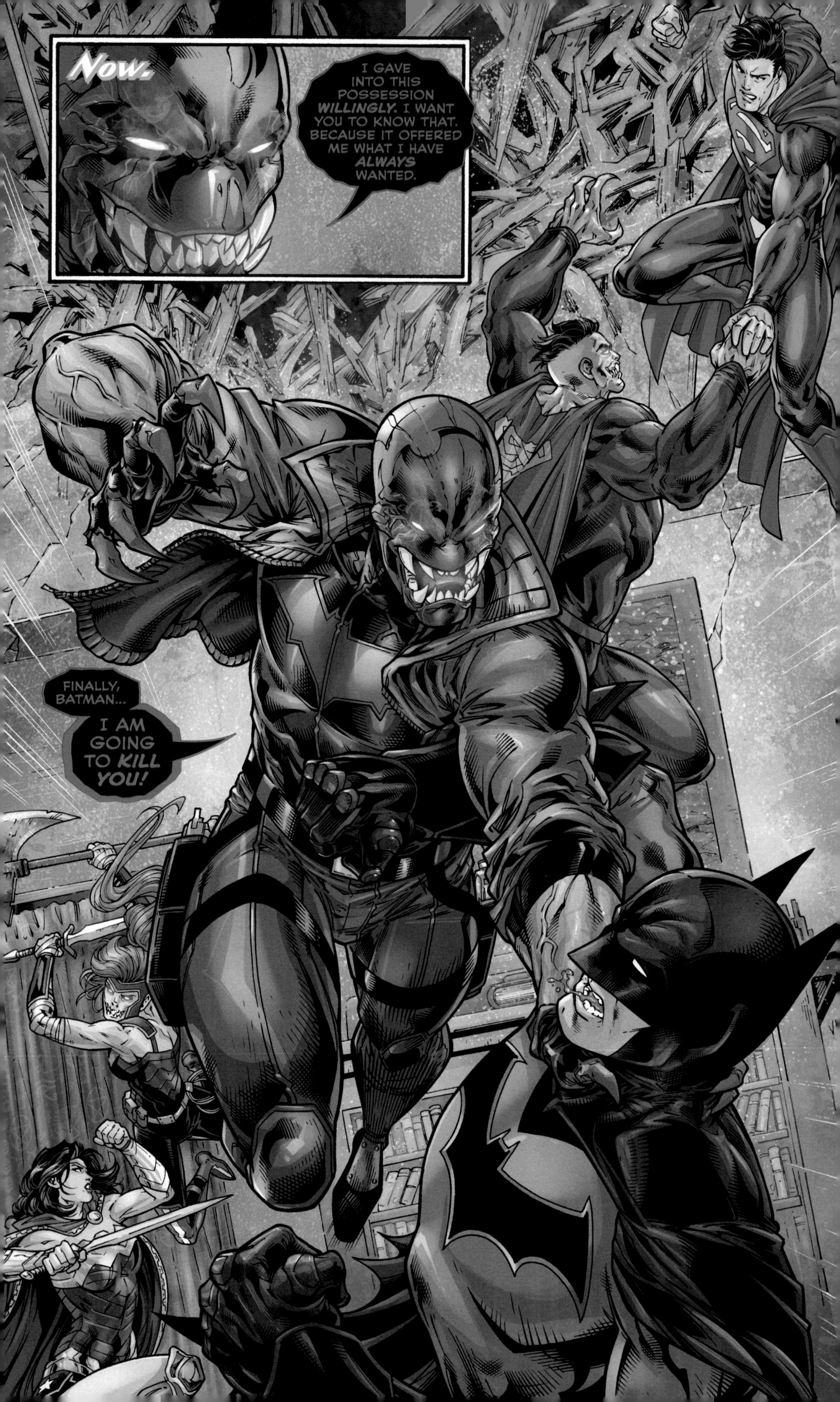
Now.
I GAVE INTO THIS POSSESSION WILLINGLY. I WANT YOU TO KNOW THAT. BECAUSE IT OFFERED ME WHAT I HAVE ALWAYS WANTED.
FINALLY, BATMAN...
I AM GOING TO KILL YOU!

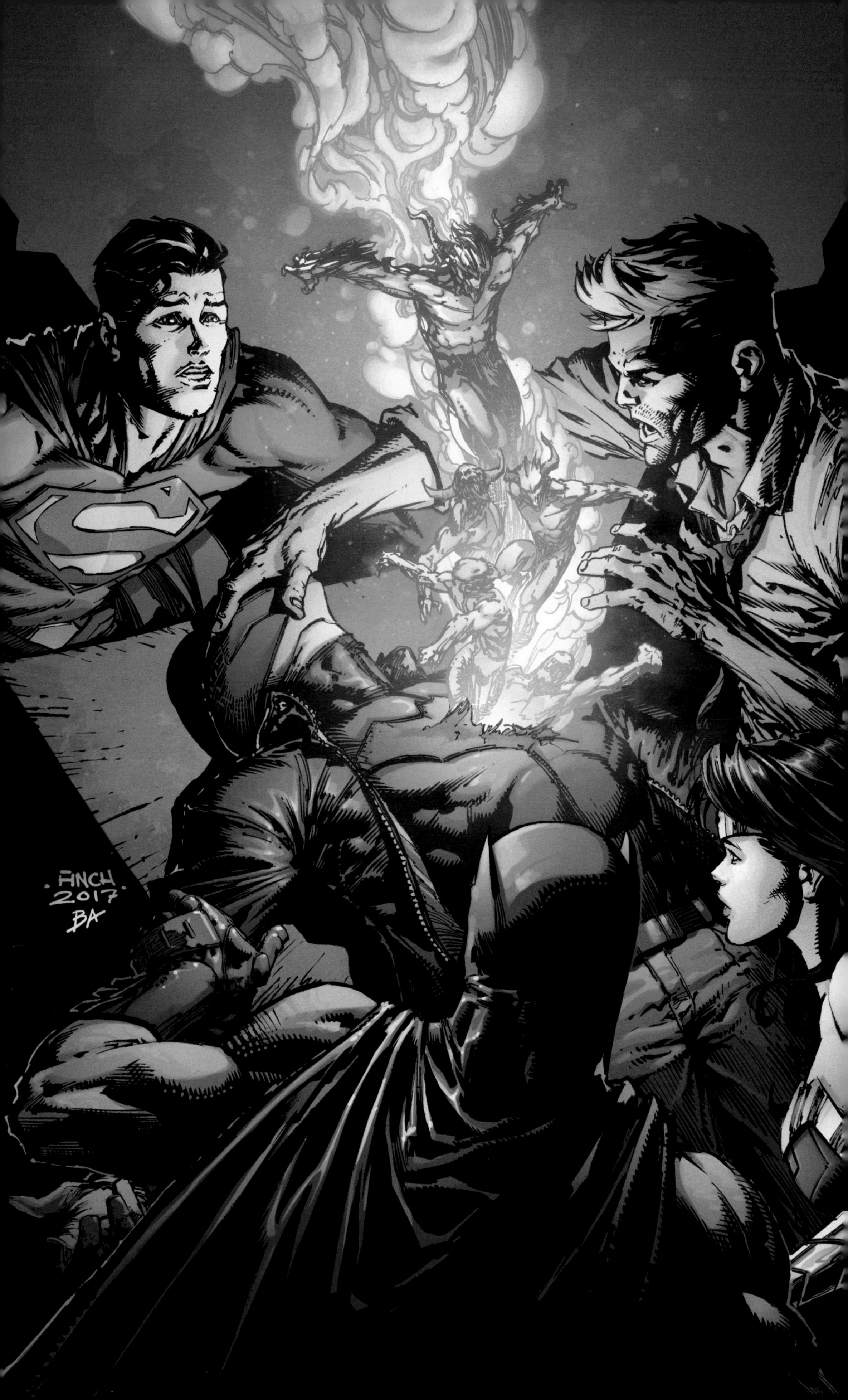
FINCH
2017
BA

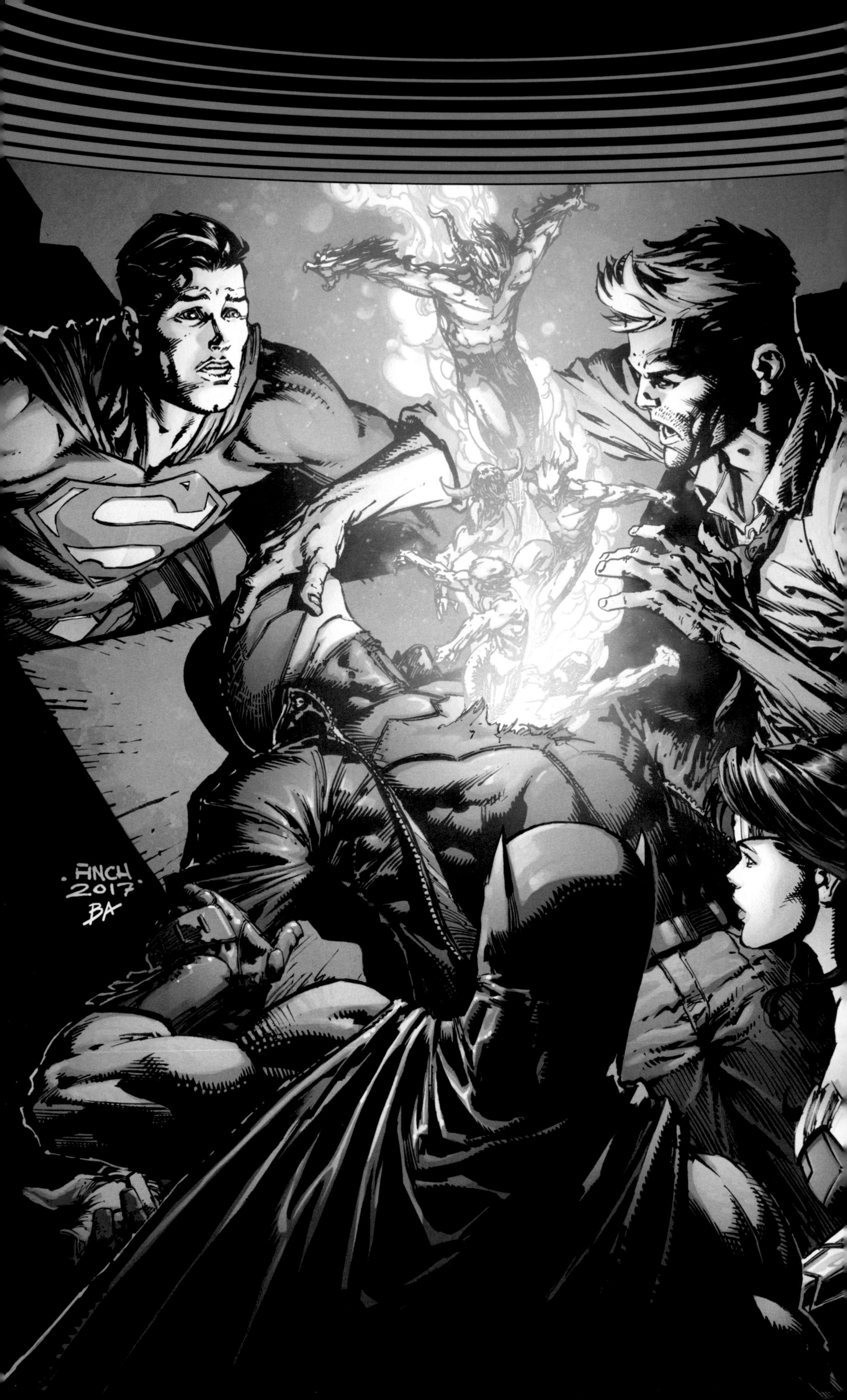
FINCH
2017
BA

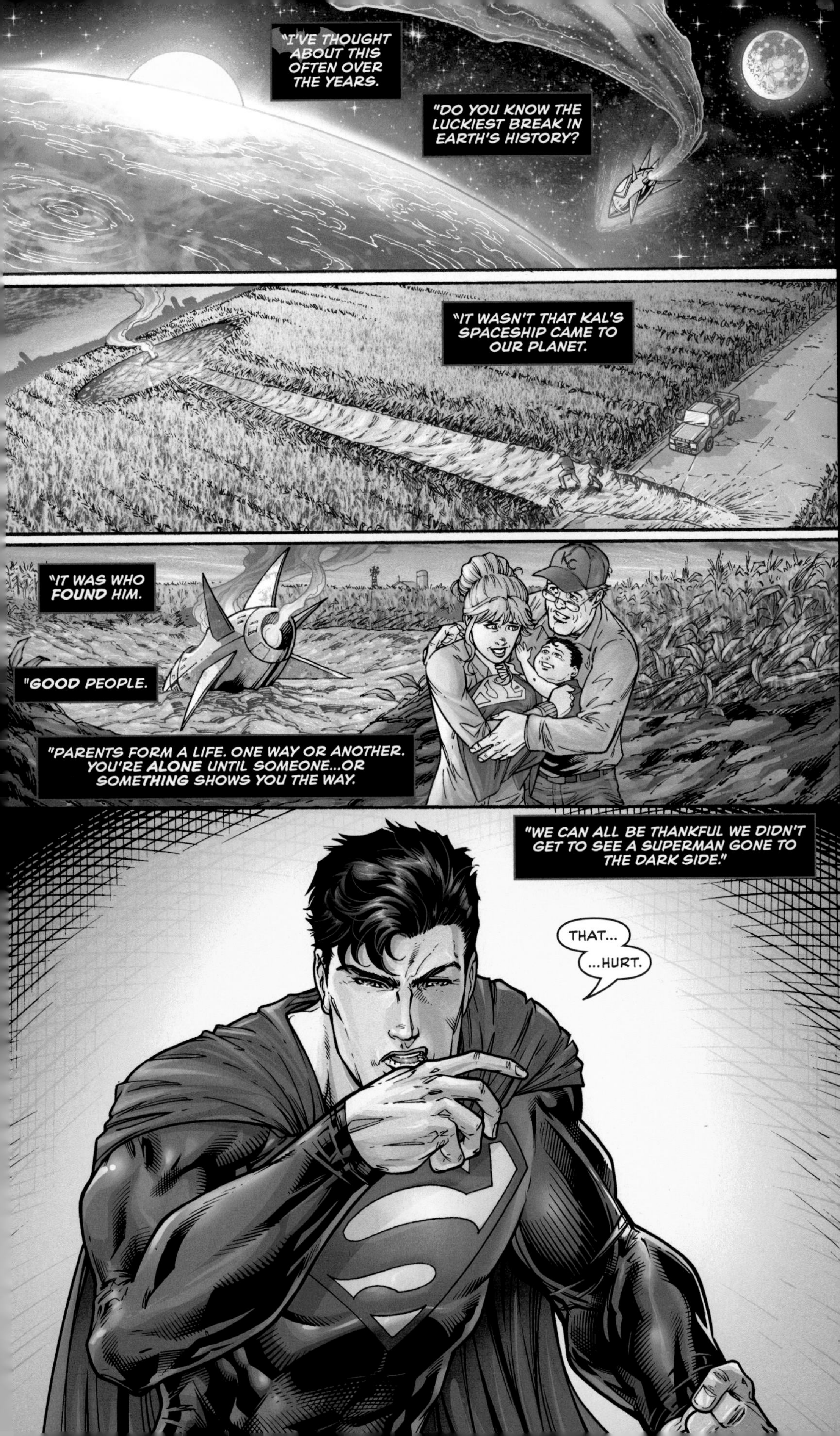
"I'VE THOUGHT ABOUT THIS OFTEN OVER THE YEARS.
"DO YOU KNOW THE LUCKIEST BREAK IN EARTH'S HISTORY?
"IT WASN'T THAT KAL'S SPACESHIP CAME TO OUR PLANET.
"IT WAS WHO FOUND HIM.
"GOOD PEOPLE.
"PARENTS FORM A LIFE. ONE WAY OR ANOTHER. YOU'RE ALONE UNTIL SOMEONE...OR SOMETHING SHOWS YOU THE WAY.
"WE CAN ALL BE THANKFUL WE DIDN'T GET TO SEE A SUPERMAN GONE TO THE DARK SIDE."
THAT...
...HURT.

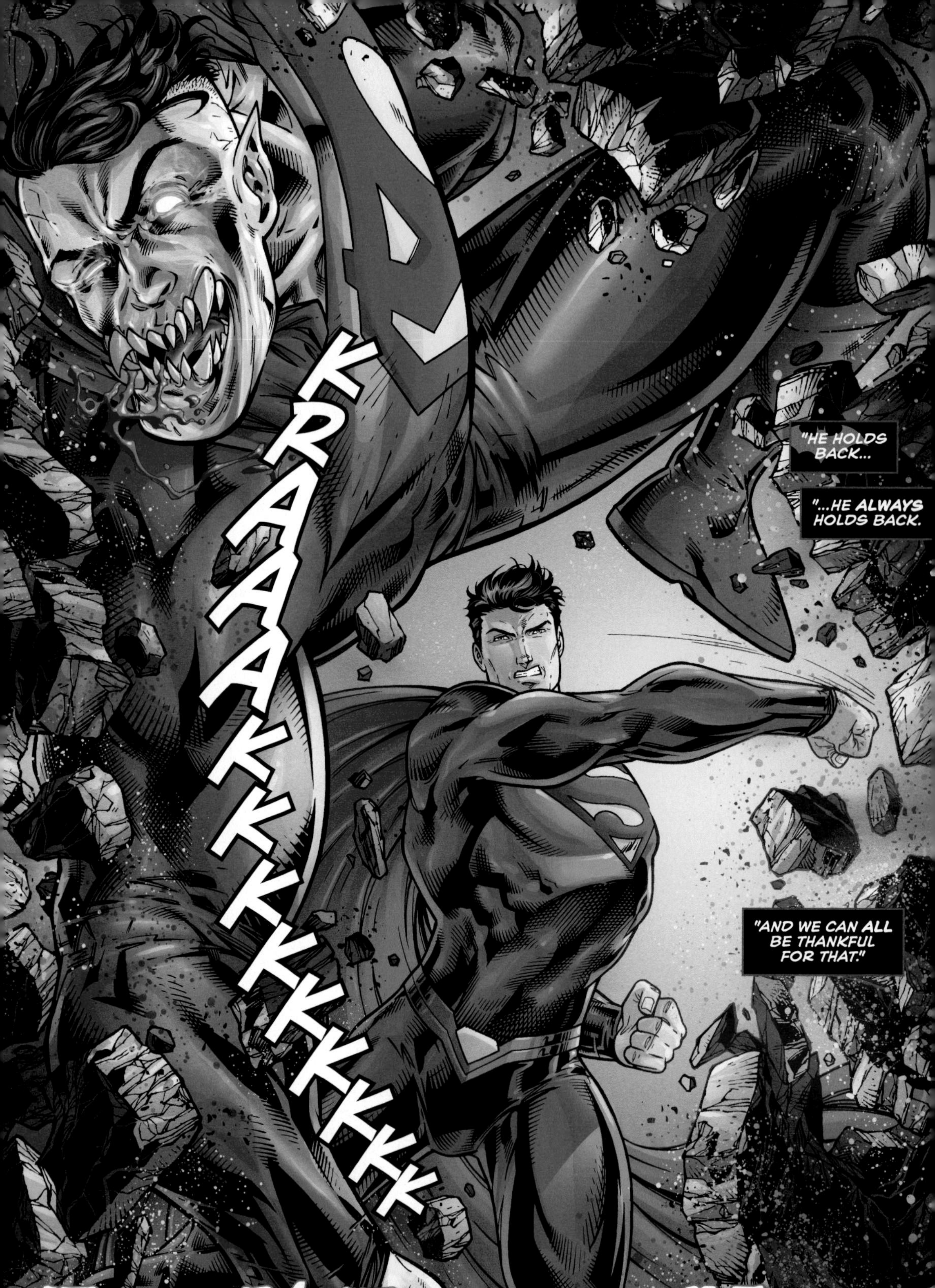
KRAAAKKKKKKK
"HE HOLDS BACK...
"...HE ALWAYS HOLDS BACK.
"AND WE CAN ALL BE THANKFUL FOR THAT."

# DARK DESTINY PART TWO

WRITER: ROB WILLIAMS ARTIST: V KEN MARION
INKS: RAY McCARTHY COLORS: DINEI RIBEIRO LETTERS: JOSH REED
COVER: DAVID FINCH & BRAD ANDERSON
ASSISTANT EDITOR: ANDREA SHEA EDITORS: PAUL KAMINSKI & EDDIE BERGANZA

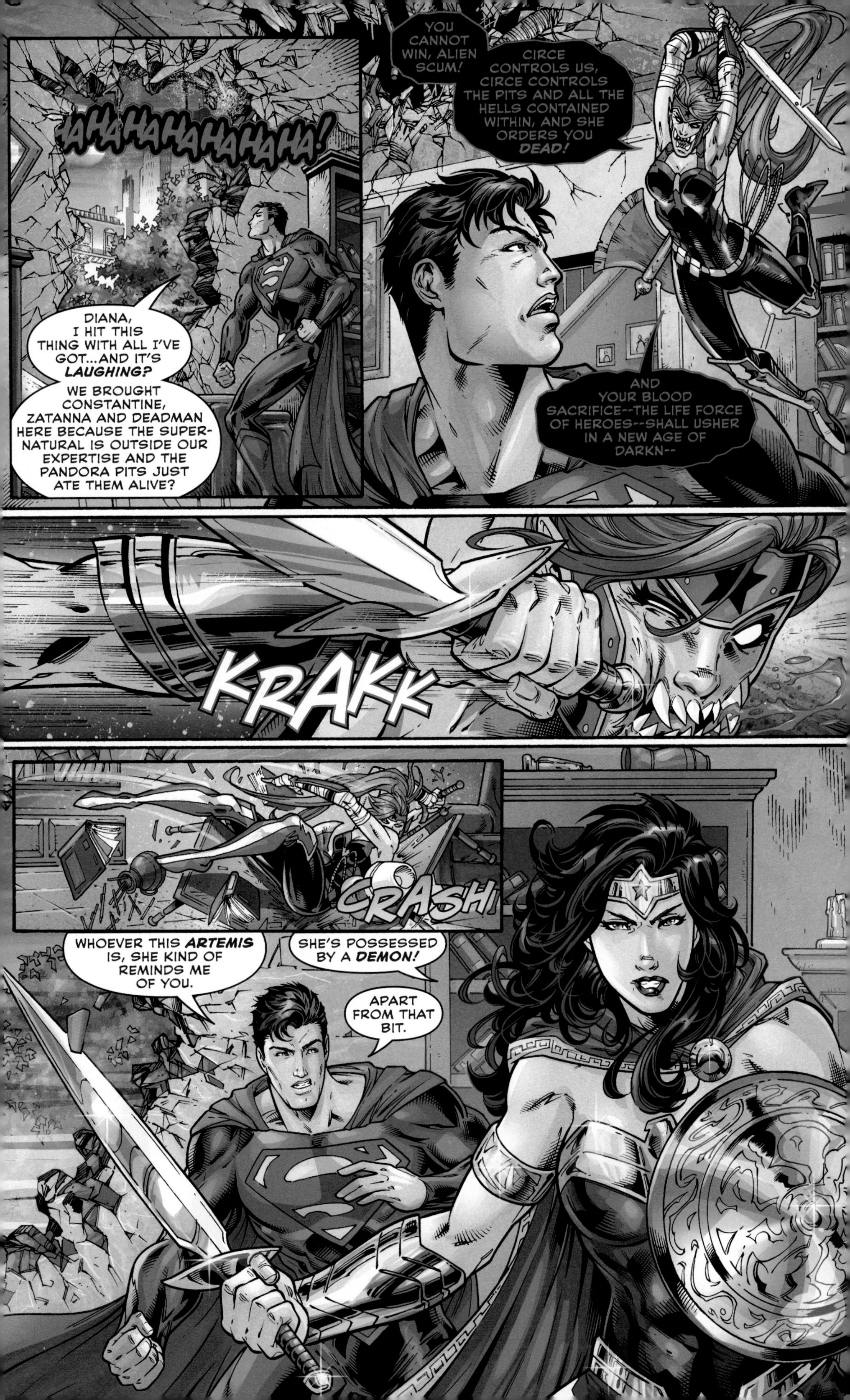
HAHAHAHAHAHAHAHA!
DIANA, I HIT THIS THING WITH ALL I'VE GOT...AND IT'S LAUGHING?
WE BROUGHT CONSTANTINE, ZATANNA AND DEADMAN HERE BECAUSE THE SUPER-NATURAL IS OUTSIDE OUR EXPERTISE AND THE PANDORA PITS JUST ATE THEM ALIVE?
YOU CANNOT WIN, ALIEN SCUM!
CIRCE CONTROLS US, CIRCE CONTROLS THE PITS AND ALL THE HELLS CONTAINED WITHIN, AND SHE ORDERS YOU DEAD!
AND YOUR BLOOD SACRIFICE--THE LIFE FORCE OF HEROES--SHALL USHER IN A NEW AGE OF DARKN--
KRAKK
CRASH
WHOEVER THIS ARTEMIS IS, SHE KIND OF REMINDS ME OF YOU.
SHE'S POSSESSED BY A DEMON!
APART FROM THAT BIT.

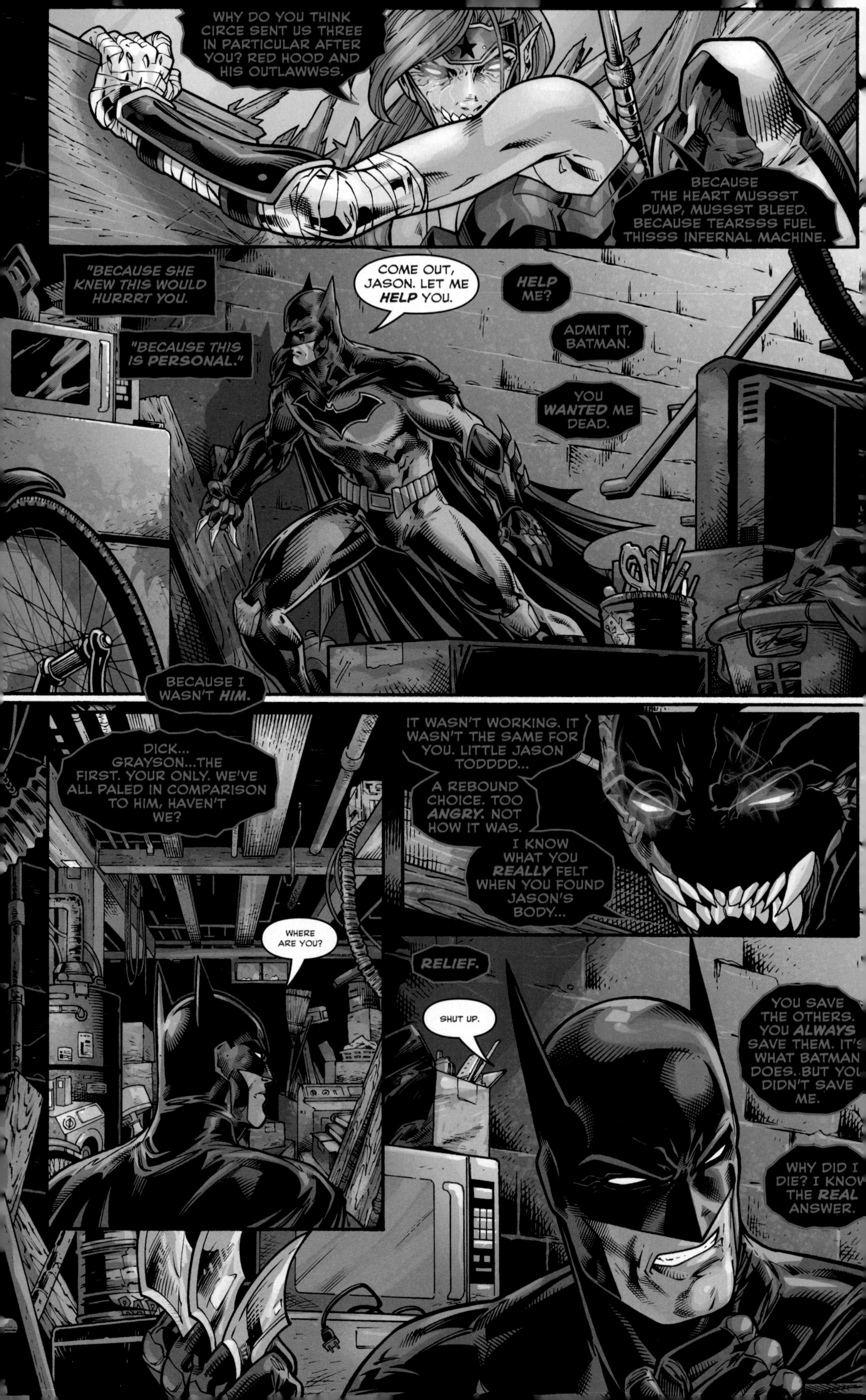
WHY DO YOU THINK CIRCE SENT US THREE IN PARTICULAR AFTER YOU? RED HOOD AND HIS OUTLAWWSS.
BECAUSE THE HEART MUSSST PUMP, MUSSST BLEED. BECAUSE TEARSSS FUEL THISSS INFERNAL MACHINE.
"BECAUSE SHE KNEW THIS WOULD HURRRT YOU.
"BECAUSE THIS IS PERSONAL."
COME OUT, JASON. LET ME HELP YOU.
HELP ME?
ADMIT IT, BATMAN.
YOU WANTED ME DEAD.
BECAUSE I WASN'T HIM.
DICK... GRAYSON...THE FIRST. YOUR ONLY. WE'VE ALL PALED IN COMPARISON TO HIM, HAVEN'T WE?
IT WASN'T WORKING. IT WASN'T THE SAME FOR YOU. LITTLE JASON TODDDD...
A REBOUND CHOICE. TOO ANGRY. NOT HOW IT WAS.
I KNOW WHAT YOU REALLY FELT WHEN YOU FOUND JASON'S BODY...
WHERE ARE YOU?
RELIEF.
SHUT UP.
YOU SAVE THE OTHERS. YOU ALWAYS SAVE THEM. IT'S WHAT BATMAN DOES..BUT YOU DIDN'T SAVE ME.
WHY DID I DIE? I KNOW THE REAL ANSWER.

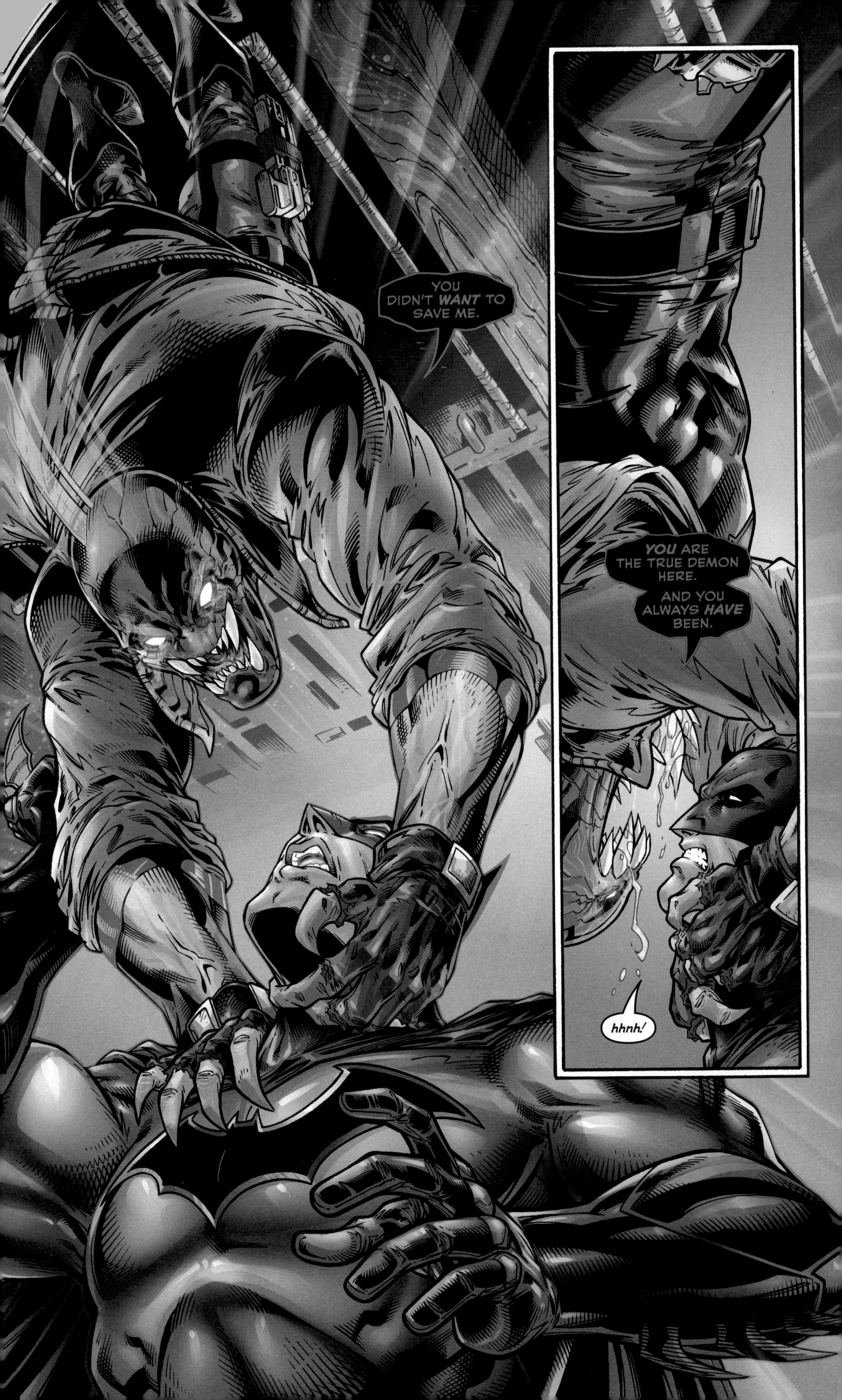
YOU DIDN'T *WANT* TO SAVE ME.
*YOU* ARE THE TRUE DEMON HERE.
AND YOU ALWAYS *HAVE* BEEN.
*hhnh!*

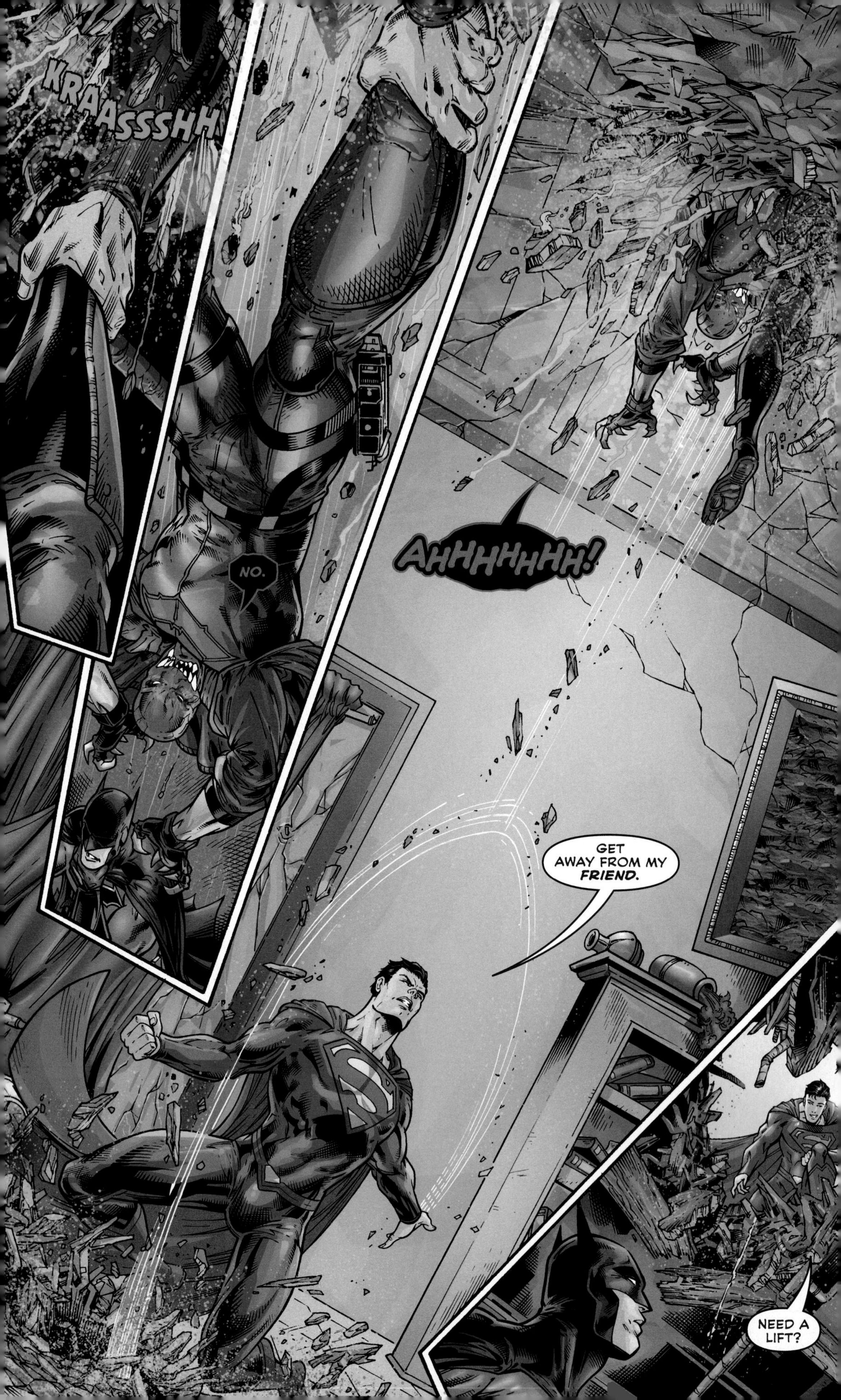

KRAASSSHH
NO.
AHHHHHHH!
GET AWAY FROM MY FRIEND.
NEED A LIFT?

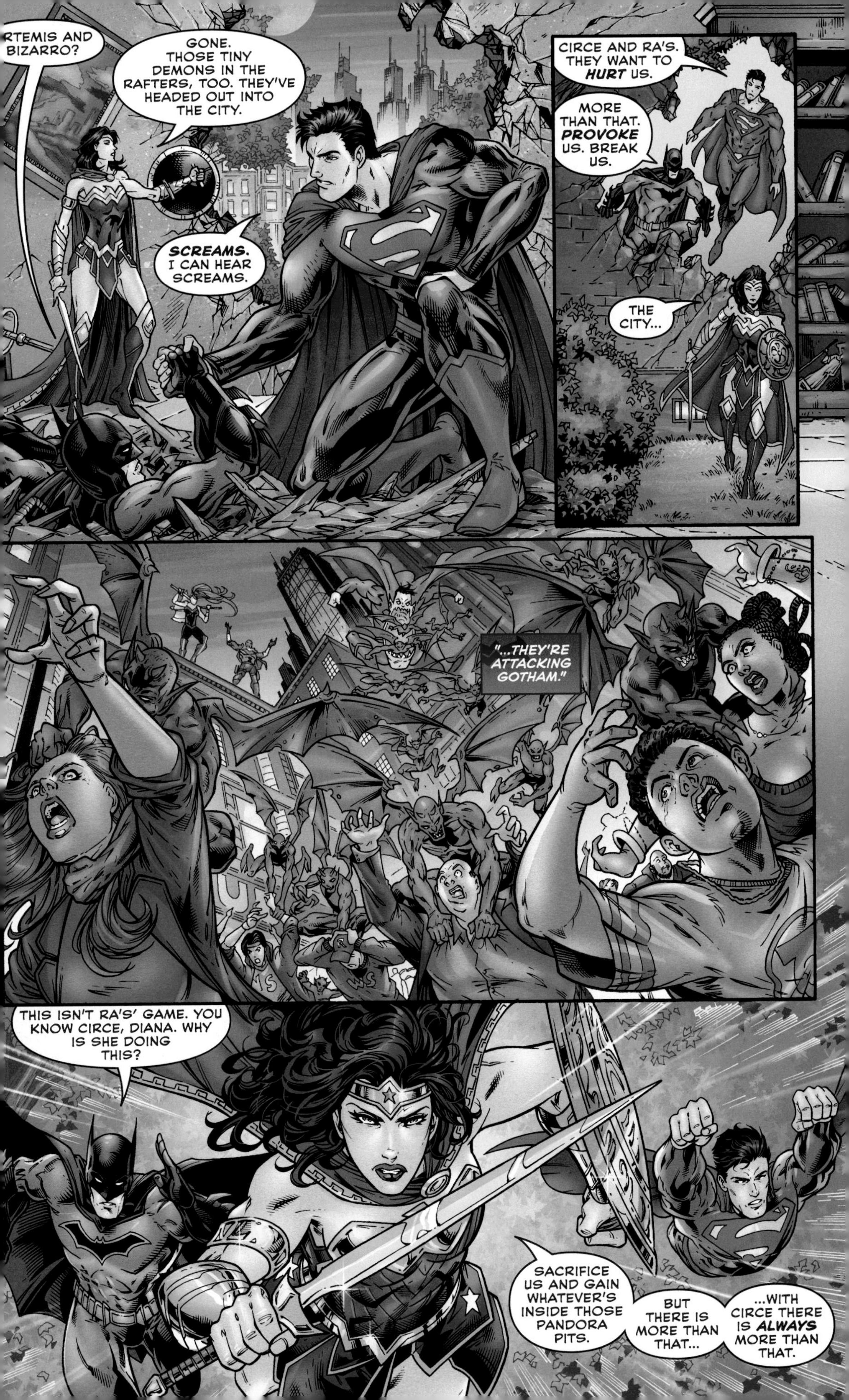
RTEMIS AND BIZARRO?
GONE. THOSE TINY DEMONS IN THE RAFTERS, TOO. THEY'VE HEADED OUT INTO THE CITY.
SCREAMS. I CAN HEAR SCREAMS.
CIRCE AND RA'S. THEY WANT TO HURT US.
MORE THAN THAT. PROVOKE US. BREAK US.
THE CITY...
"...THEY'RE ATTACKING GOTHAM."
THIS ISN'T RA'S' GAME. YOU KNOW CIRCE, DIANA. WHY IS SHE DOING THIS?
SACRIFICE US AND GAIN WHATEVER'S INSIDE THOSE PANDORA PITS.
BUT THERE IS MORE THAN THAT...
...WITH CIRCE THERE IS ALWAYS MORE THAN THAT.

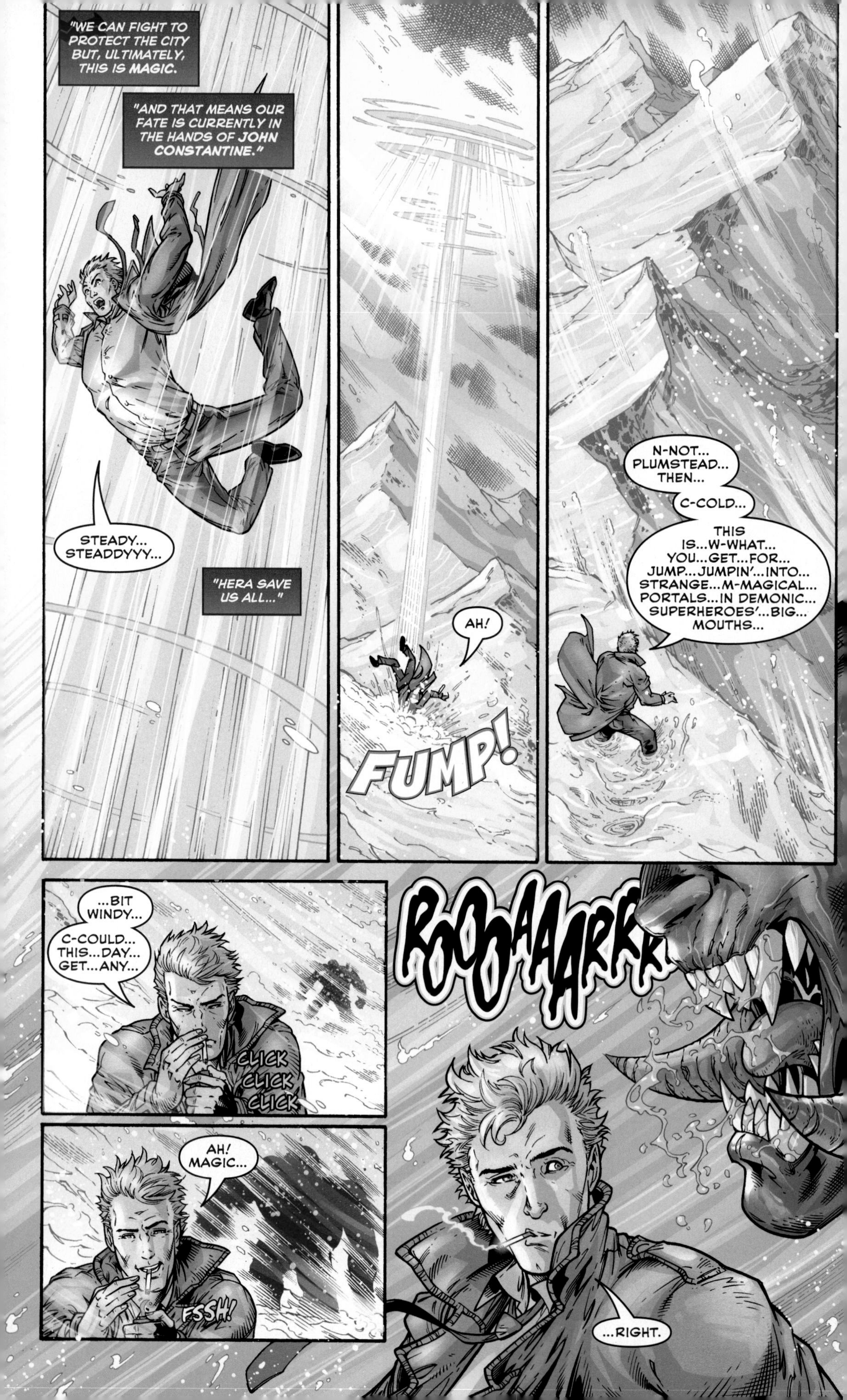
"WE CAN FIGHT TO PROTECT THE CITY BUT, ULTIMATELY, THIS IS MAGIC.
"AND THAT MEANS OUR FATE IS CURRENTLY IN THE HANDS OF JOHN CONSTANTINE."
STEADY... STEADDYYY...
"HERA SAVE US ALL..."
AH!
FUMP!
N-NOT... PLUMSTEAD... THEN...
C-COLD...
THIS IS...W-WHAT... YOU...GET...FOR... JUMP...JUMPIN'...INTO... STRANGE...M-MAGICAL... PORTALS...IN DEMONIC... SUPERHEROES'...BIG... MOUTHS...
...BIT WINDY...
C-COULD... THIS...DAY... GET...ANY...
CLICK CLICK CLICK
AH! MAGIC...
FSSH!
ROOOAAARKK
...RIGHT.

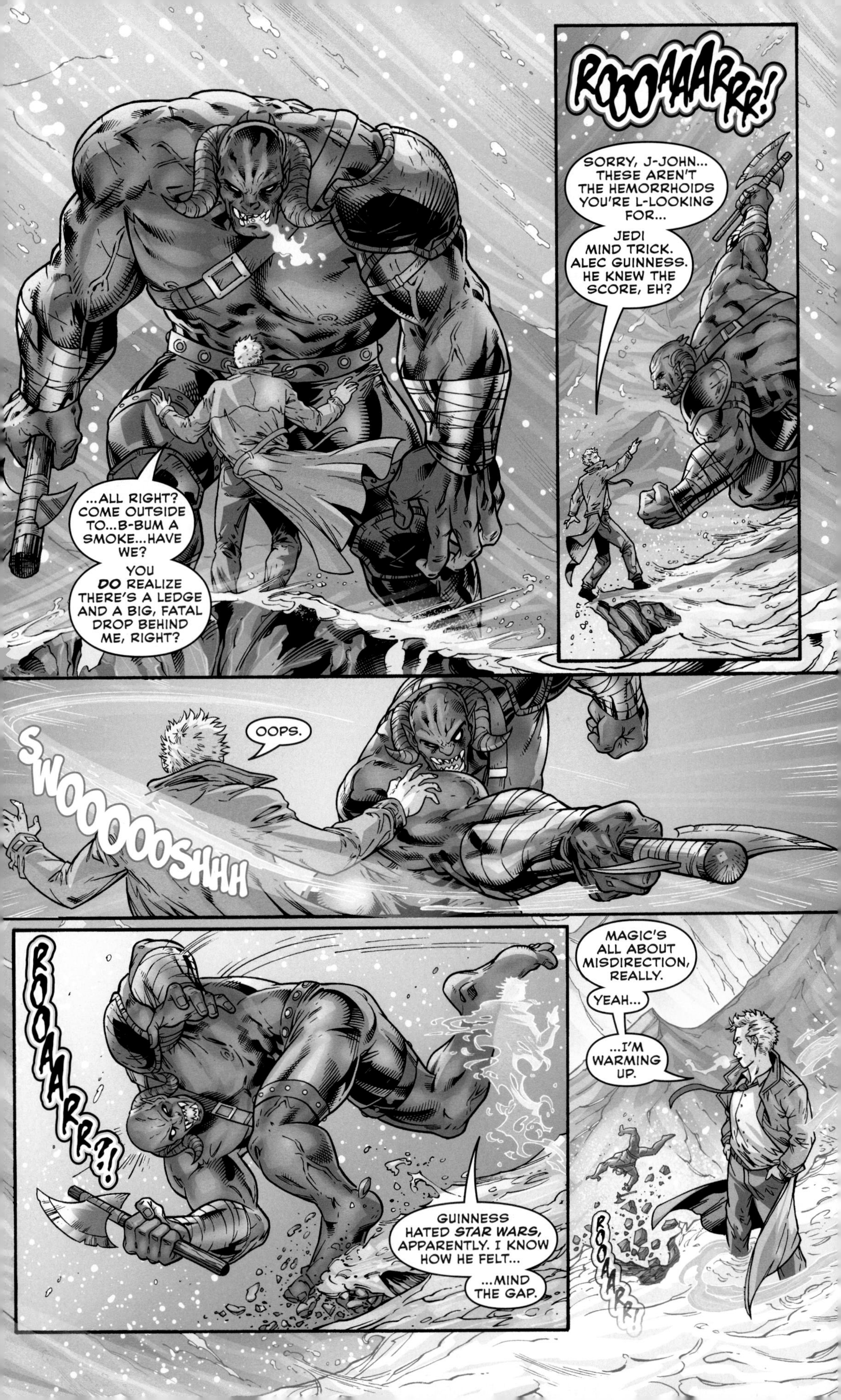

...ALL RIGHT? COME OUTSIDE TO...B-BUM A SMOKE...HAVE WE?
YOU **DO** REALIZE THERE'S A LEDGE AND A BIG, FATAL DROP BEHIND ME, RIGHT?
ROOOAAAARRRR!
SORRY, J-JOHN... THESE AREN'T THE HEMORRHOIDS YOU'RE L-LOOKING FOR...
JEDI MIND TRICK. ALEC GUINNESS. HE KNEW THE SCORE, EH?
OOPS.
SWOOOOOOSHHH
ROOAARRR?!
GUINNESS HATED *STAR WARS*, APPARENTLY. I KNOW HOW HE FELT...
...MIND THE GAP.
MAGIC'S ALL ABOUT MISDIRECTION, REALLY.
YEAH...
...I'M WARMING UP.
ROOAARR!

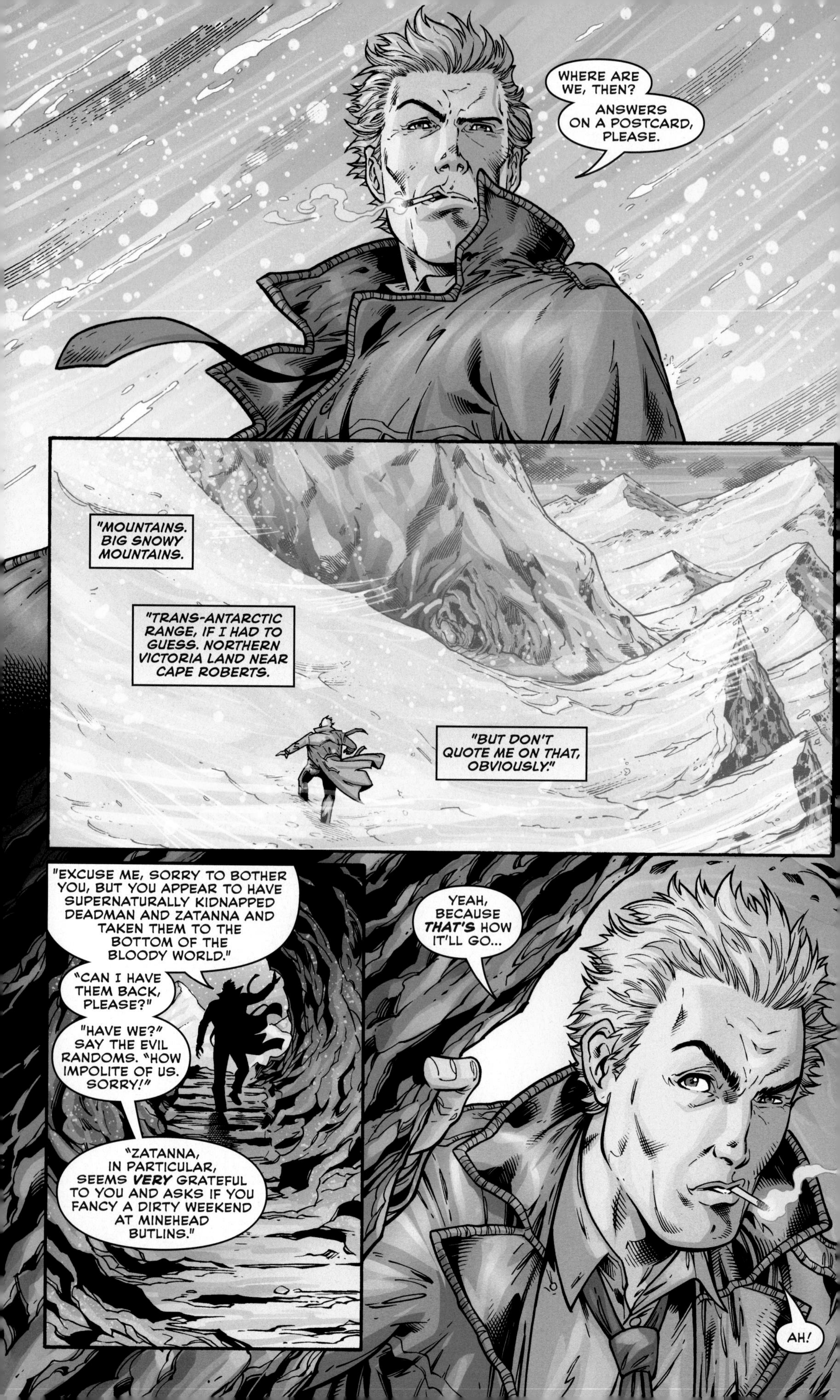
WHERE ARE WE, THEN?
ANSWERS ON A POSTCARD, PLEASE.
"MOUNTAINS. BIG SNOWY MOUNTAINS.
"TRANS-ANTARCTIC RANGE, IF I HAD TO GUESS. NORTHERN VICTORIA LAND NEAR CAPE ROBERTS.
"BUT DON'T QUOTE ME ON THAT, OBVIOUSLY."
"EXCUSE ME, SORRY TO BOTHER YOU, BUT YOU APPEAR TO HAVE SUPERNATURALLY KIDNAPPED DEADMAN AND ZATANNA AND TAKEN THEM TO THE BOTTOM OF THE BLOODY WORLD."
"CAN I HAVE THEM BACK, PLEASE?"
"HAVE WE?" SAY THE EVIL RANDOMS. "HOW IMPOLITE OF US. SORRY!"
"ZATANNA, IN PARTICULAR, SEEMS VERY GRATEFUL TO YOU AND ASKS IF YOU FANCY A DIRTY WEEKEND AT MINEHEAD BUTLINS."
YEAH, BECAUSE THAT'S HOW IT'LL GO...
AH!

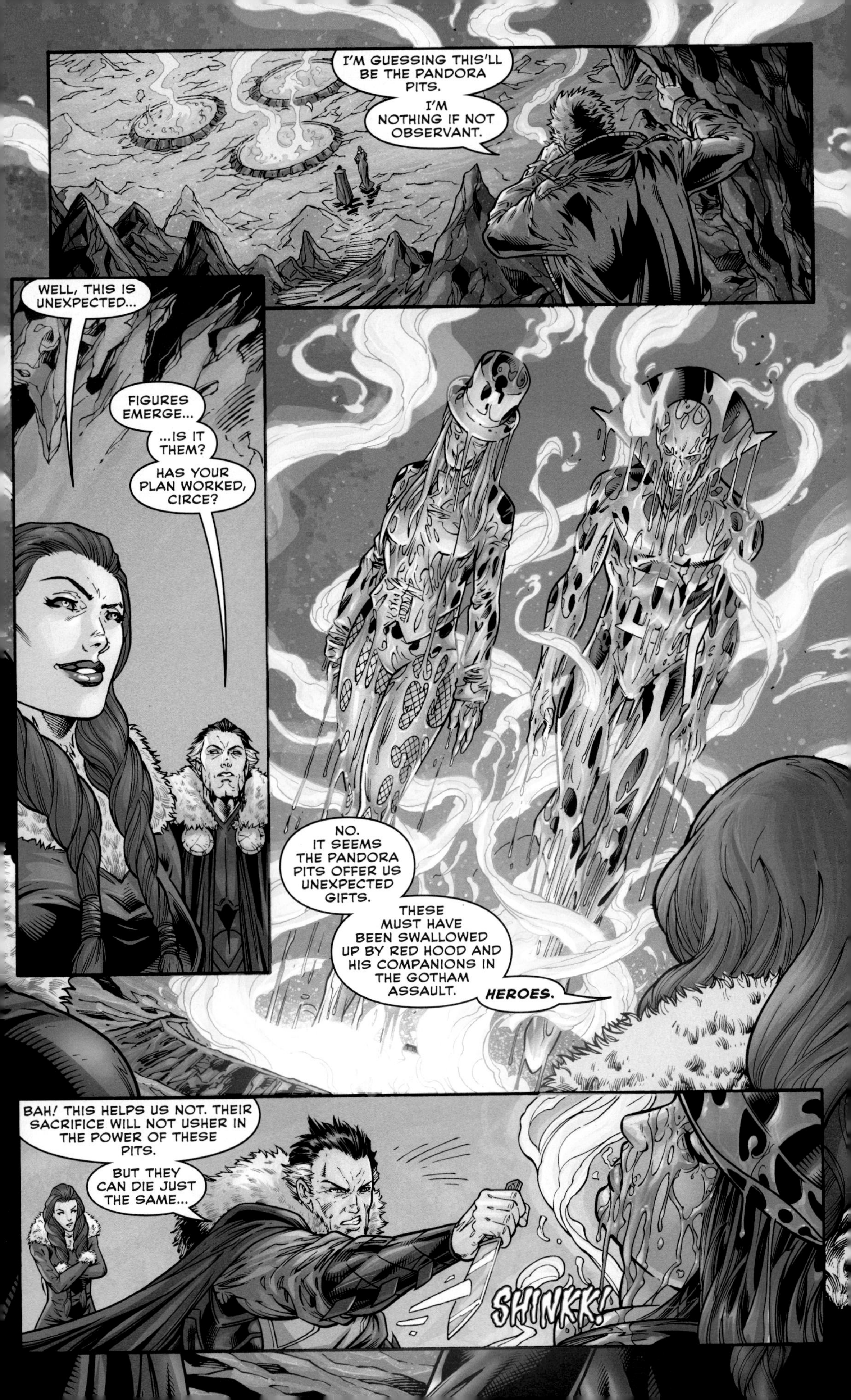

I'M GUESSING THIS'LL BE THE PANDORA PITS.
I'M NOTHING IF NOT OBSERVANT.
WELL, THIS IS UNEXPECTED...
FIGURES EMERGE...
...IS IT THEM?
HAS YOUR PLAN WORKED, CIRCE?
NO. IT SEEMS THE PANDORA PITS OFFER US UNEXPECTED GIFTS.
THESE MUST HAVE BEEN SWALLOWED UP BY RED HOOD AND HIS COMPANIONS IN THE GOTHAM ASSAULT.
HEROES.
BAH! THIS HELPS US NOT. THEIR SACRIFICE WILL NOT USHER IN THE POWER OF THESE PITS.
BUT THEY CAN DIE JUST THE SAME...
SHINKK!

WHOA! OI! HANG ABOUT! PETER CUSHING'S DIRTY UNCLE! HOLD UP...

...YOU REALLY DON'T THINK THESE THINGS THROUGH, DO YOU?

WHO--?

A MAGICIAN. A POWERFUL ONE, IF HE HAS GAINED ACCESS HERE PAST OUR SENTRIES.

YOU'D BE CIRCE, THEN. LOOKING GOOD FOR AN IMMORTAL. BOTOX WORKING...

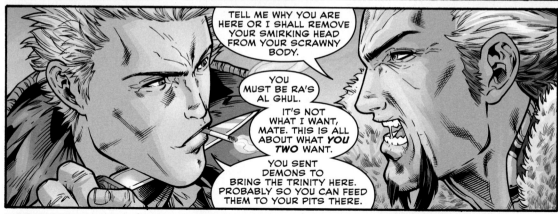

TELL ME WHY YOU ARE HERE OR I SHALL REMOVE YOUR SMIRKING HEAD FROM YOUR SCRAWNY BODY.

YOU MUST BE RA'S AL GHUL.

IT'S NOT WHAT I WANT, MATE. THIS IS ALL ABOUT WHAT *YOU TWO* WANT.

YOU SENT DEMONS TO BRING THE TRINITY HERE. PROBABLY SO YOU CAN FEED THEM TO YOUR PITS THERE.

THREE MYSTERIOUS MAGIC PITS, FILLED WITH EVIL-Y NONSENSE. ONE FOR SUPES, ONE FOR BATS AND ONE FOR THE HOTNESS.

AND YOU SENT THREE DEMONIZED SUPER-WHOEVERS AFTER THEM.

THREE. THAT'S THE MAGIC NUMBER. DE LA SOUL.

THIS IS SOME KIND OF PROPHECY DEAL, RIGHT? "LO, IT IS FATED" ETC. SO HERE'S A QUESTION FOR YOU. IF THIS IS A PROPHECY OF *THREES*...

...HOW COME THERE'S ONLY *TWO* OF YOU?

I THINK CIRCE'S SPINNING YOU A YARN, MATE.

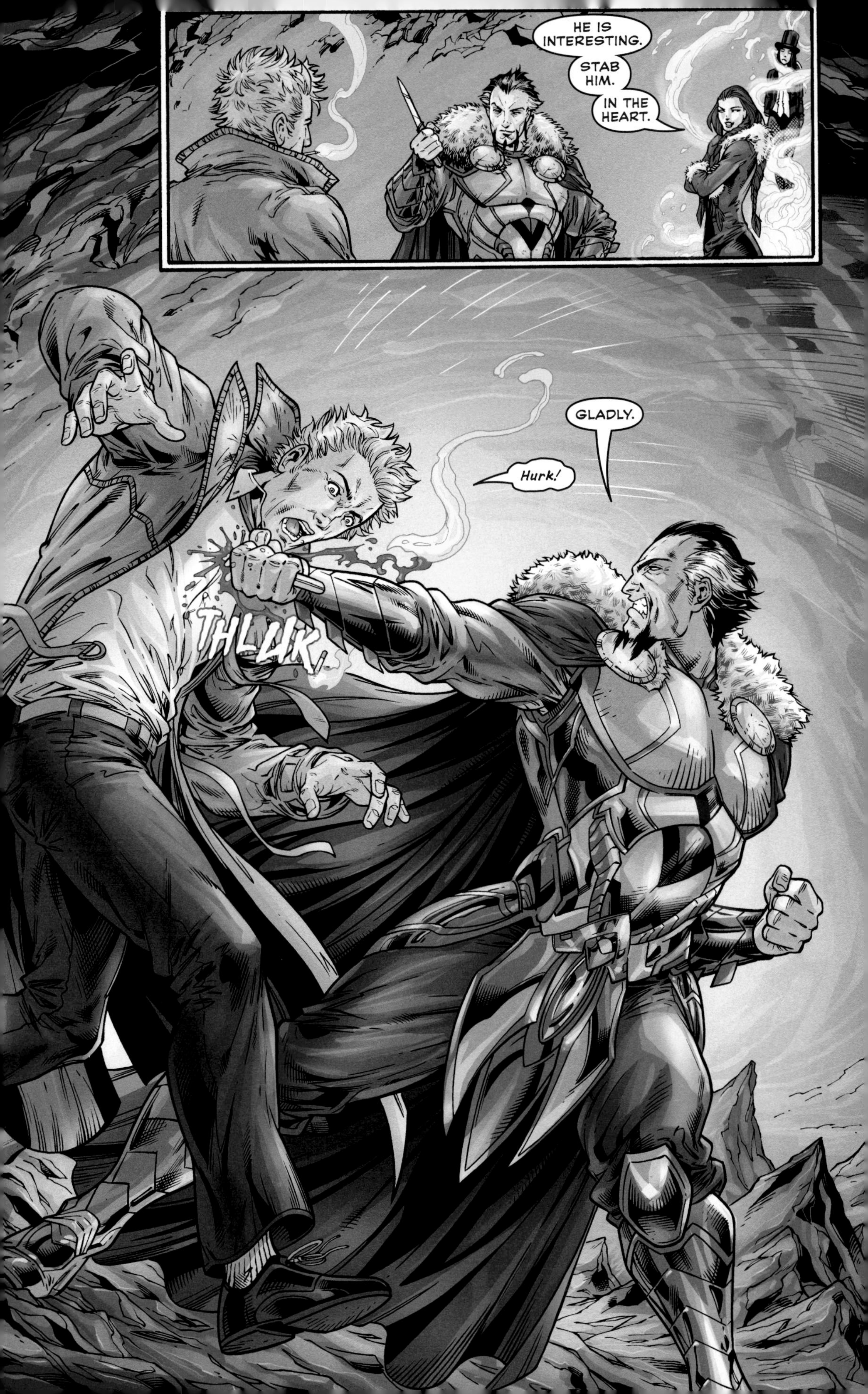
HE IS INTERESTING.
STAB HIM.
IN THE HEART.
GLADLY.
Hurk!
THLUK

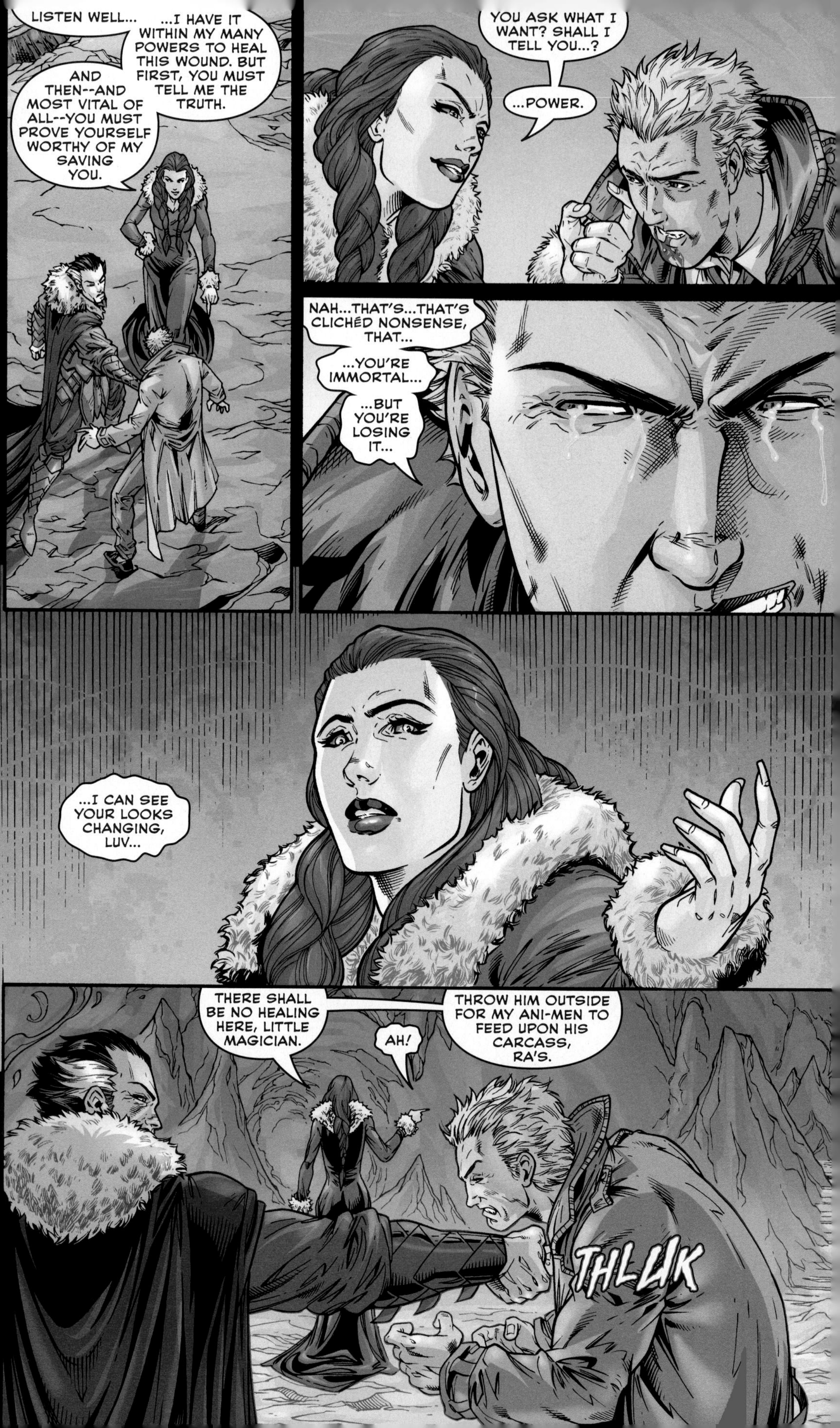
LISTEN WELL...
...I HAVE IT WITHIN MY MANY POWERS TO HEAL THIS WOUND. BUT FIRST, YOU MUST TELL ME THE TRUTH.
AND THEN--AND MOST VITAL OF ALL--YOU MUST PROVE YOURSELF WORTHY OF MY SAVING YOU.
YOU ASK WHAT I WANT? SHALL I TELL YOU...?
...POWER.
NAH...THAT'S...THAT'S CLICHÉD NONSENSE, THAT...
...YOU'RE IMMORTAL...
...BUT YOU'RE LOSING IT...
...I CAN SEE YOUR LOOKS CHANGING, LUV...
THERE SHALL BE NO HEALING HERE, LITTLE MAGICIAN.
THROW HIM OUTSIDE FOR MY ANI-MEN TO FEED UPON HIS CARCASS, RA'S.
AH!
THLUK

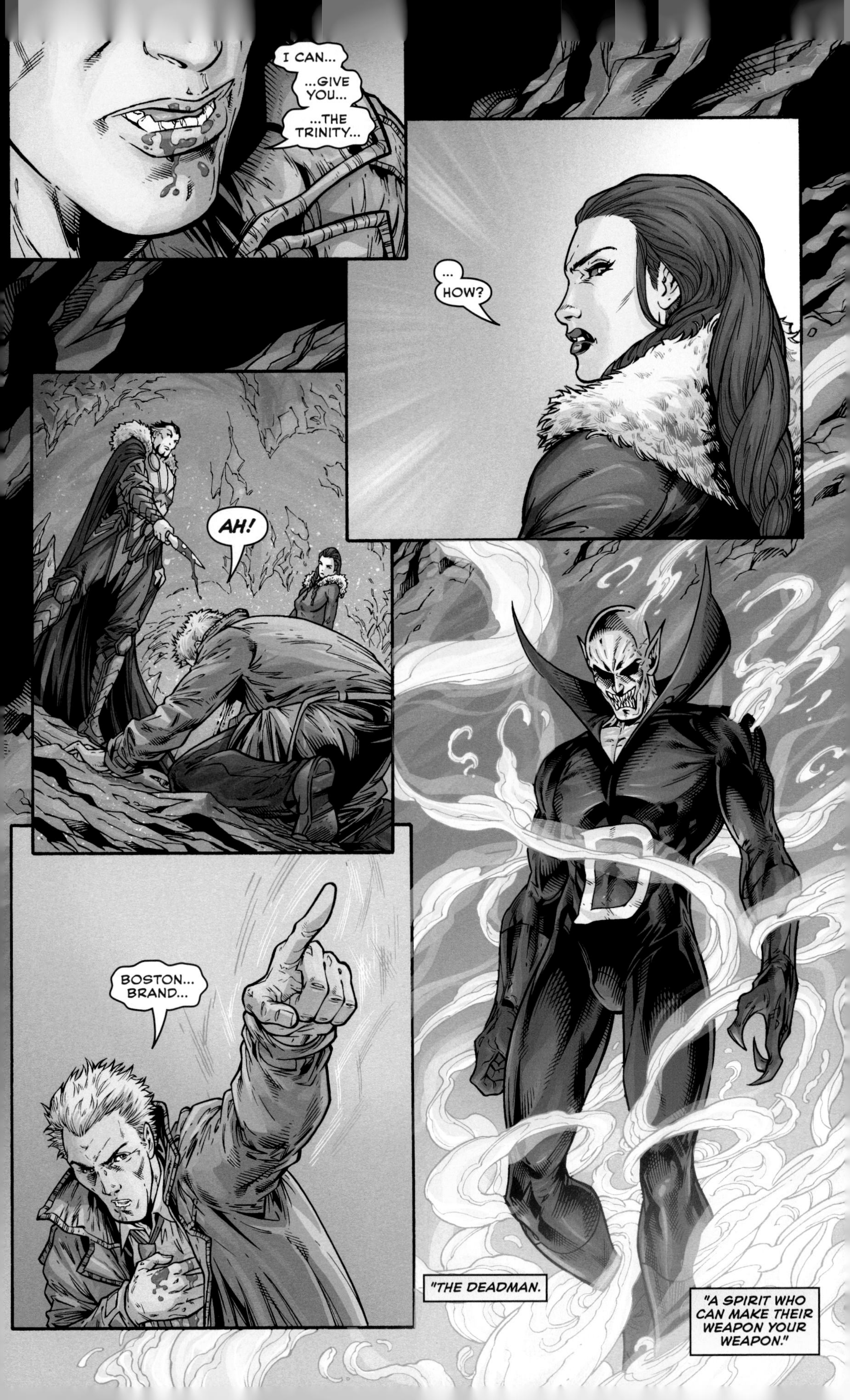
I CAN...
...GIVE YOU...
...THE TRINITY...
... HOW?
AH!
BOSTON... BRAND...
"THE DEADMAN.
"A SPIRIT WHO CAN MAKE THEIR WEAPON YOUR WEAPON."

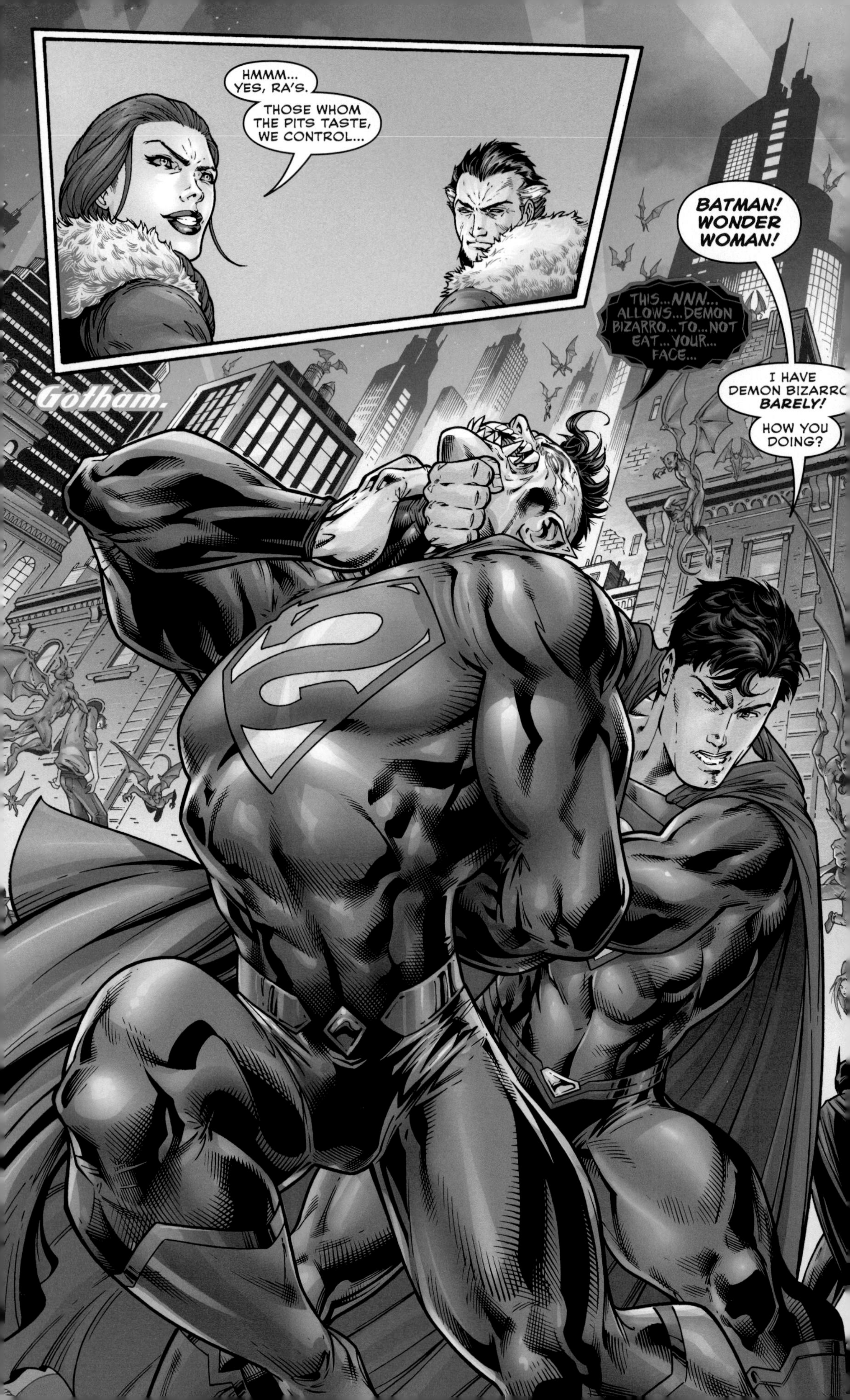
HMMM... YES, RA'S.
THOSE WHOM THE PITS TASTE, WE CONTROL...
Gotham.
BATMAN! WONDER WOMAN!
THIS...NNN... ALLOWS...DEMON BIZARRO...TO...NOT EAT...YOUR... FACE...
I HAVE DEMON BIZARRO *BARELY!*
HOW YOU DOING?

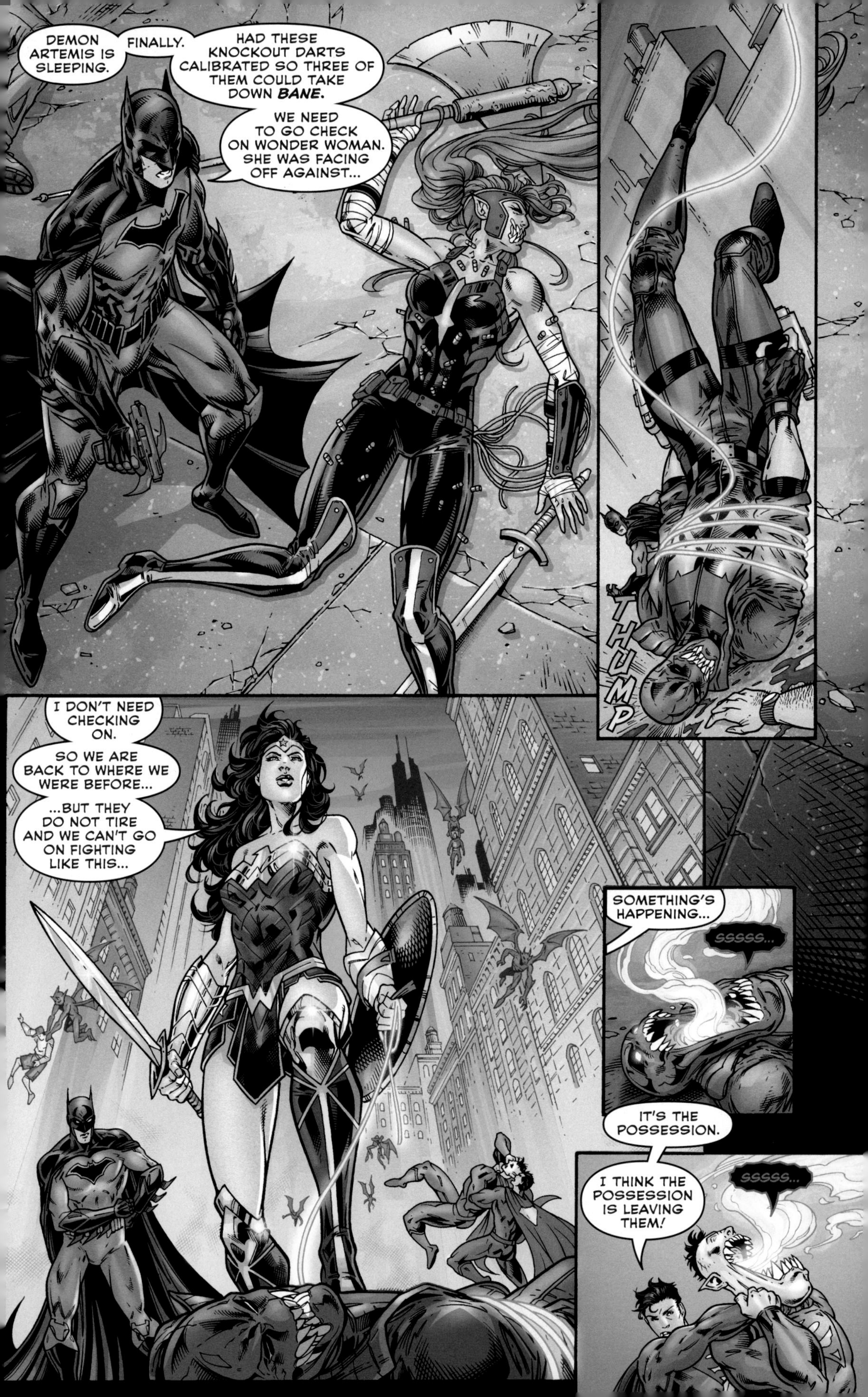
DEMON ARTEMIS IS SLEEPING.
FINALLY.
HAD THESE KNOCKOUT DARTS CALIBRATED SO THREE OF THEM COULD TAKE DOWN BANE.
WE NEED TO GO CHECK ON WONDER WOMAN. SHE WAS FACING OFF AGAINST...
THUMP
I DON'T NEED CHECKING ON.
SO WE ARE BACK TO WHERE WE WERE BEFORE...
...BUT THEY DO NOT TIRE AND WE CAN'T GO ON FIGHTING LIKE THIS...
SOMETHING'S HAPPENING...
SSSSS...
IT'S THE POSSESSION.
I THINK THE POSSESSION IS LEAVING THEM!
SSSSS...

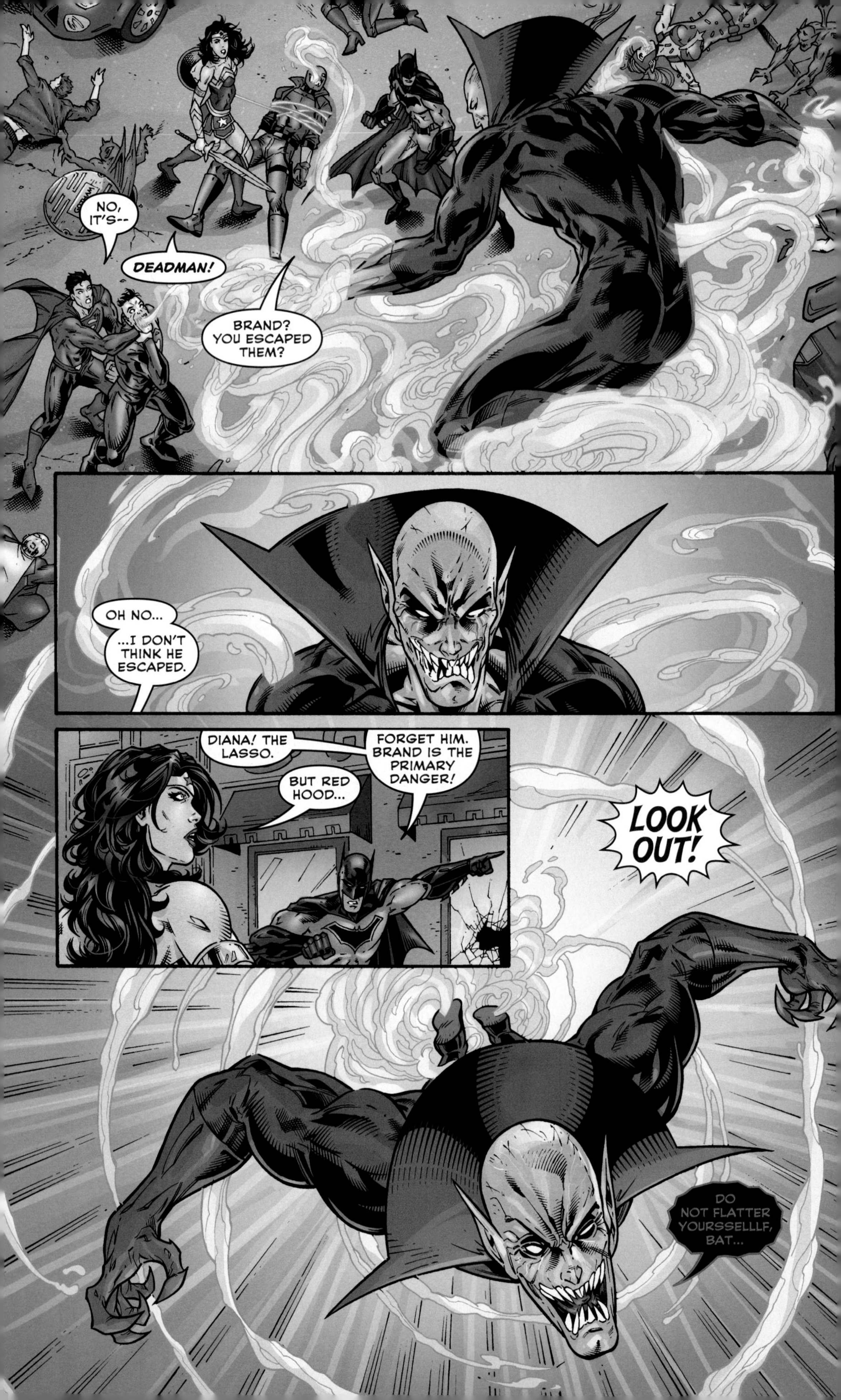
NO, IT'S--
DEADMAN!
BRAND? YOU ESCAPED THEM?
OH NO...
...I DON'T THINK HE ESCAPED.
DIANA! THE LASSO.
BUT RED HOOD...
FORGET HIM. BRAND IS THE PRIMARY DANGER!
LOOK OUT!
DO NOT FLATTER YOURSSELLLF, BAT...

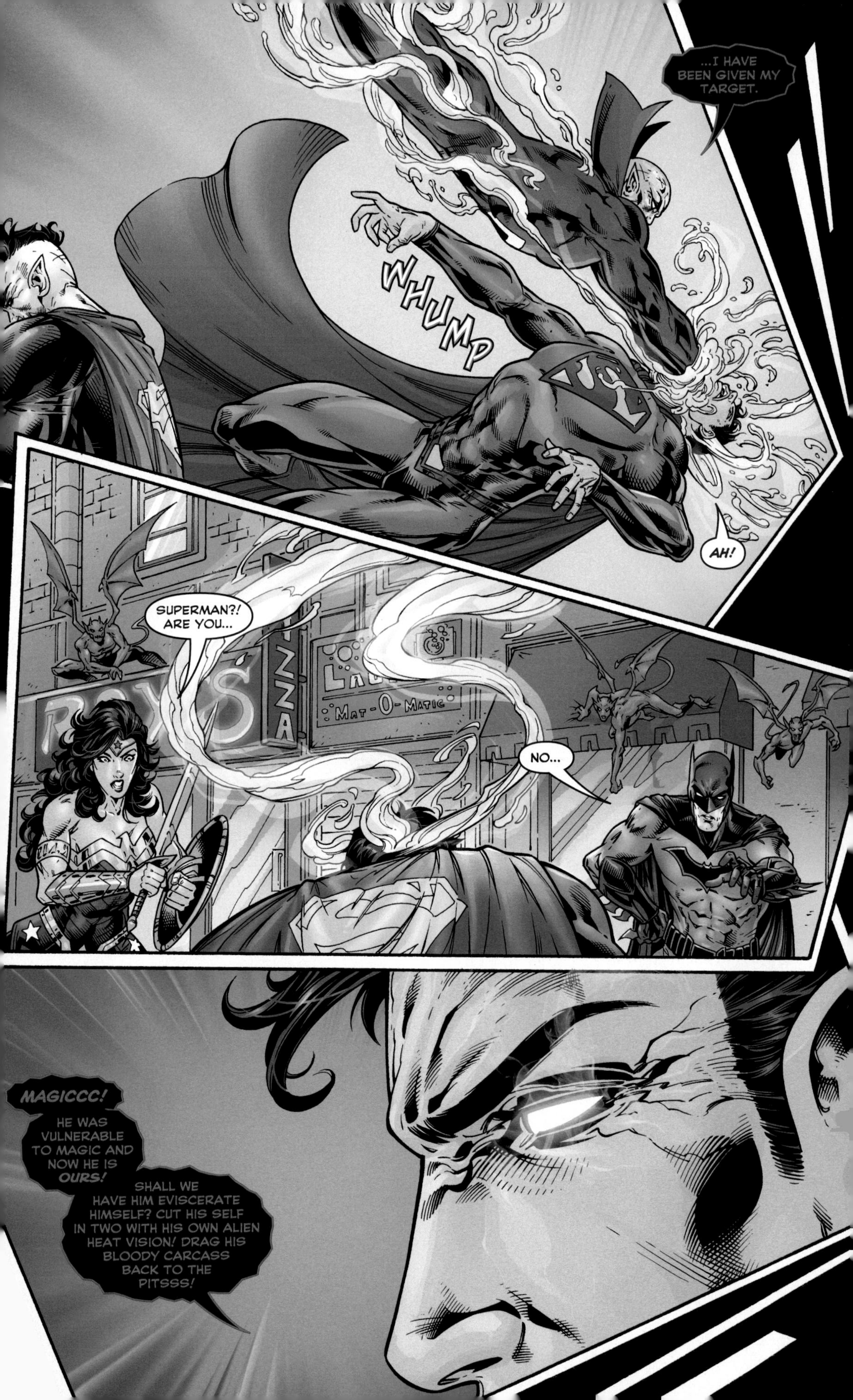
...I HAVE BEEN GIVEN MY TARGET.
WHUMP
AH!
SUPERMAN?! ARE YOU...
ZZA
Mat-O-Matic
NO...
MAGICCC!
HE WAS VULNERABLE TO MAGIC AND NOW HE IS OURS!
SHALL WE HAVE HIM EVISCERATE HIMSELF? CUT HIS SELF IN TWO WITH HIS OWN ALIEN HEAT VISION! DRAG HIS BLOODY CARCASS BACK TO THE PITSSS!

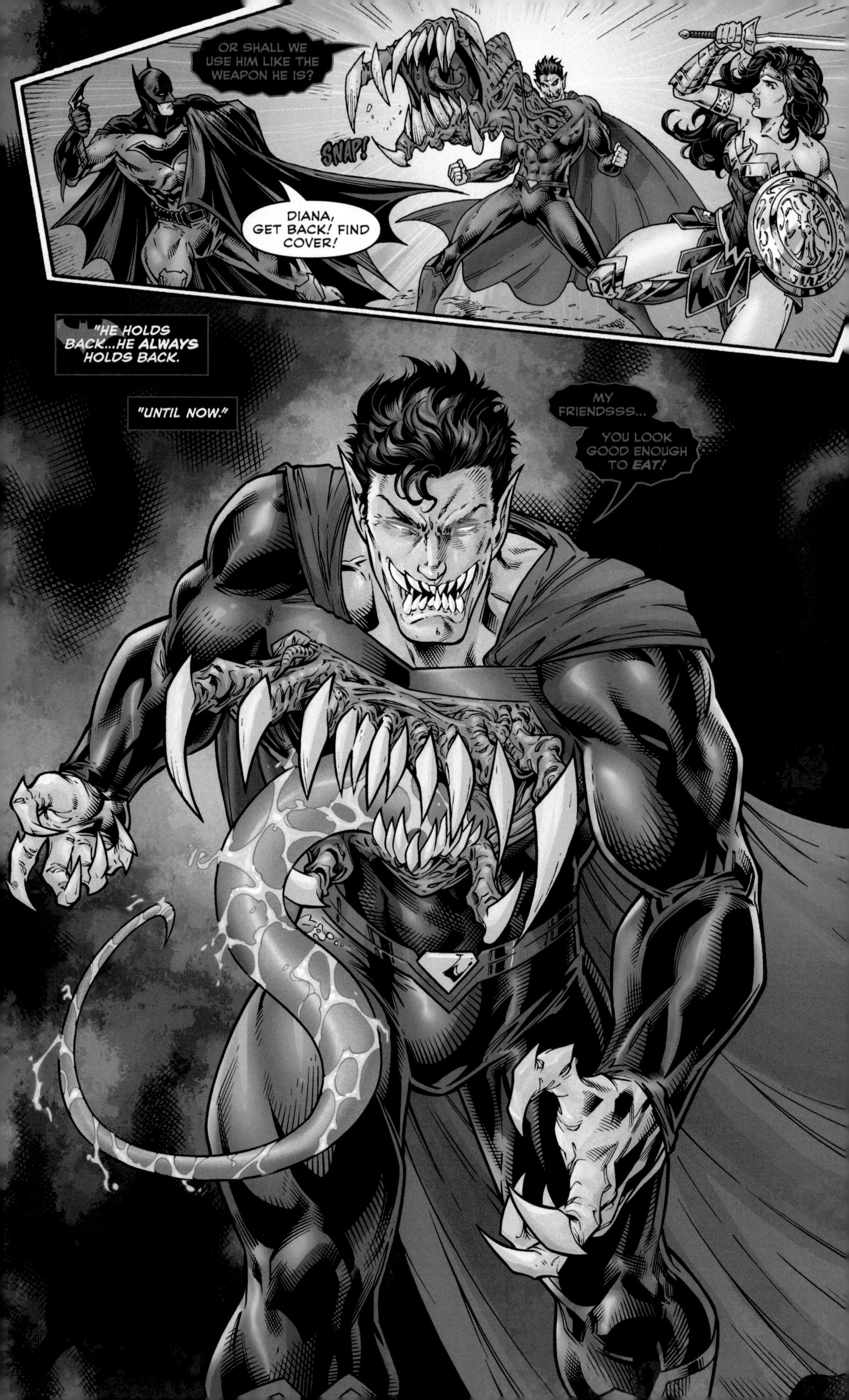
OR SHALL WE USE HIM LIKE THE WEAPON HE IS?
SNAP!
DIANA, GET BACK! FIND COVER!
"HE HOLDS BACK...HE ALWAYS HOLDS BACK.
"UNTIL NOW."
MY FRIENDSSS...
YOU LOOK GOOD ENOUGH TO EAT!

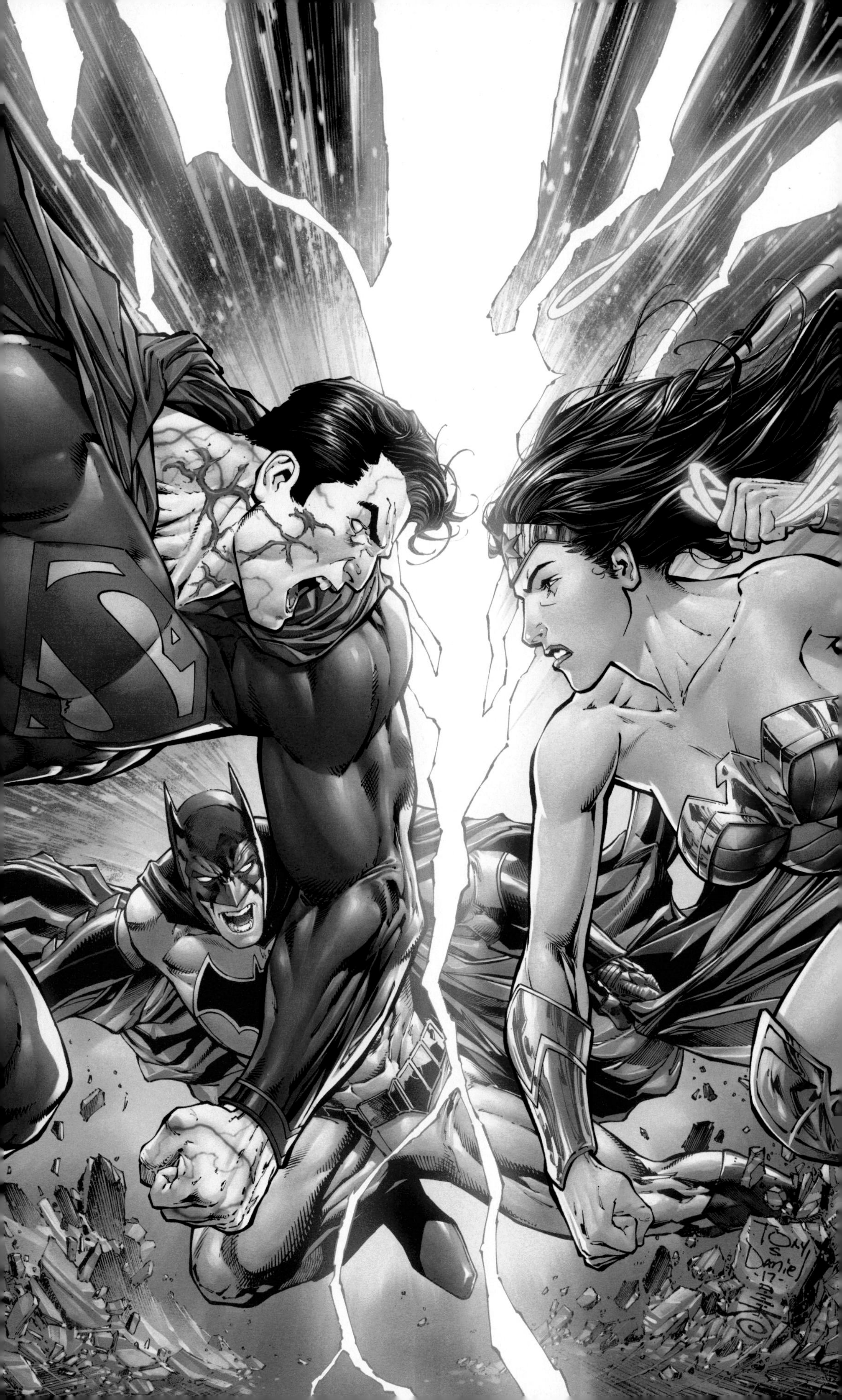

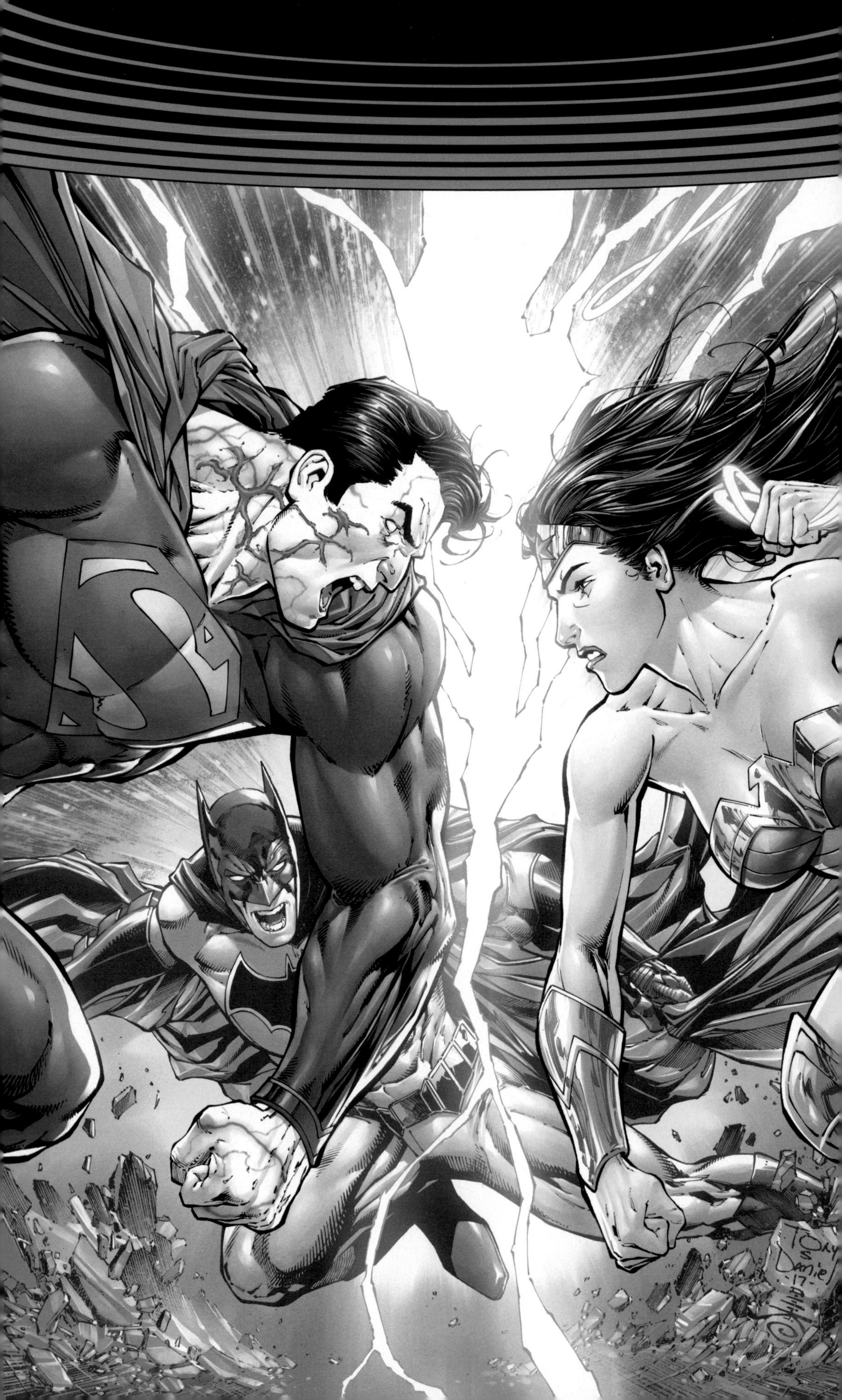
Tony S Daniel -17-

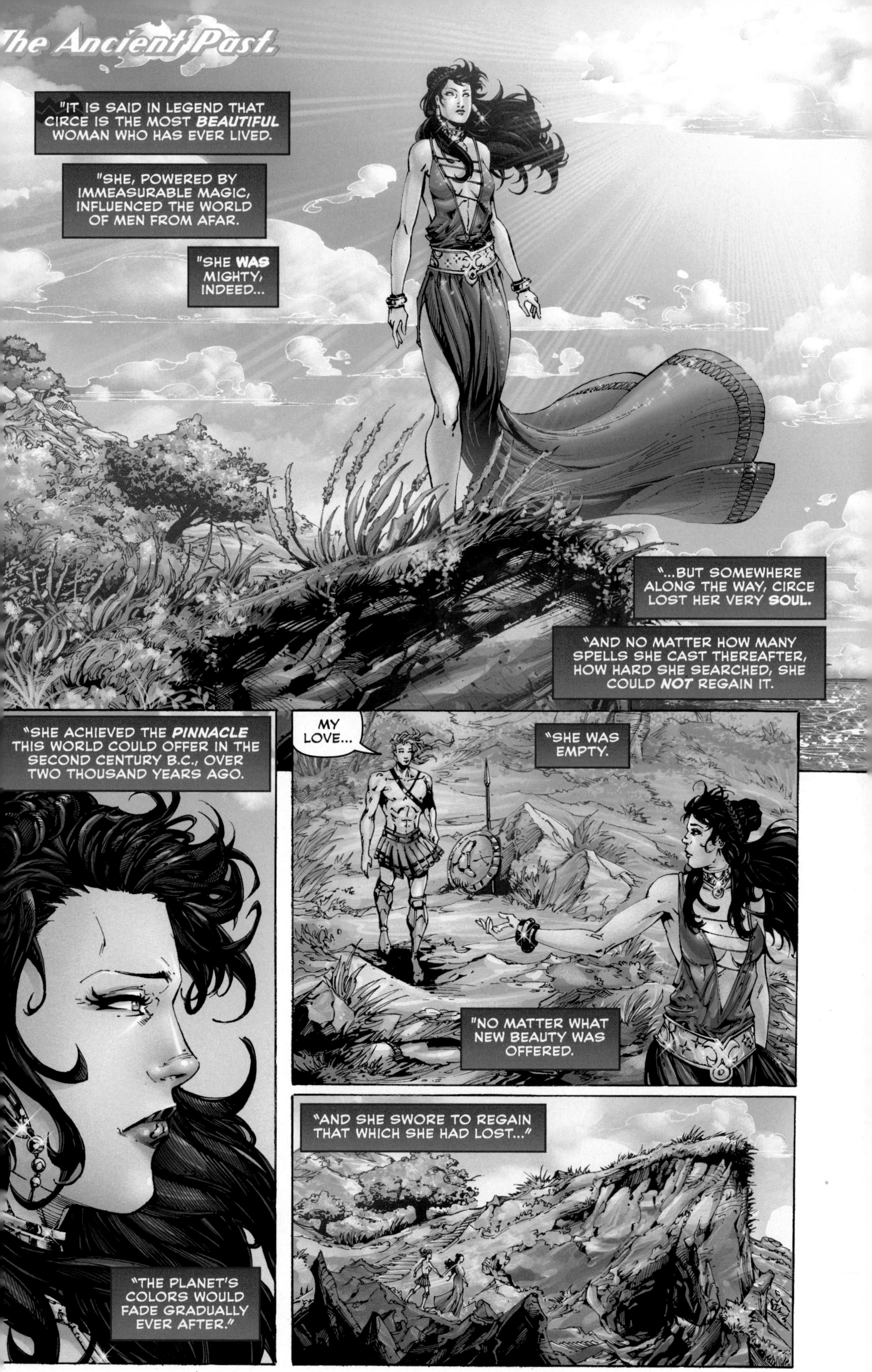
The Ancient Past.
"IT IS SAID IN LEGEND THAT CIRCE IS THE MOST BEAUTIFUL WOMAN WHO HAS EVER LIVED.
"SHE, POWERED BY IMMEASURABLE MAGIC, INFLUENCED THE WORLD OF MEN FROM AFAR.
"SHE WAS MIGHTY, INDEED...
"...BUT SOMEWHERE ALONG THE WAY, CIRCE LOST HER VERY SOUL.
"AND NO MATTER HOW MANY SPELLS SHE CAST THEREAFTER, HOW HARD SHE SEARCHED, SHE COULD NOT REGAIN IT.
"SHE ACHIEVED THE PINNACLE THIS WORLD COULD OFFER IN THE SECOND CENTURY B.C., OVER TWO THOUSAND YEARS AGO.
"THE PLANET'S COLORS WOULD FADE GRADUALLY EVER AFTER."
MY LOVE...
"SHE WAS EMPTY.
"NO MATTER WHAT NEW BEAUTY WAS OFFERED.
"AND SHE SWORE TO REGAIN THAT WHICH SHE HAD LOST..."

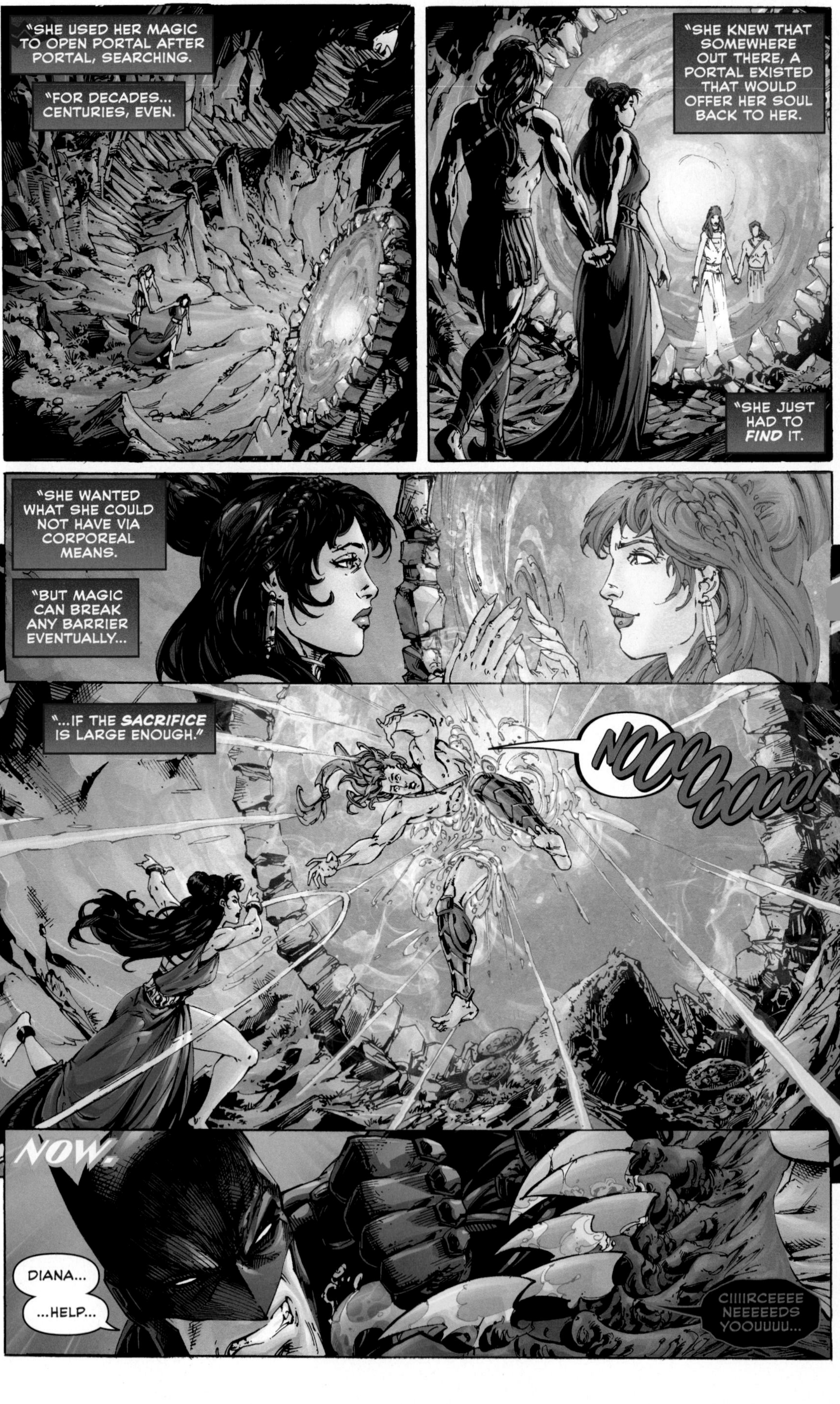
"SHE USED HER MAGIC TO OPEN PORTAL AFTER PORTAL, SEARCHING.
"FOR DECADES... CENTURIES, EVEN.
"SHE KNEW THAT SOMEWHERE OUT THERE, A PORTAL EXISTED THAT WOULD OFFER HER SOUL BACK TO HER.
"SHE JUST HAD TO FIND IT.
"SHE WANTED WHAT SHE COULD NOT HAVE VIA CORPOREAL MEANS.
"BUT MAGIC CAN BREAK ANY BARRIER EVENTUALLY...
"...IF THE SACRIFICE IS LARGE ENOUGH."
NOOOOOOOOO!
NOW.
DIANA...
...HELP...
CIIIRCEEEE NEEEEEDS YOOUUUU...

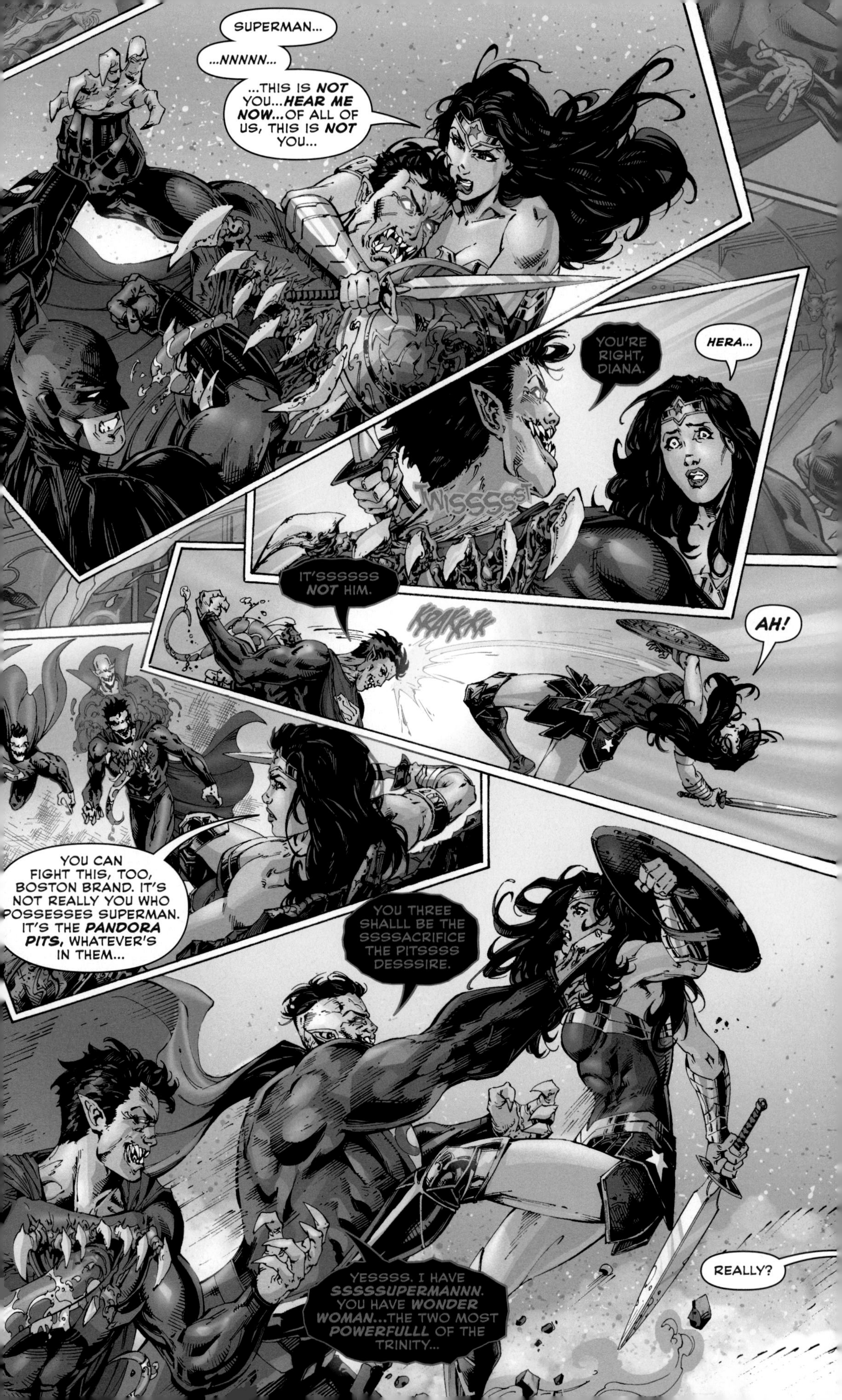
SUPERMAN...
...NNNNN...
...THIS IS NOT YOU...HEAR ME NOW...OF ALL OF US, THIS IS NOT YOU...
YOU'RE RIGHT, DIANA.
HERA...
TWISSSSST
IT'SSSSSS NOT HIM.
KRAKKKK
AH!
YOU CAN FIGHT THIS, TOO, BOSTON BRAND. IT'S NOT REALLY YOU WHO POSSESSES SUPERMAN. IT'S THE PANDORA PITS, WHATEVER'S IN THEM...
YOU THREE SHALLL BE THE SSSSACRIFICE THE PITSSSS DESSSIRE.
REALLY?
YESSSS. I HAVE SSSSSUPERMANNN. YOU HAVE WONDER WOMAN...THE TWO MOST POWERFULLL OF THE TRINITY...

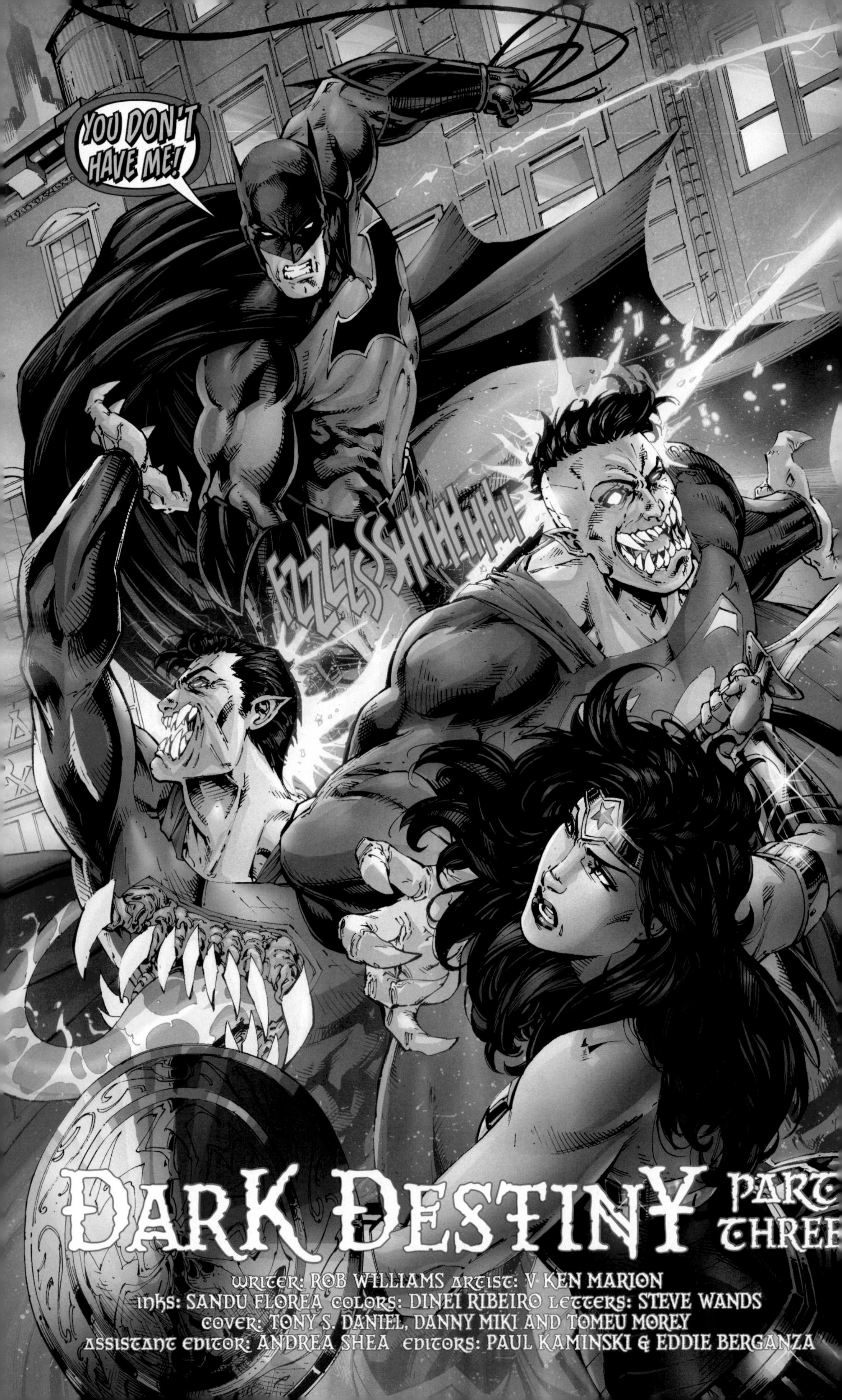

YOU DON'T HAVE ME!
FZZZZSSHHHHHHH
DARK DESTINY PART THREE
WRITER: ROB WILLIAMS ARTIST: V KEN MARION
INKS: SANDU FLOREA COLORS: DINEI RIBEIRO LETTERS: STEVE WANDS
COVER: TONY S. DANIEL, DANNY MIKI AND TOMEU MOREY
ASSISTANT EDITOR: ANDREA SHEA EDITORS: PAUL KAMINSKI & EDDIE BERGANZA

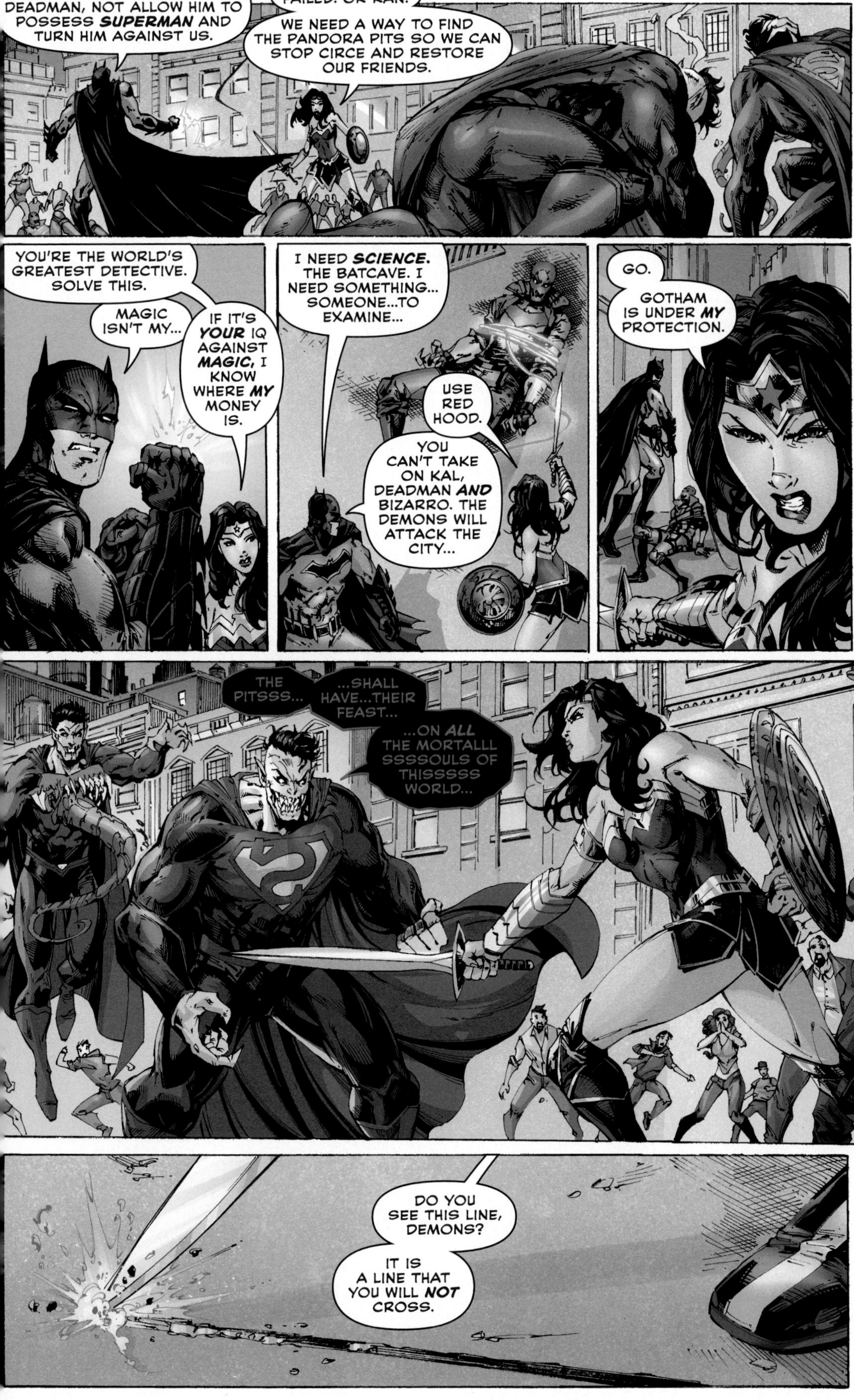
CONSTANTINE WAS SUPPOSED TO ***SAVE*** DEADMAN, NOT ALLOW HIM TO POSSESS ***SUPERMAN*** AND TURN HIM AGAINST US.
CONSTANTINE FAILED. OR RAN.
WE NEED A WAY TO FIND THE PANDORA PITS SO WE CAN STOP CIRCE AND RESTORE OUR FRIENDS.
YOU'RE THE WORLD'S GREATEST DETECTIVE. SOLVE THIS.
MAGIC ISN'T MY...
IF IT'S ***YOUR*** IQ AGAINST ***MAGIC,*** I KNOW WHERE ***MY*** MONEY IS.
I NEED ***SCIENCE.*** THE BATCAVE. I NEED SOMETHING... SOMEONE...TO EXAMINE...
USE RED HOOD.
YOU CAN'T TAKE ON KAL, DEADMAN ***AND*** BIZARRO. THE DEMONS WILL ATTACK THE CITY...
GO.
GOTHAM IS UNDER ***MY*** PROTECTION.
THE PITSSS...
...SHALL HAVE...THEIR FEAST...
...ON ***ALL*** THE MORTALLL SSSSOULS OF THISSSSS WORLD...
DO YOU SEE THIS LINE, DEMONS?
IT IS A LINE THAT YOU WILL ***NOT*** CROSS.

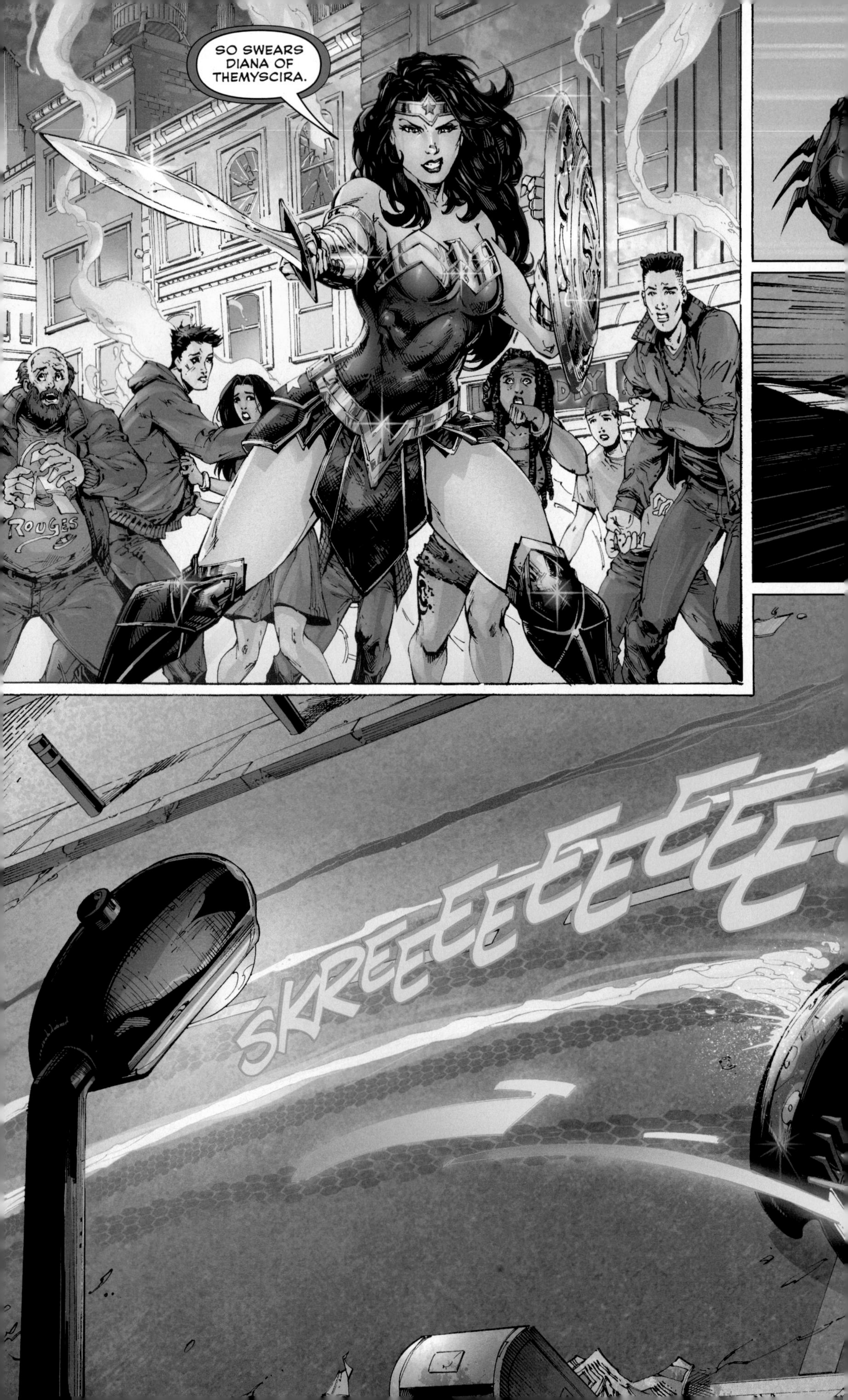
SO SWEARS DIANA OF THEMYSCIRA.
ROUGES
SKREEEEEEEEE

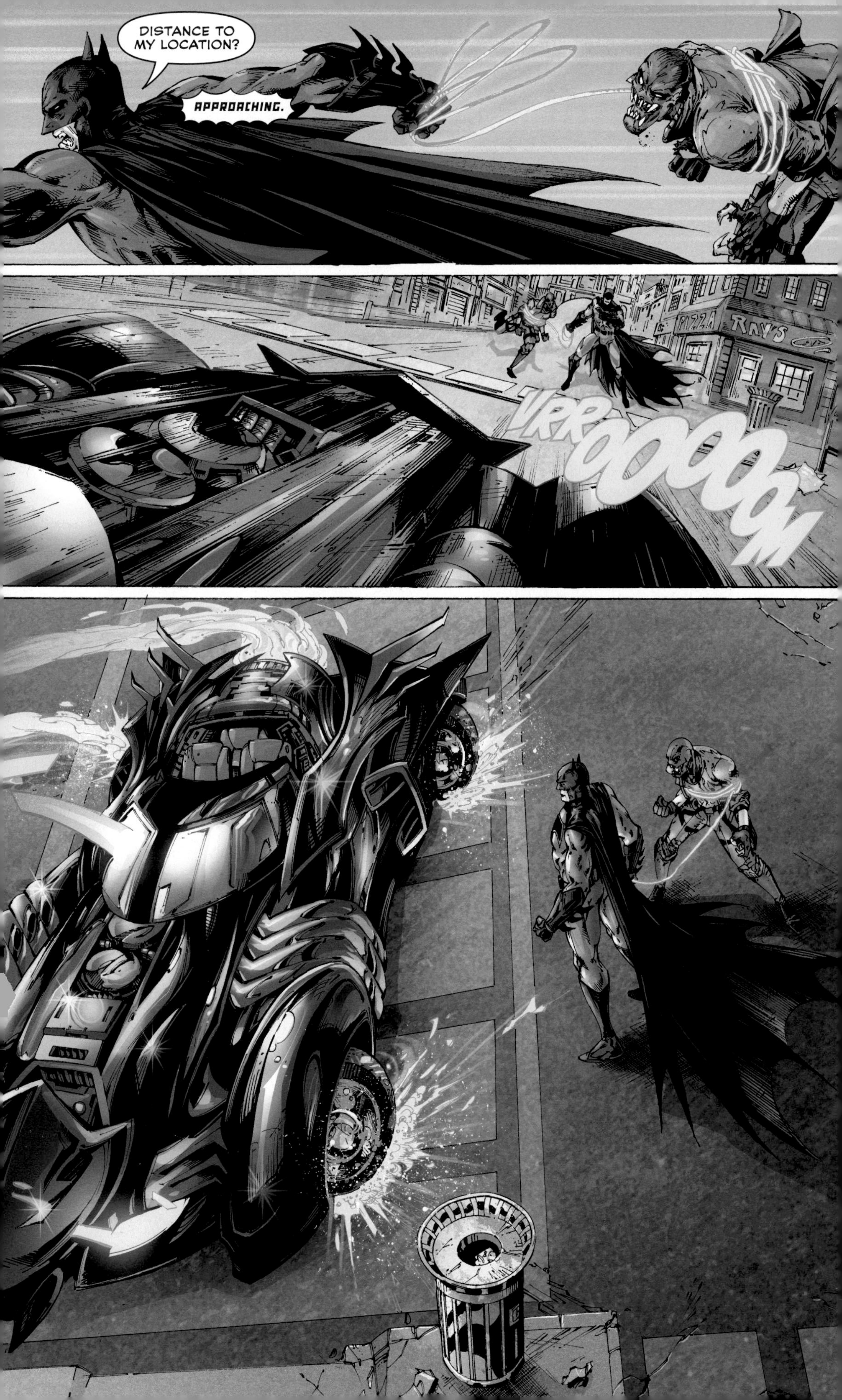
DISTANCE TO MY LOCATION?
APPROACHING.
PIZZA
RAY'S
VRROOOOOM

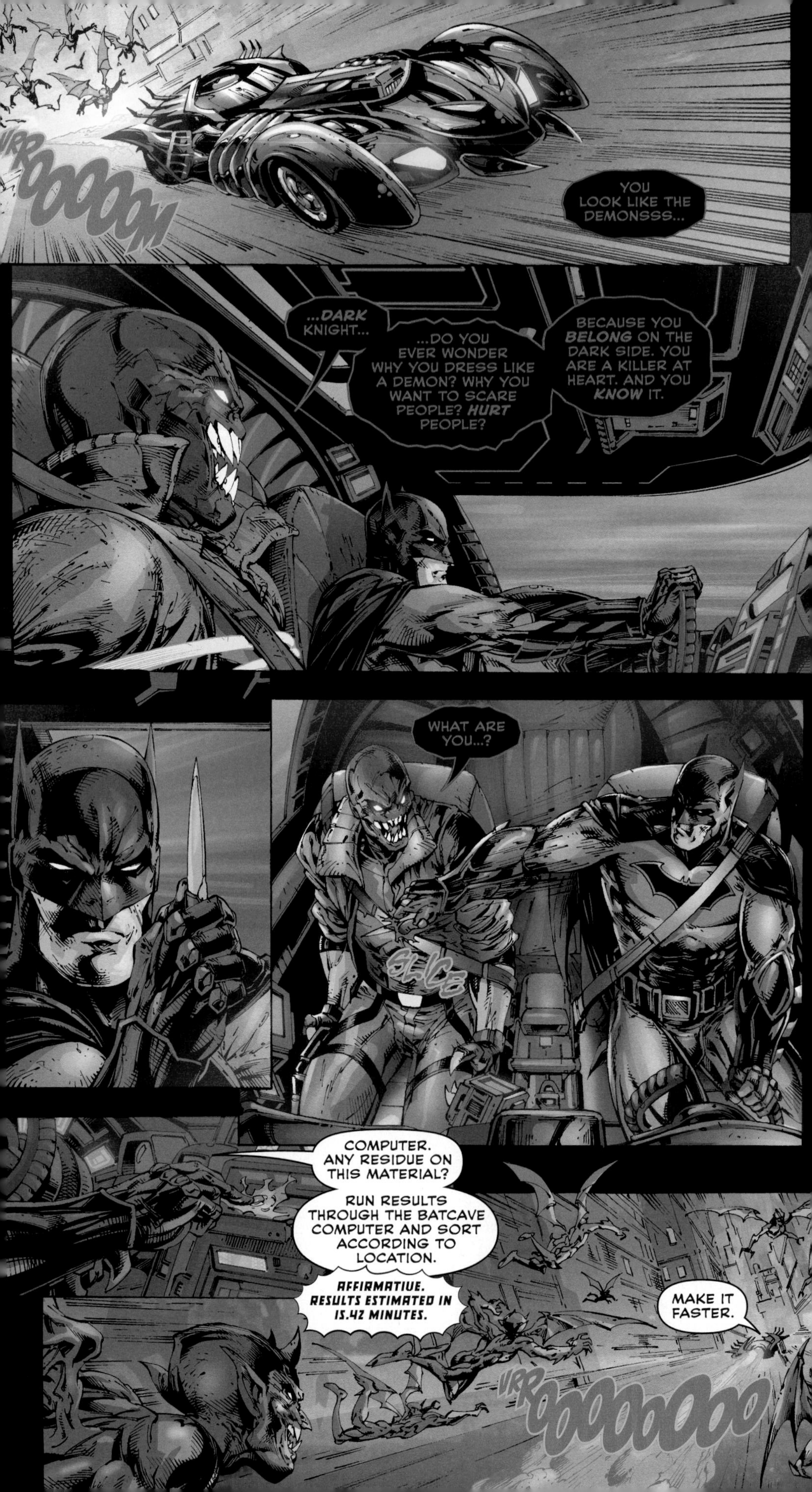
VRROOOOOM
YOU LOOK LIKE THE DEMONSSS...
...DARK KNIGHT...
...DO YOU EVER WONDER WHY YOU DRESS LIKE A DEMON? WHY YOU WANT TO SCARE PEOPLE? HURT PEOPLE?
BECAUSE YOU BELONG ON THE DARK SIDE. YOU ARE A KILLER AT HEART. AND YOU KNOW IT.
WHAT ARE YOU...?
SLICE
COMPUTER. ANY RESIDUE ON THIS MATERIAL?
RUN RESULTS THROUGH THE BATCAVE COMPUTER AND SORT ACCORDING TO LOCATION.
AFFIRMATIVE. RESULTS ESTIMATED IN 15.42 MINUTES.
MAKE IT FASTER.
VRROOOOOOOO

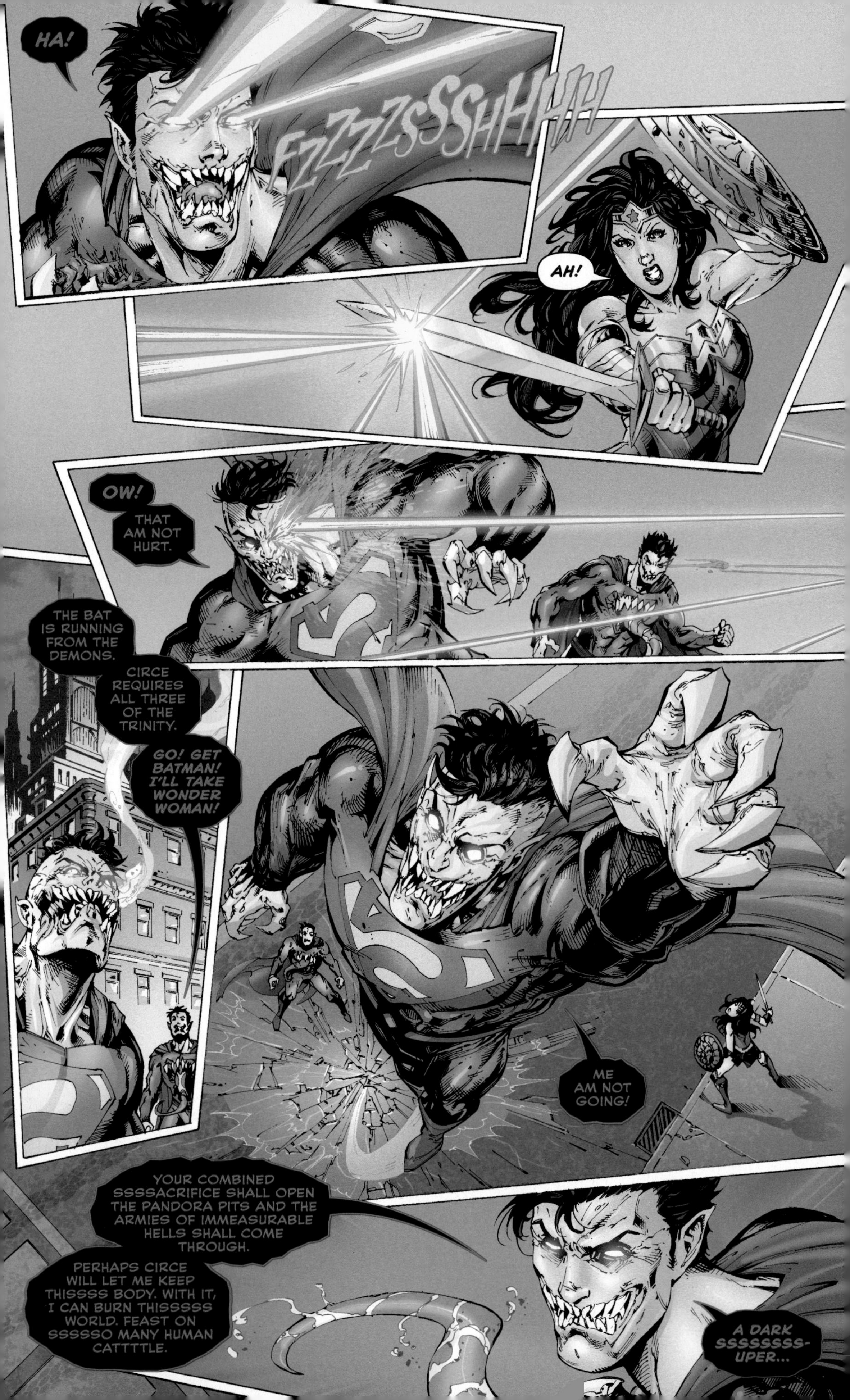
HA!
FZZZZSSSHHHHH
AH!
OW!
THAT AM NOT HURT.
THE BAT IS RUNNING FROM THE DEMONS.
CIRCE REQUIRES ALL THREE OF THE TRINITY.
GO! GET BATMAN! I'LL TAKE WONDER WOMAN!
ME AM NOT GOING!
YOUR COMBINED SSSSACRIFICE SHALL OPEN THE PANDORA PITS AND THE ARMIES OF IMMEASURABLE HELLS SHALL COME THROUGH.
PERHAPS CIRCE WILL LET ME KEEP THISSSS BODY. WITH IT, I CAN BURN THISSSSS WORLD. FEAST ON SSSSSO MANY HUMAN CATTTTLE.
A DARK SSSSSSSS-UPER...

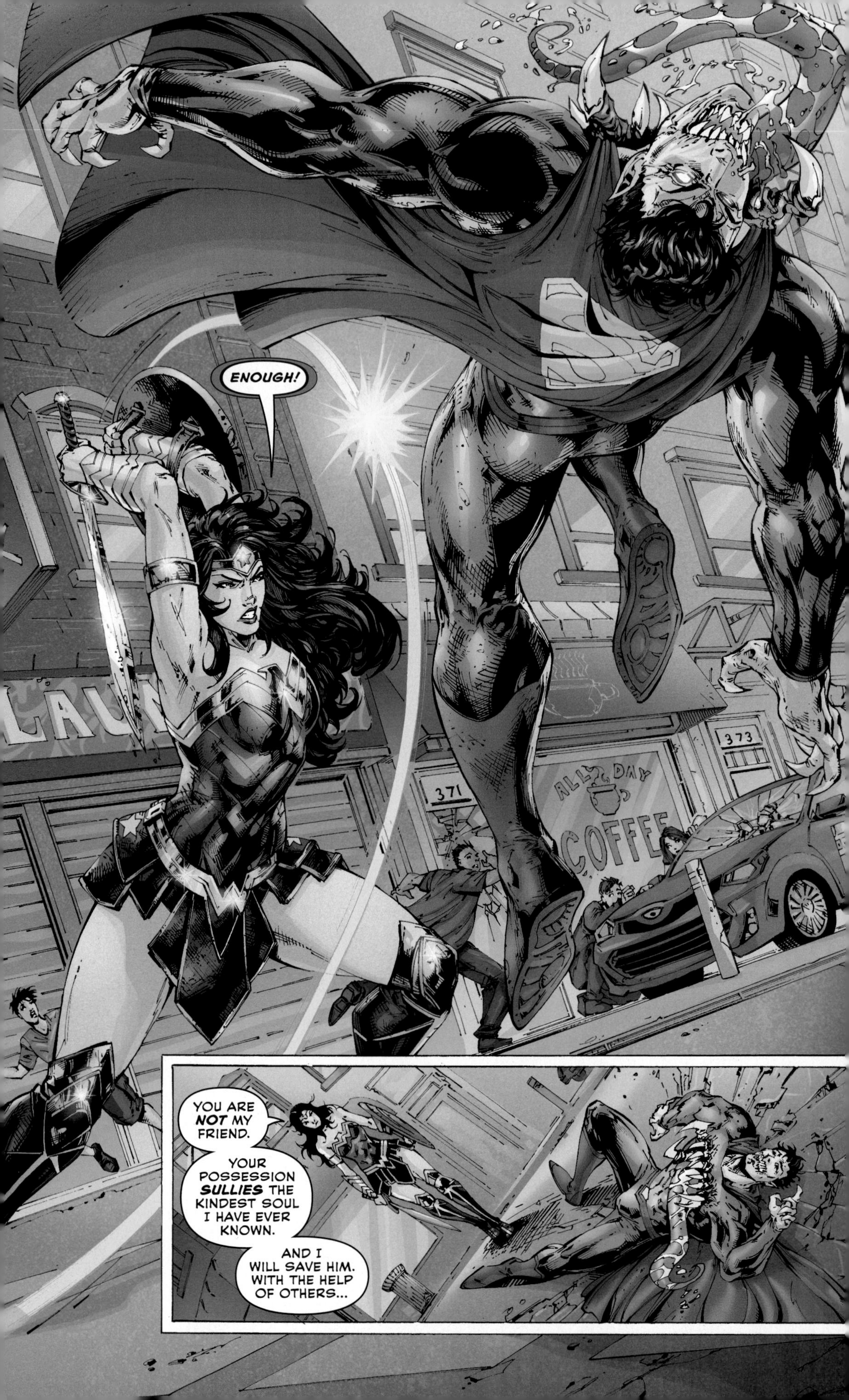
ENOUGH!
LAUN
371
ALL DAY
COFFEE
373
YOU ARE NOT MY FRIEND.
YOUR POSSESSION SULLIES THE KINDEST SOUL I HAVE EVER KNOWN.
AND I WILL SAVE HIM. WITH THE HELP OF OTHERS...

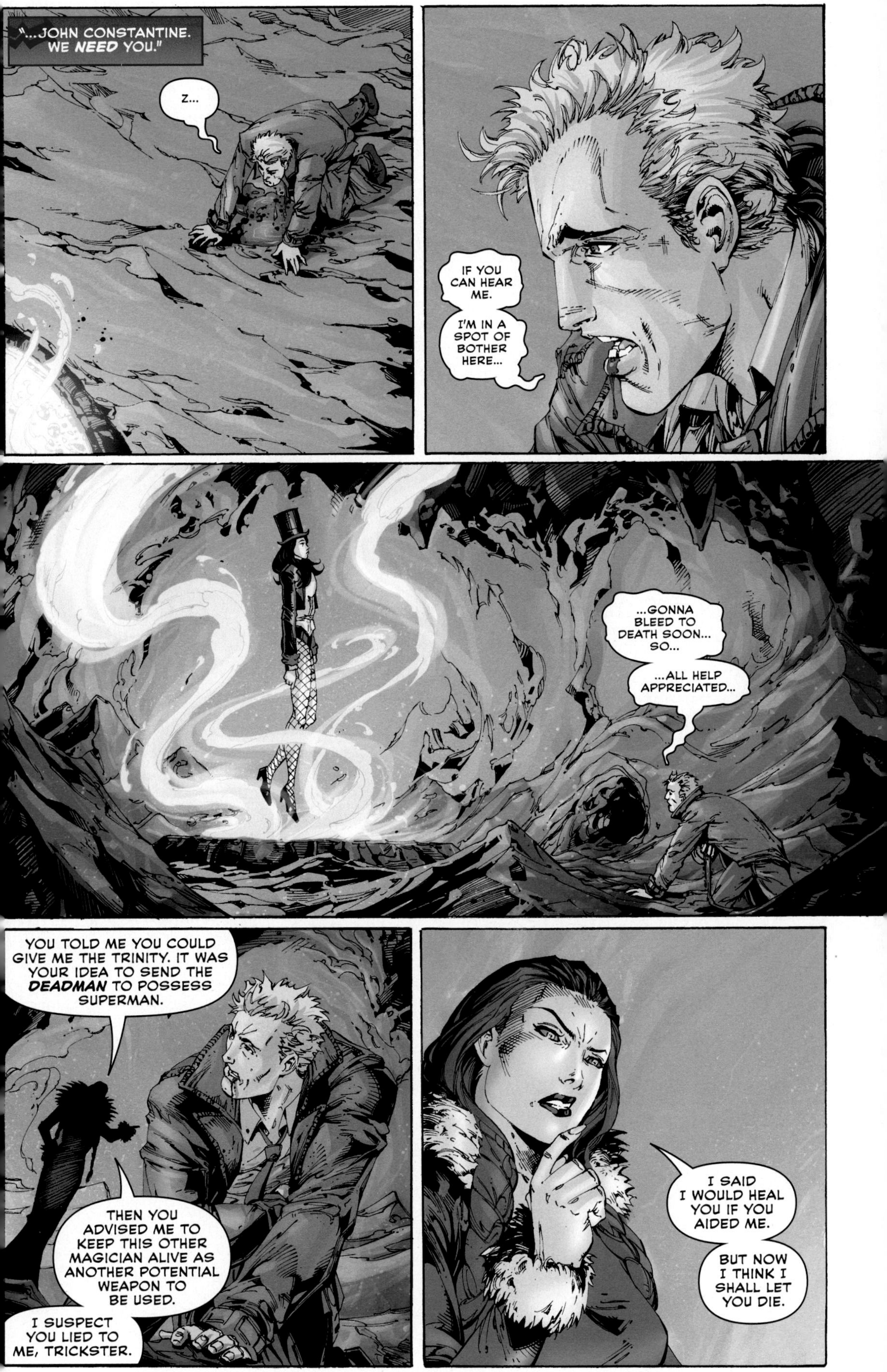
"...JOHN CONSTANTINE. WE NEED YOU."
Z...
IF YOU CAN HEAR ME.
I'M IN A SPOT OF BOTHER HERE...
...GONNA BLEED TO DEATH SOON... SO...
...ALL HELP APPRECIATED...
YOU TOLD ME YOU COULD GIVE ME THE TRINITY. IT WAS YOUR IDEA TO SEND THE DEADMAN TO POSSESS SUPERMAN.
THEN YOU ADVISED ME TO KEEP THIS OTHER MAGICIAN ALIVE AS ANOTHER POTENTIAL WEAPON TO BE USED.
I SUSPECT YOU LIED TO ME, TRICKSTER.
I SAID I WOULD HEAL YOU IF YOU AIDED ME.
BUT NOW I THINK I SHALL LET YOU DIE.

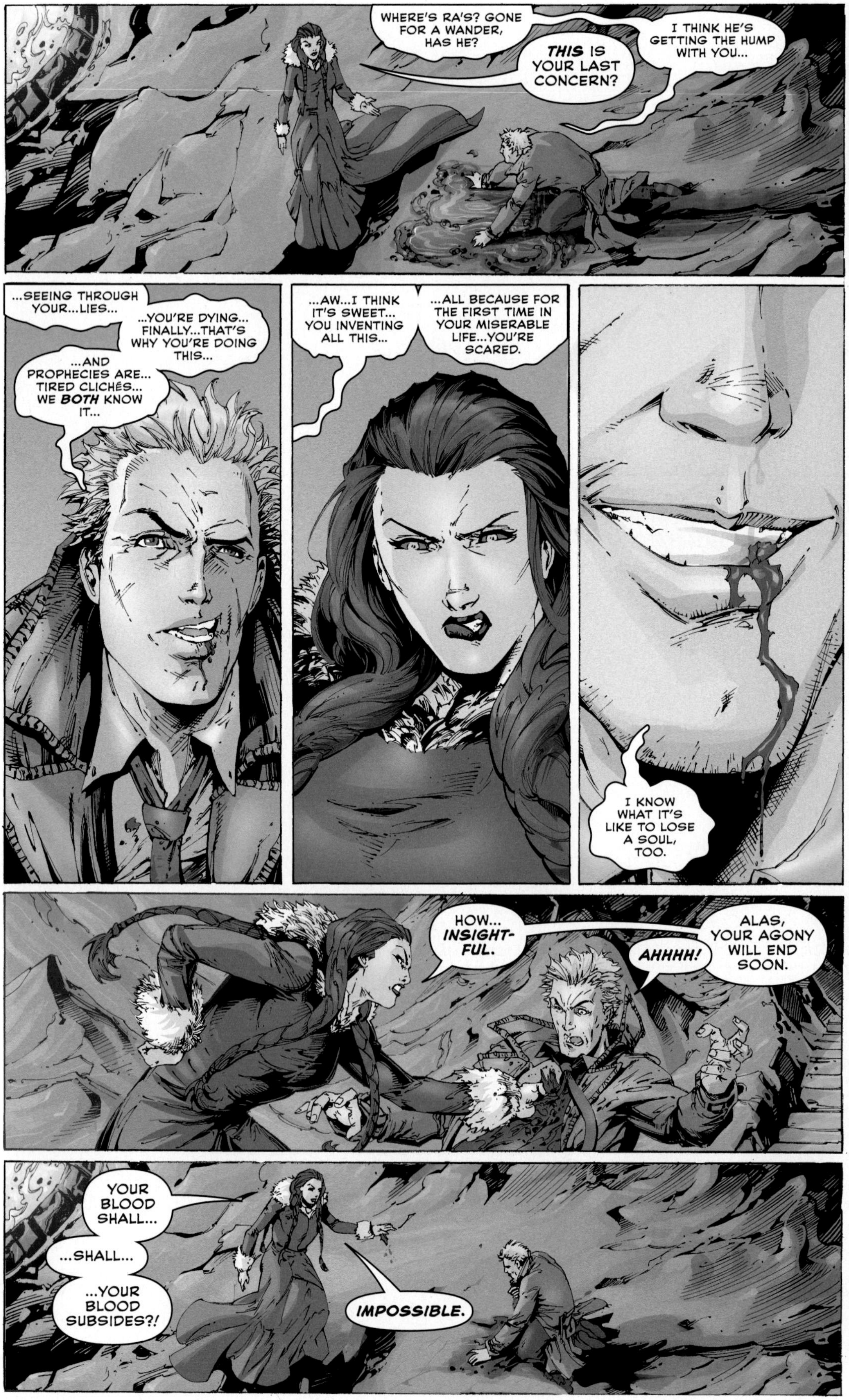
WHERE'S RA'S? GONE FOR A WANDER, HAS HE?
THIS IS YOUR LAST CONCERN?
I THINK HE'S GETTING THE HUMP WITH YOU...
...SEEING THROUGH YOUR...LIES...
...YOU'RE DYING... FINALLY...THAT'S WHY YOU'RE DOING THIS...
...AND PROPHECIES ARE... TIRED CLICHÉS... WE BOTH KNOW IT...
...AW...I THINK IT'S SWEET... YOU INVENTING ALL THIS...
...ALL BECAUSE FOR THE FIRST TIME IN YOUR MISERABLE LIFE...YOU'RE SCARED.
I KNOW WHAT IT'S LIKE TO LOSE A SOUL, TOO.
HOW... INSIGHTFUL.
AHHHH!
ALAS, YOUR AGONY WILL END SOON.
YOUR BLOOD SHALL...
...SHALL...
...YOUR BLOOD SUBSIDES?!
IMPOSSIBLE.

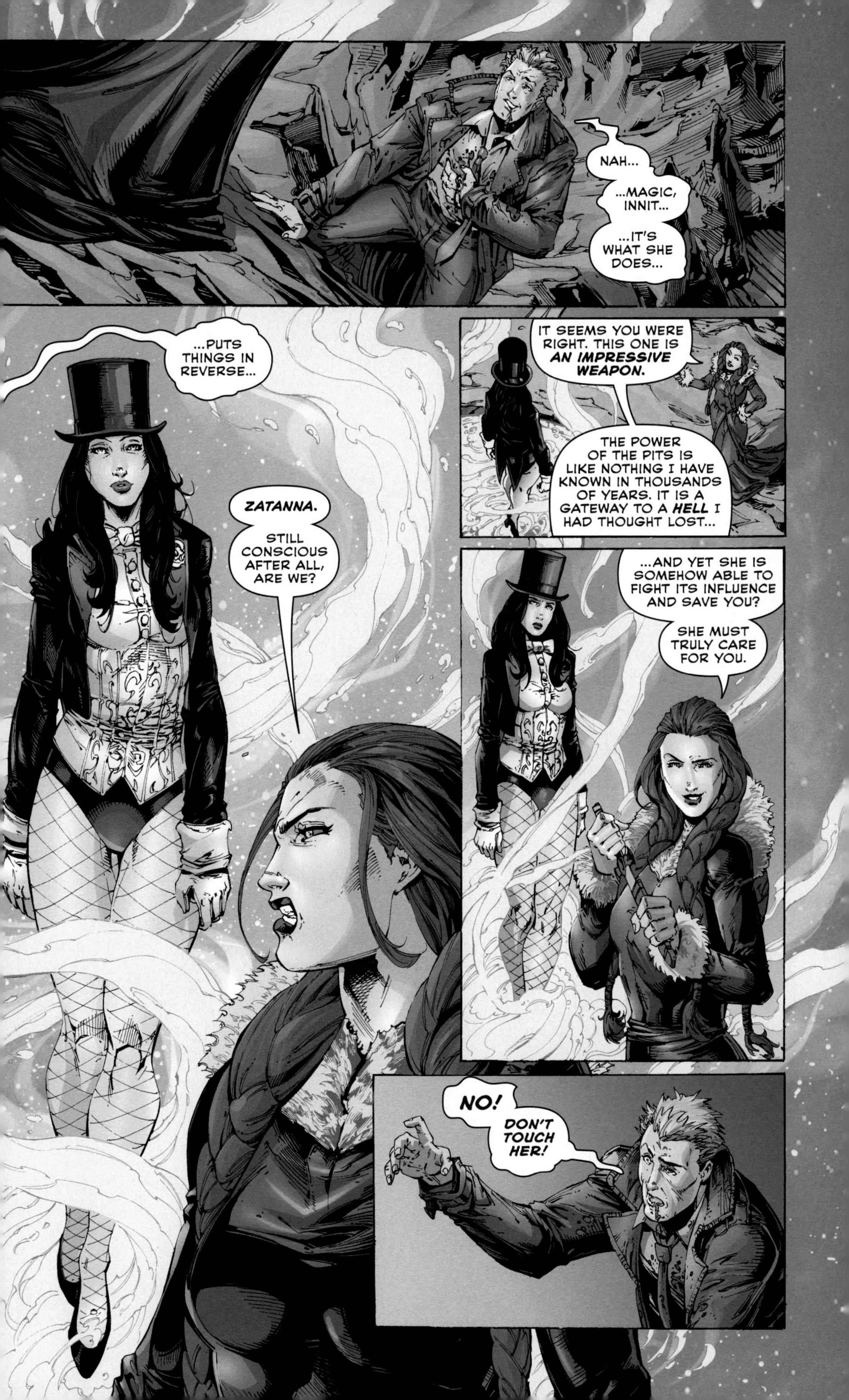
NAH...
...MAGIC, INNIT...
...IT'S WHAT SHE DOES...
...PUTS THINGS IN REVERSE...
IT SEEMS YOU WERE RIGHT. THIS ONE IS ***AN IMPRESSIVE WEAPON.***
THE POWER OF THE PITS IS LIKE NOTHING I HAVE KNOWN IN THOUSANDS OF YEARS. IT IS A GATEWAY TO A ***HELL*** I HAD THOUGHT LOST...
***ZATANNA.***
STILL CONSCIOUS AFTER ALL, ARE WE?
...AND YET SHE IS SOMEHOW ABLE TO FIGHT ITS INFLUENCE AND SAVE YOU?
SHE MUST TRULY CARE FOR YOU.
***NO!***
***DON'T TOUCH HER!***

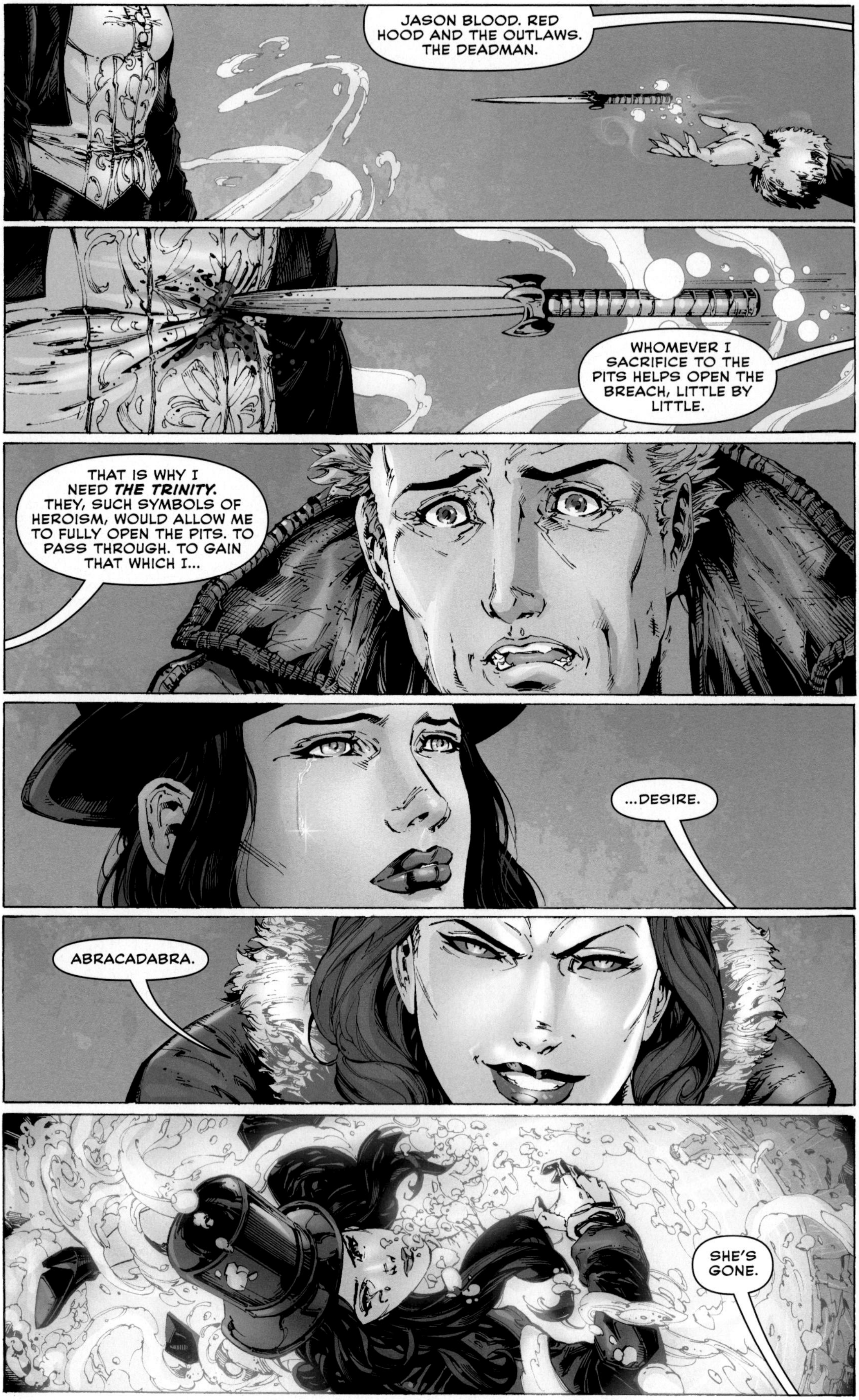
JASON BLOOD. RED HOOD AND THE OUTLAWS. THE DEADMAN.
WHOMEVER I SACRIFICE TO THE PITS HELPS OPEN THE BREACH, LITTLE BY LITTLE.
THAT IS WHY I NEED **THE TRINITY.** THEY, SUCH SYMBOLS OF HEROISM, WOULD ALLOW ME TO FULLY OPEN THE PITS. TO PASS THROUGH. TO GAIN THAT WHICH I...
...DESIRE.
ABRACADABRA.
SHE'S GONE.

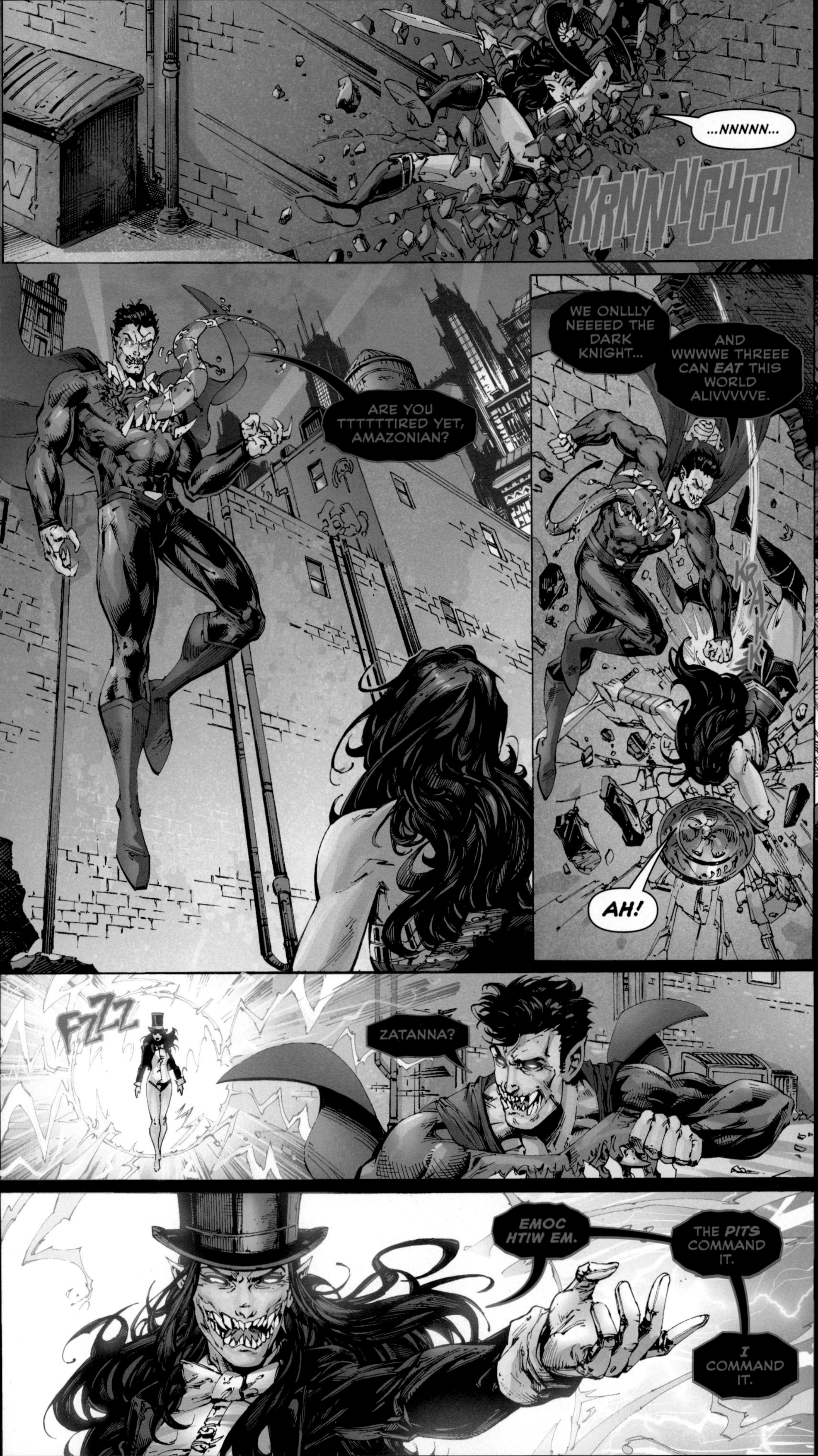

...NNNNN...
KRNNNCHHH
ARE YOU TTTTTTIRED YET, AMAZONIAN?
WE ONLLLY NEEEED THE DARK KNIGHT...
AND WWWWE THREEE CAN *EAT* THIS WORLD ALIVVVVVE.
KRAKK
AH!
FZZZ
ZATANNA?
EMOC HTIW EM.
THE *PITS* COMMAND IT.
*I* COMMAND IT.

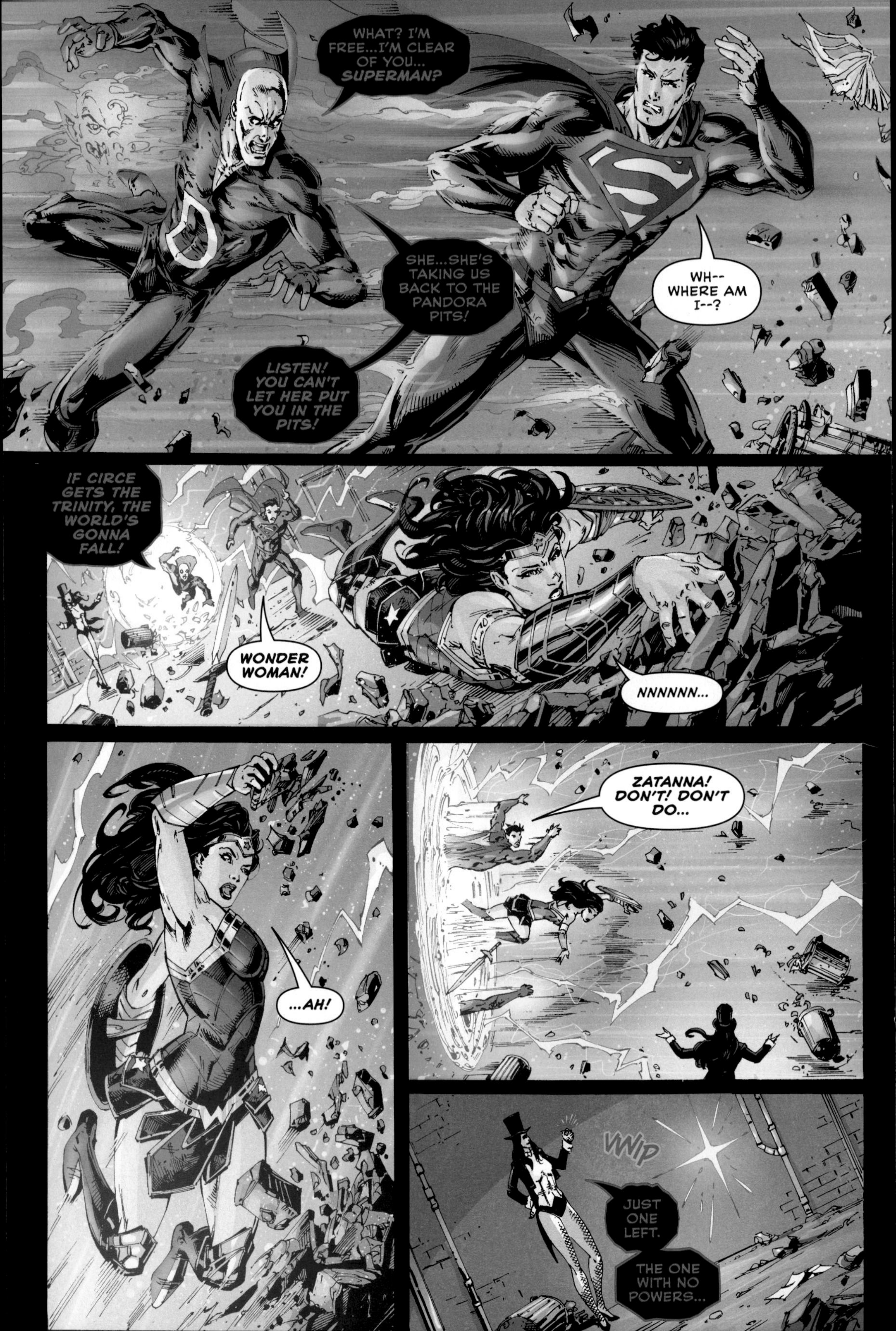
WHAT? I'M FREE...I'M CLEAR OF YOU... SUPERMAN?
SHE...SHE'S TAKING US BACK TO THE PANDORA PITS!
LISTEN! YOU CAN'T LET HER PUT YOU IN THE PITS!
WH-- WHERE AM I--?
IF CIRCE GETS THE TRINITY, THE WORLD'S GONNA FALL!
WONDER WOMAN!
NNNNNN...
...AH!
ZATANNA! DON'T! DON'T DO...
VVIP
JUST ONE LEFT.
THE ONE WITH NO POWERS...

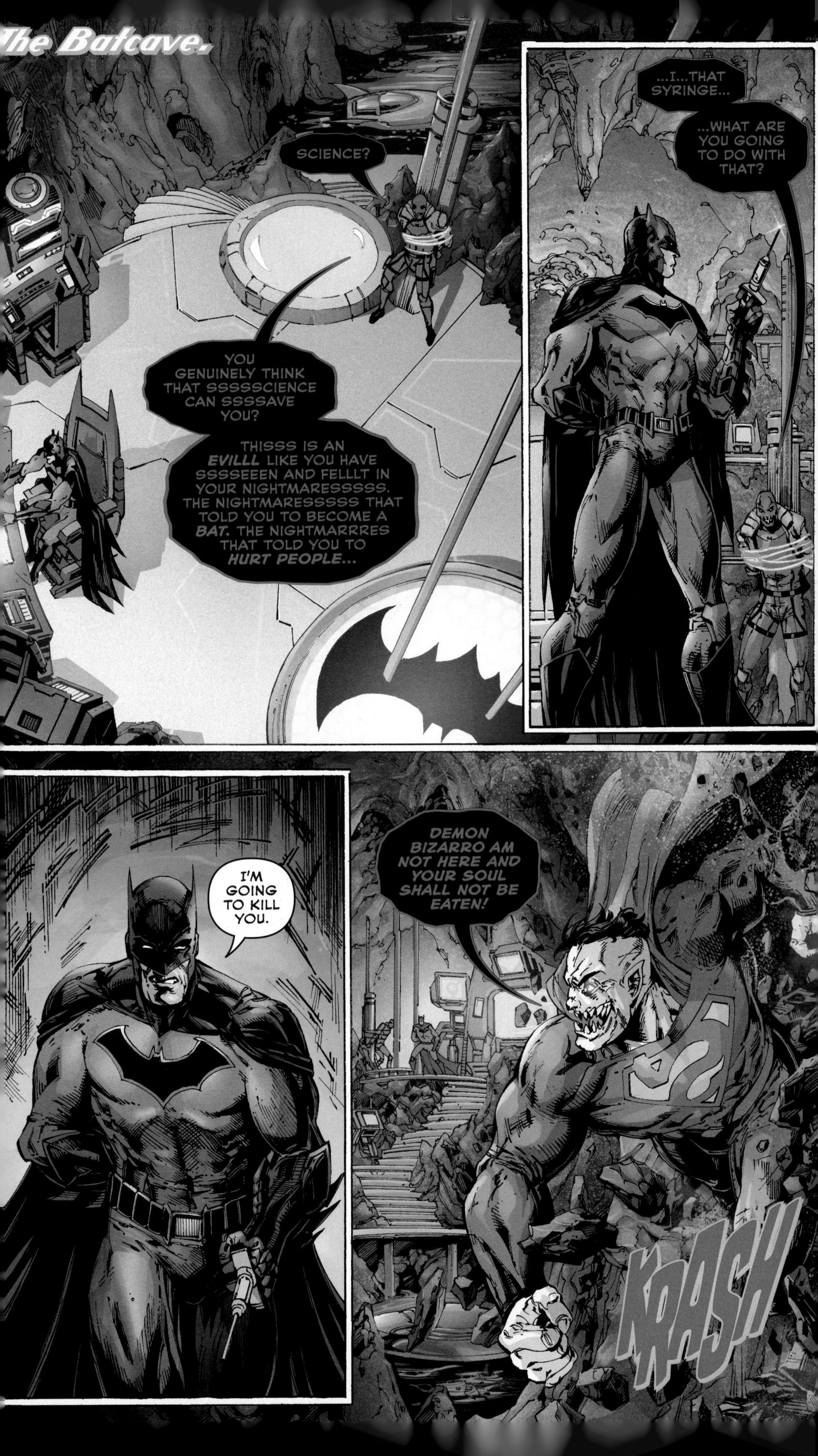
The Batcave.
SCIENCE?
YOU GENUINELY THINK THAT SSSSSCIENCE CAN SSSSAVE YOU?
THISSS IS AN EVILLL LIKE YOU HAVE SSSSEEEN AND FELLLT IN YOUR NIGHTMARESSSSS. THE NIGHTMARESSSSS THAT TOLD YOU TO BECOME A BAT. THE NIGHTMARRRES THAT TOLD YOU TO HURT PEOPLE...
...I...THAT SYRINGE...
...WHAT ARE YOU GOING TO DO WITH THAT?
I'M GOING TO KILL YOU.
DEMON BIZARRO AM NOT HERE AND YOUR SOUL SHALL NOT BE EATEN!
KRASH

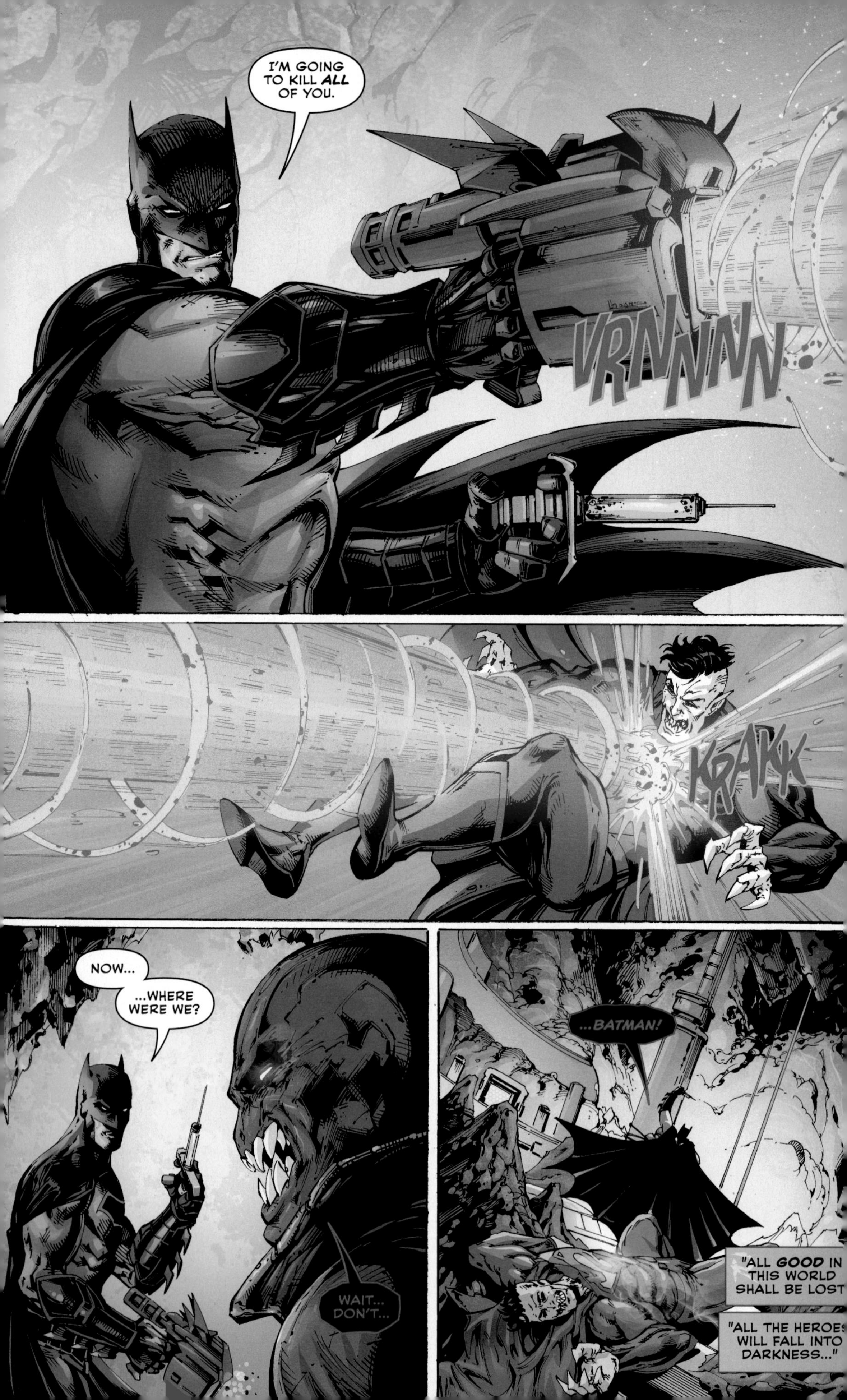

I'M GOING TO KILL ALL OF YOU.
VRNNNN
KRAKK
NOW...
...WHERE WERE WE?
WAIT... DON'T...
...BATMAN!
"ALL GOOD IN THIS WORLD SHALL BE LOST
"ALL THE HEROES WILL FALL INTO DARKNESS..."

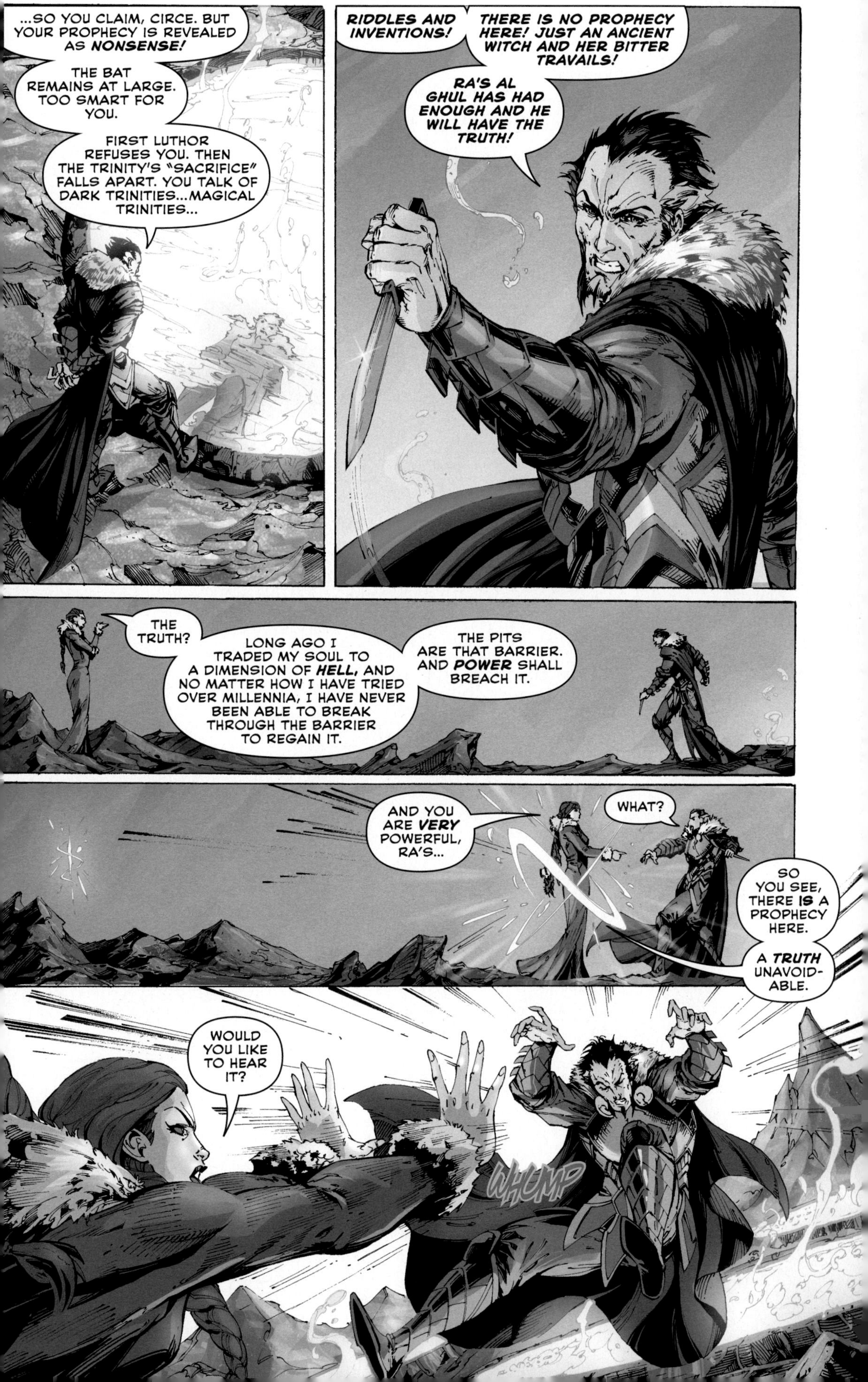

...SO YOU CLAIM, CIRCE. BUT YOUR PROPHECY IS REVEALED AS NONSENSE!
THE BAT REMAINS AT LARGE. TOO SMART FOR YOU.
FIRST LUTHOR REFUSES YOU. THEN THE TRINITY'S "SACRIFICE" FALLS APART. YOU TALK OF DARK TRINITIES...MAGICAL TRINITIES...
RIDDLES AND INVENTIONS!
THERE IS NO PROPHECY HERE! JUST AN ANCIENT WITCH AND HER BITTER TRAVAILS!
RA'S AL GHUL HAS HAD ENOUGH AND HE WILL HAVE THE TRUTH!
THE TRUTH?
LONG AGO I TRADED MY SOUL TO A DIMENSION OF HELL, AND NO MATTER HOW I HAVE TRIED OVER MILLENNIA, I HAVE NEVER BEEN ABLE TO BREAK THROUGH THE BARRIER TO REGAIN IT.
THE PITS ARE THAT BARRIER. AND POWER SHALL BREACH IT.
AND YOU ARE VERY POWERFUL, RA'S...
WHAT?
SO YOU SEE, THERE IS A PROPHECY HERE.
A TRUTH UNAVOID-ABLE.
WOULD YOU LIKE TO HEAR IT?
WHUMP

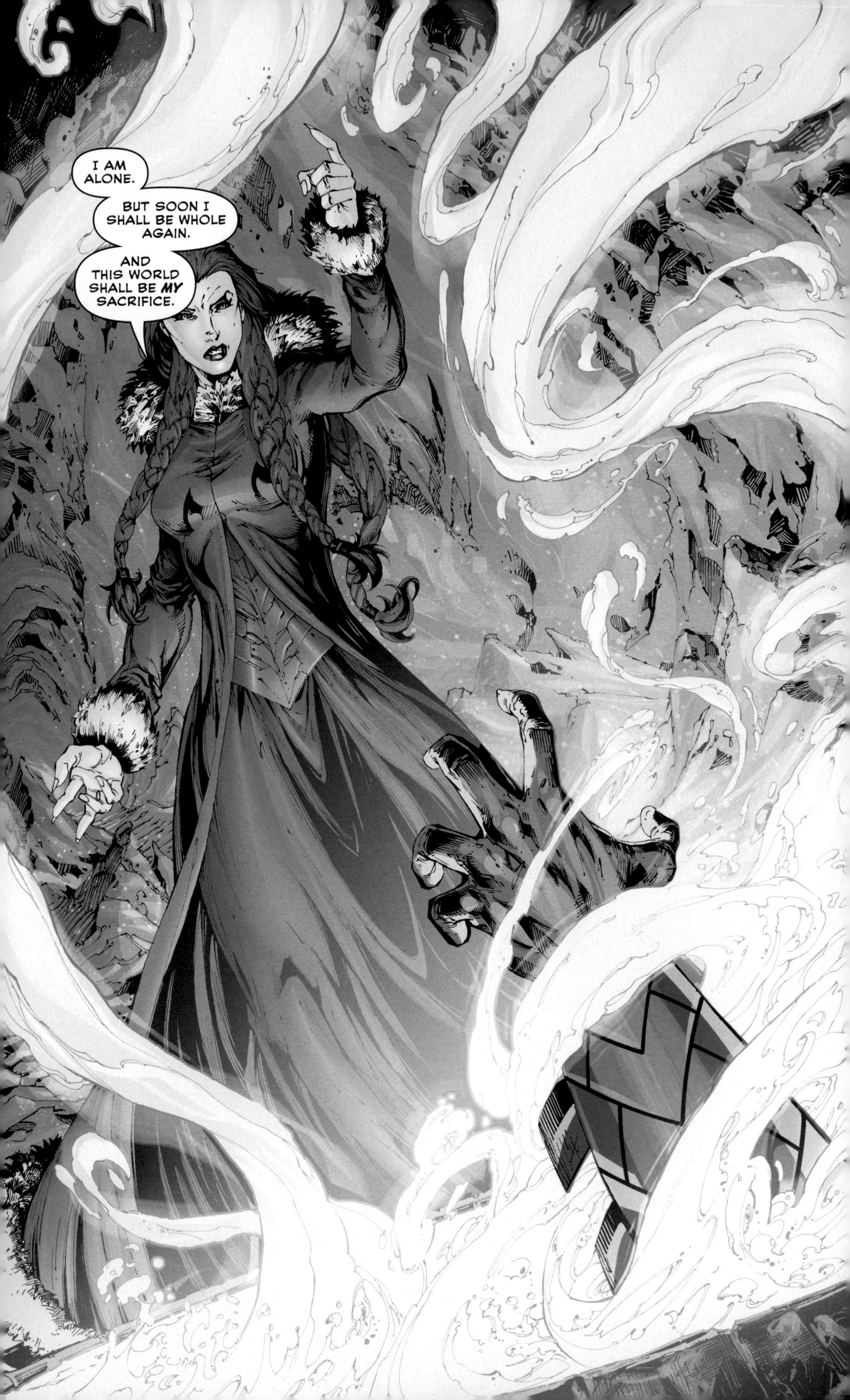
I AM ALONE.
BUT SOON I SHALL BE WHOLE AGAIN.
AND THIS WORLD SHALL BE *MY* SACRIFICE.

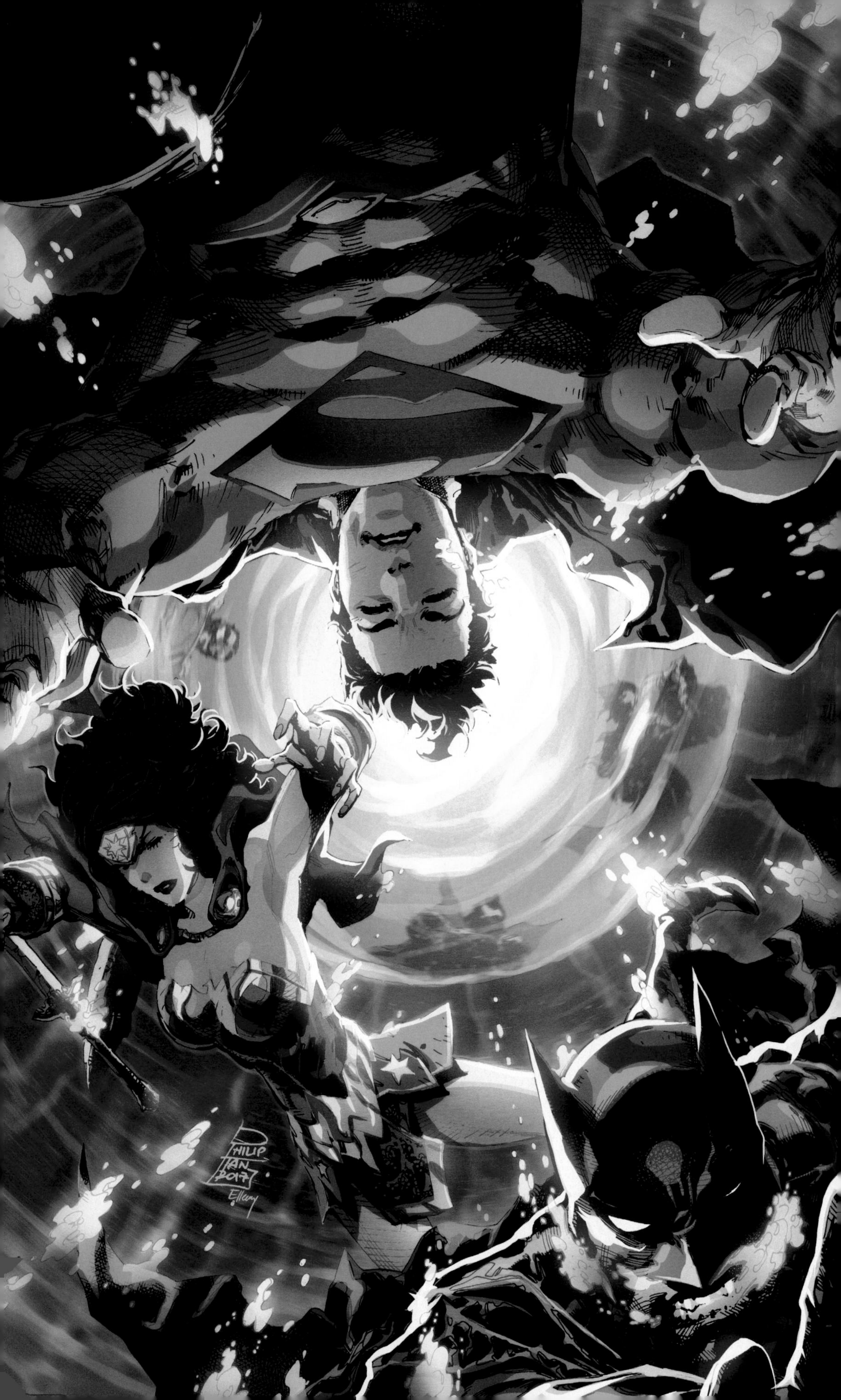
PHILIP TAN 2017

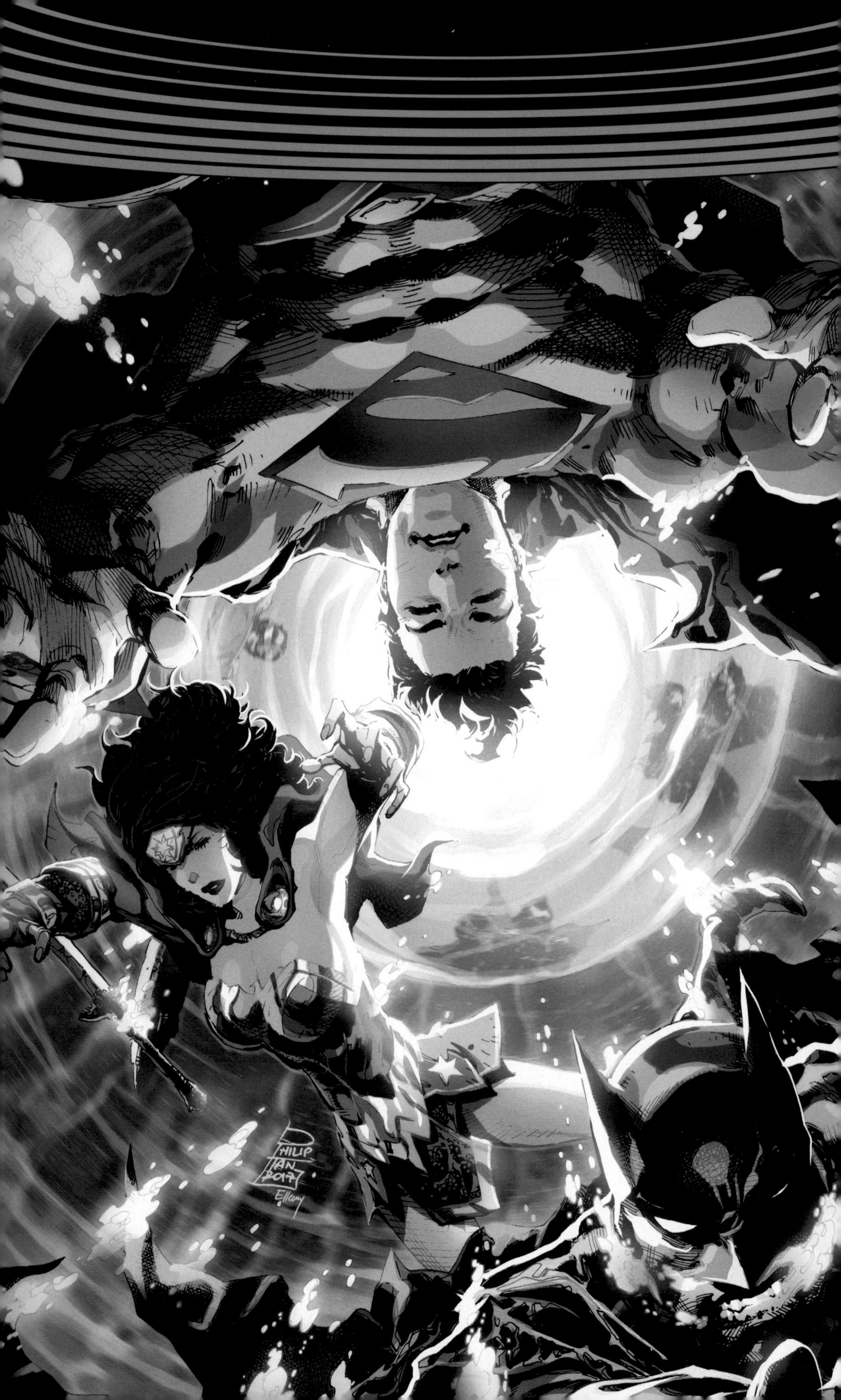

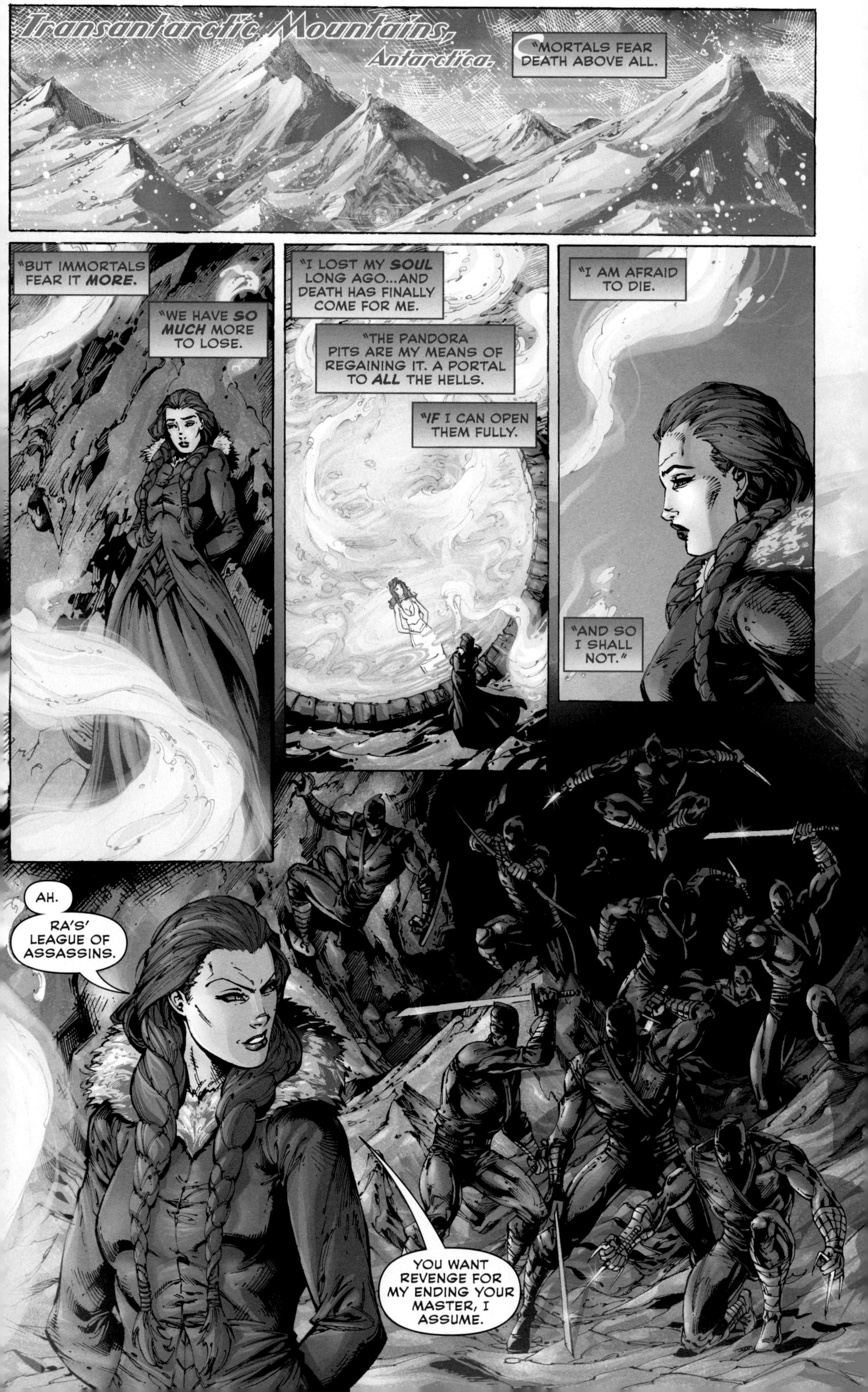
Transantarctic Mountains, Antarctica.
"MORTALS FEAR DEATH ABOVE ALL.
"BUT IMMORTALS FEAR IT MORE.
"WE HAVE SO MUCH MORE TO LOSE.
"I LOST MY SOUL LONG AGO...AND DEATH HAS FINALLY COME FOR ME.
"THE PANDORA PITS ARE MY MEANS OF REGAINING IT. A PORTAL TO ALL THE HELLS.
"IF I CAN OPEN THEM FULLY.
"I AM AFRAID TO DIE.
"AND SO I SHALL NOT."
AH.
RA'S' LEAGUE OF ASSASSINS.
YOU WANT REVENGE FOR MY ENDING YOUR MASTER, I ASSUME.

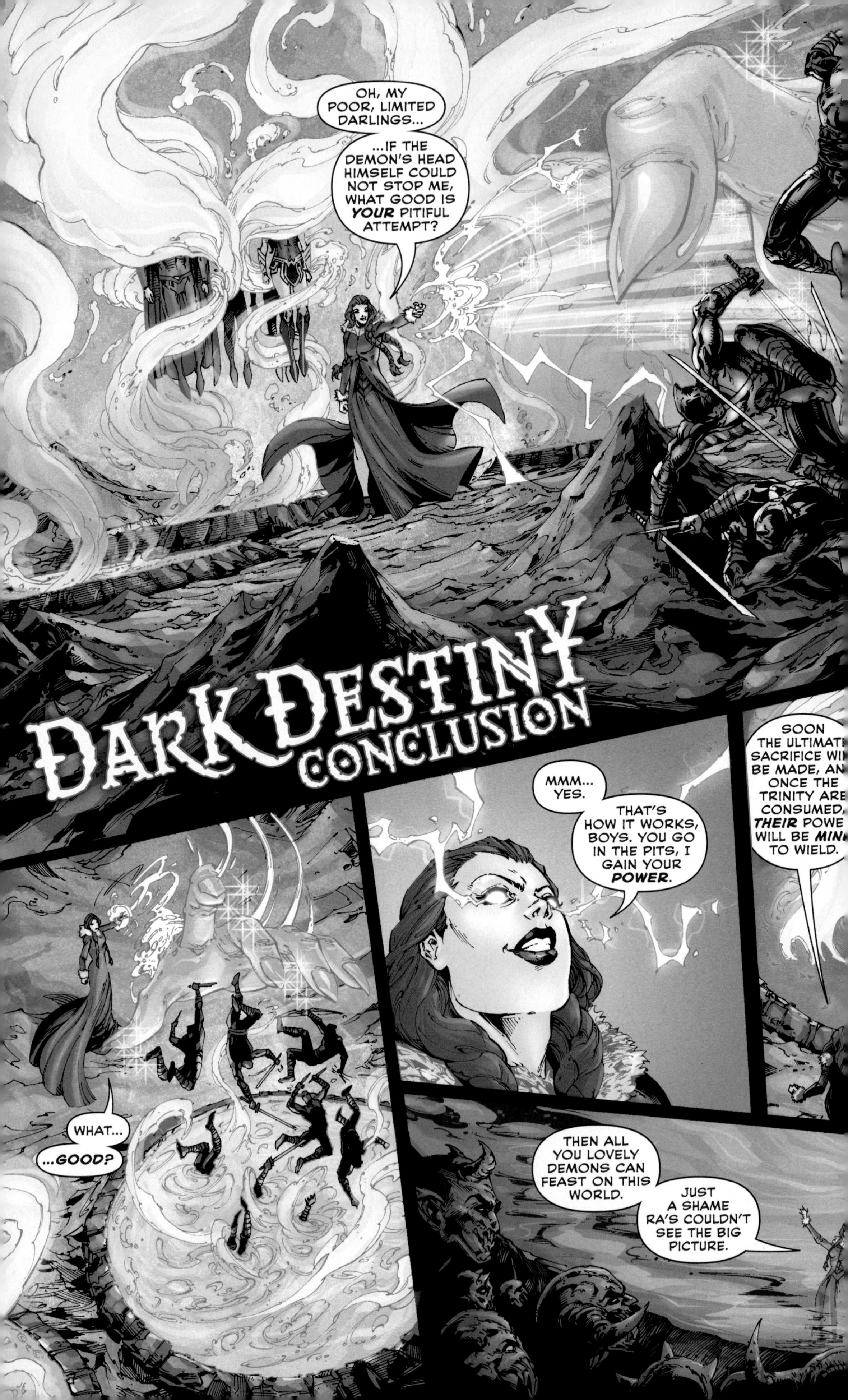
OH, MY POOR, LIMITED DARLINGS...
...IF THE DEMON'S HEAD HIMSELF COULD NOT STOP ME, WHAT GOOD IS YOUR PITIFUL ATTEMPT?
DARK DESTINY CONCLUSION
WHAT...
...GOOD?
MMM... YES.
THAT'S HOW IT WORKS, BOYS. YOU GO IN THE PITS, I GAIN YOUR POWER.
SOON THE ULTIMAT SACRIFICE WI BE MADE, AN ONCE THE TRINITY ARE CONSUMED, THEIR POWE WILL BE MIN TO WIELD.
THEN ALL YOU LOVELY DEMONS CAN FEAST ON THIS WORLD.
JUST A SHAME RA'S COULDN'T SEE THE BIG PICTURE.

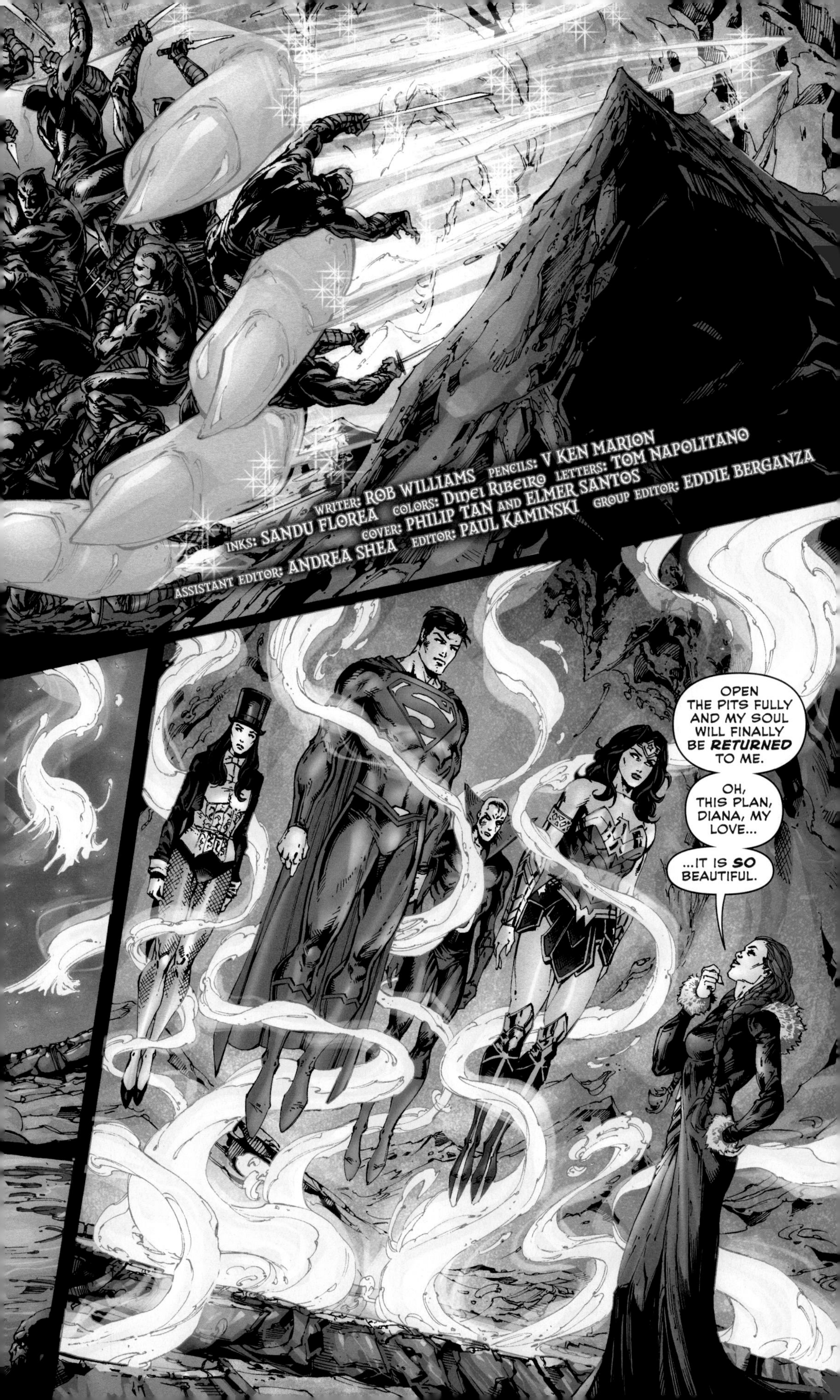

WRITER: ROB WILLIAMS PENCILS: V KEN MARION LETTERS: TOM NAPOLITANO
INKS: SANDU FLOREA COLORS: DINEI RIBEIRO
COVER: PHILIP TAN AND ELMER SANTOS
ASSISTANT EDITOR: ANDREA SHEA EDITOR: PAUL KAMINSKI GROUP EDITOR: EDDIE BERGANZA
OPEN THE PITS FULLY AND MY SOUL WILL FINALLY BE RETURNED TO ME.
OH, THIS PLAN, DIANA, MY LOVE...
...IT IS SO BEAUTIFUL.

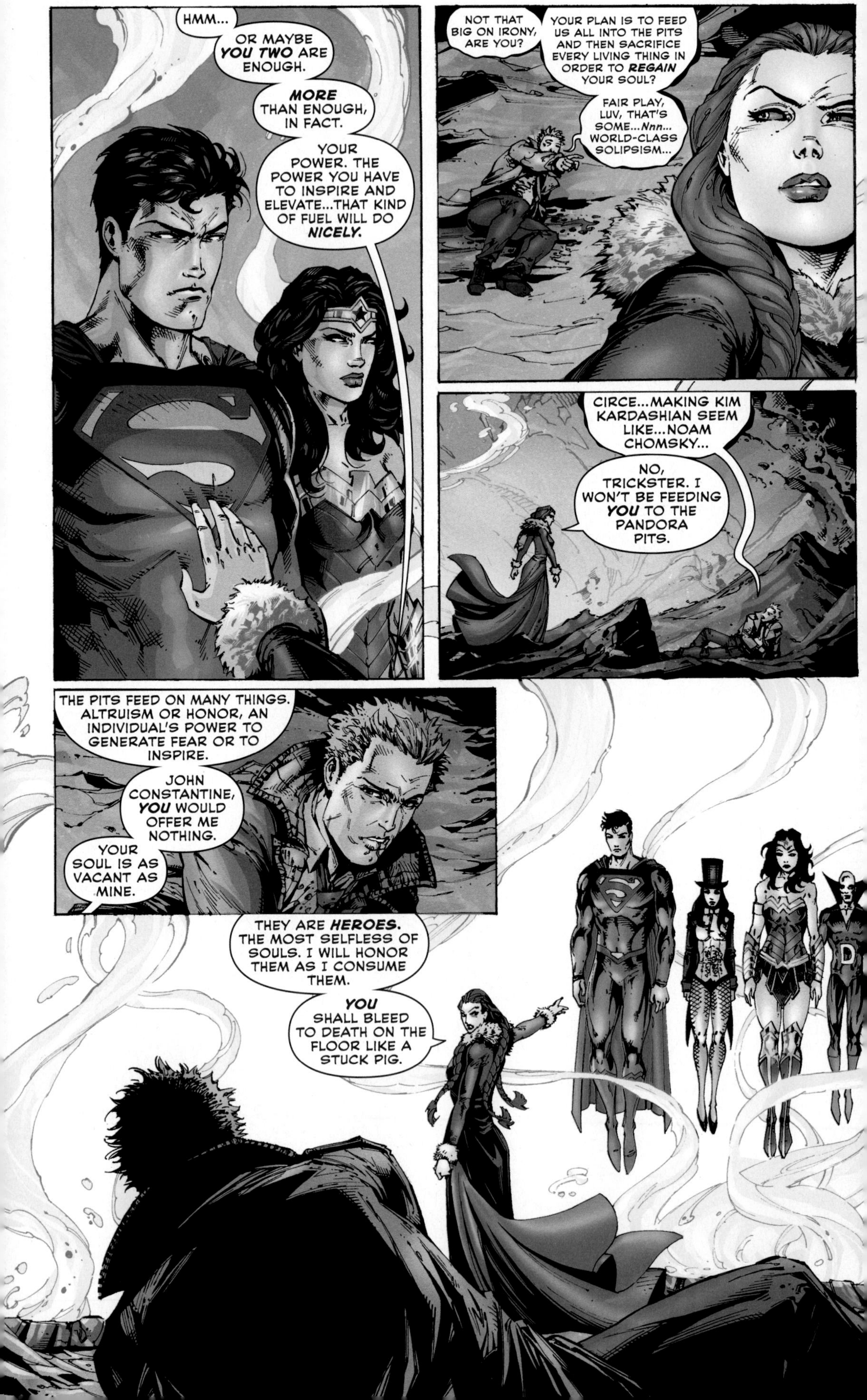

HMM...
OR MAYBE YOU TWO ARE ENOUGH.
MORE THAN ENOUGH, IN FACT.
YOUR POWER. THE POWER YOU HAVE TO INSPIRE AND ELEVATE...THAT KIND OF FUEL WILL DO NICELY.
NOT THAT BIG ON IRONY, ARE YOU?
YOUR PLAN IS TO FEED US ALL INTO THE PITS AND THEN SACRIFICE EVERY LIVING THING IN ORDER TO REGAIN YOUR SOUL?
FAIR PLAY, LUV, THAT'S SOME...Nnn... WORLD-CLASS SOLIPSISM...
CIRCE...MAKING KIM KARDASHIAN SEEM LIKE...NOAM CHOMSKY...
NO, TRICKSTER. I WON'T BE FEEDING YOU TO THE PANDORA PITS.
THE PITS FEED ON MANY THINGS. ALTRUISM OR HONOR, AN INDIVIDUAL'S POWER TO GENERATE FEAR OR TO INSPIRE.
JOHN CONSTANTINE, YOU WOULD OFFER ME NOTHING.
YOUR SOUL IS AS VACANT AS MINE.
THEY ARE HEROES. THE MOST SELFLESS OF SOULS. I WILL HONOR THEM AS I CONSUME THEM.
YOU SHALL BLEED TO DEATH ON THE FLOOR LIKE A STUCK PIG.

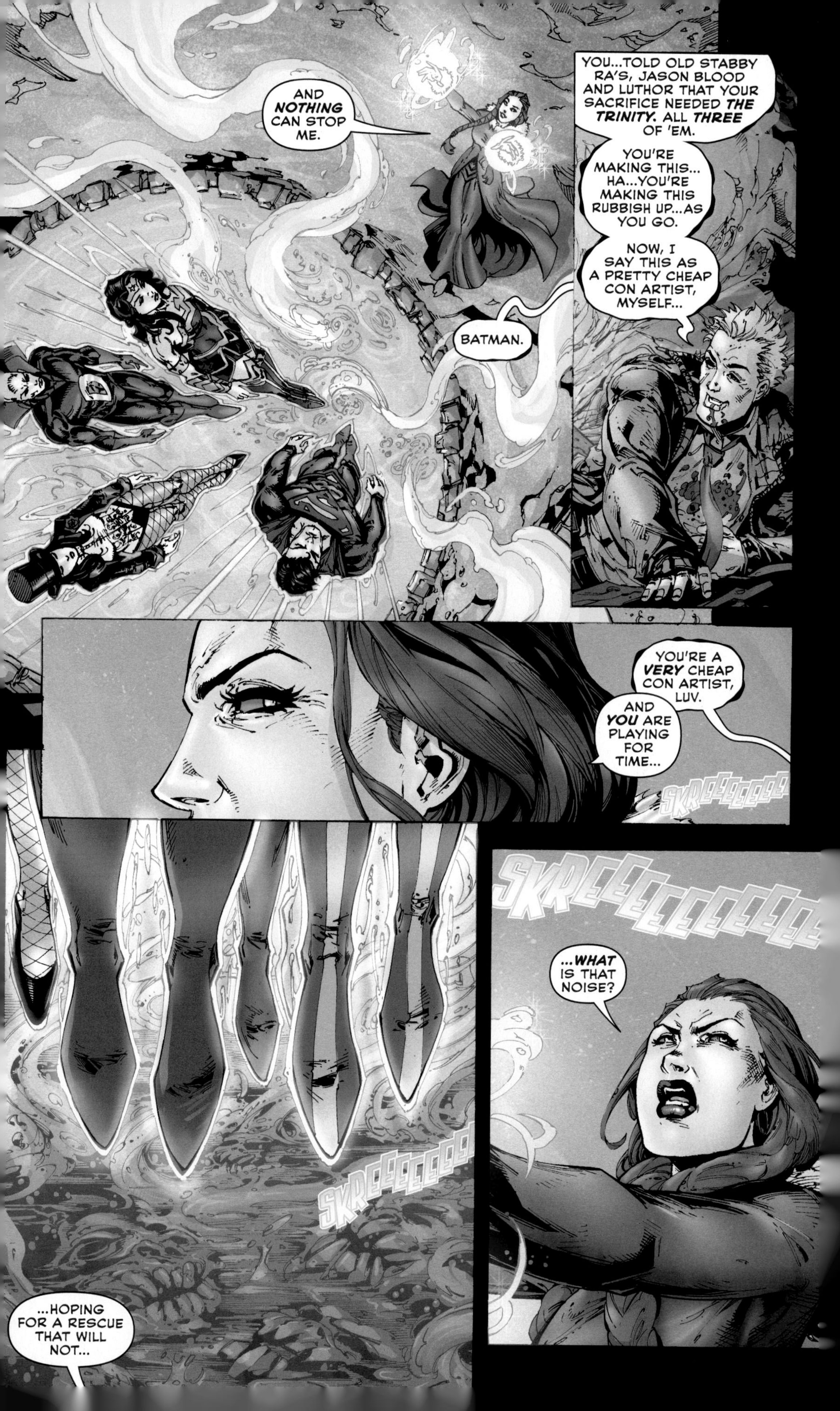

AND NOTHING CAN STOP ME.
YOU...TOLD OLD STABBY RA'S, JASON BLOOD AND LUTHOR THAT YOUR SACRIFICE NEEDED THE TRINITY. ALL THREE OF 'EM.
YOU'RE MAKING THIS... HA...YOU'RE MAKING THIS RUBBISH UP...AS YOU GO.
NOW, I SAY THIS AS A PRETTY CHEAP CON ARTIST, MYSELF...
BATMAN.
YOU'RE A VERY CHEAP CON ARTIST, LUV.
AND YOU ARE PLAYING FOR TIME...
SKREEEEEEEE
SKREEEEEEEE
...HOPING FOR A RESCUE THAT WILL NOT...
SKREEEEEEEEEEEE
...WHAT IS THAT NOISE?

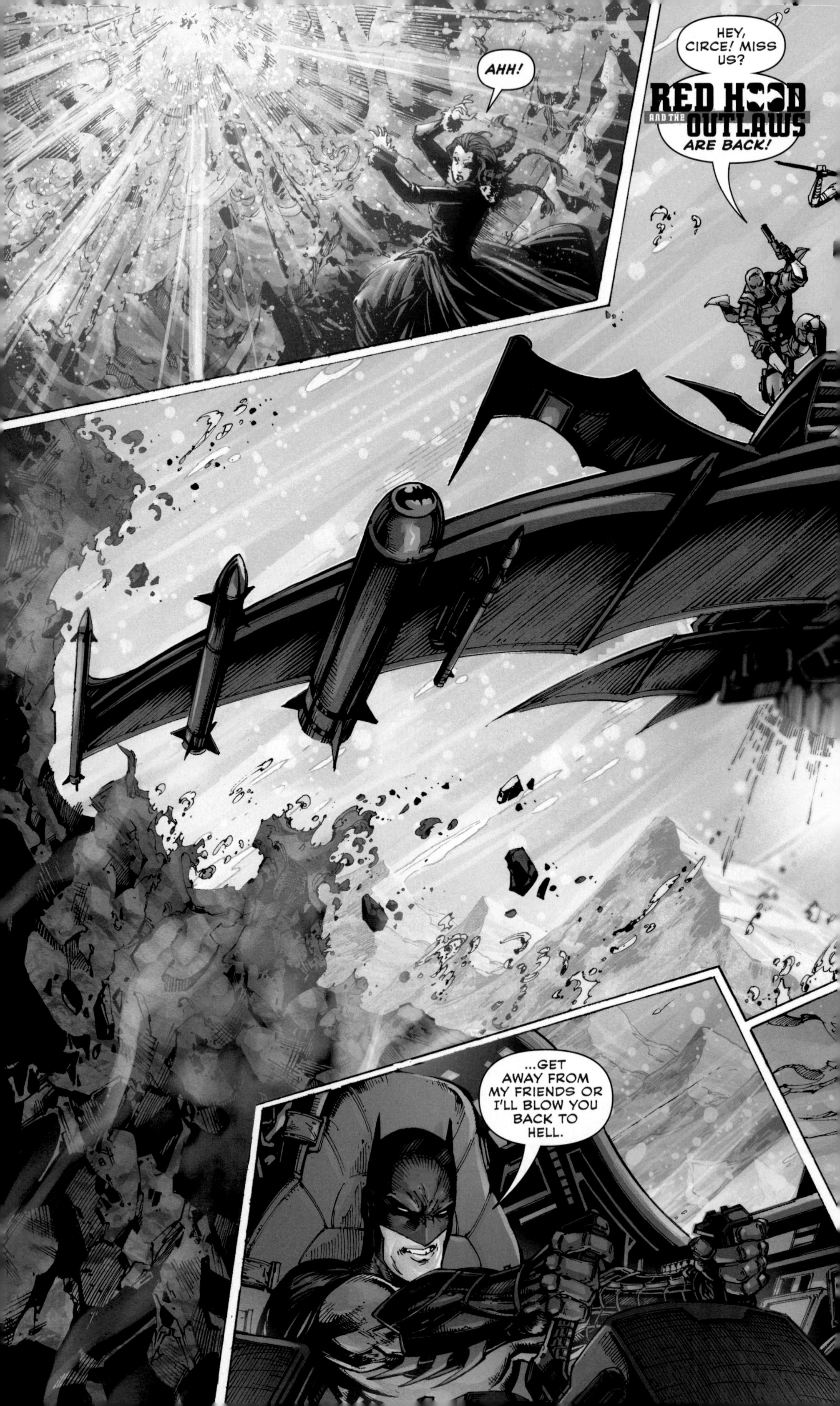
AHH!
HEY, CIRCE! MISS US?
RED HOOD AND THE OUTLAWS ARE BACK!
...GET AWAY FROM MY FRIENDS OR I'LL BLOW YOU BACK TO HELL.

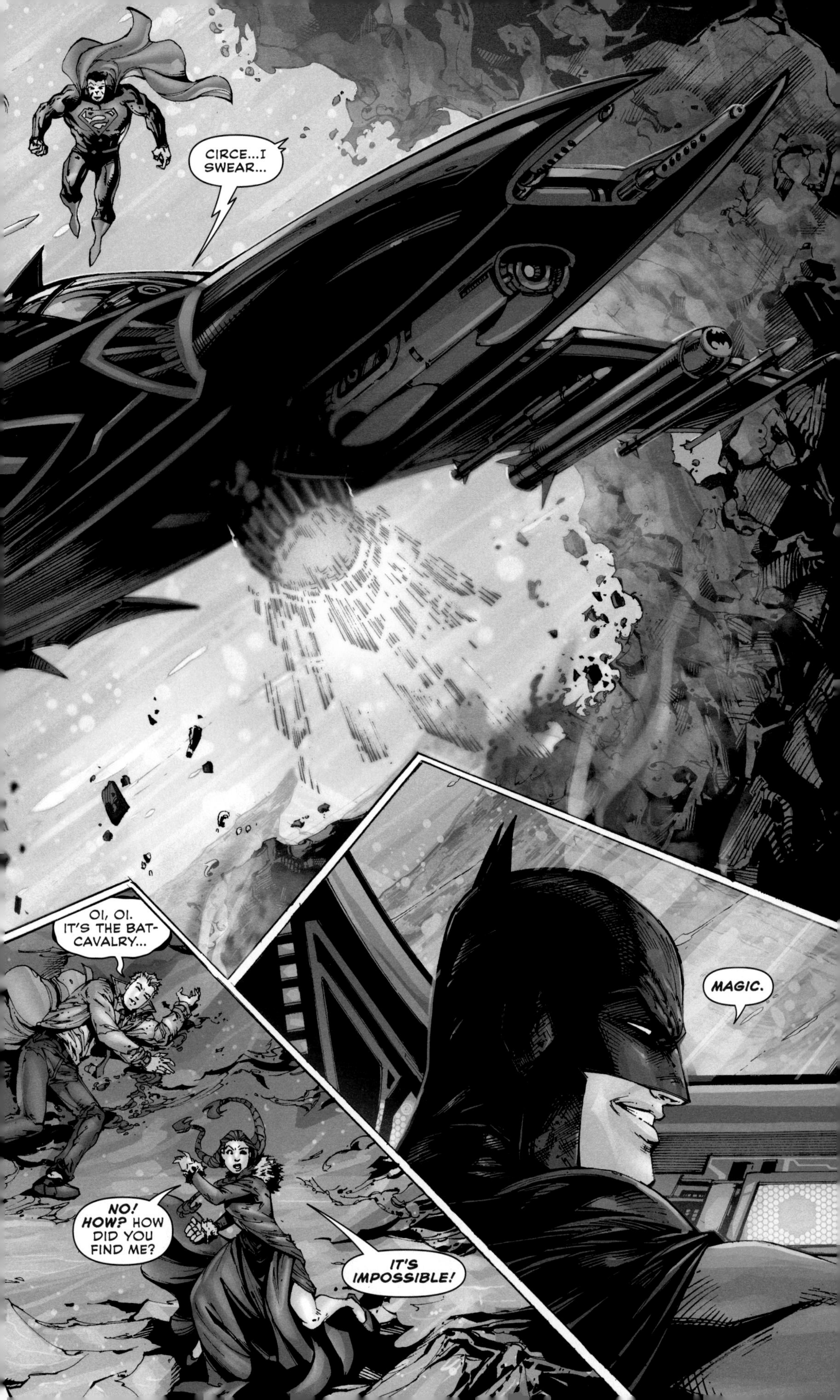
CIRCE...I SWEAR...
OI, OI. IT'S THE BAT-CAVALRY...
MAGIC.
NO! HOW? HOW DID YOU FIND ME?
IT'S IMPOSSIBLE!

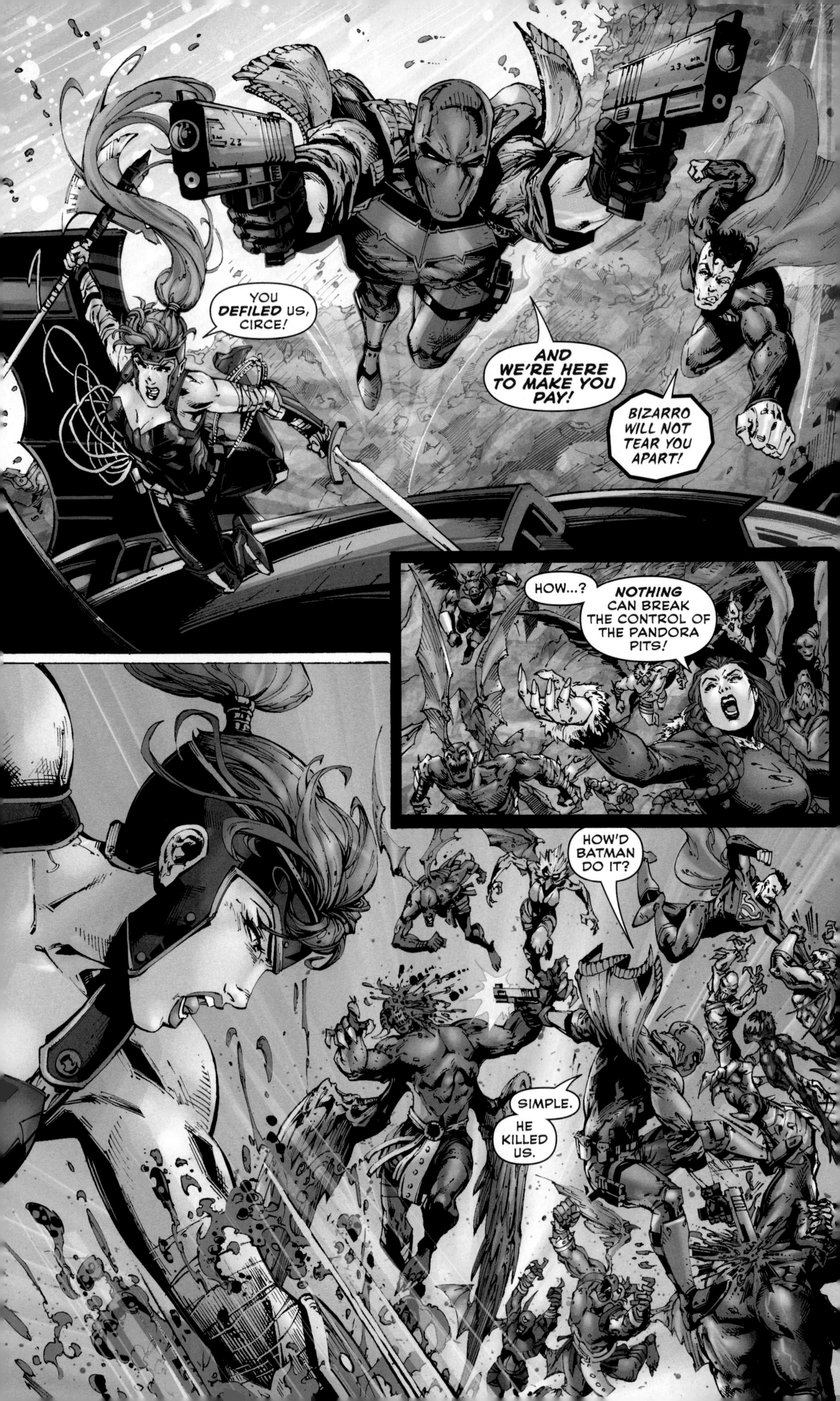

YOU DEFILED US, CIRCE!
AND WE'RE HERE TO MAKE YOU PAY!
BIZARRO WILL NOT TEAR YOU APART!
HOW...?
NOTHING CAN BREAK THE CONTROL OF THE PANDORA PITS!
HOW'D BATMAN DO IT?
SIMPLE.
HE KILLED US.

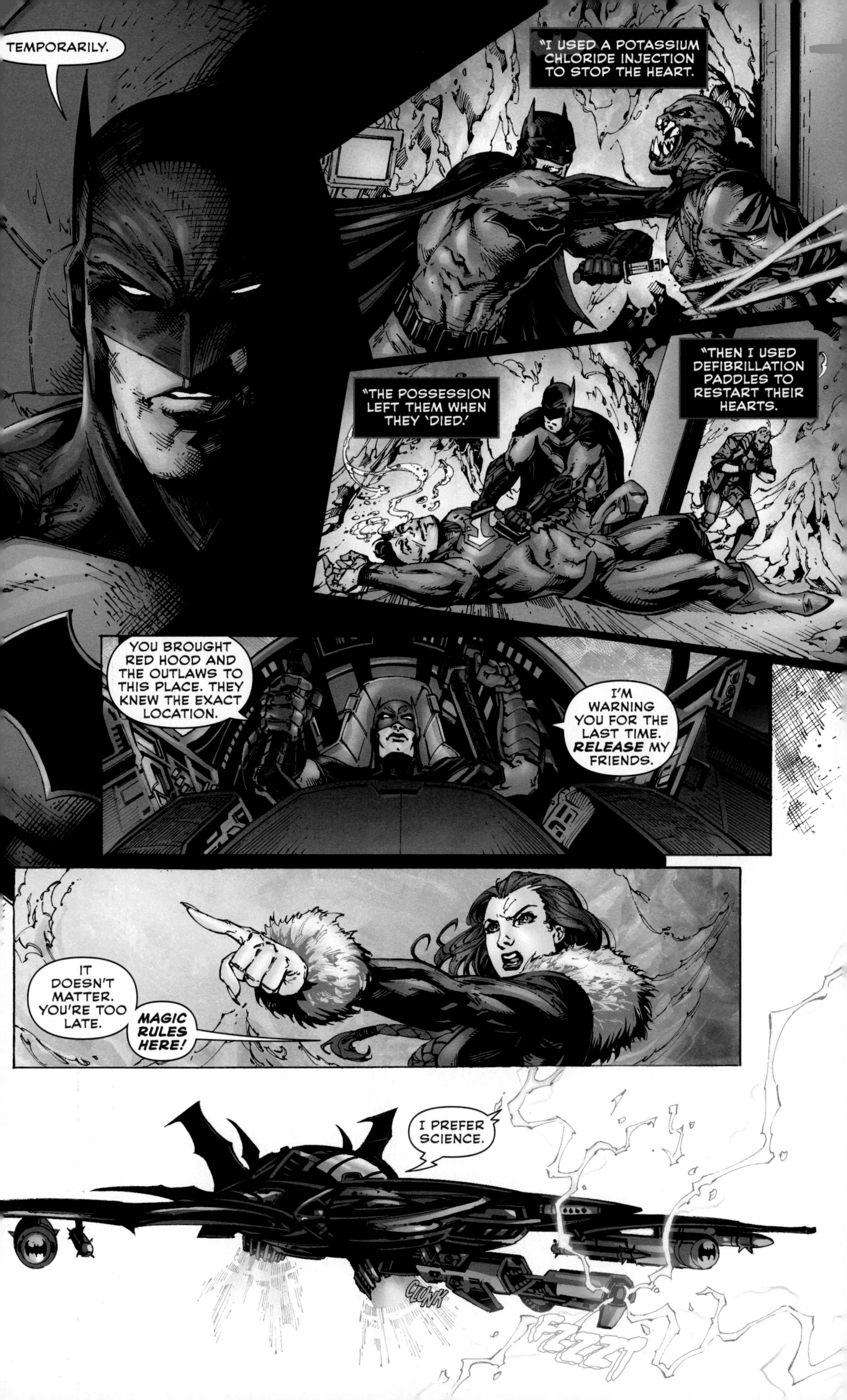
TEMPORARILY.
"I USED A POTASSIUM CHLORIDE INJECTION TO STOP THE HEART.
"THE POSSESSION LEFT THEM WHEN THEY 'DIED.'
"THEN I USED DEFIBRILLATION PADDLES TO RESTART THEIR HEARTS.
YOU BROUGHT RED HOOD AND THE OUTLAWS TO THIS PLACE. THEY KNEW THE EXACT LOCATION.
I'M WARNING YOU FOR THE LAST TIME. RELEASE MY FRIENDS.
IT DOESN'T MATTER. YOU'RE TOO LATE.
MAGIC RULES HERE!
I PREFER SCIENCE.
CLUNK
FZZZT

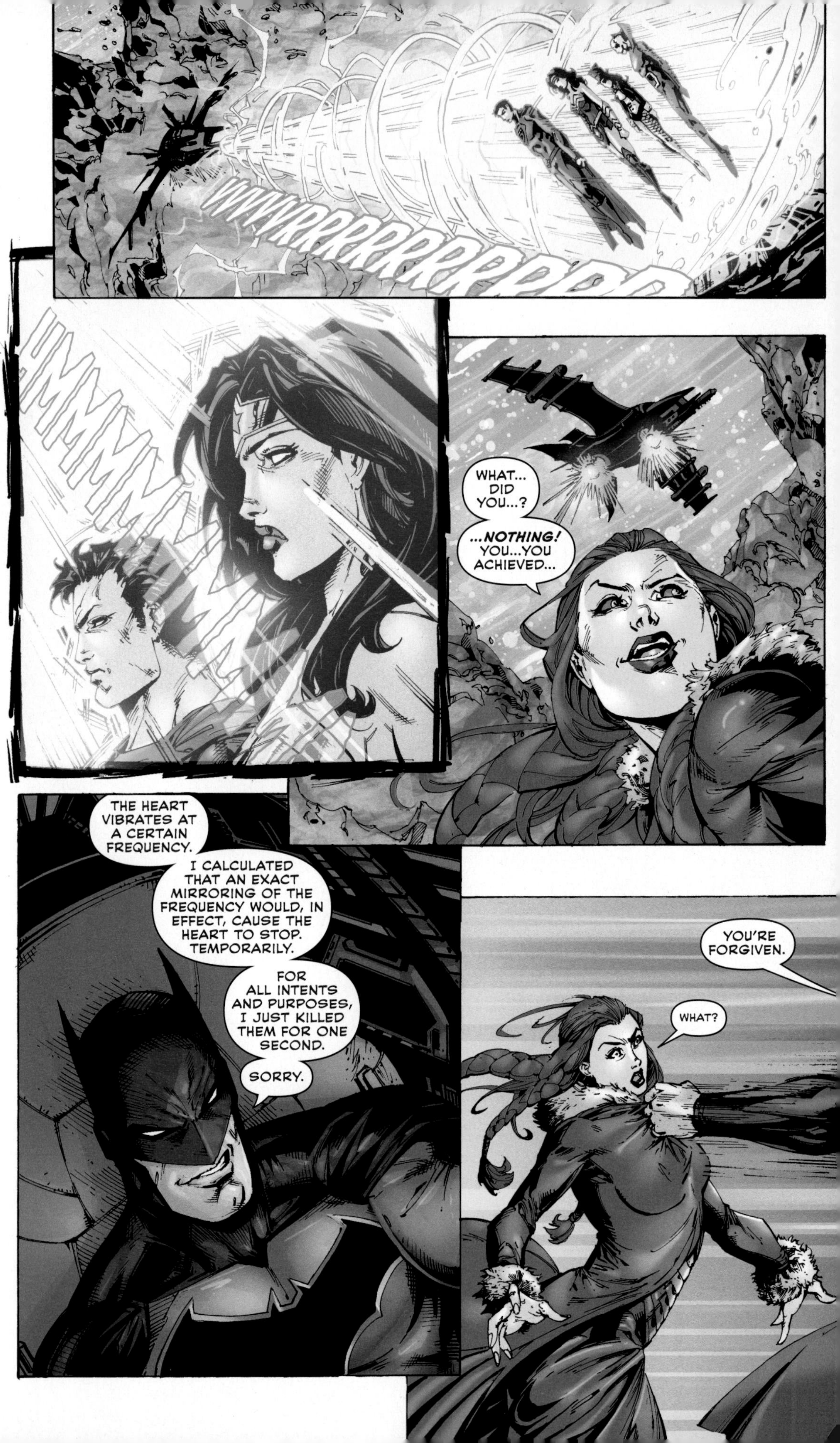
VVVVRRRRRRRRRRRR
HMMMMMMM
WHAT... DID YOU...?
...NOTHING! YOU...YOU ACHIEVED...
THE HEART VIBRATES AT A CERTAIN FREQUENCY.
I CALCULATED THAT AN EXACT MIRRORING OF THE FREQUENCY WOULD, IN EFFECT, CAUSE THE HEART TO STOP. TEMPORARILY.
FOR ALL INTENTS AND PURPOSES, I JUST KILLED THEM FOR ONE SECOND.
SORRY.
YOU'RE FORGIVEN.
WHAT?

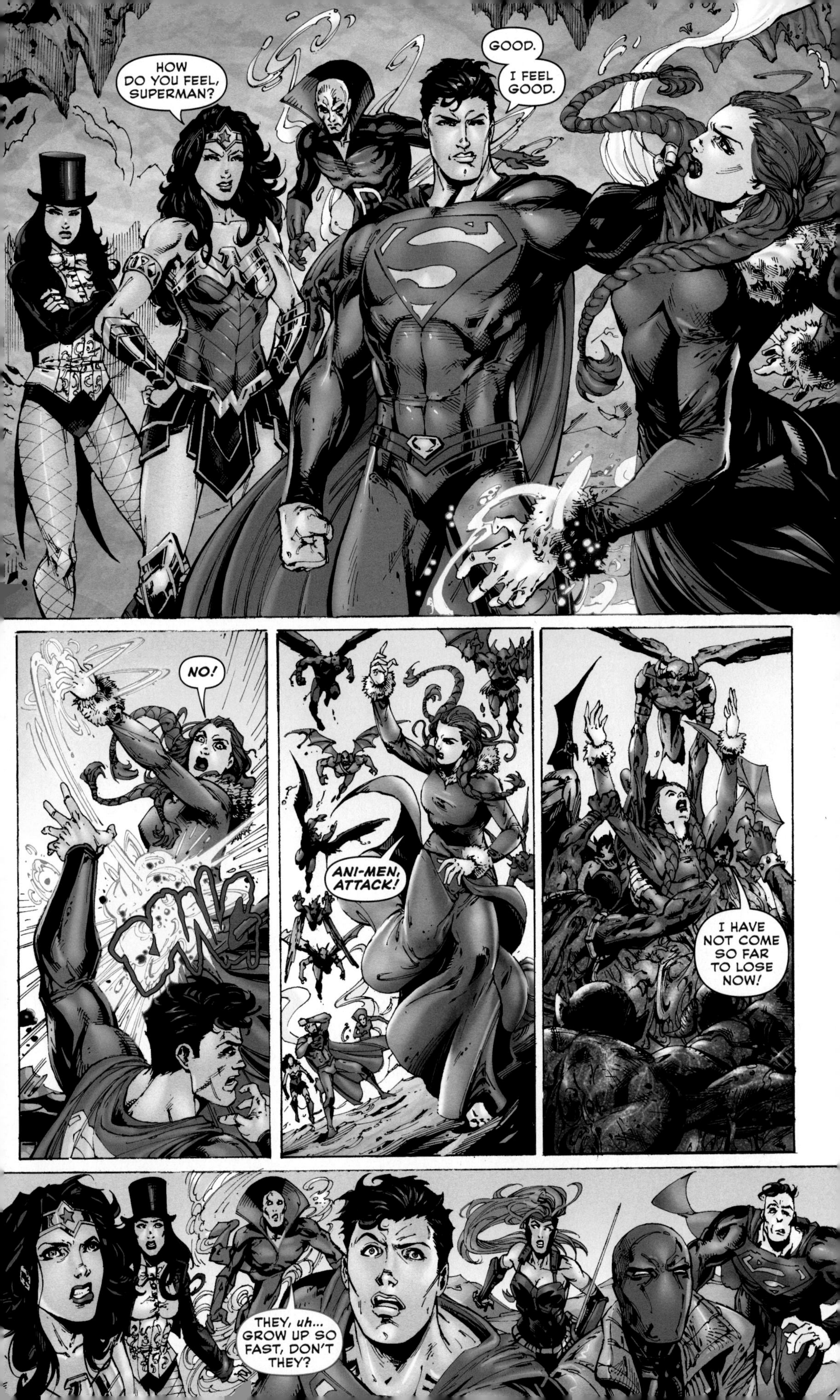
HOW DO YOU FEEL, SUPERMAN?
GOOD.
I FEEL GOOD.
NO!
ANI-MEN, ATTACK!
I HAVE NOT COME SO FAR TO LOSE NOW!
THEY, *uh*... GROW UP SO FAST, DON'T THEY?

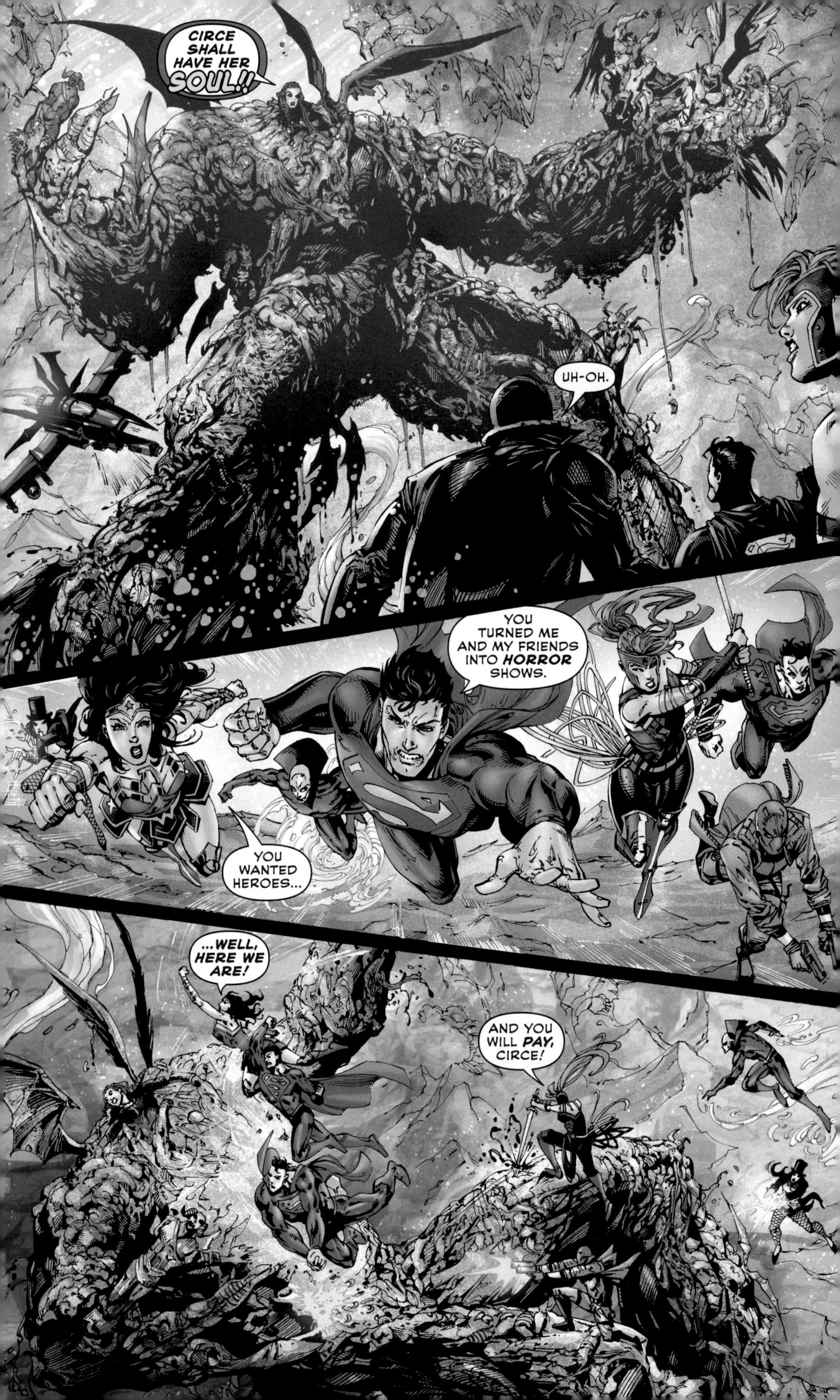
CIRCE SHALL HAVE HER SOUL!!
UH-OH.
YOU TURNED ME AND MY FRIENDS INTO HORROR SHOWS.
YOU WANTED HEROES...
...WELL, HERE WE ARE!
AND YOU WILL PAY, CIRCE!

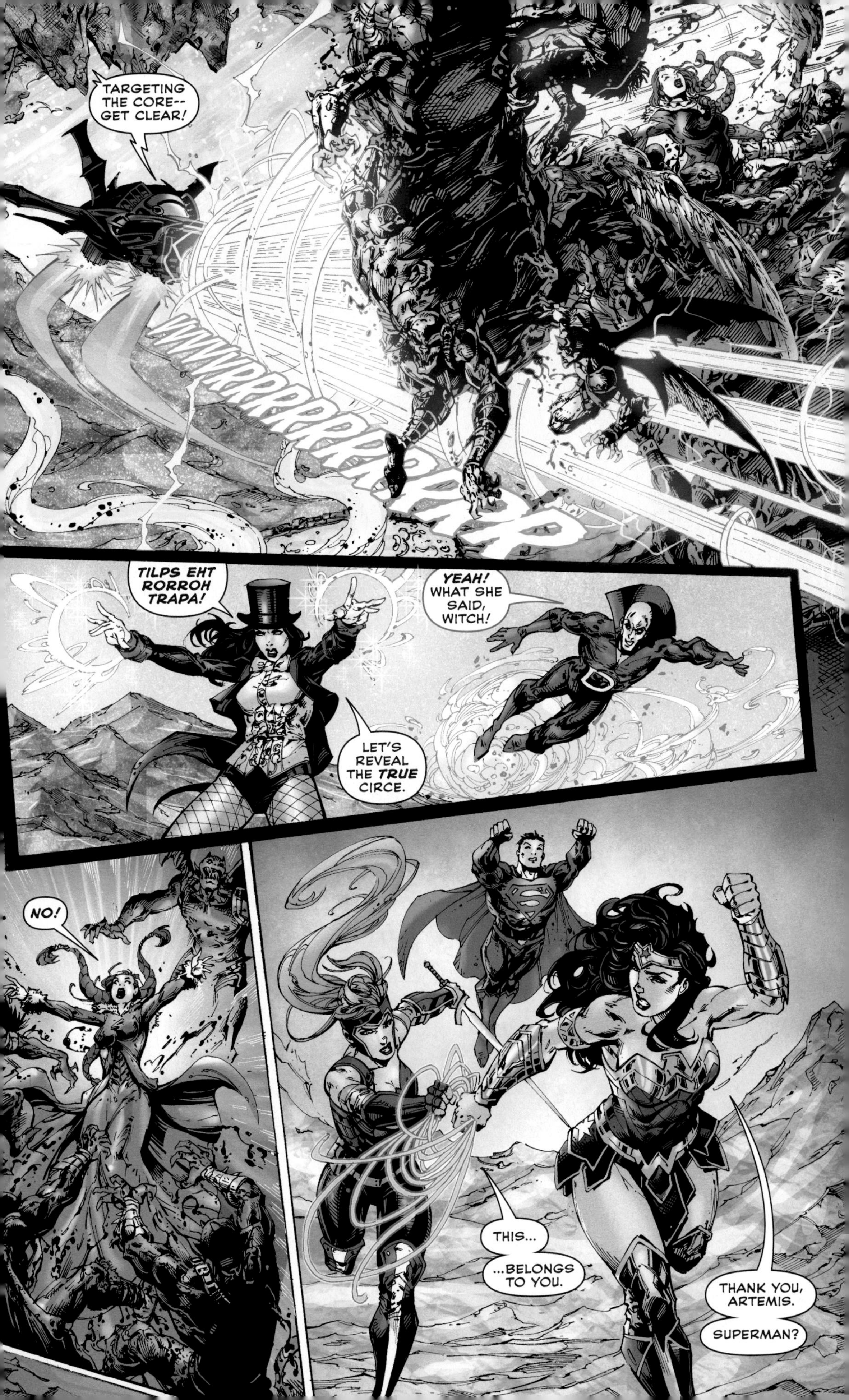
TARGETING THE CORE-- GET CLEAR!
WWWRRRRRRRRRRR
TILPS EHT RORROH TRAPA!
YEAH! WHAT SHE SAID, WITCH!
LET'S REVEAL THE TRUE CIRCE.
NO!
THIS...
...BELONGS TO YOU.
THANK YOU, ARTEMIS.
SUPERMAN?

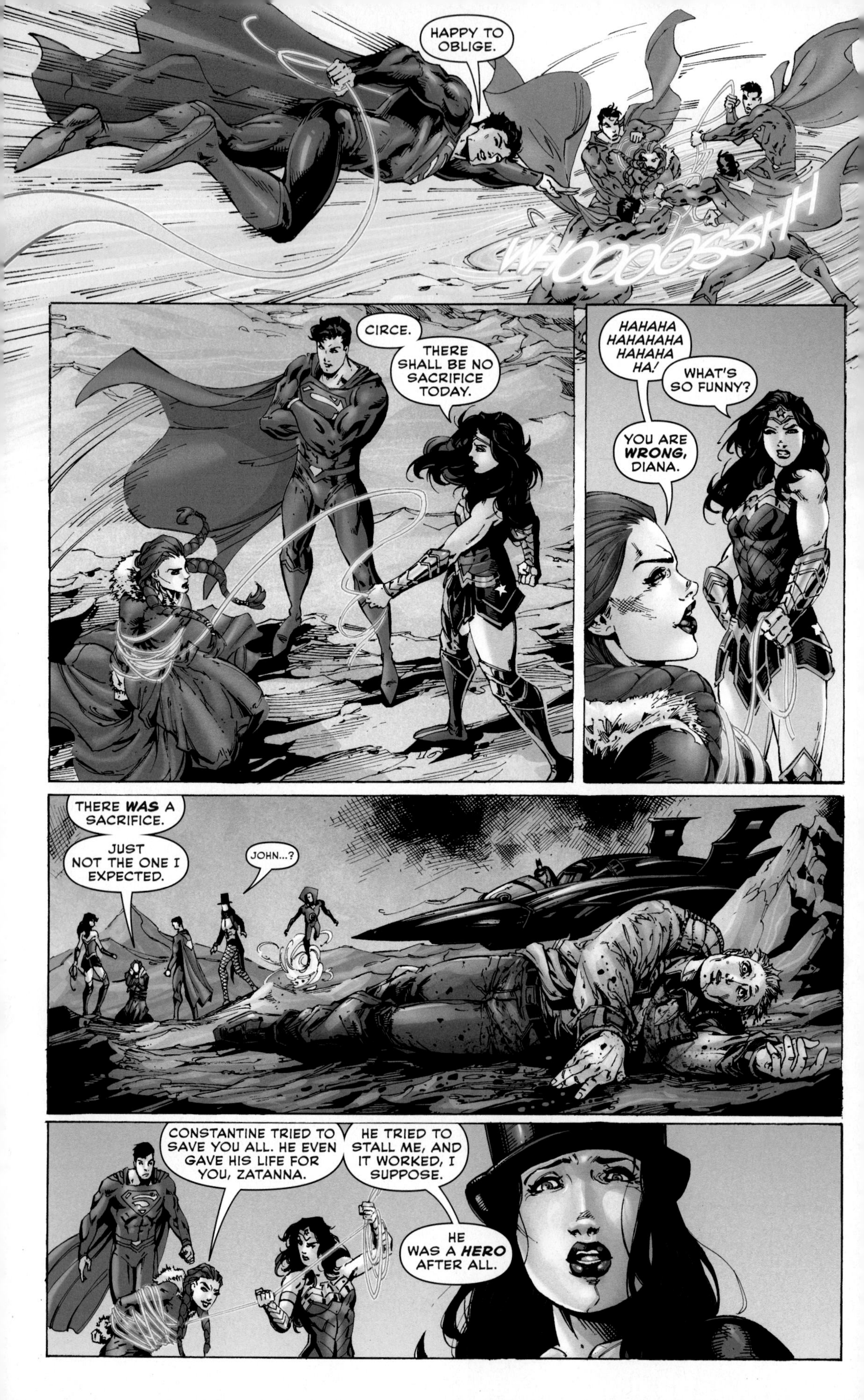
HAPPY TO OBLIGE.
WHOOOOSSHH
CIRCE.
THERE SHALL BE NO SACRIFICE TODAY.
HAHAHA HAHAHAHA HAHAHA HA!
WHAT'S SO FUNNY?
YOU ARE WRONG, DIANA.
THERE WAS A SACRIFICE.
JUST NOT THE ONE I EXPECTED.
JOHN...?
CONSTANTINE TRIED TO SAVE YOU ALL. HE EVEN GAVE HIS LIFE FOR YOU, ZATANNA.
HE TRIED TO STALL ME, AND IT WORKED, I SUPPOSE.
HE WAS A HERO AFTER ALL.

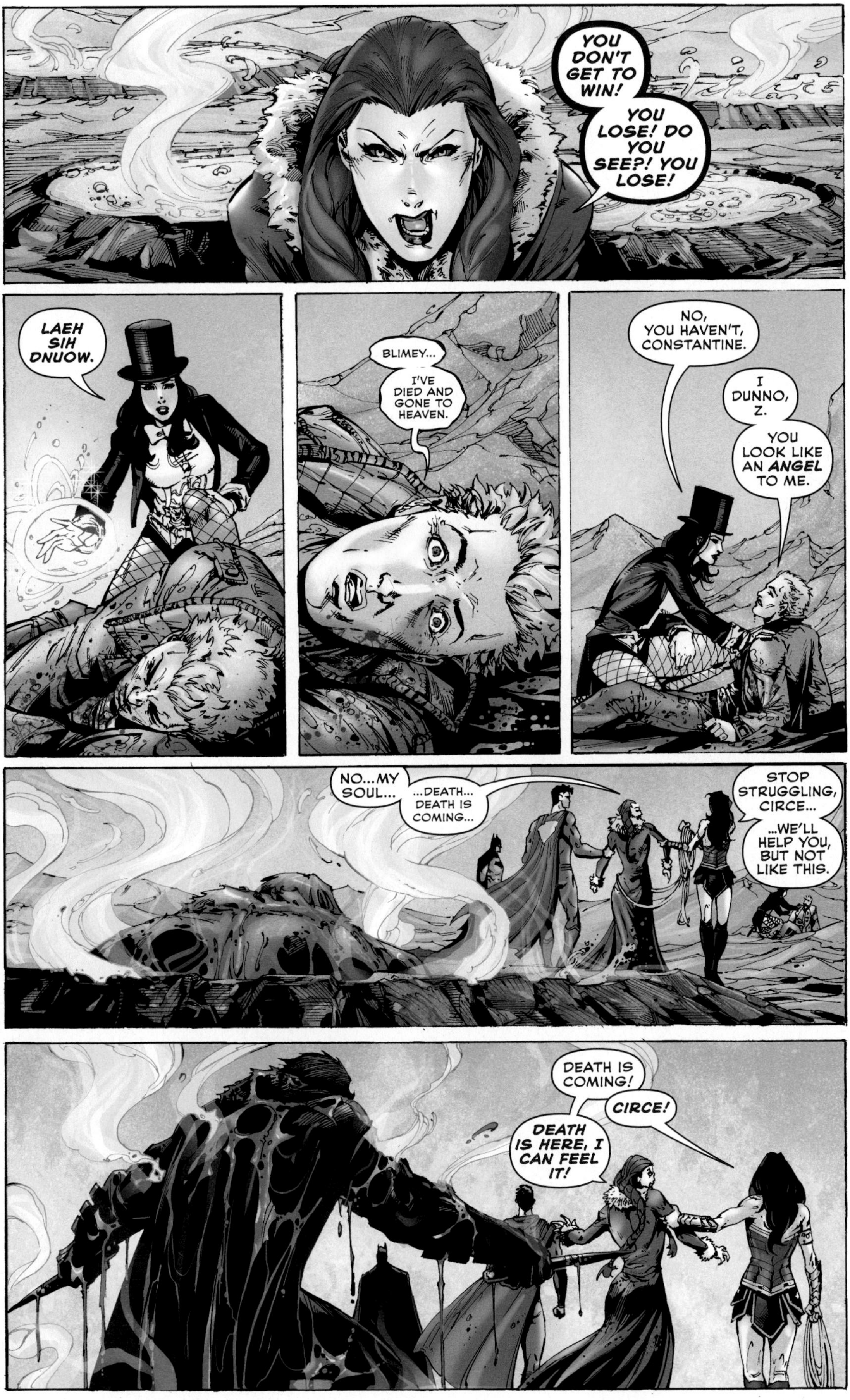
YOU DON'T GET TO WIN!
YOU LOSE! DO YOU SEE?! YOU LOSE!
LAEH SIH DNUOW.
BLIMEY...
I'VE DIED AND GONE TO HEAVEN.
NO, YOU HAVEN'T, CONSTANTINE.
I DUNNO, Z.
YOU LOOK LIKE AN ANGEL TO ME.
NO...MY SOUL...
...DEATH... DEATH IS COMING...
STOP STRUGGLING, CIRCE...
...WE'LL HELP YOU, BUT NOT LIKE THIS.
DEATH IS COMING!
CIRCE!
DEATH IS HERE, I CAN FEEL IT!

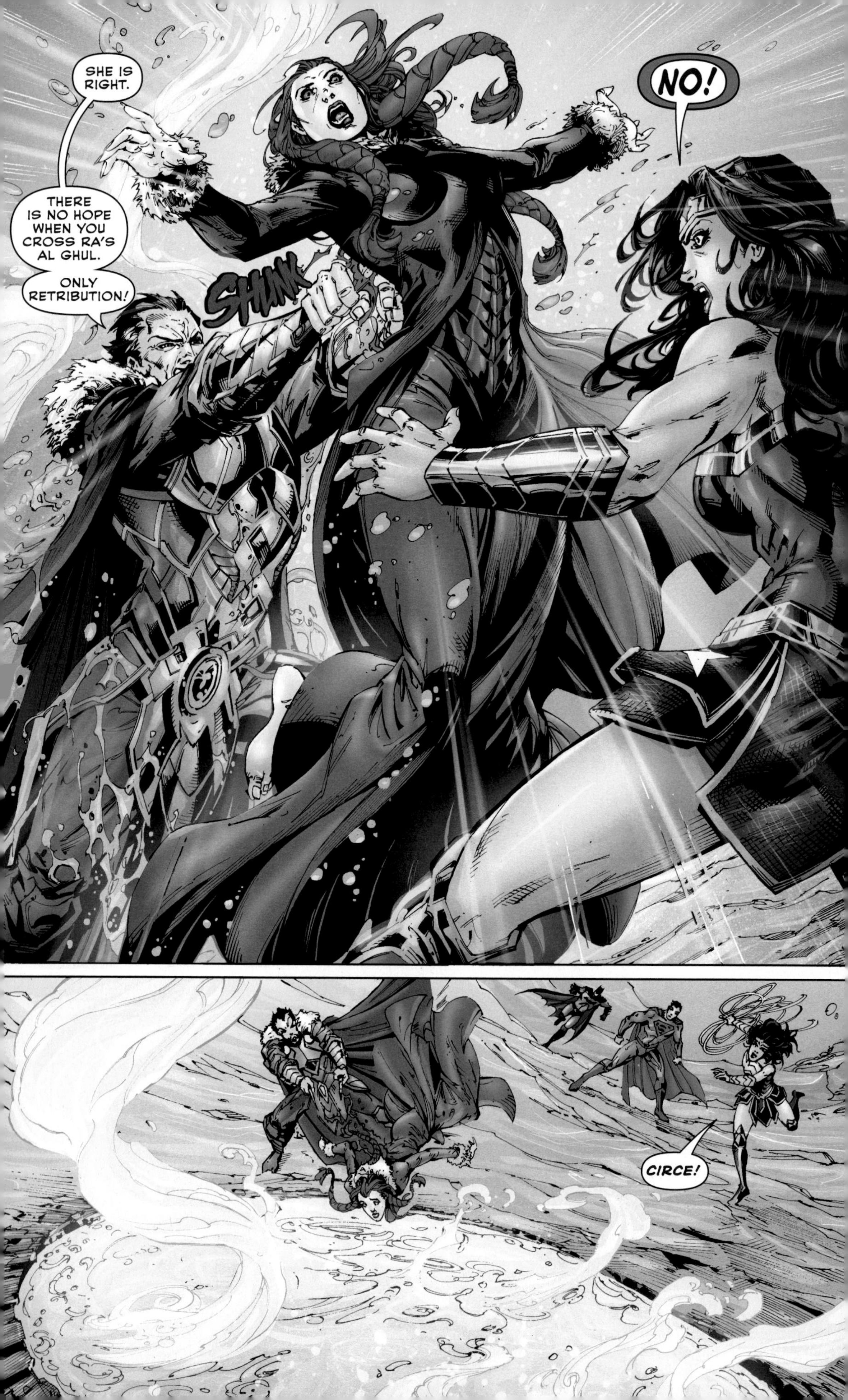
SHE IS RIGHT.
THERE IS NO HOPE WHEN YOU CROSS RA'S AL GHUL.
ONLY RETRIBUTION!
SHUNK
NO!
CIRCE!

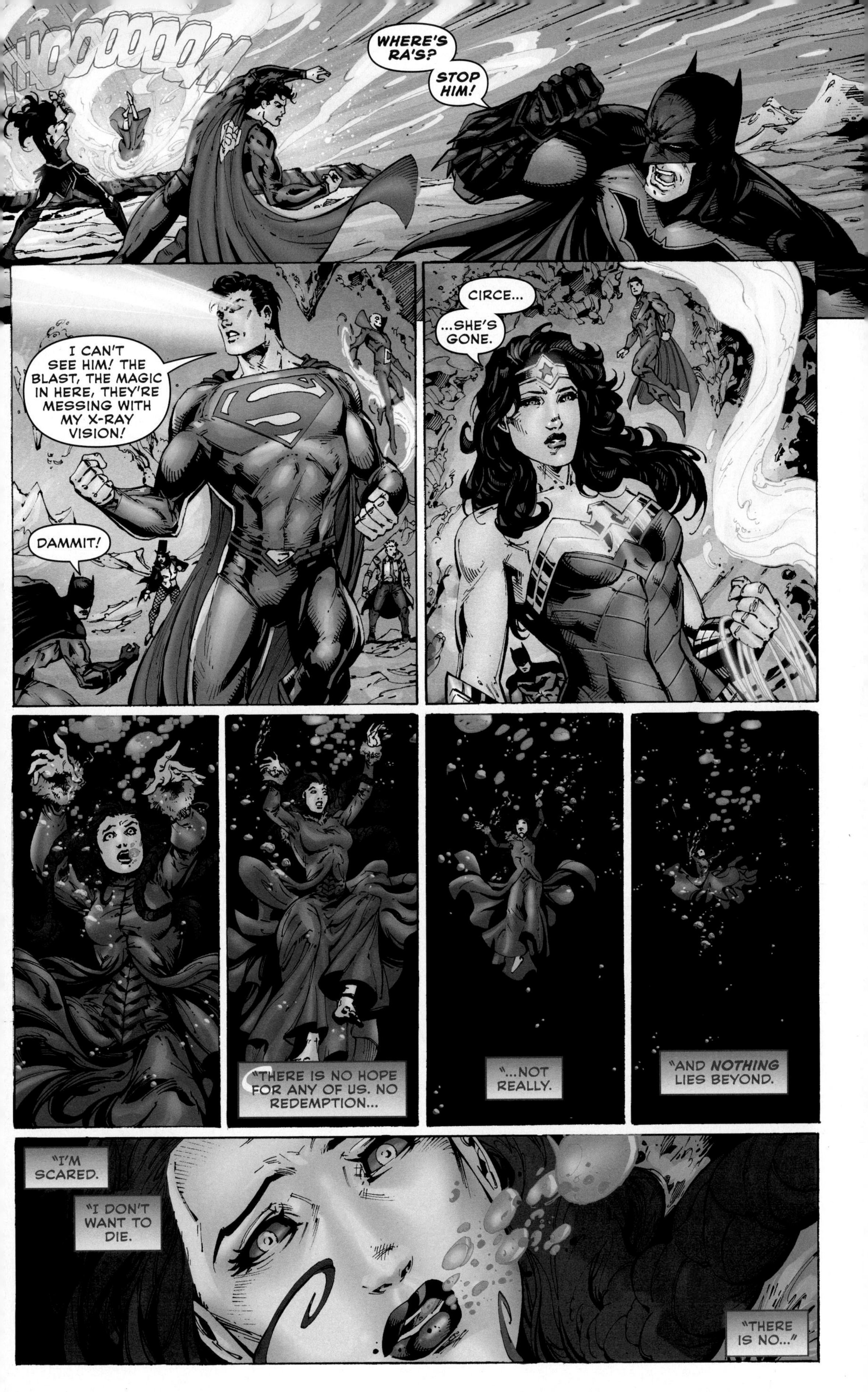
HOOOOOOM
WHERE'S RA'S?
STOP HIM!
I CAN'T SEE HIM! THE BLAST, THE MAGIC IN HERE, THEY'RE MESSING WITH MY X-RAY VISION!
DAMMIT!
CIRCE...
...SHE'S GONE.
"THERE IS NO HOPE FOR ANY OF US. NO REDEMPTION...
"...NOT REALLY.
"AND NOTHING LIES BEYOND.
"I'M SCARED.
"I DON'T WANT TO DIE.
"THERE IS NO..."

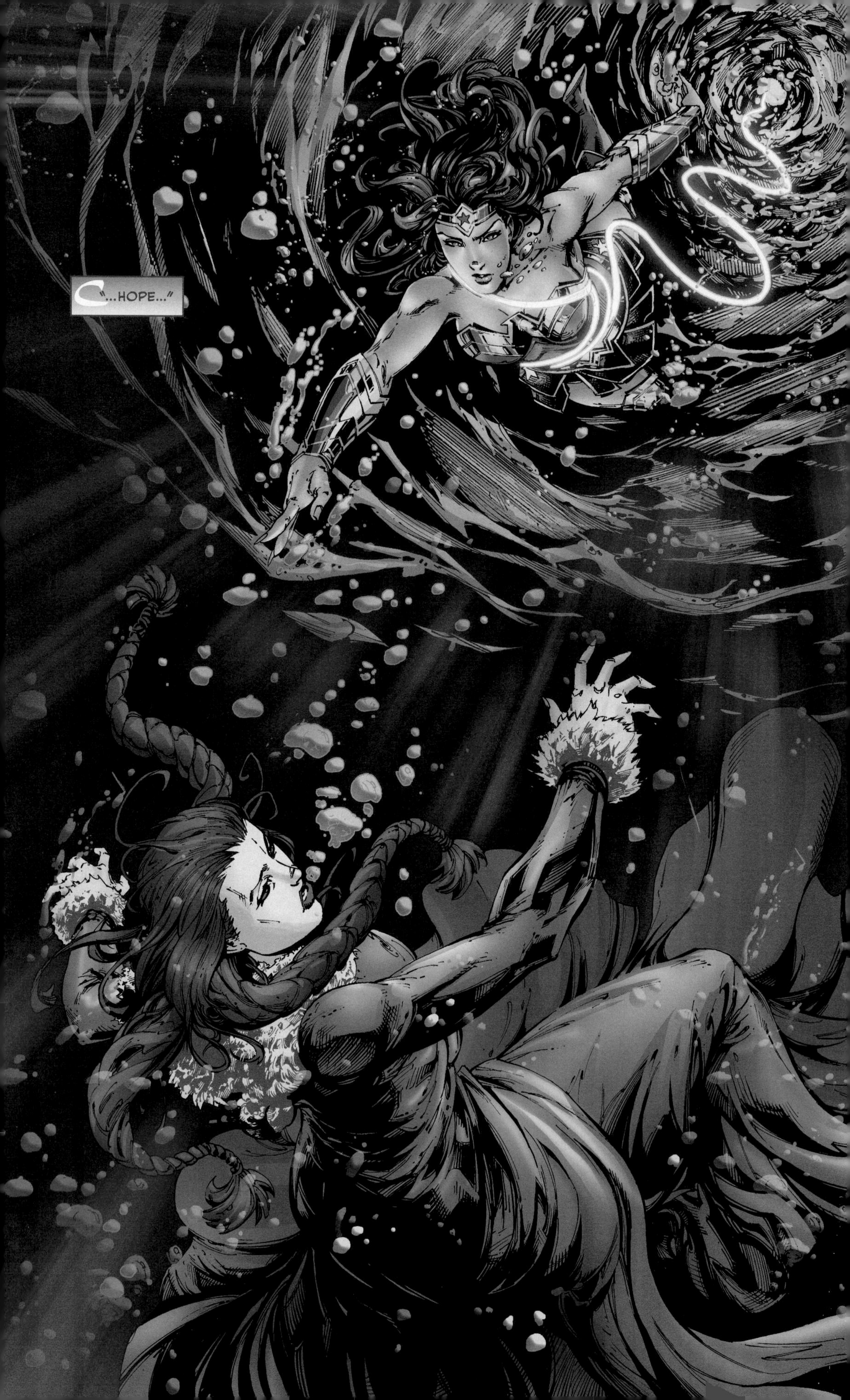
"...HOPE..."

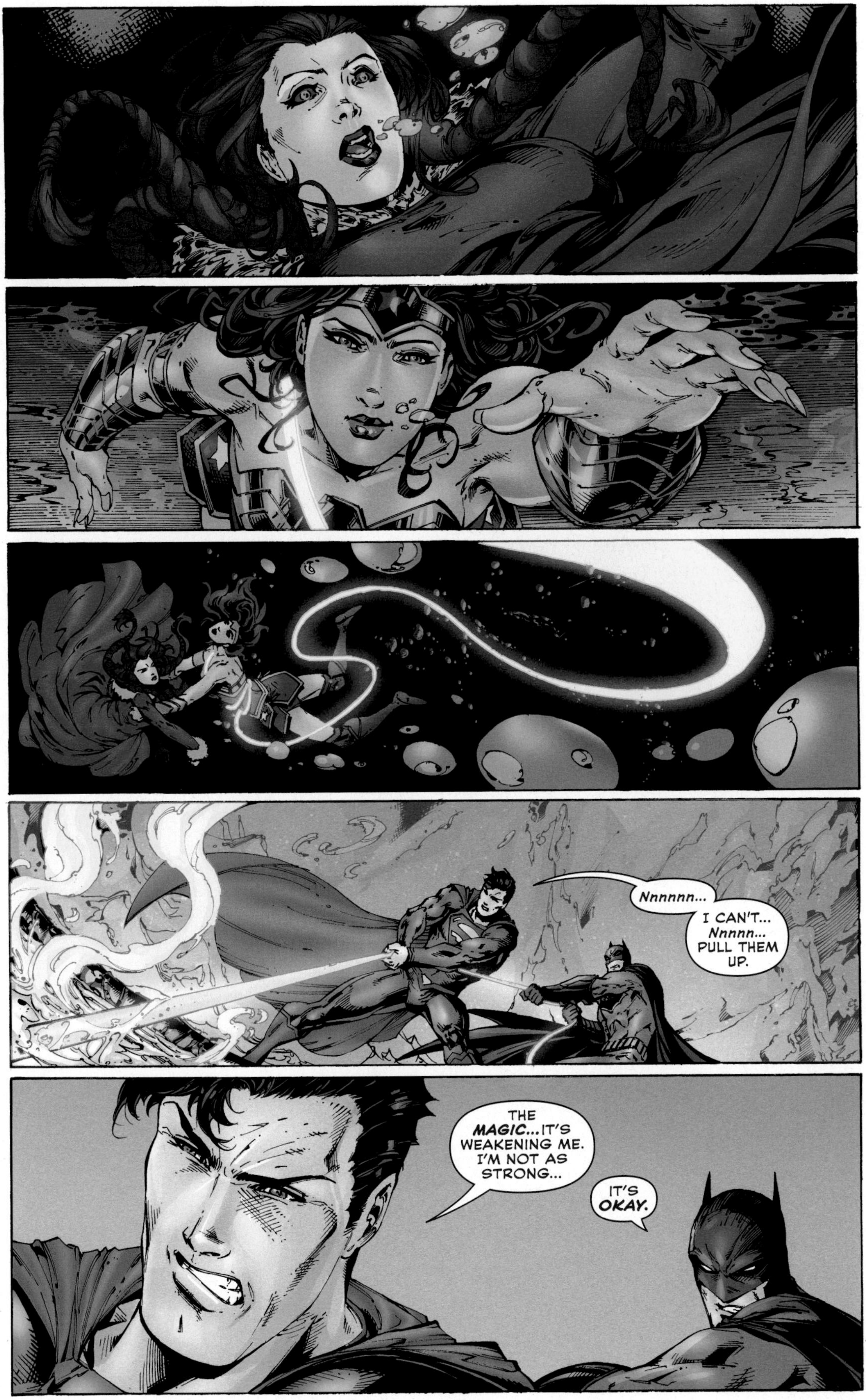
Nnnnnn...
I CAN'T... Nnnnn... PULL THEM UP.
THE MAGIC...IT'S WEAKENING ME. I'M NOT AS STRONG...
IT'S OKAY.

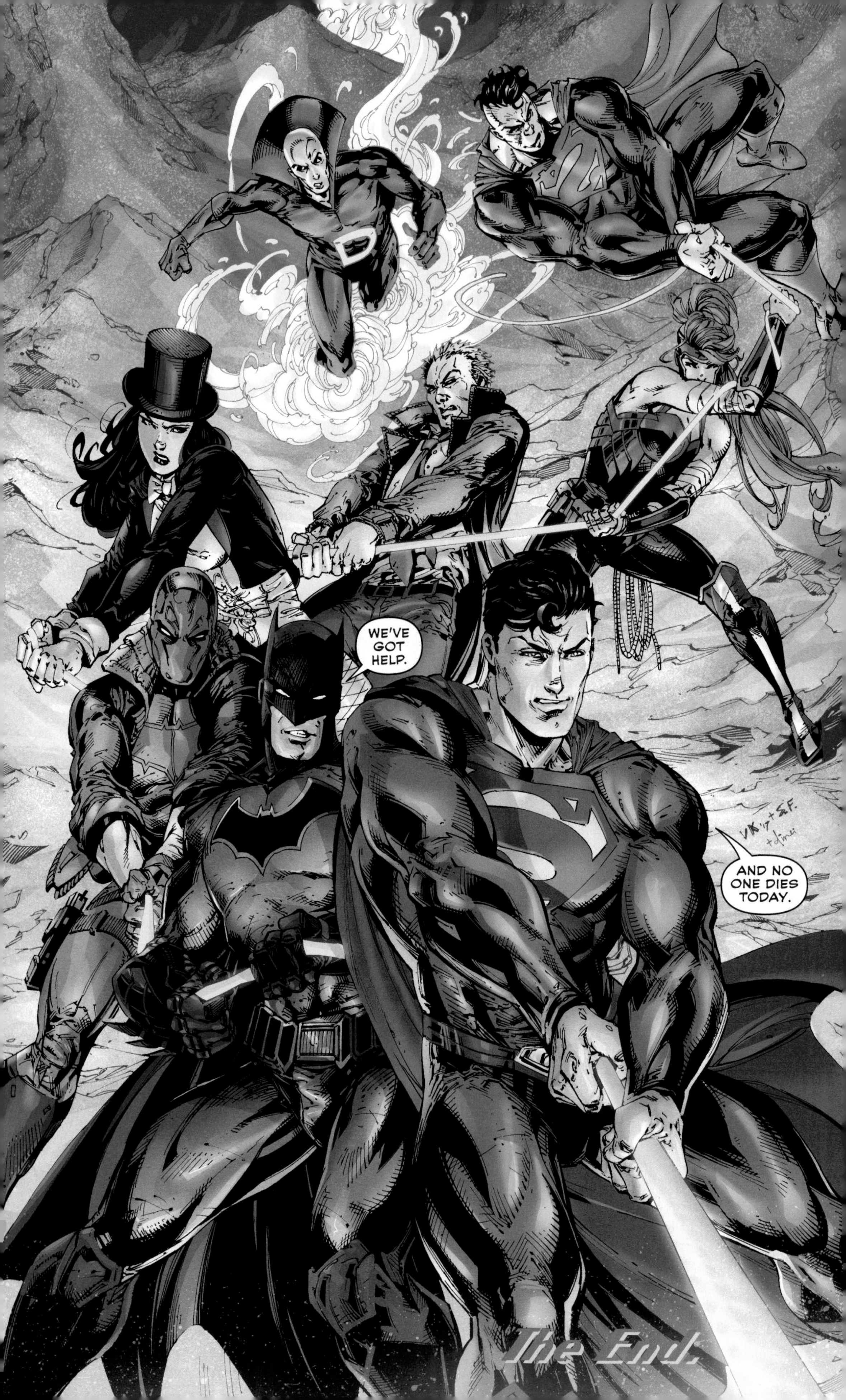
WE'VE GOT HELP.
AND NO ONE DIES TODAY.
The End.

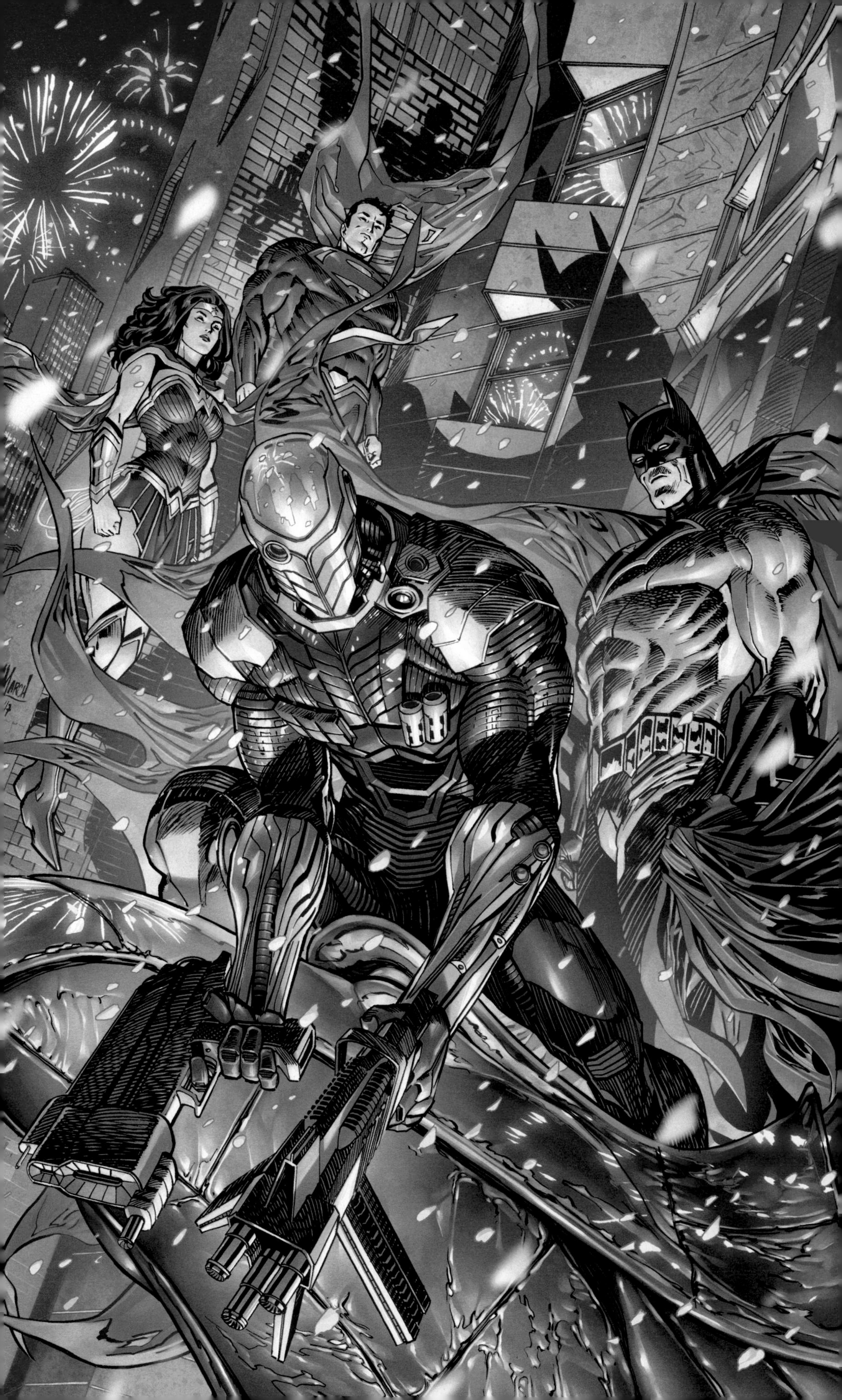

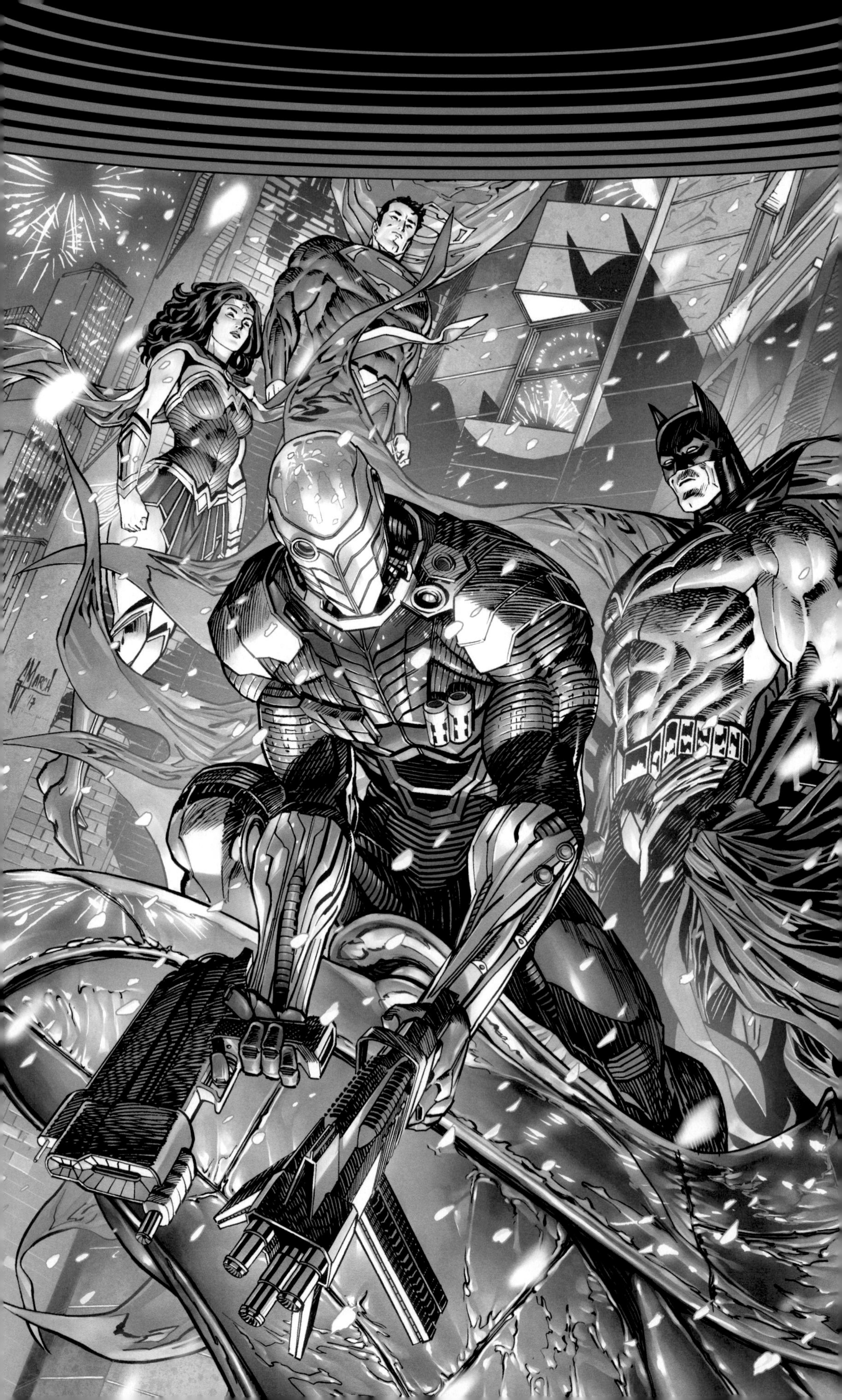

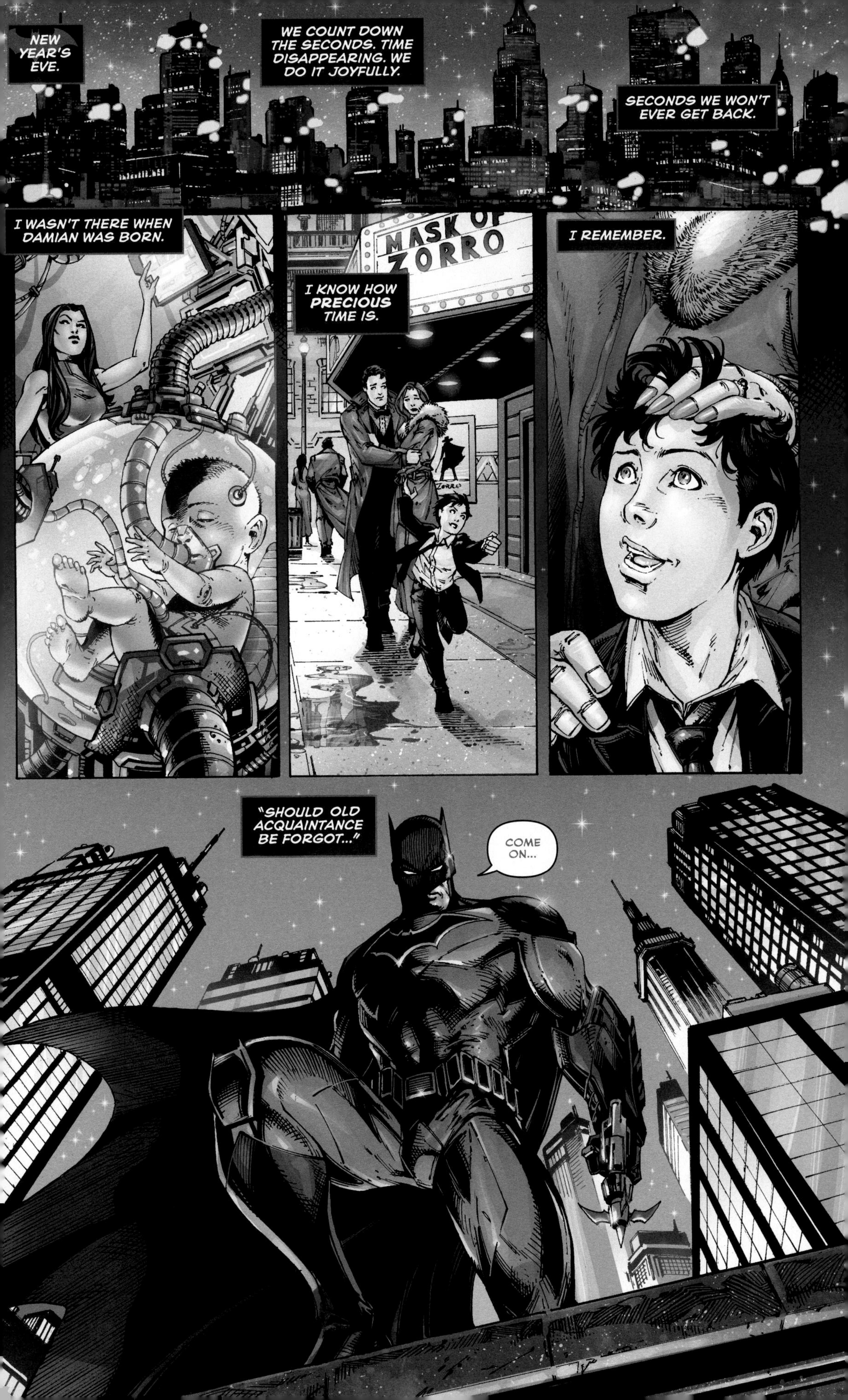
NEW YEAR'S EVE.
WE COUNT DOWN THE SECONDS. TIME DISAPPEARING. WE DO IT JOYFULLY.
SECONDS WE WON'T EVER GET BACK.
I WASN'T THERE WHEN DAMIAN WAS BORN.
MASK OF ZORRO
I KNOW HOW PRECIOUS TIME IS.
I REMEMBER.
"SHOULD OLD ACQUAINTANCE BE FORGOT..."
COME ON...

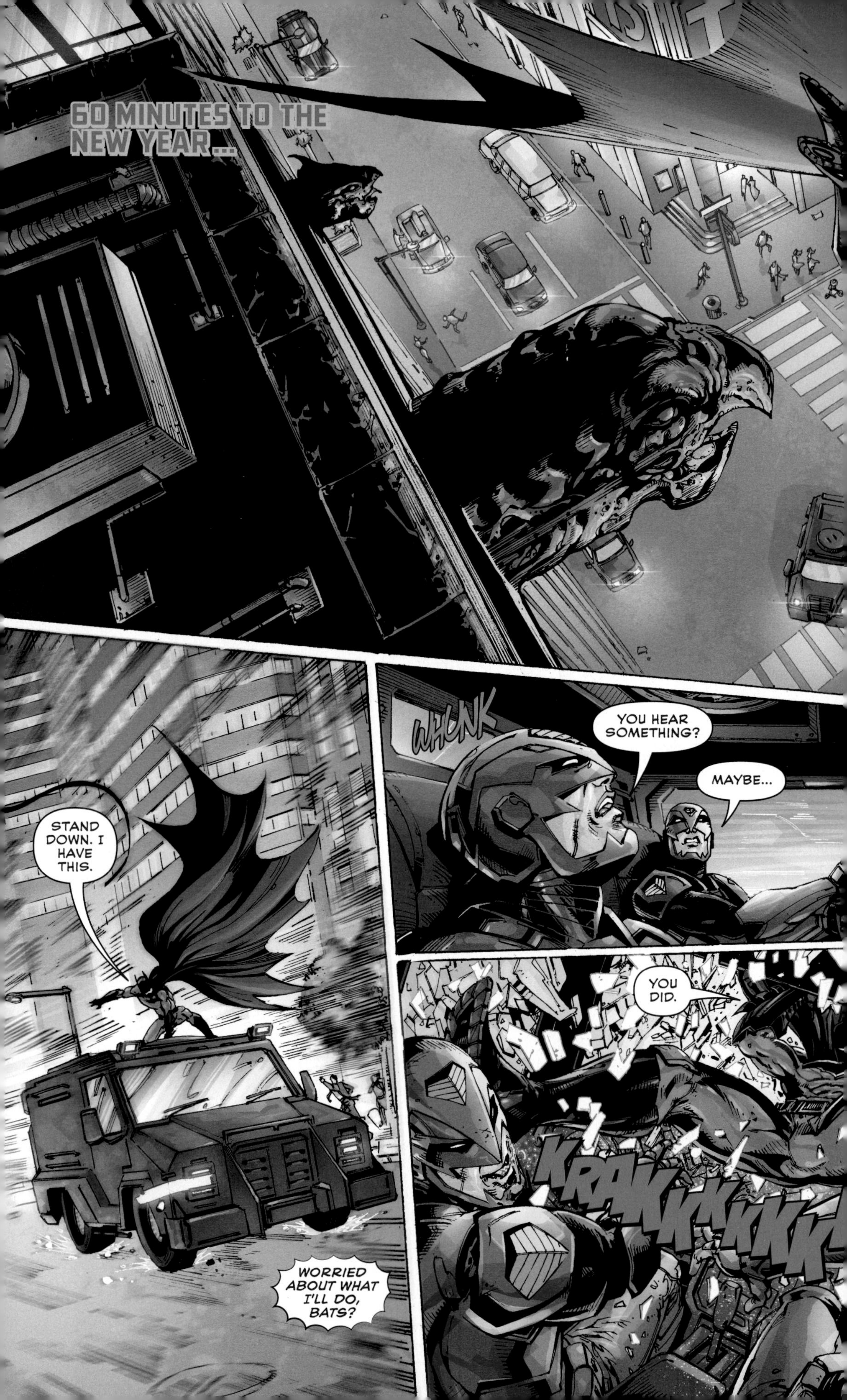
60 MINUTES TO THE NEW YEAR...
STAND DOWN. I HAVE THIS.
WHUNK
YOU HEAR SOMETHING?
MAYBE...
YOU DID.
KRAKKKKKKK
WORRIED ABOUT WHAT I'LL DO, BATS?

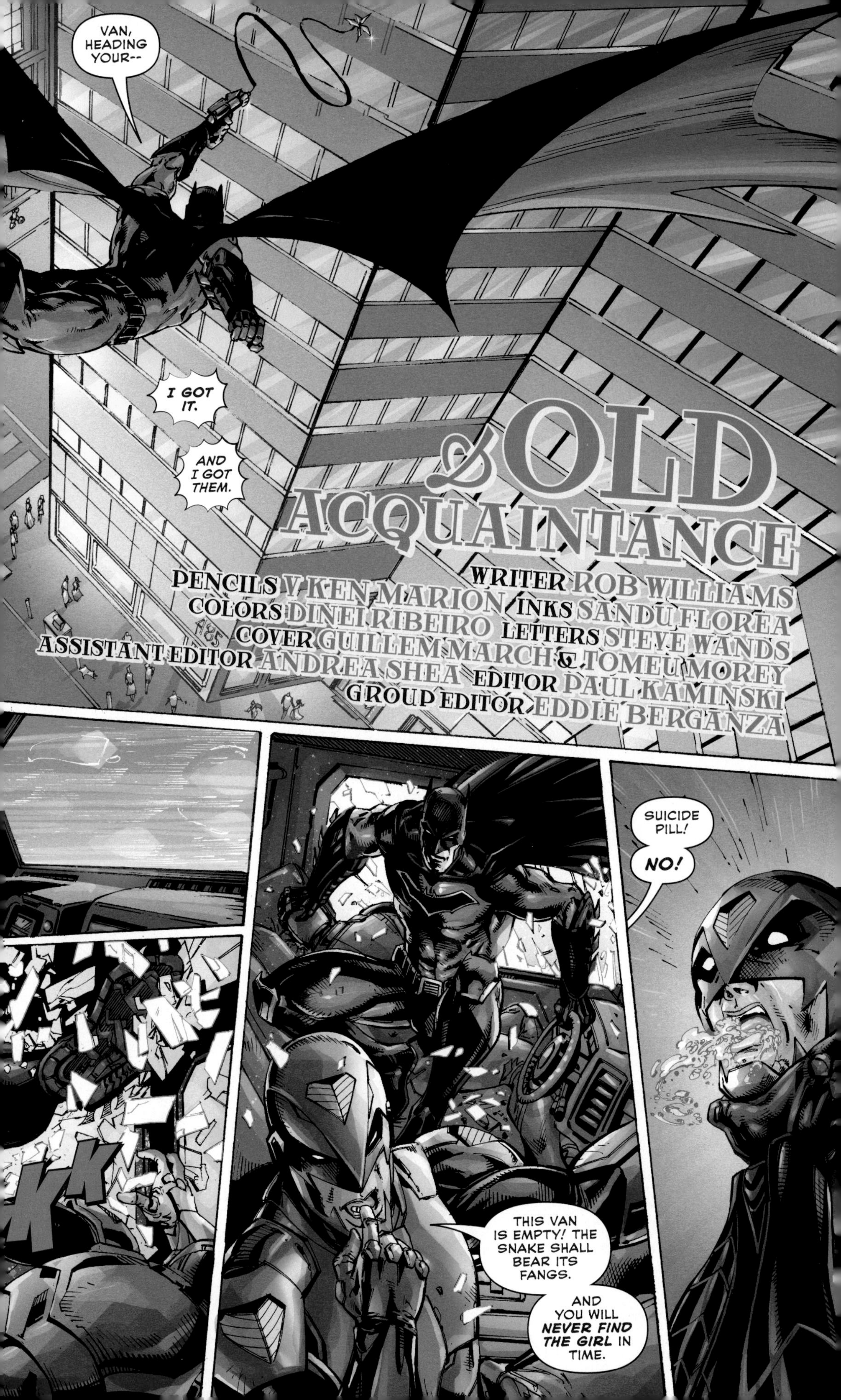

VAN, HEADING YOUR--
I GOT IT.
AND I GOT THEM.
OLD ACQUAINTANCE
WRITER ROB WILLIAMS
PENCILS V KEN MARION INKS SANDU FLOREA
COLORS DINEI RIBEIRO LETTERS STEVE WANDS
COVER GUILLEM MARCH & TOMEU MOREY
ASSISTANT EDITOR ANDREA SHEA EDITOR PAUL KAMINSKI
GROUP EDITOR EDDIE BERGANZA
SUICIDE PILL!
NO!
THIS VAN IS EMPTY! THE SNAKE SHALL BEAR ITS FANGS.
AND YOU WILL NEVER FIND THE GIRL IN TIME.

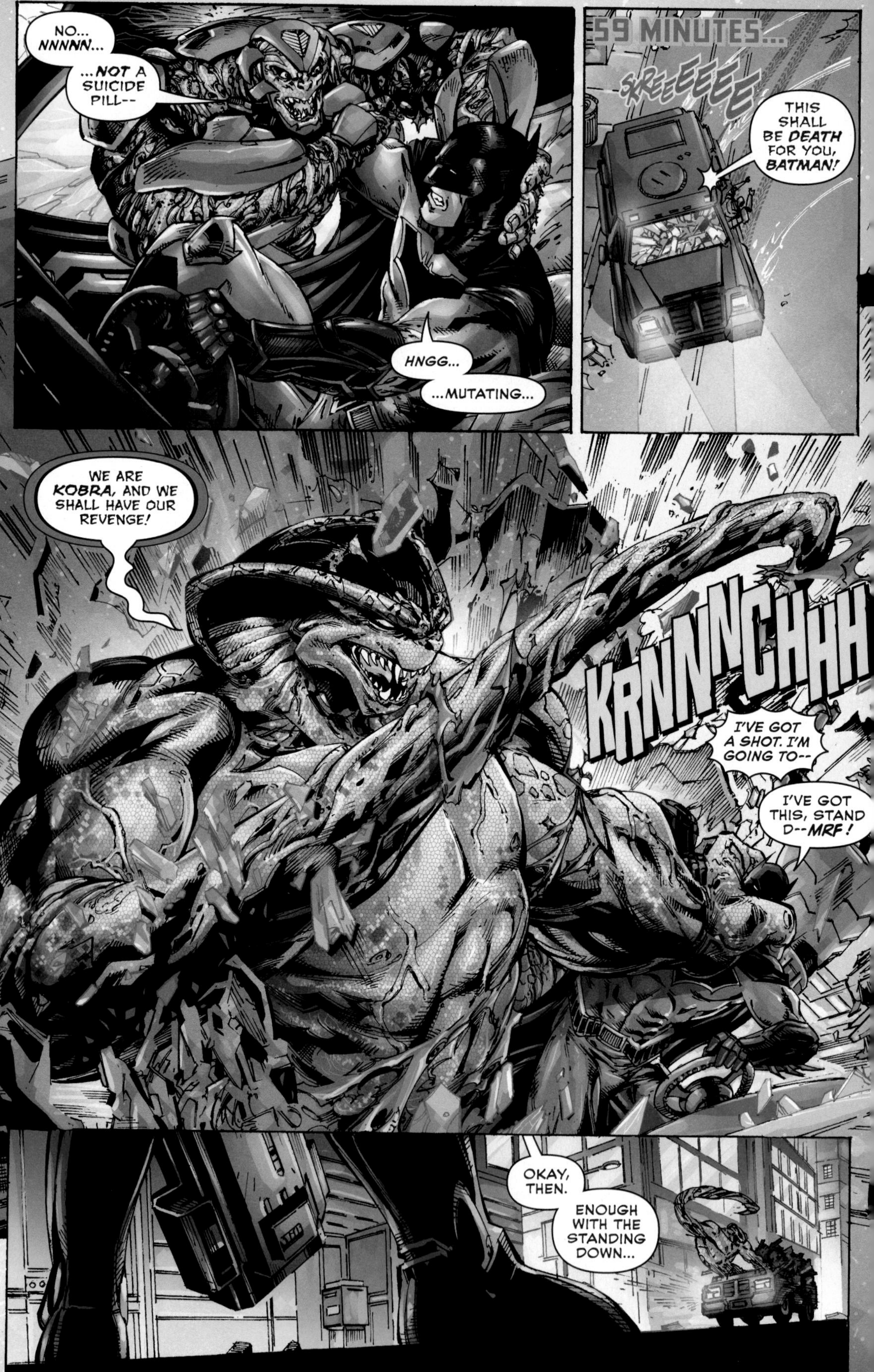
NO... NNNNN... ...NOT A SUICIDE PILL--
HNGG... ...MUTATING...
59 MINUTES...
SKREEEEEEE
THIS SHALL BE DEATH FOR YOU, BATMAN!
WE ARE KOBRA, AND WE SHALL HAVE OUR REVENGE!
KRNNNCHHH
I'VE GOT A SHOT. I'M GOING TO--
I'VE GOT THIS, STAND D--MRF!
OKAY, THEN.
ENOUGH WITH THE STANDING DOWN...

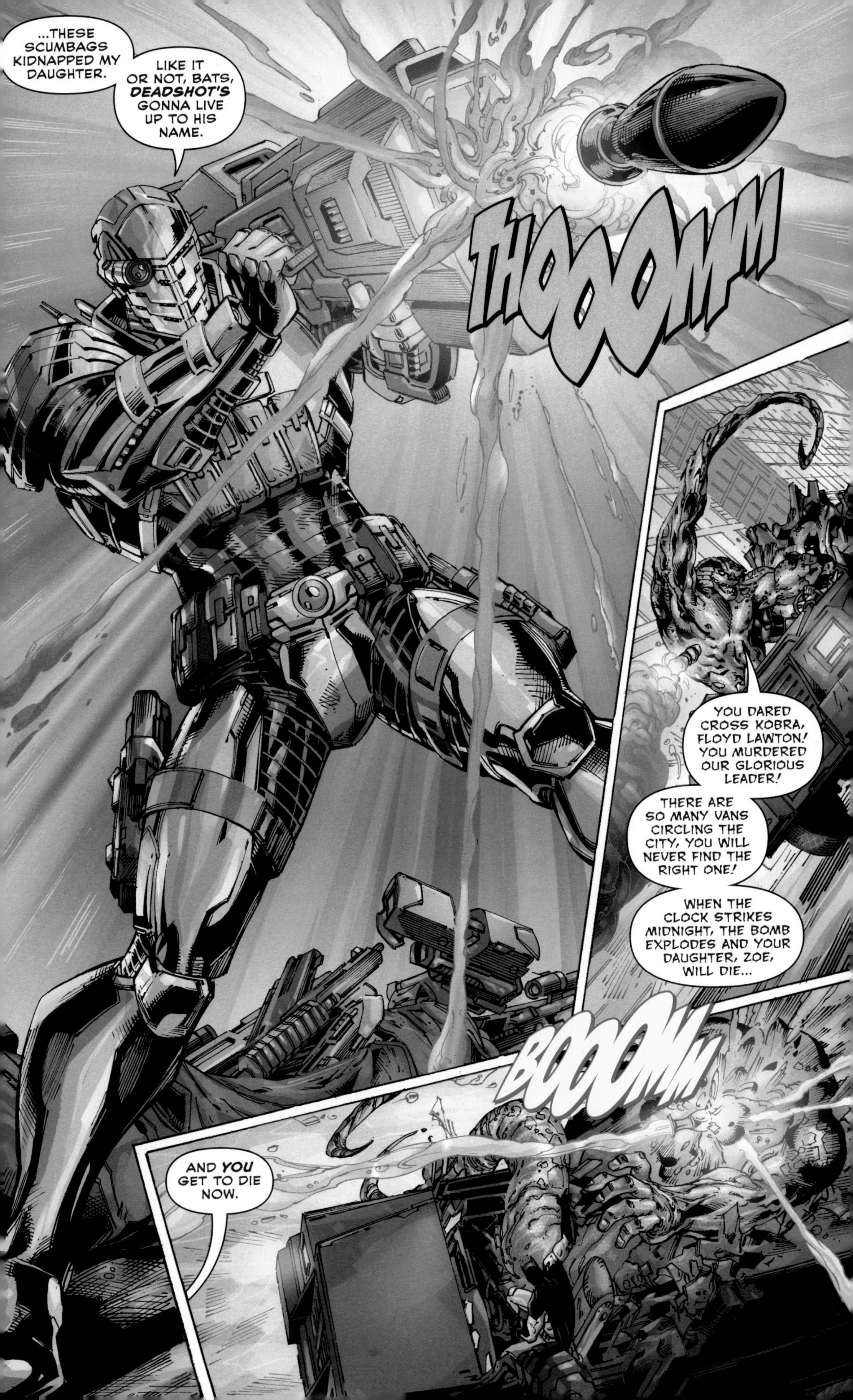
...THESE SCUMBAGS KIDNAPPED MY DAUGHTER.
LIKE IT OR NOT, BATS, *DEADSHOT'S* GONNA LIVE UP TO HIS NAME.
THOOOMM
YOU DARED CROSS KOBRA, FLOYD LAWTON! YOU MURDERED OUR GLORIOUS LEADER!
THERE ARE SO MANY VANS CIRCLING THE CITY, YOU WILL NEVER FIND THE RIGHT ONE!
WHEN THE CLOCK STRIKES MIDNIGHT, THE BOMB EXPLODES AND YOUR DAUGHTER, ZOE, WILL DIE...
BOOOMM
AND *YOU* GET TO DIE NOW.

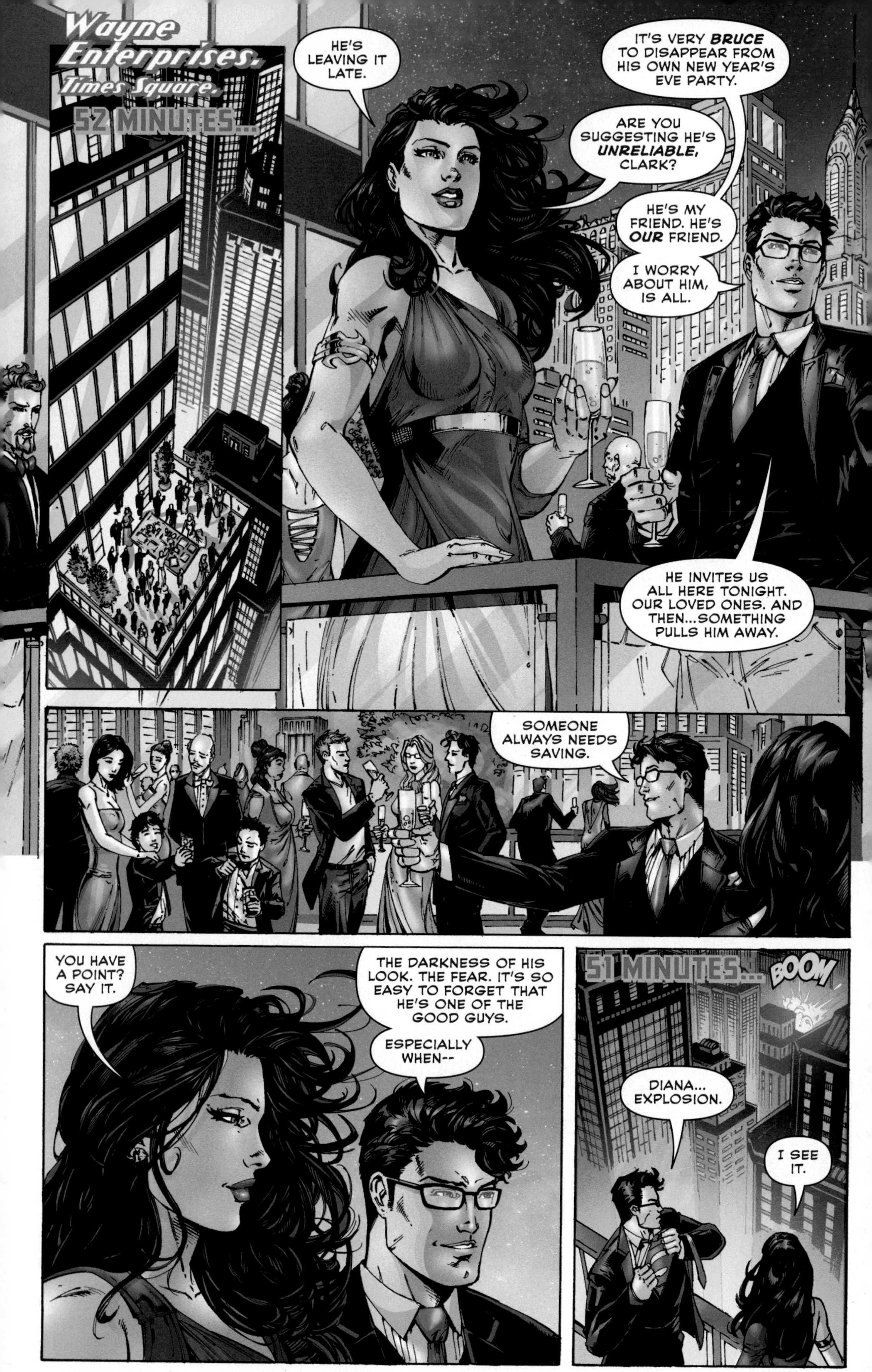
Wayne Enterprises. Times Square.
52 MINUTES...
HE'S LEAVING IT LATE.
IT'S VERY BRUCE TO DISAPPEAR FROM HIS OWN NEW YEAR'S EVE PARTY.
ARE YOU SUGGESTING HE'S UNRELIABLE, CLARK?
HE'S MY FRIEND. HE'S OUR FRIEND.
I WORRY ABOUT HIM, IS ALL.
HE INVITES US ALL HERE TONIGHT. OUR LOVED ONES. AND THEN...SOMETHING PULLS HIM AWAY.
SOMEONE ALWAYS NEEDS SAVING.
YOU HAVE A POINT? SAY IT.
THE DARKNESS OF HIS LOOK. THE FEAR. IT'S SO EASY TO FORGET THAT HE'S ONE OF THE GOOD GUYS.
ESPECIALLY WHEN--
51 MINUTES...
BOOM
DIANA... EXPLOSION.
I SEE IT.

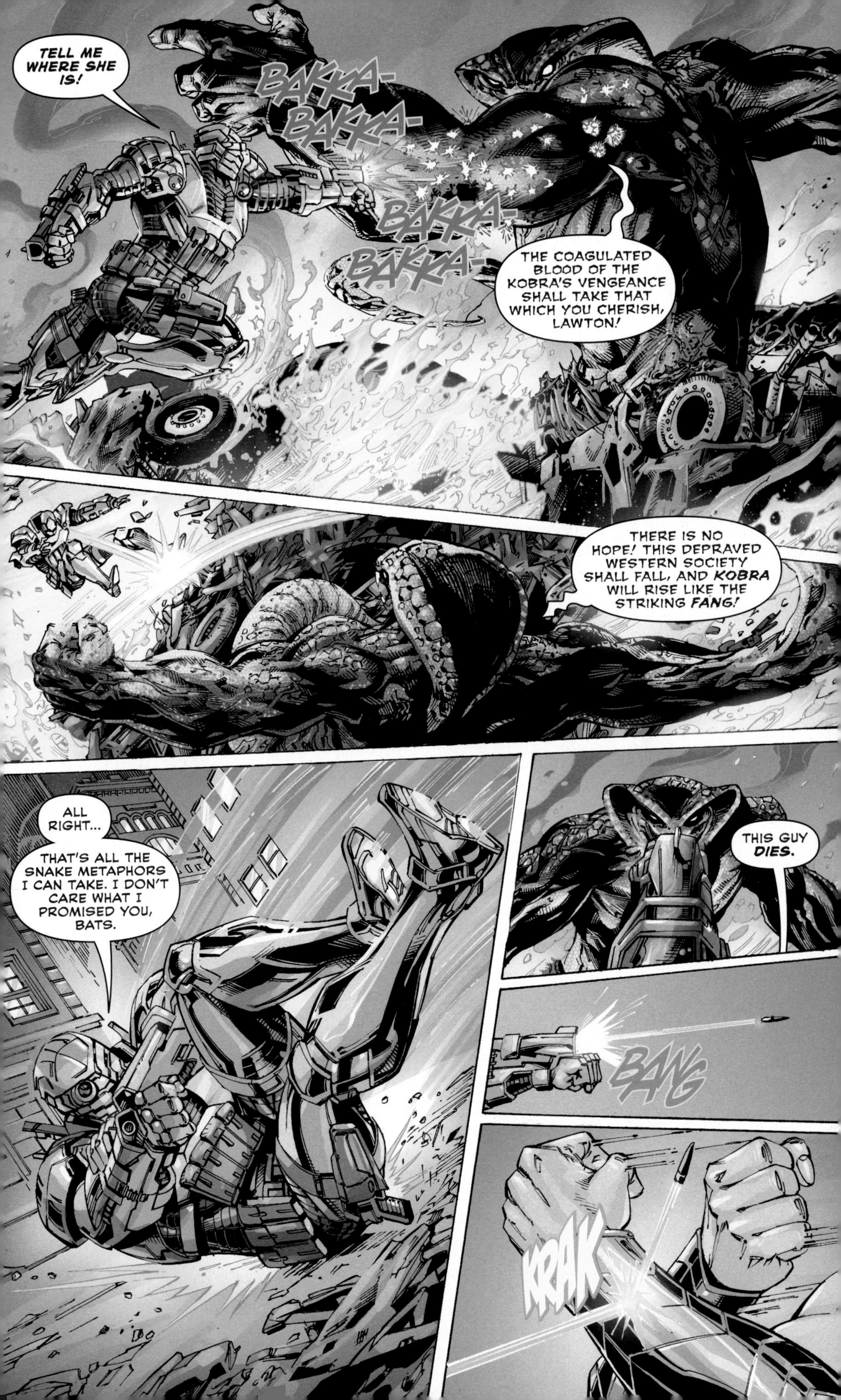
TELL ME WHERE SHE IS!
BAKKA-BAKKA-
BAKKA-BAKKA-
THE COAGULATED BLOOD OF THE KOBRA'S VENGEANCE SHALL TAKE THAT WHICH YOU CHERISH, LAWTON!
THERE IS NO HOPE! THIS DEPRAVED WESTERN SOCIETY SHALL FALL, AND KOBRA WILL RISE LIKE THE STRIKING FANG!
ALL RIGHT...
THAT'S ALL THE SNAKE METAPHORS I CAN TAKE. I DON'T CARE WHAT I PROMISED YOU, BATS.
THIS GUY DIES.
BANG
KRAK

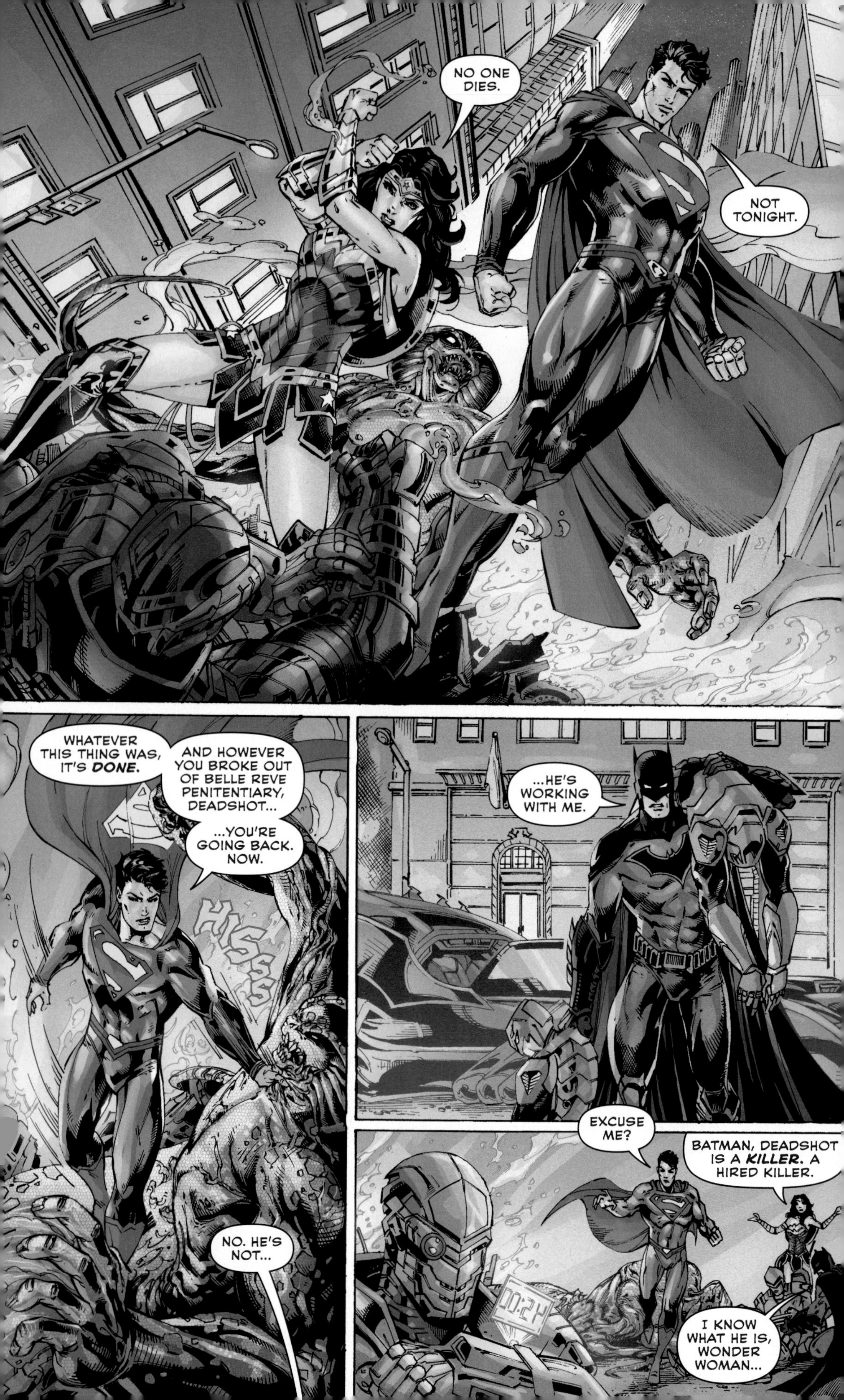
NO ONE DIES.
NOT TONIGHT.
WHATEVER THIS THING WAS, IT'S **DONE.**
AND HOWEVER YOU BROKE OUT OF BELLE REVE PENITENTIARY, DEADSHOT...
...YOU'RE GOING BACK. NOW.
HISSS
...HE'S WORKING WITH ME.
NO. HE'S NOT...
EXCUSE ME?
BATMAN, DEADSHOT IS A **KILLER.** A HIRED KILLER.
00:24
I KNOW WHAT HE IS, WONDER WOMAN...

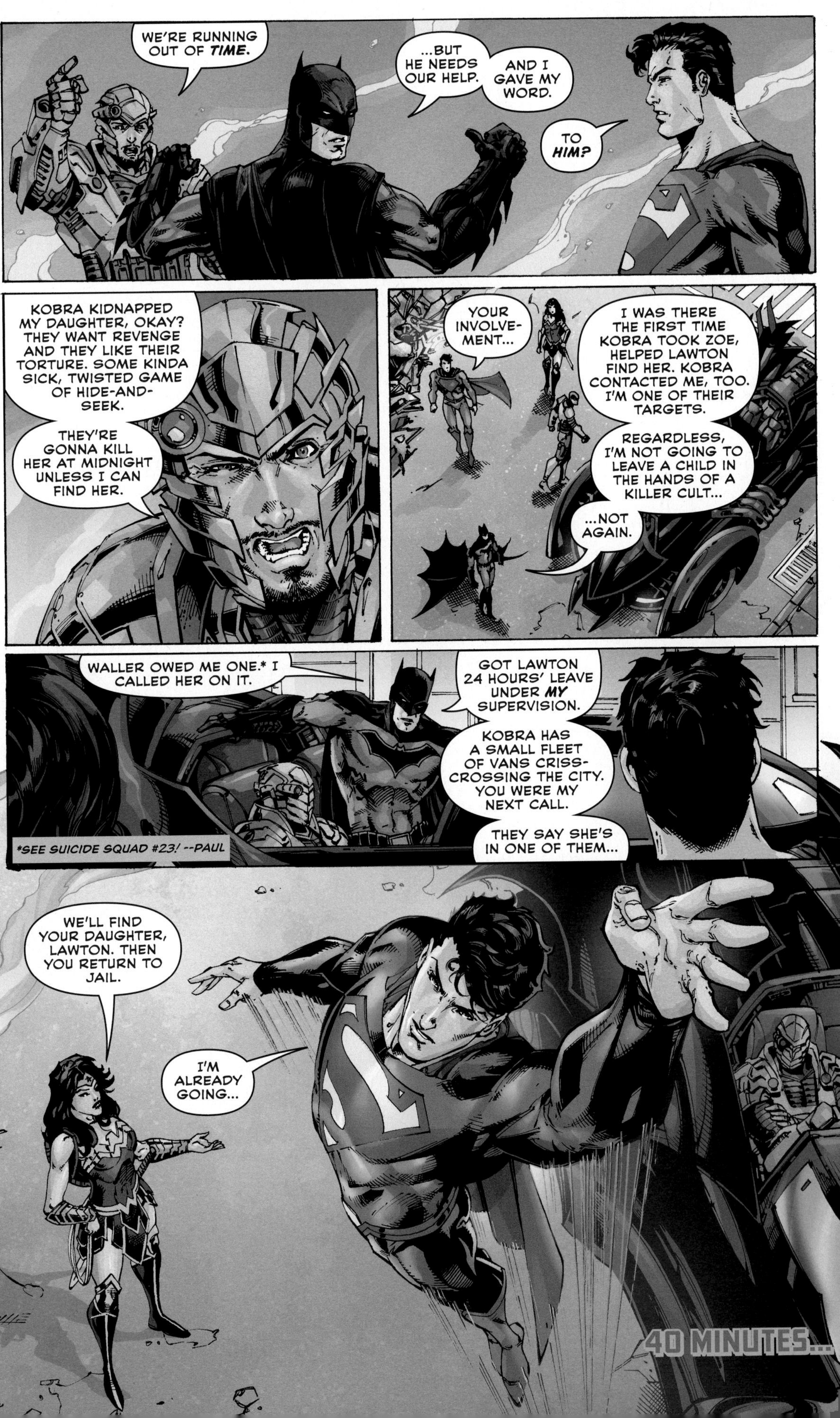
WE'RE RUNNING OUT OF TIME.
...BUT HE NEEDS OUR HELP.
AND I GAVE MY WORD.
TO HIM?
KOBRA KIDNAPPED MY DAUGHTER, OKAY? THEY WANT REVENGE AND THEY LIKE THEIR TORTURE. SOME KINDA SICK, TWISTED GAME OF HIDE-AND-SEEK.
THEY'RE GONNA KILL HER AT MIDNIGHT UNLESS I CAN FIND HER.
YOUR INVOLVEMENT...
I WAS THERE THE FIRST TIME KOBRA TOOK ZOE, HELPED LAWTON FIND HER. KOBRA CONTACTED ME, TOO. I'M ONE OF THEIR TARGETS.
REGARDLESS, I'M NOT GOING TO LEAVE A CHILD IN THE HANDS OF A KILLER CULT...
...NOT AGAIN.
WALLER OWED ME ONE.* I CALLED HER ON IT.
GOT LAWTON 24 HOURS' LEAVE UNDER MY SUPERVISION.
KOBRA HAS A SMALL FLEET OF VANS CRISS-CROSSING THE CITY. YOU WERE MY NEXT CALL.
THEY SAY SHE'S IN ONE OF THEM...
*SEE SUICIDE SQUAD #23! --PAUL
WE'LL FIND YOUR DAUGHTER, LAWTON. THEN YOU RETURN TO JAIL.
I'M ALREADY GOING...
40 MINUTES...

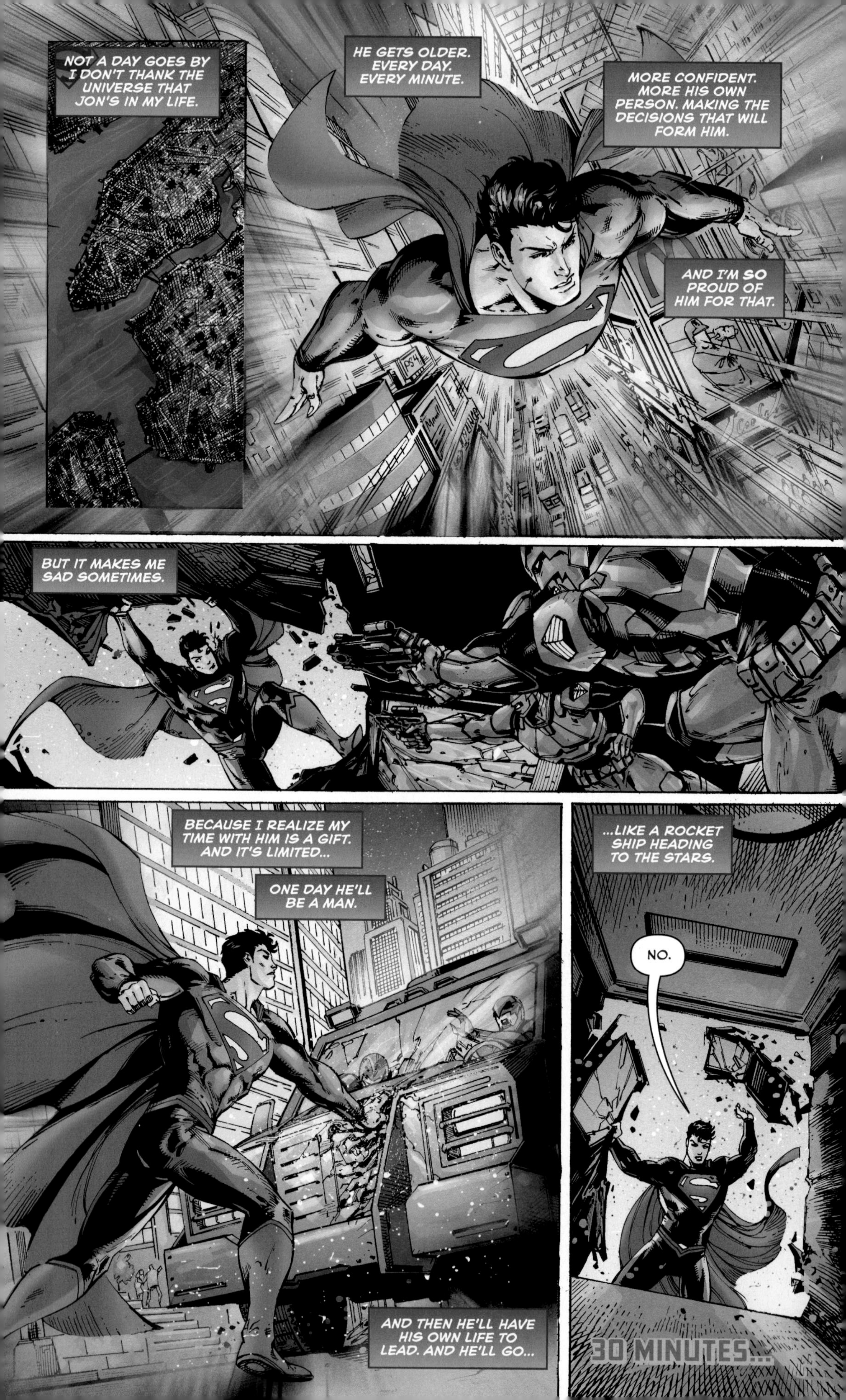
NOT A DAY GOES BY I DON'T THANK THE UNIVERSE THAT JON'S IN MY LIFE.
HE GETS OLDER. EVERY DAY. EVERY MINUTE.
MORE CONFIDENT. MORE HIS OWN PERSON. MAKING THE DECISIONS THAT WILL FORM HIM.
AND I'M SO PROUD OF HIM FOR THAT.
BUT IT MAKES ME SAD SOMETIMES.
BECAUSE I REALIZE MY TIME WITH HIM IS A GIFT. AND IT'S LIMITED...
ONE DAY HE'LL BE A MAN.
AND THEN HE'LL HAVE HIS OWN LIFE TO LEAD. AND HE'LL GO...
...LIKE A ROCKET SHIP HEADING TO THE STARS.
NO.
30 MINUTES...

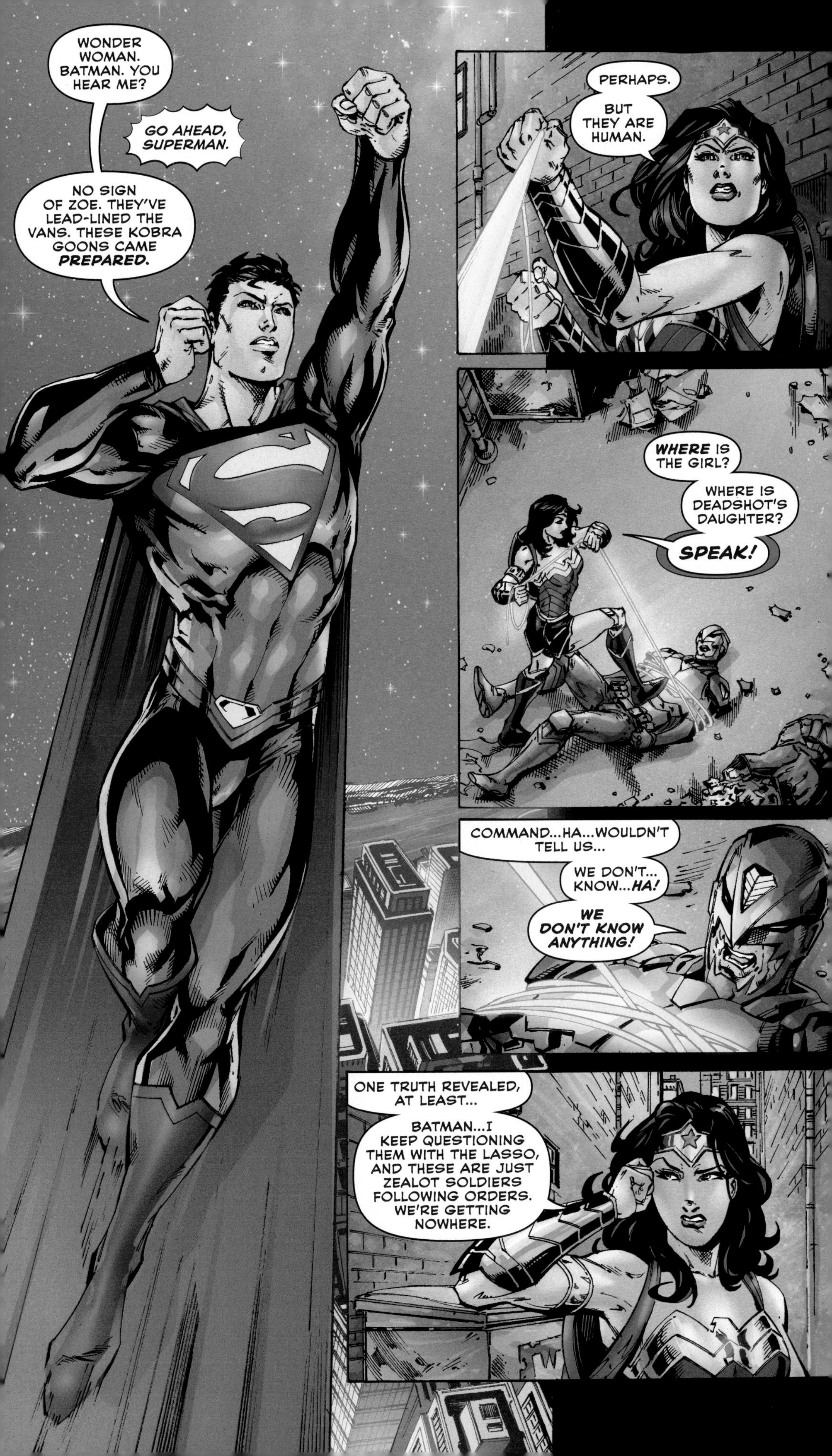
WONDER WOMAN. BATMAN. YOU HEAR ME?
GO AHEAD, SUPERMAN.
NO SIGN OF ZOE. THEY'VE LEAD-LINED THE VANS. THESE KOBRA GOONS CAME PREPARED.
PERHAPS.
BUT THEY ARE HUMAN.
WHERE IS THE GIRL?
WHERE IS DEADSHOT'S DAUGHTER?
SPEAK!
COMMAND...HA...WOULDN'T TELL US...
WE DON'T... KNOW...HA!
WE DON'T KNOW ANYTHING!
ONE TRUTH REVEALED, AT LEAST...
BATMAN...I KEEP QUESTIONING THEM WITH THE LASSO, AND THESE ARE JUST ZEALOT SOLDIERS FOLLOWING ORDERS. WE'RE GETTING NOWHERE.

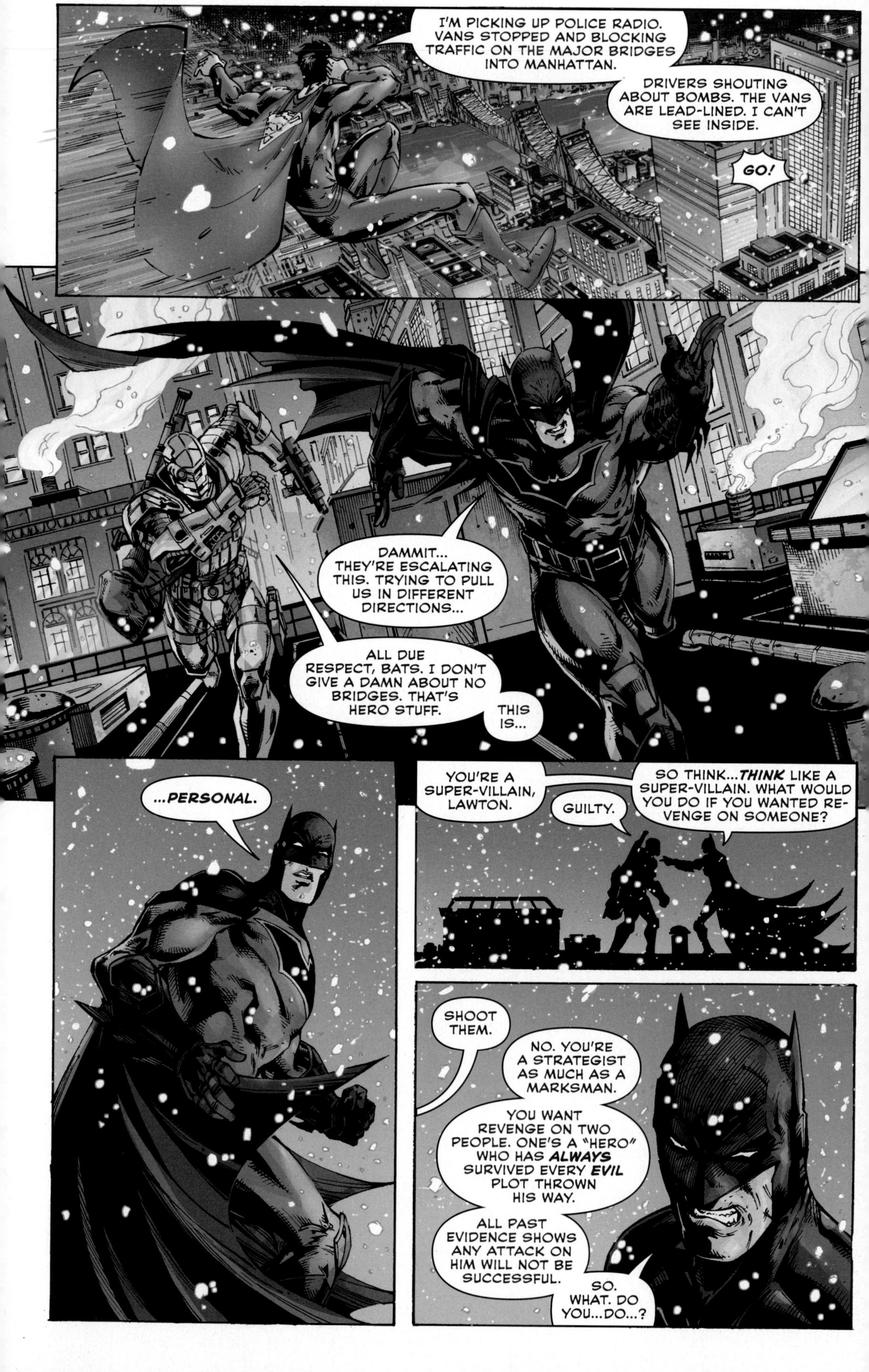
I'M PICKING UP POLICE RADIO. VANS STOPPED AND BLOCKING TRAFFIC ON THE MAJOR BRIDGES INTO MANHATTAN.
DRIVERS SHOUTING ABOUT BOMBS. THE VANS ARE LEAD-LINED. I CAN'T SEE INSIDE.
GO!
DAMMIT... THEY'RE ESCALATING THIS. TRYING TO PULL US IN DIFFERENT DIRECTIONS...
ALL DUE RESPECT, BATS. I DON'T GIVE A DAMN ABOUT NO BRIDGES. THAT'S HERO STUFF.
THIS IS...
...PERSONAL.
YOU'RE A SUPER-VILLAIN, LAWTON.
GUILTY.
SO THINK...THINK LIKE A SUPER-VILLAIN. WHAT WOULD YOU DO IF YOU WANTED REVENGE ON SOMEONE?
SHOOT THEM.
NO. YOU'RE A STRATEGIST AS MUCH AS A MARKSMAN.
YOU WANT REVENGE ON TWO PEOPLE. ONE'S A "HERO" WHO HAS ALWAYS SURVIVED EVERY EVIL PLOT THROWN HIS WAY.
ALL PAST EVIDENCE SHOWS ANY ATTACK ON HIM WILL NOT BE SUCCESSFUL.
SO. WHAT. DO YOU...DO...?

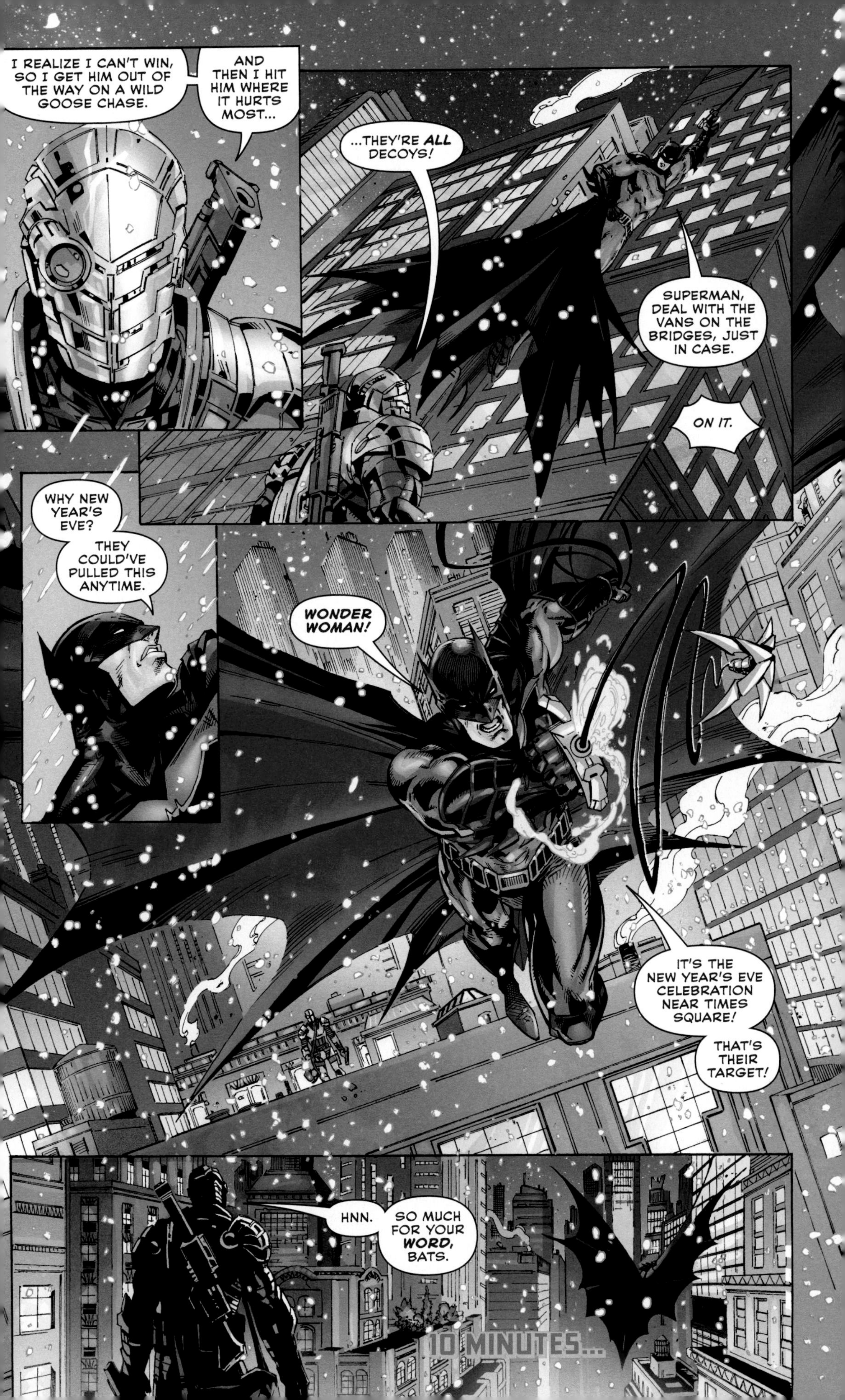
I REALIZE I CAN'T WIN, SO I GET HIM OUT OF THE WAY ON A WILD GOOSE CHASE.
AND THEN I HIT HIM WHERE IT HURTS MOST...
...THEY'RE ALL DECOYS!
SUPERMAN, DEAL WITH THE VANS ON THE BRIDGES, JUST IN CASE.
ON IT.
WHY NEW YEAR'S EVE?
THEY COULD'VE PULLED THIS ANYTIME.
WONDER WOMAN!
IT'S THE NEW YEAR'S EVE CELEBRATION NEAR TIMES SQUARE!
THAT'S THEIR TARGET!
HNN.
SO MUCH FOR YOUR WORD, BATS.
10 MINUTES...

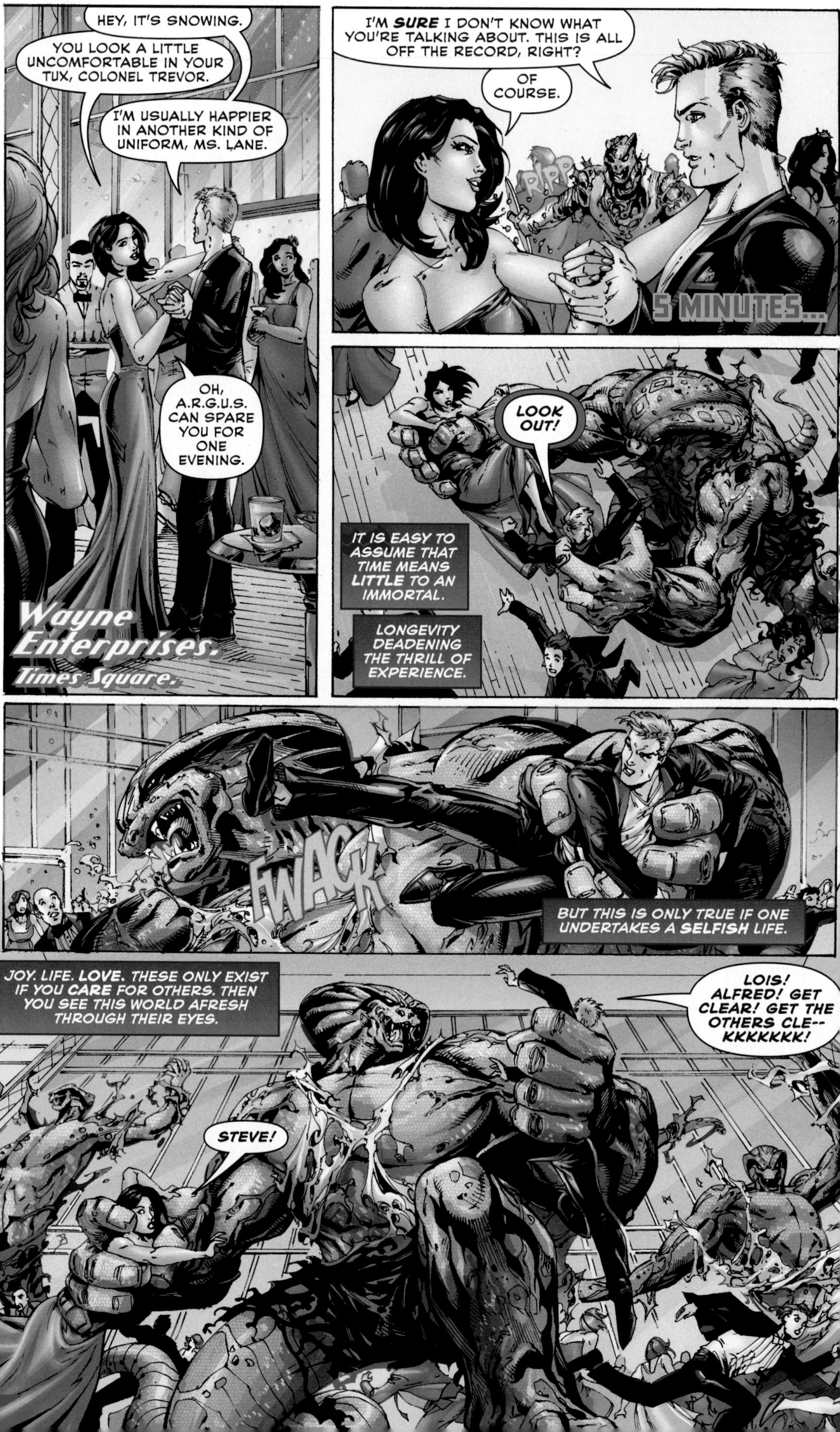
HEY, IT'S SNOWING.
YOU LOOK A LITTLE UNCOMFORTABLE IN YOUR TUX, COLONEL TREVOR.
I'M USUALLY HAPPIER IN ANOTHER KIND OF UNIFORM, MS. LANE.
OH, A.R.G.U.S. CAN SPARE YOU FOR ONE EVENING.
Wayne Enterprises. Times Square.
I'M SURE I DON'T KNOW WHAT YOU'RE TALKING ABOUT. THIS IS ALL OFF THE RECORD, RIGHT?
OF COURSE.
RIPP
5 MINUTES...
LOOK OUT!
IT IS EASY TO ASSUME THAT TIME MEANS LITTLE TO AN IMMORTAL.
LONGEVITY DEADENING THE THRILL OF EXPERIENCE.
FWACK
BUT THIS IS ONLY TRUE IF ONE UNDERTAKES A SELFISH LIFE.
JOY. LIFE. LOVE. THESE ONLY EXIST IF YOU CARE FOR OTHERS. THEN YOU SEE THIS WORLD AFRESH THROUGH THEIR EYES.
LOIS! ALFRED! GET CLEAR! GET THE OTHERS CLE--KKKKKKK!
STEVE!

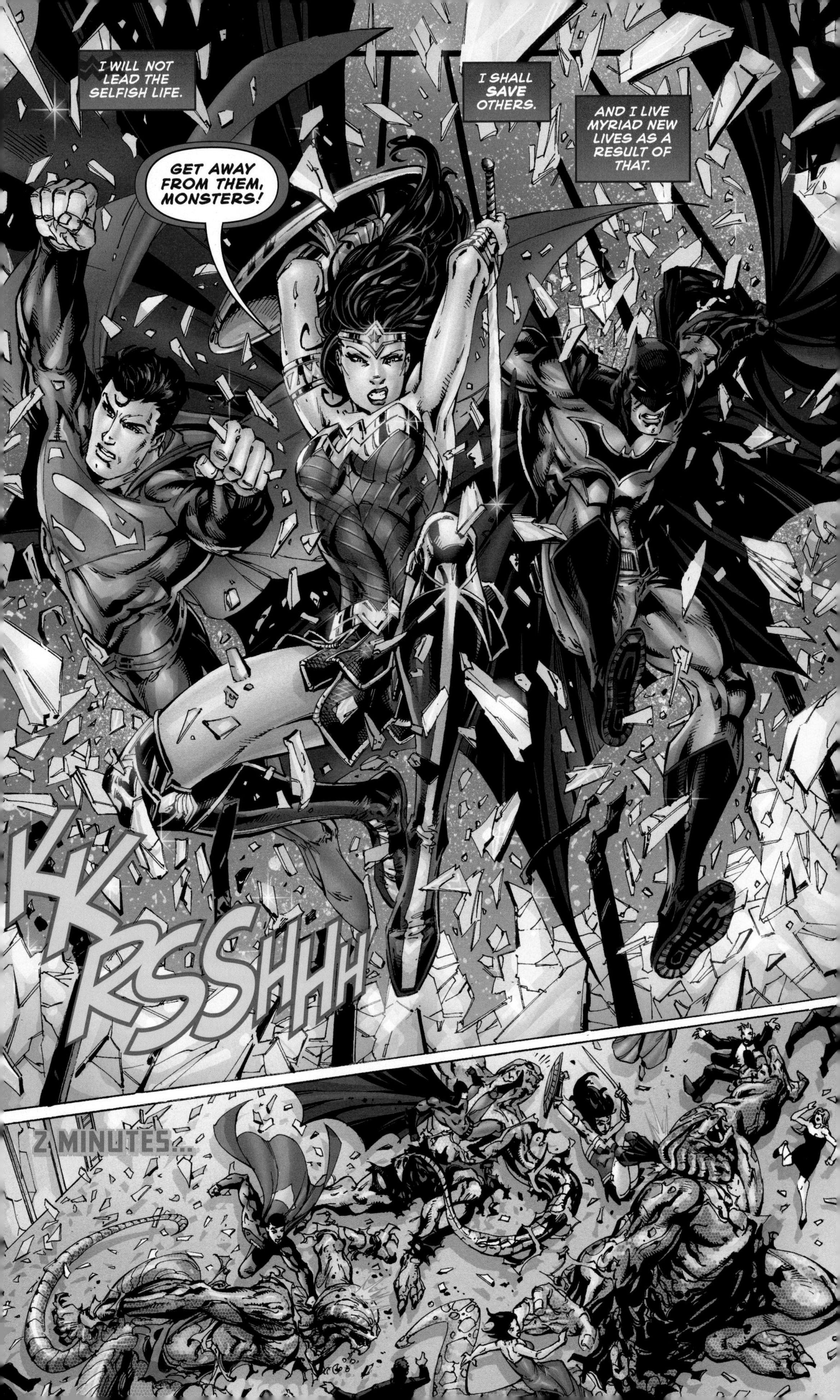
I WILL NOT LEAD THE SELFISH LIFE.
GET AWAY FROM THEM, MONSTERS!
I SHALL SAVE OTHERS.
AND I LIVE MYRIAD NEW LIVES AS A RESULT OF THAT.
KKRSSHHH
2 MINUTES...

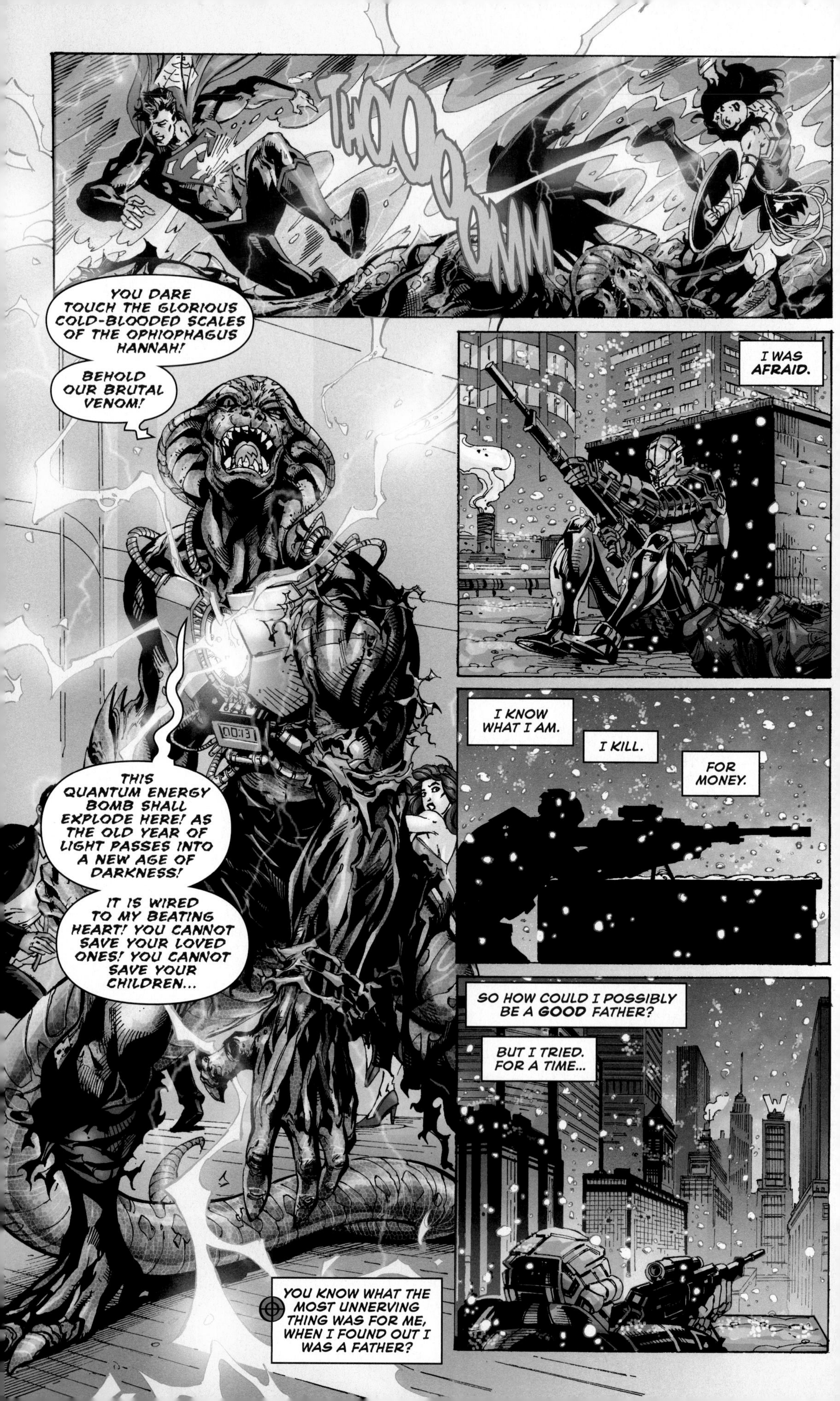
THOOOOOMM
YOU DARE TOUCH THE GLORIOUS COLD-BLOODED SCALES OF THE OPHIOPHAGUS HANNAH!
BEHOLD OUR BRUTAL VENOM!
00:13
THIS QUANTUM ENERGY BOMB SHALL EXPLODE HERE! AS THE OLD YEAR OF LIGHT PASSES INTO A NEW AGE OF DARKNESS!
IT IS WIRED TO MY BEATING HEART! YOU CANNOT SAVE YOUR LOVED ONES! YOU CANNOT SAVE YOUR CHILDREN...
YOU KNOW WHAT THE MOST UNNERVING THING WAS FOR ME, WHEN I FOUND OUT I WAS A FATHER?
I WAS AFRAID.
I KNOW WHAT I AM.
I KILL.
FOR MONEY.
SO HOW COULD I POSSIBLY BE A GOOD FATHER?
BUT I TRIED. FOR A TIME...

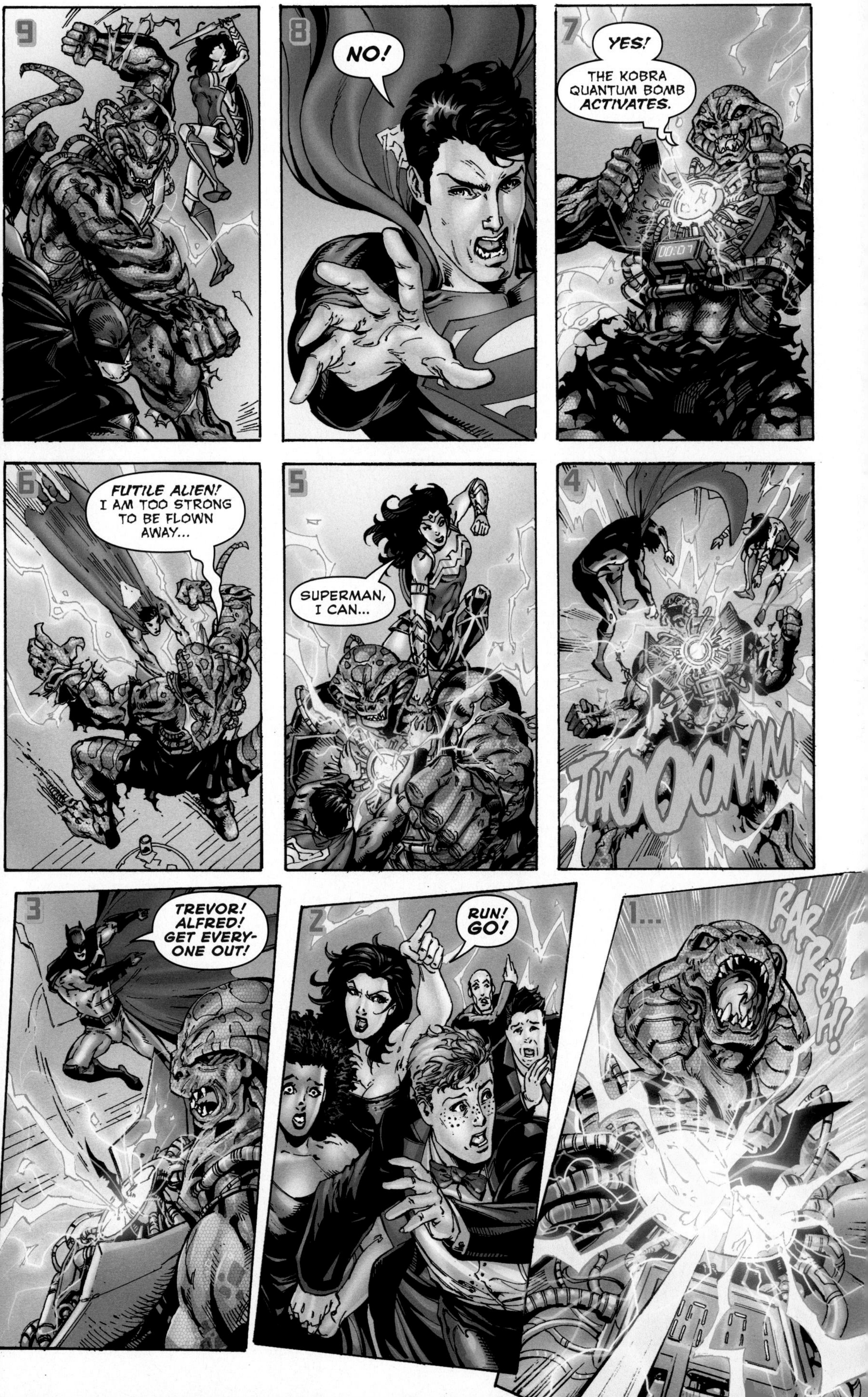
9
8
NO!
7
YES!
THE KOBRA QUANTUM BOMB ACTIVATES.
00:07
6
FUTILE ALIEN! I AM TOO STRONG TO BE FLOWN AWAY...
5
SUPERMAN, I CAN...
4
THOOOMM
3
TREVOR! ALFRED! GET EVERY-ONE OUT!
2
RUN! GO!
1...
RARRGH!!

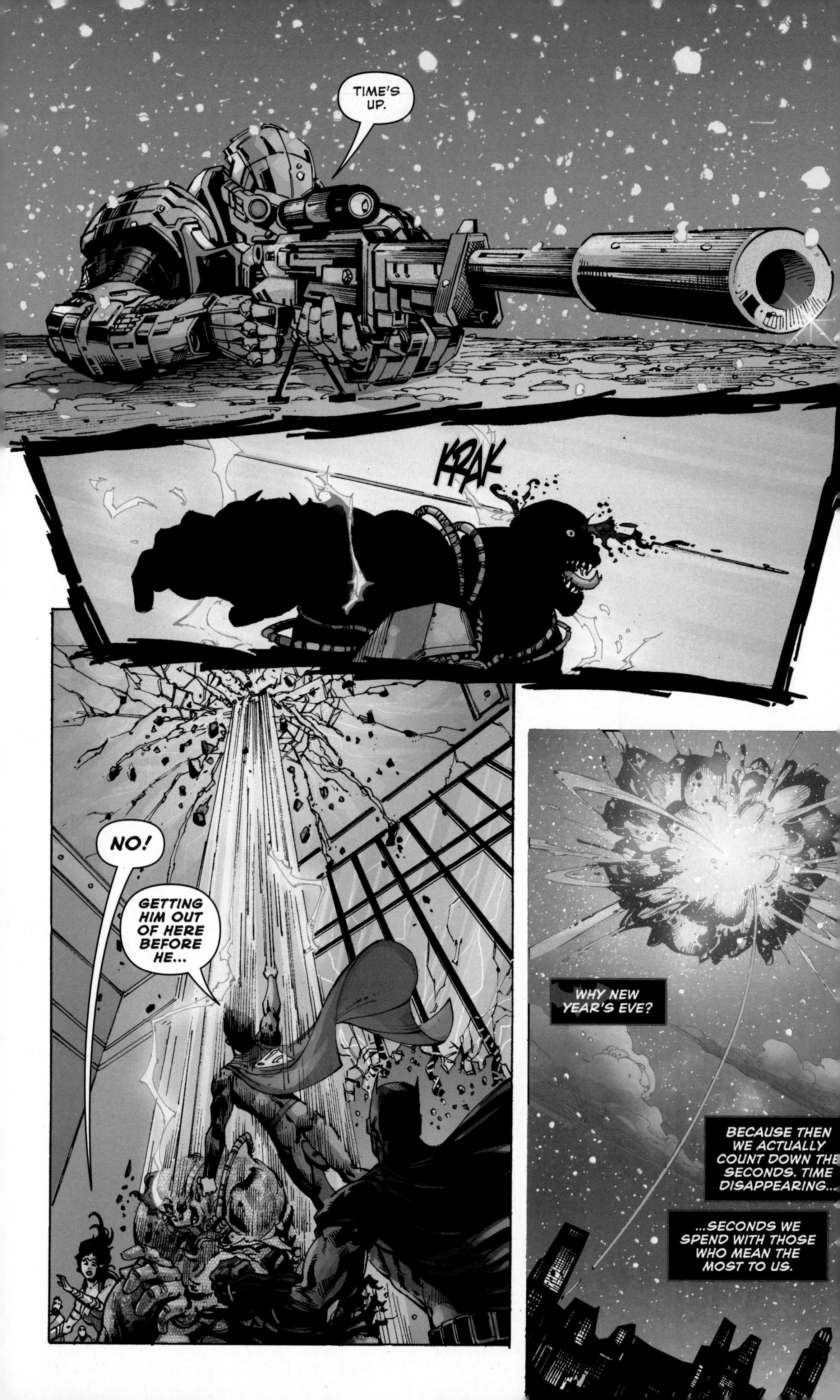
TIME'S UP.
KRAK
NO!
GETTING HIM OUT OF HERE BEFORE HE...
WHY NEW YEAR'S EVE?
BECAUSE THEN WE ACTUALLY COUNT DOWN THE SECONDS. TIME DISAPPEARING...
...SECONDS WE SPEND WITH THOSE WHO MEAN THE MOST TO US.

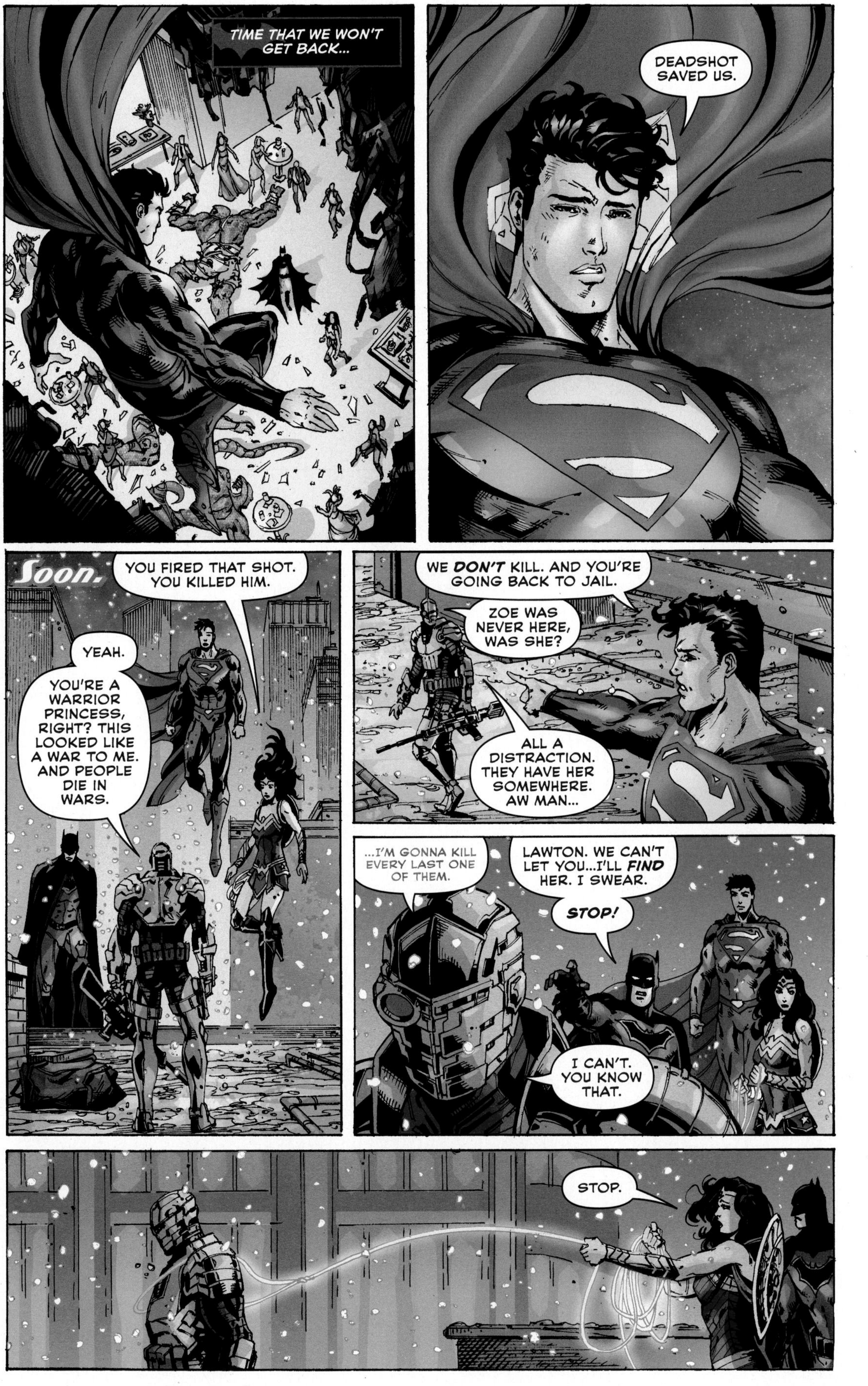

TIME THAT WE WON'T GET BACK...
DEADSHOT SAVED US.
Soon.
YOU FIRED THAT SHOT. YOU KILLED HIM.
YEAH.
YOU'RE A WARRIOR PRINCESS, RIGHT? THIS LOOKED LIKE A WAR TO ME. AND PEOPLE DIE IN WARS.
WE DON'T KILL. AND YOU'RE GOING BACK TO JAIL.
ZOE WAS NEVER HERE, WAS SHE?
ALL A DISTRACTION. THEY HAVE HER SOMEWHERE. AW MAN...
...I'M GONNA KILL EVERY LAST ONE OF THEM.
LAWTON. WE CAN'T LET YOU...I'LL FIND HER. I SWEAR.
STOP!
I CAN'T. YOU KNOW THAT.
STOP.

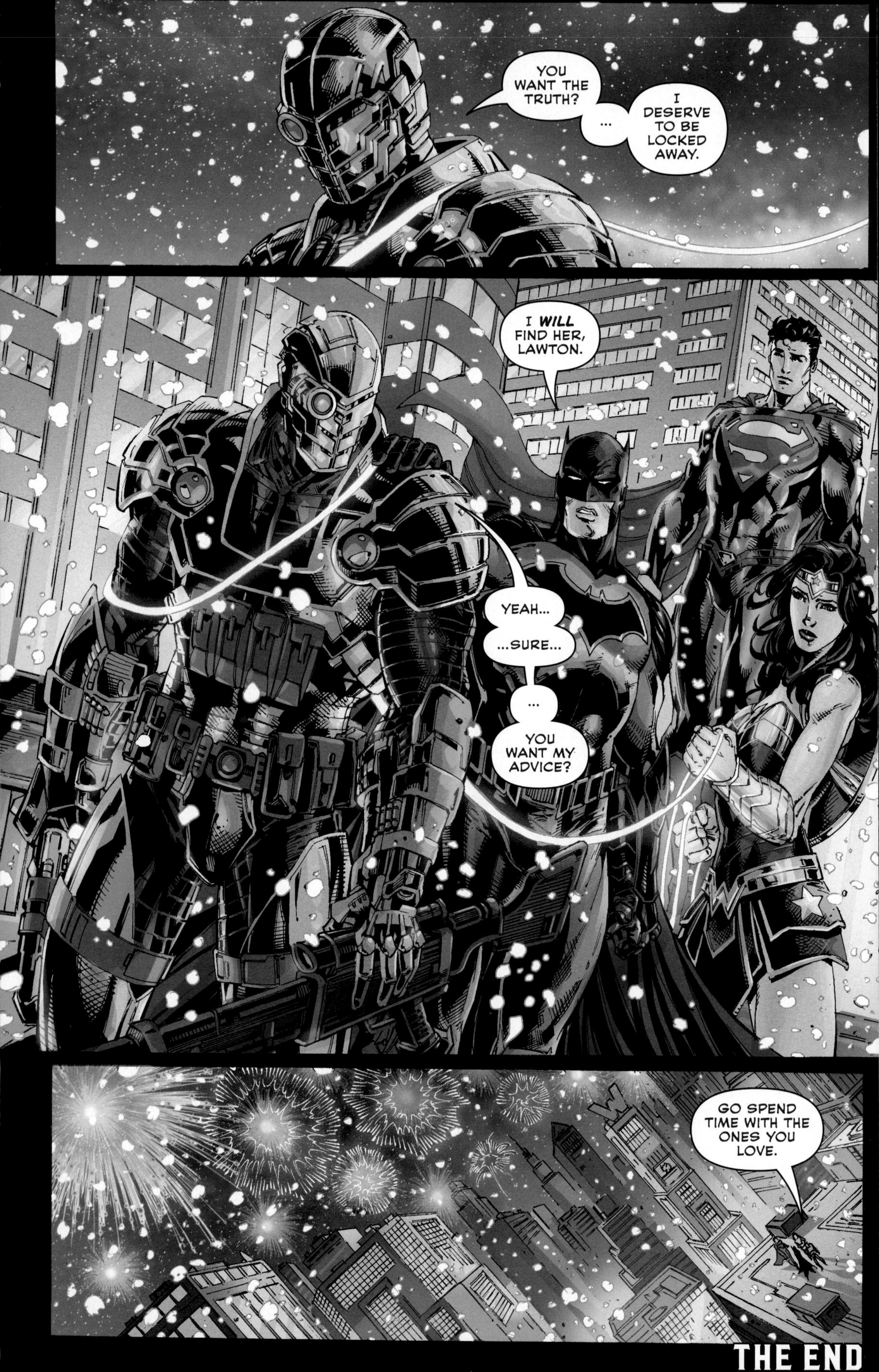
YOU WANT THE TRUTH?
...
I DESERVE TO BE LOCKED AWAY.
I WILL FIND HER, LAWTON.
YEAH...
...SURE...
...
YOU WANT MY ADVICE?
GO SPEND TIME WITH THE ONES YOU LOVE.
THE END

BATMAN ★ WONDER WOMAN ★ SUPERMAN

# TRINITY

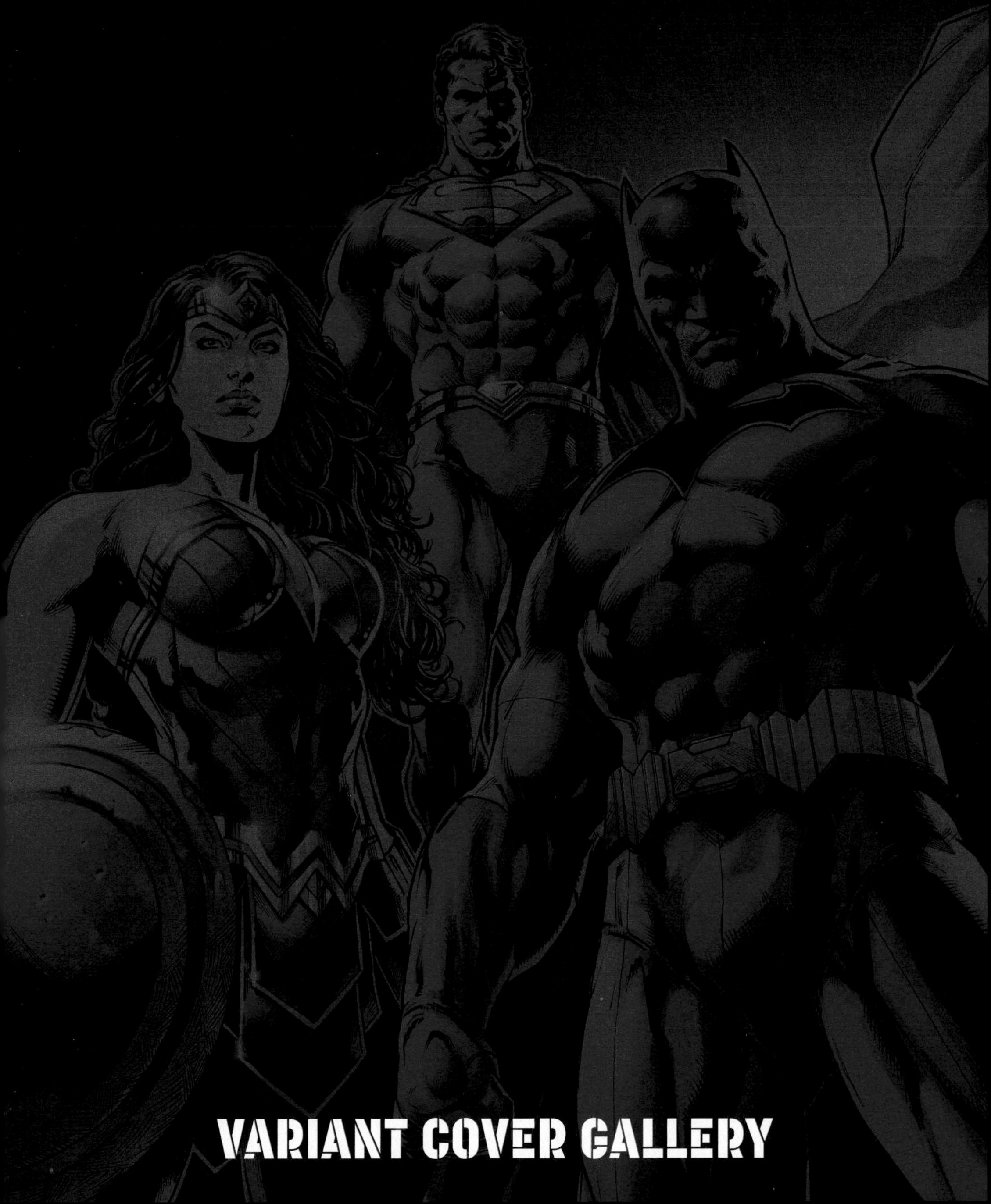

## VARIANT COVER GALLERY

TRINITY #12 variant cover by BILL SIENKIEWICZ

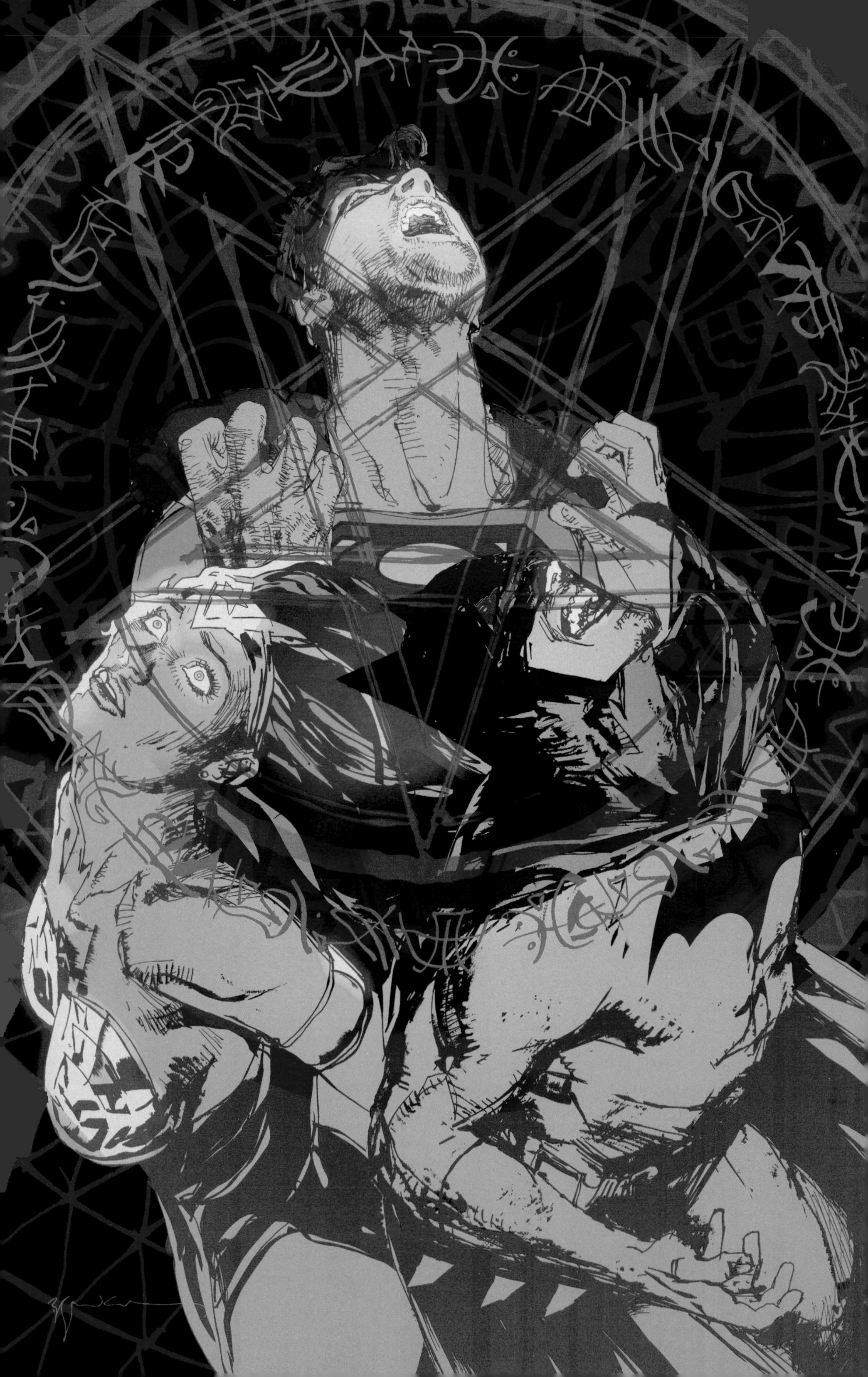

TRINITY #13 variant cover by BILL SIENKIEWICZ

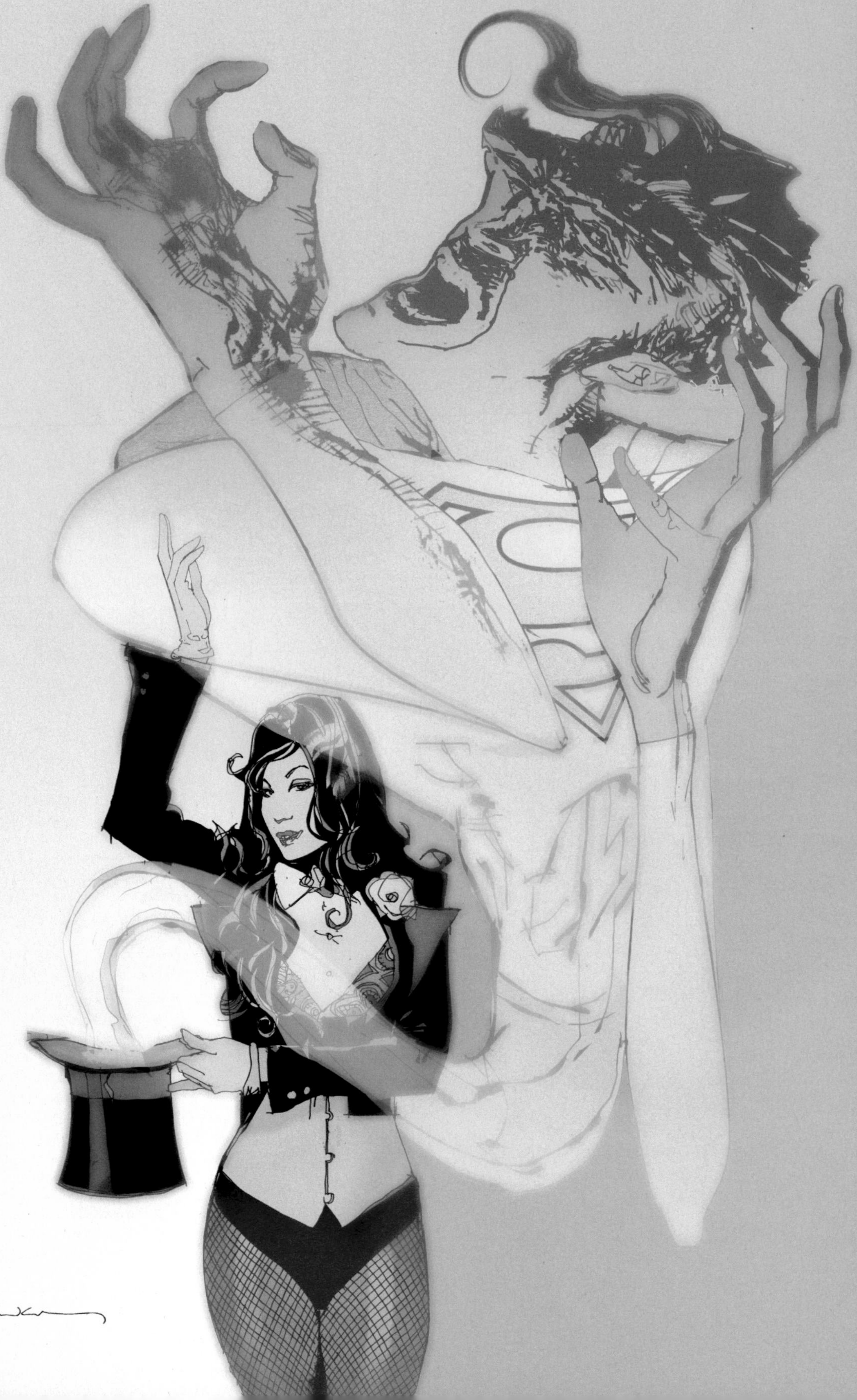

TRINITY #14 variant cover by BILL SIENKIEWICZ

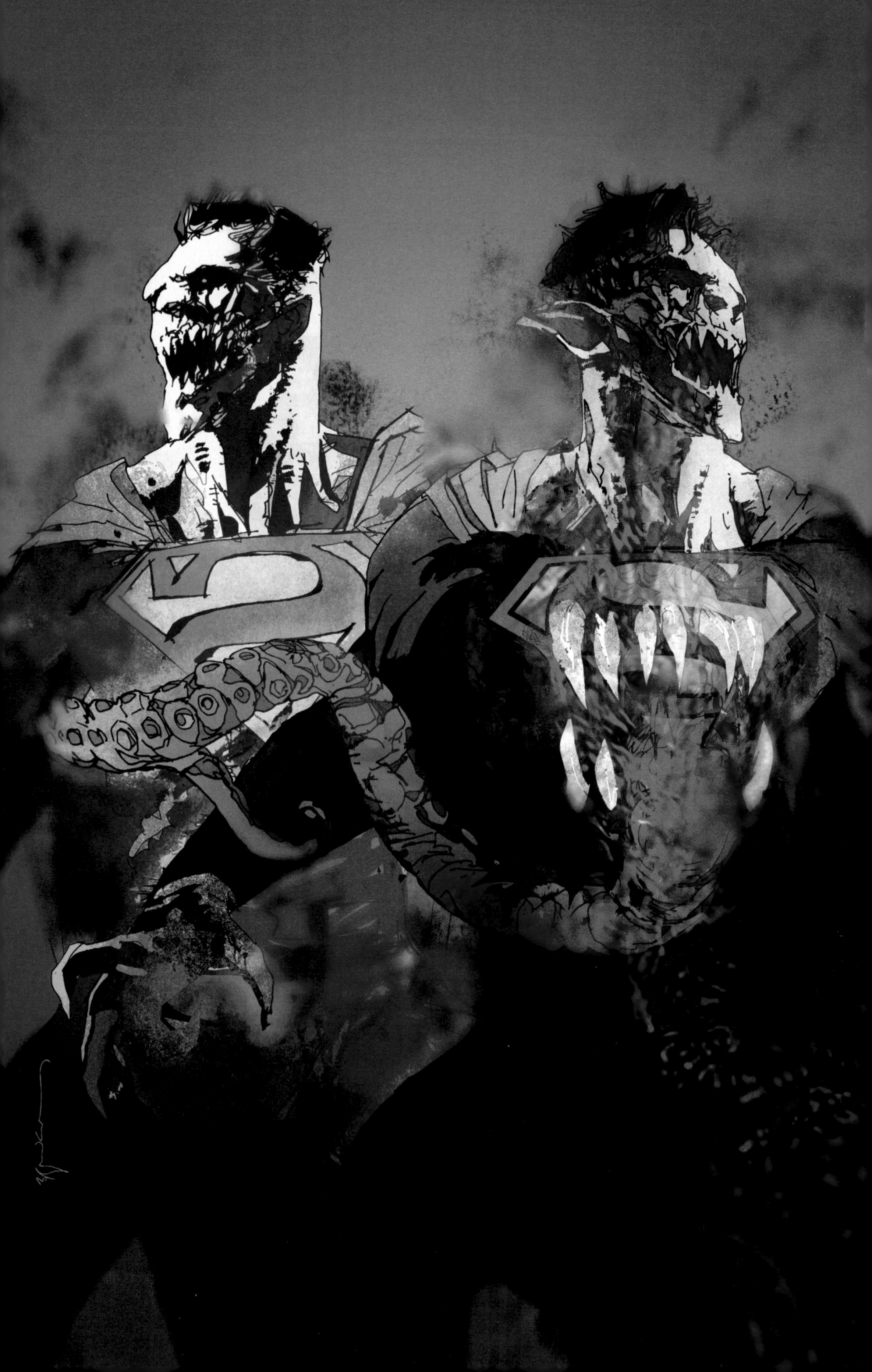

TRINITY #15 variant cover by BEN OLIVER

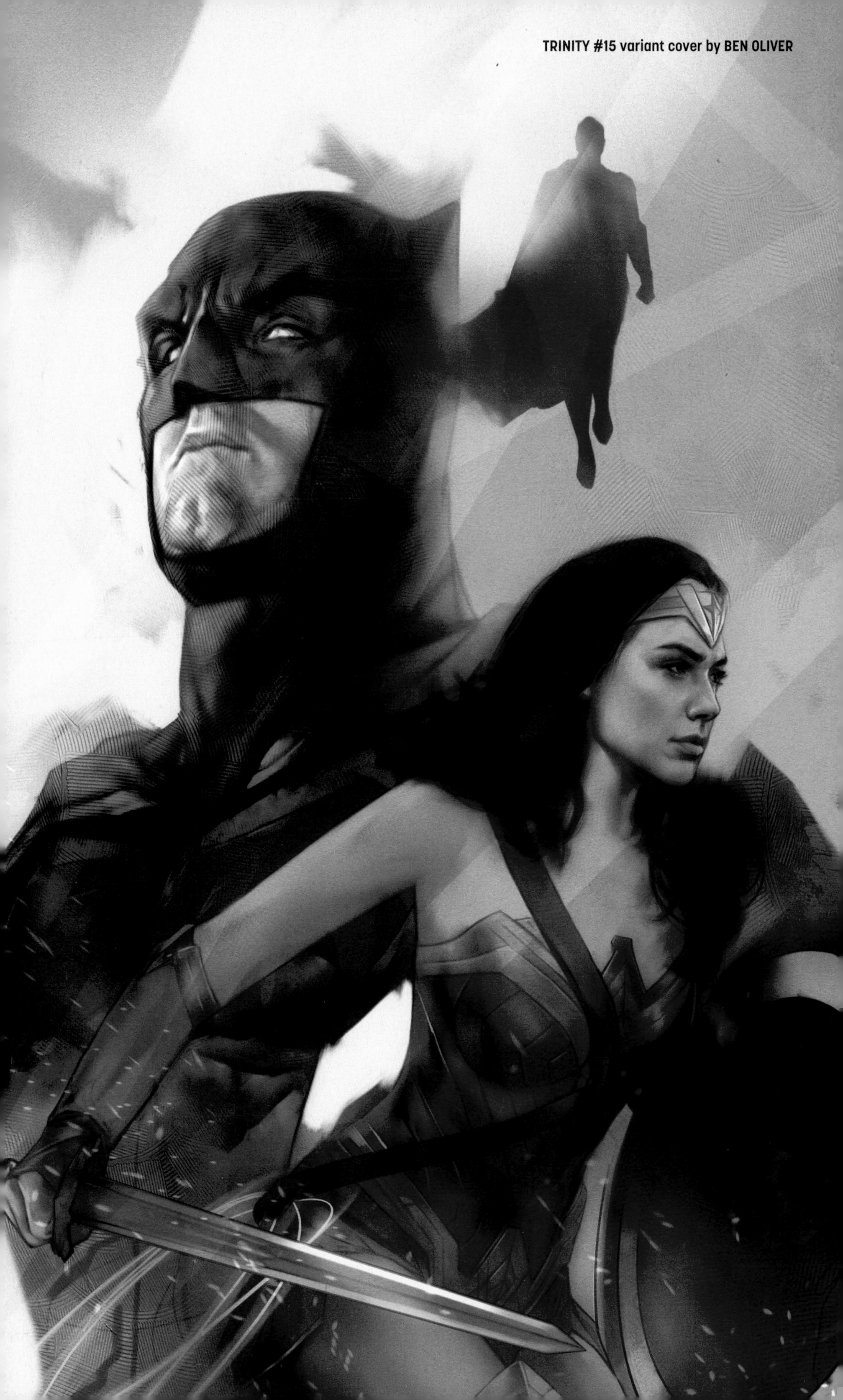

TRINITY #16 variant cover by JASON FABOK and BRAD ANDERSON

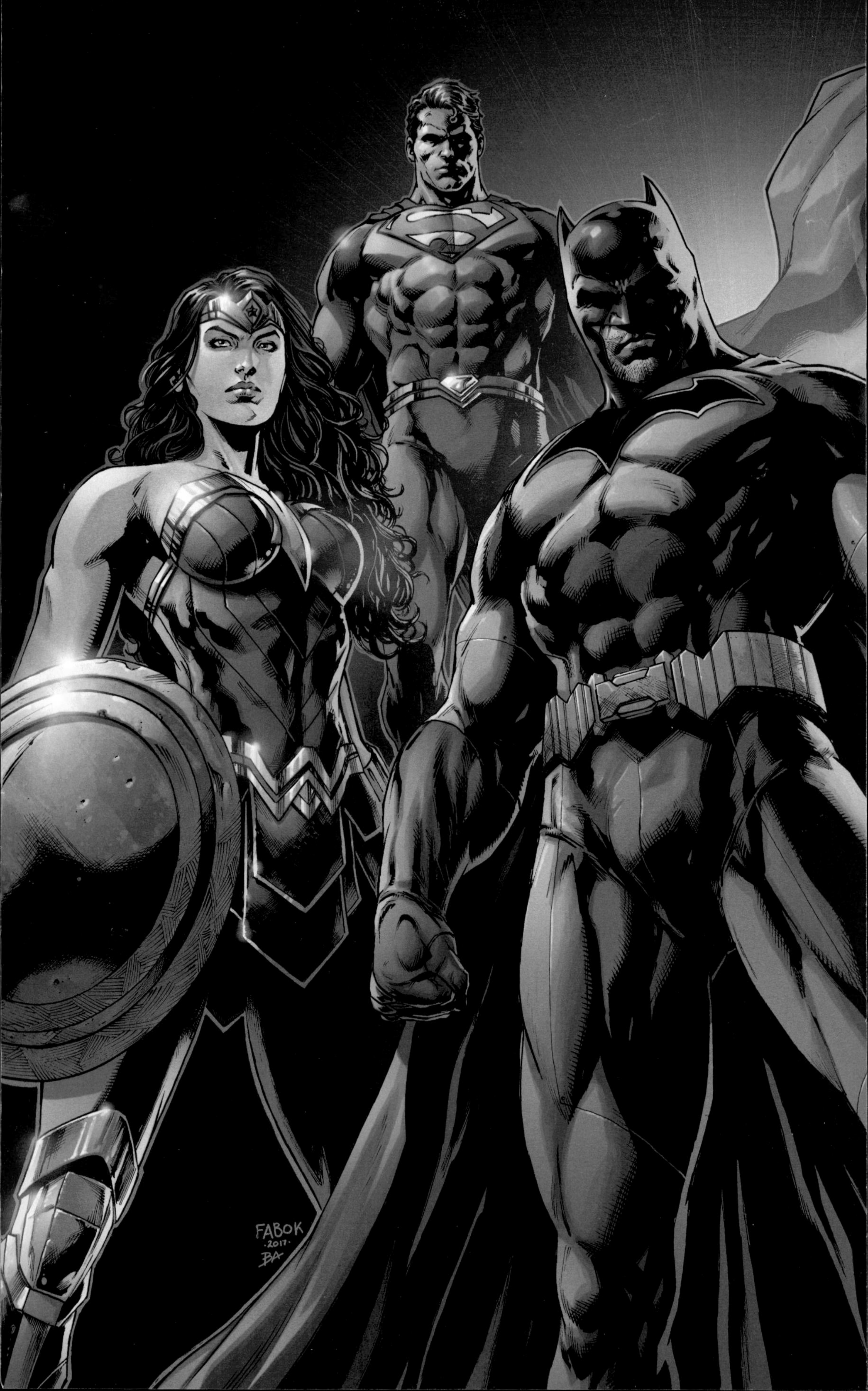
FABOK
·2017·
BA